Preface and

Writing Lives emerged from a series of reflections and conversations which occurred during the completion of our *Reading, Society and Politics*. Even since the publication of that volume, scholars in a number of fields and disciplines—even those not directly concerned with literature and its receptions—have discovered the insights and rewards of an engagement with theories and histories of reading and interpretation and with the broader critical perspectives opened by the history of the book—its materialities, its economies, its circulation, its social authority and energy. What struck us was how biography seemed to be the one genre uninfluenced and untroubled by such critical perspectives and moves; indeed biography has been the genre least inflected by the theoretical preoccupations and critical innovations of the last two or three decades. Such immunity, we would suggest, has not been accidental. Many of the theoretical dogmas of recent years—the erasure of authorship, the insistence on textual instability, the critical address to elisions and fissures, most of all the emphasis on the self as a site of fracture rather than coherence—not only question the methods, they might seem fundamentally to have undermined the very project of biography.

Of course rumours of the death of the author and the end of literature now seem rather exaggerated. In some forms, biography appears to thrive as never before; and there obviously remains a readership, indeed an appetite, for literary biography despite theory's condescension. While it is clear that criticism and biography have both flourished, they have not much engaged in conversation, the methods and approaches of criticism and theory scarcely informing the premises or arts of biography. The dominance of theory in the academy has diminished, some would say passed; but whatever one's position in these culture wars, most of us would agree that over the last two decades important insights have emerged, still more, new questions have been asked about the ways in which we interrogate and appreciate literature.

It occurred to us that such enquiry, rather than threaten, might enhance and extend the biographical archive and project. In particular, as early modern scholars we felt that the biographical model as it emerged as a stable form and practice in the eighteenth century has been a distorting lens onto early modern lives. In the Renaissance and early modern period, rather than biography's organic and developmental narratives of a coherent subject, lives were written and represented in a, to us, bewildering array of textual sites and generic forms. And such lives were clearly imagined and written not to entertain or even simply to inform, but to edify, instruct, and counsel. It is only when we understand how early moderns imagined and narrated lives that we can newly conceive the meaning of those lives and begin to rewrite their histories free of the imperatives and teleologies of Enlightenment. Whatever the value of theoretical and critical questions and perspectives for our own writing of early modern lives, it is only, as revisionists have insisted, through a full return to history, an exact historicizing, that we can begin to answer such questions.

In conceiving a collection of studies of early modern lives and life writing, we approached colleagues who were not for the most part conventional biographers, but literary scholars, cultural critics, historians of ideas and visual media. All these scholars have been or are currently engaged both with early modern conceptions of the life and our own conceptualizing of the biographical project. We invited them to reflect on such problems from the various and particular perspectives of their own research and in the form of case studies animated by new questions, even speculations. From the beginning, our interest was in the conversations between these cases and among our contributors. Accordingly most of our contributors met together in a colloquium and conference in which earlier ideas and drafts were presented and discussed both among themselves and within a larger gathering of early modern scholars. The conference clearly revealed that rather than at an end, critical conversations about early modern biography and life writing are in some respects beginning anew. It is our hope that this volume might stimulate further conversations.

For their hosting and generous support of the conference held in the summer of 2006, we express our thanks to the School of English and Drama and the Centre for Editing Lives and Letters, Queen Mary, University of London, and in particular Julia Boffey and Lisa Jardine, and Beverley Stewart and Alistair Daniel. We would also like to thank all our contributors for their interest in and commitment to this volume, and especially Stella Tillyard for the set of broad and provocative reflections that opened our conference. We would both like to thank the Departments of English and History at Washington University, St Louis, and in particular Derek Hirst, Gerald Izenberg, and Joe Loewenstein, and colleagues in the School of English at Queen Mary, especially Warren Boutcher, Jerry Brotton, David Colclough, and Lisa Jardine. Beyond these institutions, we thank for their interest and support Chris D'Addario, Jane Ohlmeyer, and Greg Walker. For showing such enthusiasm for the collection from beginning to end, we wish to express warm thanks to Andrew McNeillie of Oxford University Press. For assistance with the final preparation of the manuscript we thank Matthew Augustine. And to Alexandra Lumbers and Judith Zwicker our thanks for helping to write our lives.

Contents

List of Illustrations

List of Illustrations

Abbreviations

ADN	Archives of the Département du Nord
AHR	*American Historical Review*
BL	British Library
CLRO	City of London Record Office
CSP	*Calendar of State Papers*
CSPD	*Calendar of State Papers Domestic*
EEBO	Early English Books Online
ELH	*English Literary History*
ELR	*English Literary Renaissance*
HMC	Historical Manuscripts Commission
MLQ	*Modern Language Quarterly*
NLS	National Library of Scotland
ODNB	*Oxford Dictionary of National Biography*
PMLA	*Proceedings of the Modern Language Association*
PRO	Public Record Office
Wing	Donald Wing, *Short-Title Catalogue of Books Printed in England, Scotland, Ireland, Wales and British American, and of English Books Printed in Other Countries 1641–1700*

Introducing Lives

Kevin Sharpe and Steven N. Zwicker

We began to think about this subject—surely not coincidentally—as Oxford University brought to fruition the largest project in humanities research in modern times: a full revision and extension of the *Dictionary of National Biography*, an ongoing biographical database of the most notable English men and women through history. The *ODNB* is a monument of modern scholarship, but one need only enter a local bookstore or scan the pages of the weekend supplements to see that biography is also a thriving and popular form. From literary and historical lives to the biographies of sporting heroes and of course celebrities, lives are the predominant form of non-fiction. The very popularity of biography and the authority of the *ODNB* seem to have so naturalized the form that we seldom pause to ask questions about the origins and the emergence of biography, or about the changes in the form through centuries of economic, social, and intellectual transformations. When was it, we might ask, that biography emerged as a distinct form? How does biography relate to—and how has it negotiated with—other modes of imagining, scripting, and depicting lives? Biography is of course not an exclusively national genre, but we should ask, as Stella Tillyard suggests, how and in what ways biography is shaped by cultural styles and national habits of recording, memorializing, and celebrating lives. Most fundamentally, we ask, why do people write and read lives, or, to pose the question historically, what have been the purposes and uses of biographies and other forms of life writing?

Writing Lives is concerned with these questions, most particularly with early modern England, the place and time in which what we recognize, and what contemporaries began to describe, as biography emerged from myriad forms of representing lives. The predominant form of life writing that had emerged by the end of the seventeenth century was not only biography but national biography. While we have taken for granted the national identity of biographies, we must remind ourselves that in this early modernity marked an important departure. The medieval lives of saints and martyrs were of course catholic, universal, and the models and heroes of hagiography and of spiritual combat were not of nations but of European Christendom. Though Renaissance 'lives' were less preoccupied with crusades and eschatologies, they were no less conceived as international, as lives to be imagined within a European republic of letters and written in the international language of scholarship. Classical antiquity gave Renaissance humanism not only its language and its literatures but also its exemplary lives of stoic self-restraint, civic virtue, and public duty. We are familiar with the ways in which the Reformation fractured European Christendom, but less attention has been paid to how reformations shaped conceptions of lives in new confessional, local, and even national terms. The models of Reformation and Counter-Reformation spirituality rather than European and Catholic, were Protestant and Roman, Lutheran and Zwinglian, vernacular, provincial, and even national. In the case of England, the course of the Reformation is inseparable from the story of nationhood; and English modes of life writing cannot be separated from emergent notions of Elect Nation. Though the Renaissance exemplary life remained an important model, over the course of the sixteenth century it gave place, at least in terms of popularity, to the lives forged through Reformation struggle: Foxe's martyrs and puritan worthies. By the end of the sixteenth century, models of life writing in England were often inseparable from confessional and national identities.

Elect Nation was not just the geography but the driving force of sixteenth-century English lives. Elect Nation was not a descriptive but a polemical discourse and design, a Protestant defence against the ultramontane and the popish. But for all the tension between them, Protestantism was still part of a humanist culture than cannot be defined and delimited by nation. Who would confine Sir Philip Sidney or John Milton to national boundaries? Whatever their importance to an emergent notion of a national literature, both were and conceived themselves as European men of letters, conversant with antiquity, and as members of a humanist community. If we may at times feel that even in these cases the European dimension of intellectual formation and identity has not been fully registered, not fully acknowledged in our reading of Sidney's and Milton's lives and works, it is generally the case that vernacular nationalism has occluded those aspects of the life lived across national boundaries and borders. National identities are of course forged always in relation to—albeit in tension with—other identities. As Alastair Bellany demonstrates, the most powerful courtier in Jacobean England fashioned his authority, indeed his identity, as much from the tropes and signs of European baroque culture as of English and Protestant idioms. In Milton's case, his design for a godly republic was situated fully within, was indeed dependent on, an education in European letters.[1] Lisa Jardine insists that the life of a figure like Constantine Huygens—at home within and an agent between republic and monarchy, confederacy and nation state—cannot be fully imagined or adequately written as national biography. Huygens offers a powerful example of the need to situate early modern lives beyond national boundaries. But in the English case, he also raises the question of the *longue durée* of the European republic of letters in the face of an increasingly powerful and polemically insistent emphasis on Britishness. By the end of the seventeenth century, British identity is beginning to determine not only a national literature but as well national biography.[2]

The emergence of the nation as a determining force on life writing is a phenomenon that we date to the end of our period. We should also recognize that the very term biography emerges late in the seventeenth century.[3] And just as emergent nationalism has flattened the full textures of lives lived across national boundaries, we might also argue that the conception of life writing as biography—the organic

---

[1] In *The History of Britain*, Milton argued that 'many civil virtues must be imported into our minds from foreign writings and examples of best ages, we shall else miscarry', Milton, *History of Britain*, in the *Complete Prose Works of John Milton*, ed. D. Wolfe et al. (New Haven and London, 1971), v. 450; and see Milton's programme of moral, literary, and rhetorical learning in *Of Education*, *Complete Prose Works*, ii. 357–415.

[2] See Linda Colley's celebrated *Britons: Forging the Nation, 1707–1837* (New Haven and London, 1992).

[3] The *OED* identifies the emergence of the word in English with Dryden's *Life of Plutarch* (1683), but, as Ian Donaldson points out, the term 'biography' was already in use twenty years earlier in *The Life of . . . Thomas Fuller* (1661); see Donaldson, 'National Biography and the Art of Memory', *Mapping Lives: The Uses of Biography* (Oxford, 2002), 67.

and developmental narrative of a life—imposes an anachronistic and circumscribed model on the writing of early modern lives, indeed on those lives themselves. Our endeavour in this volume is to set aside the dominant Enlightenment model of biography in order to explore the variety and the complexities of all the forms in which early modern lives were written. Furthermore, it is by returning to the full panoply of early modern forms that we may more fully, more closely inhabit and reimagine those lives—rewrite them and refashion our conception of biography itself.

Such a recovery must begin with the simple but fundamental question: what were the purposes of life writing in early modernity? Even a casual perusal of early modern lives discloses quite different intentions and purposes to those of the modern biography: where, for example, the modern biographer focuses on childhood, development, psychology, and individuality, early modern lives are more concerned with community, with spirituality, but most of all with the life as exemplar. Indeed, exemplarity is at the heart of early modern lives and early modern life writing. From classical antiquity and medieval hagiography, Renaissance writers inherited, edited, and re-presented exemplary lives of scholarship, sanctity, and civic virtue. Such lives were consumed as pedagogic texts, as counsel and guide, as models for the life of the mind and spirit. And the exemplary life was more often than not a polemical as much as pedagogic text, an ethical example, an ideological formation, but also a political argument. Early modern lives were above all lives written for use. The uses and purposes of early modern lives are inseparable from forms of life writing quite different from our own. The modern biography is above all a free-standing text, the narrative of an individual and of individuality self-contained in form as in subject. Early modern lives are more often written and read in collections and as collectives, folded into histories, prefacing and appended to a myriad of early modern books. While the free-standing 'life' is not unknown in early modern England—Roper's *Life* of More is an obvious example— from editions of Plutarch's *Lives* to Clarendon's *History* exemplary and polemical lives were more often encountered within the pages of other texts and bound to other lives. For all the scholarly attention to self-fashioning, to the celebration of the individual, the most common forms of early modern life writing caution us that individuality itself is fashioned out of collectives, typologies, and exemplars. The conventions and materials, the very forms of early modern life writing, are to an extent that we have not fully appreciated central to our understanding of early modern lives.

Out of what materials was the early modern 'life' constituted? And what place might their materials of life writing have in our imagining and writing of their lives? To begin with the example of the early modern literary life, modern biographers have anxiously sought to distinguish the archival records—the locus of fact, event, and truth—from the literature and fictions of their subjects, to police the fictive and privilege the factual. It is such anxious discriminations that long characterized, even limited, so many modern lives of the greatest of Renaissance literary figures, not least the lives of Marlowe and Shakespeare. By contrast, in our collection Andrew Hadfield identifies a Spenser who self-consciously writes himself into his own fictions, perhaps plots his own life, certainly his own aspirations from those fictions. Rather than a nervous resistance to such moments, Hadfield urges the full embrace of the fictive as evidence of life writing. The life imagined, even fantasized, within the work becomes then the archive of biography. Traditional biography would be quick to record and narrate the fact of Spenser's marriage; Hadfield turns our attention to Spenser's fantasy of his own wedding night in which a voyeuristic queen peers in envy through his bedroom window and Hadfield invites us to find in such a fantasy a deeper truth about Spenser's imagination and life: his erotic selfhood, his domestic economy, his transgressive political daring. In the case of Milton, early modern lives are, albeit differently, as at great a distance from modern biographical preoccupations. The modern biographies have privileged the poet's high ideals, his spirituality, his ideological engagement and public service, and of course his epic literary achievement. But as Thomas Corns reminds us, this is hardly the Milton written into or out of his early lives, lives which subordinate spiritual development and political engagement for stories and rumours of illicit sexuality. Such early rumours and innuendoes have been accorded little place and play in modern lives of Milton, yet the insistence and in some cases the anxiety with which early modern lives of Milton engage what we have been inclined to dismiss as trivia surely invite us to admit rumour and innuendo into the archive of biography. Harold Love urges us not only to acknowledge gossip as the very material of early modern life writing but to see gossip as constitutive of personality and identity, recognition and reputation, we might say the life itself.[4] In Love's formulation, gossip by underpinning social norms partakes of a conventionality that might well evoke the Renaissance exemplar; but gossip at the same time depends on particularity and idiosyncrasy. In the early modern world, gossip constituted a social selfhood; but often it was the instrument of defamation, of the destruction of reputation and identity. Because rumour and gossip are often the fragmentary residues of fuller lives and histories, modern biography in its quest for organic wholeness and linear narrative has often elided gossip in the construction of early modern lives, not only on the grounds of unreliability but on account of its fragmentary nature. Our contributors in accord with other critical and historiographical moves, and perhaps with some scepticism about master narratives, have variously privileged the fragmentary as a window onto historical circumstances and contingences, and therefore as an especially rich material for early modern lives.

To identify and insist on the importance of the various materials of early moderns' life writing for our own writing of early modern lives raises a set of questions about method. Of all literary forms biography has least been troubled by issues of method, by that series of critical enquiries that has so insistently raised questions about textuality, about our own position in relation to interpretation, about the stability of texts, and about issues of reception and the construction of meaning. Ian Donaldson has suggested the value of such textual and rhetorical awareness in the biographical project; to apply such perspectives is radically to disrupt the stabilities of traditional biography, even most radically to read the life itself as a text.[5] Certainly the rhetorics of all the materials of early modern life writing—and of Renaissance lives— demand our critical attention. We may be familiar with the rhetoric of the royal declaration or parliamentary address, but in our roles as biographers we need to extend such alertness to the rhetoricity of all early modern written, spoken, and visual forms. We need, that is, a deeper sense of the rhetoric of the early modern life.

---

[4] Harold Love valuably extends our recovery of early modern orality in Ch. 5, 'Biography and Gossip'; see also Adam Fox, *Oral and Literate Culture in England*: *1500–1700* (Oxford, 2000), and Bernard Capp, *When Gossips Meet*: *Women, Family, and Neighborhood in Early Modern England* (Oxford, 2003).

[5] See Donaldson, *Ben Jonson's Magic Houses*: *Essays in Interpretation* (Oxford, 1997), 4.

Renaissance rhetorical theory fully recognized that the meaning of texts was as much made—as we have latterly recognized—by readers as by authors. We might suggest that some greater attention to the receptions of lives should inform our understanding of how lives themselves were written, represented, even lived. As Alastair Bellany observes, in the very act of fashioning his life Buckingham anxiously anticipated not only different but contestatory readings, indeed writings, of that life. And finally, we would urge the application to biography of the new bibliography and history of the book which have so enriched our understanding of the performance of early modern texts. At the simplest level, little attention has been paid to the very materiality of the materials of early modern life writing, to, that is, the presence of the hand, to multiple scripts, to emendation, to address and subscription. Leah Marcus attributes considerable significance to the varying size and position of Elizabeth's signature in explicating the purposes and meanings of her letters. And Marcus reminds us that the relationships among materiality, meaning, and reception are by no means the business only of the manuscript archive. Elizabeth may have written her prayers, but her readers read them and viewed them within the paratextual and marginal illustrations that surely complicated and perhaps contested not only Elizabeth's meanings but her authorially represented life. In the case of James II's 'Life' we cannot begin to think about the life outside its material circumstances: its gaps and fragmentary slips, the scribal copies, the published compilations, the contested versions. We need to return early modern lives to the material forms from which they were written and in which they were first consumed and interpreted.

Recent critical perspectives have not only insisted on the multiplicities, instabilities, and materialities of texts, they have raised questions about the critical categories and determinations of genre. Such critical perspectives open valuably onto the relations between genre and early modern life writing. For the modern biography that relation appears untroubled; nothing is more obvious about modern biography than the stability of its genre and forms, and nothing could be less the case with early modern life writing. As we have discussed, the very sites of early modern life writing in prefaces, paratexts, dedications, and epistles themselves preclude the notion of an established or even predominant genre of life writing. Early modern readers consumed lives in and through the texts that we assign to a variety of other genres: history, romance, travel narrative, classical translation, hagiography, biblical exegesis. Even to discuss the 'early modern life', as perforce we find ourselves doing, is to fix and stabilize forms and modes that were varied, in flux, indeterminate, and for much of our period undetermined. At some level this claim may seem surprising. Early modern publishers, writers, and readers after all spoke and wrote of 'lives'; they described lives in the language of literary genres—epic and romance, tragedy and burlesque. They even recognized such sub-genres as religious lives and royal lives. Yet when we turn to those lives, it is less their generic fixity than generic multiplicity and instability that strike us. Foxe's *Lives*, for example, could be and was read as martyrology, confessional identity and argument, counsel, providential history, and political polemic. Are not the lives in Clarendon's *History* simultaneously characters, texts of memory, exemplars, sites of ideology, and protagonists of party? In the case of royal lives, as Paulina Kewes vividly asserts, 'lives of princes were located at the intersection of chronicle, political history, panegyric, martyrology, hagiography, confessional polemic, and other more ephemeral forms such as ballads, poems, sermons, pageants, and plays'.[6] That Kewes's list virtually runs the gamut of all early modern literary forms underlines the myriad of genres within whose forms early modern lives were imagined, published, and read. If, as seems the case, generic uncertainty is more a feature of the beginning than of the end of the seventeenth century we need to ask what drove the transformation? What purposes did generic openness serve? And how, subsequently, did generic fixity address new cultural and political circumstances, new conditions of writing and reading? While the relation may be difficult precisely to determine, we surely can be in no doubt that civil war, regicide, and revolution transformed not only the lives lived through these events but as well all lives written in their shadows. Surely by the end of this period what begins to be recognizable as the stable genre 'biography' emerged from the political instability of mid-century.

For all the emergence of a stable genre of biography—and indeed increasingly of history—Clarendon immediately alerts us to the interdependences, sometimes tensions, between biography and history. Today the modern biography—particularly political biography—is as

[6] See Ch. 9, p. 187.

much a 'times' as a 'life'; and today once again historians, no longer in sympathy with grand structural explanations be they Marxist or Annaliste, accord considerable influence to the shaping force of individual men and women. If today history and biography are inseparable in the recently theorized field of memory and memorialization, we should immediately remind ourselves of the self-conscious polemics of memory in post-civil war England. Memory is of course a fact of all historical argument—the medieval chronicle, Renaissance antiquities, civic histories. But in the wake of sectarian division and political contest, history writing was more obviously, more deliberately deployed for polemical and partisan purposes. When Andrea Walkden writes of Walton's *Lives* as 'the guardian of great men after death', she reminds us of the centrality of commemoration to Restoration biography.[7] Though we read them as biography, Walton's and Clarke's 'lives' were conceived and almost certainly read as texts of collective memory in the service of confessional and political causes. The polemics of Clarke's 'Lives', Peter Lake shows, did not depend on the exemplary force of great men. Indeed, at the centre of Michael McKeon's argument is the suggestion that by the end of the seventeenth century the exemplary figure no longer depended on social greatness or political prominence. Ordinariness itself—common humanity—now most powerfully spoke to readers. The twenty-first-century reader immediately recognizes ordinary humanity written into popular celebrity in countless biographies and cultural histories. But what we more specifically would suggest is the need to consider the implications of new forms of exemplarity and life writing for Enlightenment conceptions and practices of history.

The traditional modern history with its clear notions of evidence and archive has permitted little space for what we might call the records of representation which only following the work of Roger Chartier and others has entered the historical narrative. In early modernity, by contrast, representations were the essential materials of history, not least because lives were lived as representations. And not only were they lived as representations, they were imagined and performed as representations. Famously Stephen Greenblatt has characterized the condition of early modernity—of socialities as well individuals—as one of self-fashioning, that is of the artful constructions of identities, selfhoods,

---

[7] See Ch. 15, p. 333.

public lives. Certainly in the case of such courtiers as the Duke of Buckingham, not only the public authority but the personal identity were produced through a series of constructions and performances. In the theatre of modernity, our own inclination—even desire—is to believe in an essential self, a core being beneath all roles, all fashioning and formulation. In Buckingham's case Alastair Bellany asks whether there was a 'real' self outside representation. He shows how, even if there were, the duke was defined, and certainly by the end of his life trapped, by his images and representations.[8] Scholars now may be familiar—wearily familiar—with the concept of self-fashioning; ironically, however, as biographers we have not embraced in our own writings of early modern lives the full immersion, in some cases submersion, of selfhood in representation. Bellany gestures to a new biography in which the archives of the life are signs, symbols, and mythologies. Even for lives less obviously theatrical, less insistently represented, modern biography needs to find greater space for the symbolic and performative as essentials of the early modern life. Only recently have we begun to appreciate how the symbolic, the performative, the figured, not only enriches but in some sense transforms the life of Oliver Cromwell as read and contested by contemporaries and even as chronicled by us.[9] While we urge the full application of the concepts of representation and self-fashioning to the writing of early modern lives, we must also allow the critique of a new historicism that has, in emphasizing the social and secular, underplayed interiority and spirituality.[10] Frances Harris, by recovering the courtier Robert Moray's personal motto 'to be rather than to seem', more broadly challenges a fashionable emphasis on image and theatricality: 'one needs' Harris insists 'to go beyond outward appearance and (mis)representation'.[11] While we would not ourselves fully endorse a scepticism that takes all acts of representation as misrepresentation, Harris's corrective is an important one. Not least because it returns our attention to the interior life, to,

---

[8] Bellany here follows Peter Burke's pioneering study of the *Fabrication of Louis XIV* (New Haven and London, 1992).

[9] See Laura Knoppers, *Constructing Cromwell: Ceremony, Portrait, and Print, 1645–1661* (Cambridge, 2000).

[10] See esp. Debora Suger, *Habits of Thought in the English Renaissance: Religion, Politics, and the Dominant Culture* (Berkeley, 1990).

[11] See Ch. 13, p. 288.

of course, the spiritual, but as well to the affective, the sexual, the psychological.

Sex and sexuality have of course a prominent place in almost every modern biography, and not only for commercial reasons. In a post-Freudian world, it could not be otherwise. Whether or not we have read Freud, we have interiorized the sexual as the defining condition of the self: of childhood, development, adult formation, the psyche— of the life narrated, of the life narrative. Fear of anachronism may have reinforced earlier moral sensibilities in leading us to elide or subordinate the sexual in our narrating of early modern lives. In some respects early modernity itself encourages such subordinations. Rather than a self fulfilled in copulation, even fornication, the hegemonic discourse of early modernity is a discourse of self-abnegation and of sexual self-regulation. Where religious instruction proscribed sex outside marriage and procreation, neo-stoic philosophy instructed a subjugation of base appetite to rational soul. We may read these as denials of the self, but for early modernity the scripts of self-regulation were texts for the full realization of the rational self. Post-Freudian psychology suggests that in ubiquitous discourses of self-denial there always lurks a fear of the overwhelming force of desire; but early modernity itself seems to recognize, if not in psychological language, the powerful—and destructive— undercurrents of appetite, desire, of the undisciplined body. Scholars have underscored the prominence of the discourse of the body in early modernity; we would remark how those discourses fully recognized, even as they sought to regulate, sexuality.[12] Because the various discourses of the body were early modernity's idioms of sexuality, perhaps they deserve a greater place in our own narrations of early modern lives. We could even go further and say that because the discourses of the body were so ubiquitously public and political, their recovery for the biographical project makes a significant and a seamless link between what we distinguish as the private and the public. In the middle of the seventeenth century, the body and the appetites were the very matter not only of politics but of political theory and philosophy.

---

[12] For important recent studies, see Jonathan Sawday, *The Body Emblazoned: Dissection and the Human Body in Renaissance Culture* (London, 1995); Michael C. Schoenfeldt, *Bodies and Selves in Early Modern England* (Cambridge, 1999); and Gail K. Paster, *Humoring the Body: Emotions and the Shakespearean Stage* (Chicago, 2004).

Hobbes's new theory of state, as we know, was founded upon a recognition of appetites; what has been less remarked is how profound were the implications of Hobbes's naturalizing of the appetites for early modern sexuality. There can be little doubt that the figure of Hobbes lies behind the full expression and publication of sex and sexuality in the Restoration, or that Restoration lives on the stage, at court, indeed in St James's Park, in poetry, print, and portrait were fully lives of sexual appetite and desire.[13] Julia Alexander demonstrates that sex and sexuality have a newly, a recognizably modern, place in the lives of Restoration subjects, and most especially Restoration women. While we have appreciated this for Castlemaine and Nell Gwynn, we need more fully to acknowledge and to psychologize the sexual in narrating Restoration lives.[14]

Frances Harris's recent and rich study of John Evelyn and Margaret Godolphin counsels not to conceive Restoration sexuality too narrowly, for as well as the blatant and the pornographic, Restoration sexuality embraced the erotic and affective in public as well as private lives.[15] In this collection, Harris's portrait of Robert Moray discloses, somewhat surprisingly, the degree to which the life of the senior public servant, Presbyterian gentleman, founding member of the Royal Society, scientist and alchemist, makes little sense without a centring of the amorous and affective. Moray's emblem 'agape' announces his own conception of a life with love, in the broadest sense of that word, at the centre of identity. In Moray's case the archive—although previously underexplored—fully opens the affective dimension. In the case of Pepys, though the sexual life has long been apparent, scholars have now begun to explicate the full force of the affective in the life of a highly placed civil servant.[16] Even where we lack such rich archival resources of extensive personal memoirs and diaries, we must not lose sight of the affective dimension; and in the case of apparently colourless

---

[13] For Hobbes's influence on Rochester, see Warren Chernaik, *Sexual Freedom in Restoration Literature* (Cambridge, 1995), ch. 1, 'Hobbes and the Libertines'; James Grantham Turner, *Libertines and Radicals in Early Modern London: Sexuality, Politics and Literary Culture, 1630–85* (Cambridge, 2002).

[14] See James Grantham Turner, 'Pepys and the Private Parts of Monarchy', in Gerald MacLean (ed.), *Culture and Society in the Stuart Restoration* (Cambridge, 1995), 95–110.

[15] Harris, *Transformations of Love: The Friendship of John Evelyn and Margaret Godolphin* (Oxford, 2002).

[16] See Claire Tomalin, *Samuel Pepys, The Unequalled Self* (New York, 2002).

bureaucrats we must retain a sense of the force of the affective in a Restoration culture more than ever inflected by the affective no less than the sexual. In writing the affective life, even when the archives are extensive, explication demands empathies and imaginings; when the archive is silent perhaps we should not entirely resist 'emotional speculations'.[17]

The sexual and affective have been most fully explored and theorized in modern scholarship through the prism of gender. For some time gender theory, contesting assertions of essentialist difference, urged the constructedness and porousness of male and female and implicitly argued that biography and life writing ought not to be delimited by traditional constructions of gender. And yet, when we turn to early modernity we cannot but be struck by rigid categories of gender and the relentless gendering of lives written and lived. Such categories compel us to ask: how different were early modern women's lives? How differently were they represented and written? And how do we as modern scholars both recognize and critically interrogate the early modern texts and signs of difference? As we have suggested, the predominant purpose of early modern life writing was exemplarity. The exemplary life, most commonly that of a figure of public standing or greatness, was perforce male; female exemplarity was seldom written as biography and was restricted to the spheres of private devotion and household economy, and to the gendered virtues of silence and chastity. The recovery of women's lives has largely emerged out of the texts of domesticity and devotion. In particular, social historians have uncovered the shared traces of women's lives in courtesy manuals, devotional tracts, household accounts. For all the riches of such histories, we have not yet recovered a highly individuated sense of female lives, of lives self-fashioned, engaged, active. The lives of female monarchs would seem to provide an exception; they are after all and most obviously the lives of public figures, exemplars, models of religious leadership and civic engagement. And yet for all that, and perhaps because of all that, in some measure their femaleness and their relation to other female lives have not been sufficiently studied, especially in the case of Mary Tudor. We have of course some examples of women who have written themselves into and out of spaces and genres which early modernity had not gendered—letters, memoirs, portraits.

---

[17] See Ch. 5, p. 101.

Lady Anne Clifford forged both an identity and public authority from acts of representation—reading, writing, narrating her own life.[18] It is such sites in which women wrote themselves and lived their own lives that draw our critical attention as biographers. Annabel Patterson rereads the life of Elizabeth Cary not only as a biographical form but as a text of the processes through which an early modern woman crafted her familial and social relations, her identity, her very self. Reading and rereading between the lines of this life, Patterson allows us to hear a distinct female voice and to glimpse a highly individual female life. Early modern women's lives were defined by, lived within, not only spheres but also what we categorize and they recognized as genres. As Patterson observes, the sponsoring institutions of life writing—the church, the university—were male domains. Though we have not yet fully explored the subject, there can be little doubt that changes in women's lives, both lived and written, were mapped and enabled in the history of early modern genres. Protestantism, still more religious radicalism, opened new genres and spaces for female biography and autobiography. And as the ubiquitous male complaint long evidenced, the romance was a site within which and out of which female identity—often transgressive— was formed. In the Restoration there was an obvious broadening of generic opportunity which is inseparable from the emergence of women into public life and publicity. Obviously, infamously, the stage, but also the portrait, the public park, became not only genres and sites for new representations of females, but female spaces and geographies, and not least of a highly erotic and explicitly sexual character. In any narrative of the relations of genre and gender we turn naturally to the emergence of the novel, not least because contemporaries worried those relations. For the novel was not only anxiously regarded as licensing, emancipating, dangerous femininities, it was suspected as the solvent of masculinity and of gender difference itself. The novel provides a new script for the representation of female lives, but perhaps more importantly it fashions new modes of writing and reading, that is to say, experiencing, female lives—all readers' lives.

---

[18]   G. Parry, 'The Great Portrait of Lady Anne Clifford', in D. Howardth (ed.), *Art and Patronage at the Caroline Court* (Cambridge, 1993), 202–19; M. E. Lamb, 'The Agency of the Split Subject: Lady Anne Clifford and the Uses of Reading', *English Literary Renaissance* 12 (1992), 347–68; Barbara K. Lewalski, *Writing Women in Jacobean England* (Cambridge, Mass., 1993), ch. 5.

The history of the novel is not only intertwined with the cultural and social histories of the late seventeenth century, but with architectures of the mind, with the emergence of a new psychology of the self.[19] And as historians of the novel have observed, the emergence of the form cannot be separated from the foundation of what we would recognize as the field of psychology and in particular with the determining force of childhood and with the concept of development. The moment of the novel and Lockean psychology are historically specific and mark the end of our period and perhaps of early modernity. Yet, today, as historians, as literary critics, as students of the human sciences, we cannot deny the powerful impulse, the need, to identify psychological affinities with the subjects of early modernity, to, in the words of Paul Johnson's life of Elizabeth, know our subject 'with a fair degree of intimacy'.[20] The question then poses itself: are we able to interpret and write an early modern history and biography which incorporates the psychological without the cardinal sin of anachronism?

While early modernity was obviously not concerned with developmental psychology and the emotional dynamics of early childhood, Renaissance culture was deeply concerned with the lives, the training, the formation and regulation of youth.[21] Humanist pedagogy was directed not only to learning but to the shaping of spiritual, moral, and civic lives. The modern sensibility finds in pedagogic manuals and habits not only the texts of instruction but disciplinary practices and discourses which undoubtedly spoke to the erotics of early modern education.[22] Nor are the erotics of what we would categorize as adolescence entirely absent from the texts and archives of early modern life. We are familiar with the story of Elizabeth's adolescent encounter with her

[19] Michael McKeon, *The Origins of the English Novel 1600–1740* (Baltimore, 1987); John Bender, *Imagining The Penitentiary: Fiction and the Architecture of Mind in Eighteenth-Century England* (Chicago, 1987); see also, now, McKeon, *The Secret History of Domesticity: Public, Private, and the Division of Knowledge* (Baltimore, 2005).

[20] Paul Johnson, *Elizabeth I* (New York, 1974), 195, as quoted by Leah Marcus in Ch. 10.

[21] See Philippe Aries's classic study, *Centuries of Childhood: A Social History of Family Life* (New York, 1962); and, more recently, I. Ben-Amos, *Adolescence and Youth in Early Modern England* (New Haven and London, 1994), and Matthew Harkins, 'Poetics of Youth in Early Modern England', unpublished Ph.D. thesis, Washington University in St Louis (2003).

[22] See Alan Stewart, *Close Readers: Humanism and Sodomy in Early Modern England* (Princeton, 1997).

guardian and kinsman Lord Admiral Thomas Seymour; but in the main, historians and biographers have moved swiftly and even embarrassedly over the archival hints of what we would unquestionably call abuse. By laying aside the discomforts not only of adult and improper male desire, still more the sexual infatuation of an adolescent girl and princess, Marcus opens a psychological dimension of life critical to history and biography.

Our modern sensitivities to the psychologies of childhood sexuality, abuse, and paedophilia may open further historical and biographical subjects. A recent rereading of a poet at the heart of the early modern literary canon exposes an Andrew Marvell that we could not have imagined let alone written a decade ago. While we have long if nervously acknowledged the children in Marvell's poetry and imagination, it is the modern diagnosis of paedophilia that brings out the full and illicit powers of that attraction. And beyond that, we can now suspect and in the psychological as well as critical sense analyse the traces of childhood trauma and even abuse in that hitherto impenetrable lyric, *The unfortunate Lover*, in which Marvell imagines and perhaps discloses the history of a life, his own biography.[23] Such enquiry surely opens other texts, most especially fictions, to the discovery of elisions and repressions which are fundamental to the life, if not as obviously to early modern life writing. We need in other words to lay aside our discomforts— perhaps our own repressions and elisions—in order fully to understand the desires and traumas that determined early modern lives no less than our own.

Though the modern sensibility locates the psychological first and foremost in the sexual, for early modernity it was spiritual desire and anxiety that was at the heart of selfhood. Frances Harris cautions a modern biographer saturated in secularism that 'where we are preoccupied with the self, they were with the soul'.[24] Harris's axiom neatly summarizes for us entire literatures and discourses—sermons, spiritual guides, homilies—that urge the surrender of self, the giving of the life

[23] See Derek Hirst and Steven Zwicker, 'Eros and Abuse: Imagining Andrew Marvell', *ELH* 74 (2007), 371–95.

[24] See Ch. 13, p. 290. Quite appositely McKeon, writing of the very end of our period, reverses this formula, observing 'The gradual replacement of "soul"—by "self"— terms over the span of this period', as well as 'the growth of both secularization and the sociological imagination', p. 349 of the present volume.

to God and to others. Further, the reference to soul underscores the entirely different temporality in which the life was lived, and an entirely different narrative of its writing. Modern biography of course frames life narrative between the historical moments of birth and death. The religious life, by contrast, has its origins in considerations of the first man and woman, of the fall, of original sin, of infant innocence; its terminus is not of course the death of the body but the translation of the soul and the life fulfilled in a return to the Lord's embrace. The afterlife, which only occasionally features in the modern biography as an epilogue of reputation, of historical and social memory, was for the early modern life anything but an appendix. The afterlife was the realization of the life—what gave the life its meaning. Though of course historians and biographers have fully charted denominational histories and spiritual lives, it may be that the modern biographical form of narrative as well as our scepticism and secularism accord too little place to the obsession with the hereafter as a determining force in the early modern life. And yet the contrast of selves and souls may separate what contemporaries experienced and often disturbingly as integral. For all the literatures of self-subordination, the discourses of self-righteousness, spiritual ambition, and pride inhabit early modern texts from the pulpit to the stage. The ubiquitous recognition and satirizing of hypocrisy evidences a deep concern that the spiritual was all too often the worldly. The tensions between the secular and the sacred need to be brought to the fore in our writing of all early modern lives.

In the case of rulers, we have histories and biographies that comprehend the sacred and secular, the history of kings and queens as heads of church and state. What we have inadequately interrogated is the early modern configuring of the secular and sacred in rule and the person of the ruler. Ernst Kantorowitz's famous explication of the theory of the king's two bodies has rightly influenced our histories of political thought and in some measure political practice. But this concept has seldom driven or even much informed the narration of early modern royal life.[25] And yet almost all early modern monarchs drew attention to their corporeal and spiritual bodies and selves in public addresses but more revealingly in poems, portraits, and prayers. When James II's

---

[25] E. H. Kantorowicz, *The King's Two Bodies: A Study in Medieval Political Theology* (Princeton, 1957).

devotions have been discussed at all, they have been treated as a text of Whig and Jacobite polemic; they surely invite rereading as a text of intense personal spirituality, of complex psychology and fractured subjectivity. For James II as for Charles I we have spiritual memoirs that can be opened as biography; what we might recognize is that a myriad of spiritual discourses open not simply onto the spiritual but onto all the dimensions of the life less familiar to us as the spiritual.

Religious histories and biographies have understandably been written as the stories of confession and denomination; we familiarly describe in titles and subtitles early modern English men and women as Anglican, Calvinist, Puritan; we might note in passing that only recently has historical and biographical attention been given to the Catholic lives subordinated by confessional polemic.[26] Such denominational terminology serves the needs of religious history and even of straightforward biographical description; what we would urge is a deeper consideration of the relation between confessional identity and the full contours of the self. The theological and liturgical differences between Catholic and Protestant have defined religious history in early modern as in our own histories. But what did it mean to inhabit soteriological systems, to interiorize the different scripts of salvation and damnation, to live the spiritual life according to the different prescriptions of works and grace? The few experiments in the psychobiography of spiritual figures have perhaps understandably deterred scholars from a full psychology of the spiritual life, but the ubiquitous literature of spiritual anxiety and struggle has not been accorded its full place in the life of character, of the formation of the whole personality.[27] Though contemporaries

---

[26] For the principal works on the recovery of Catholic history see J. Bossy, *The English Catholic Community 1570–1850* (Oxford, 1975); C. Haigh, *Reformation and Resistance in Tudor Lancashire* (Cambridge, 1975); C. Haigh, *English Reformations* (Oxford, 1993); E. Duffy, *The Stripping of the Altars* (New Haven and London, 1992); M. Questier, *Catholicism and Community in Early Modern England: Politics, Aristocratic Patronage and Religion, c. 1550–1640* (Cambridge, 2006); P. Lake, *The Antichrist's Lewd Hat: Protestants, Papists and Players in Post-Reformation England* (New Haven and London, 2002); Alison Shell, *Catholicism, Controversy and the English Literary Imagination* (Cambridge, 1999); Arthur Marotti, *Religious Identity and Cultural Fantasy: Catholic and Anti-Catholic Discourses in Early Modern England* (Notre Dame, Ind., 2005); Frances Dolan, *Whores of Babylon: Catholicism, Gender and Seventeenth Century Culture* (Ithaca, NY, 1999).

[27] See, most famously, Erik Erikson's controversial biography of Luther, *Young Man Luther* (New York, 1958).

and modern scholars have often written religious lives as the stories of spiritual companionship and community, attention to all the tremors of the spirit may help to illuminate the particular and individual spiritual experience. Once we recognize that early modern spiritual texts are texts not only of the devotional life, it is important to acknowledge that texts of spirituality should not be confined by denomination—the Protestant, the Puritan, the Catholic. The texts and conceptions of what have often been deemed spiritual esoterica—the cabalistic, the neoplatonic, the Hermetic—must be, as the case of Moray demonstrates, integrated into the entire life, and into the writing of that life.

The early modern life as we have seen was, above all, a site of exemplarity, and written for use. In any divided culture, however, notions of exemplarity and perceptions of use are inevitably matters of debate, contest, and division. There is no doubting the consequences of Reformation for life writing as for all literary forms in early modern England. In Protestant and Catholic martyrologies, in spiritual biographies, in scaffold life narratives, in wills and testaments, spiritual struggles as well as identities were forged and published. The Reformation was the impetus for collective biography and individual lives which were written, circulated, often printed, not only as exemplary models but also as confessional polemic. If sixteenth-century lives were written in the wake of Reformation fractures, how much more obviously and powerfully did political division across the seventeenth century define and drive the imagining and writing of the life. Most obviously civil war, republic, restoration, and revolution wrote and were written by biographical narratives: the lives of heroes, political martyrs and traitors, protagonists for lofty principles or good old cause. Even after military contest in civil war was subdued by the temporary stabilities of Restoration, life writing remained central to continuing polemical warfare. As Andrea Walkden remarks, 'the life narrative [is] the battleground of the Restoration'.[28] Civil war and revolution not only and inevitably wrote and rewrote lives as texts of party and cause, they fashioned a desire, an appetite and market for lives, old and new, a market which printers and publishers rushed to satisfy. As well as the established figures of government and court, warfare and republican experiment brought to the fore as subjects a new cast of characters—brilliant parliamentary

---

[28] See Ch. 15, p. 335.

generals, cavalier heroes, charismatic preachers. Such figures became the subjects of life narration and representation in print, in portrait, in engraving and woodcut, on medal, in memento, in verse and ballad. The life of Cromwell—a hitherto obscure provincial gentleman—is only the most obvious example of a public life represented, indeed created, in civil contest; in the cases of Henry Ireton, Charles Fleetwood, Colonel Wildman, James Naylor, the most obscure and lowly figures became the subjects of fame and infamy.

During the 1640s and 1650s lives, old and new, were not only written in and for the new demands of a public sphere; the commerce of print was everywhere embedded in partisanship and conflict. Though scholars have yet fully to interrogate the ideological identities and relations of publishers, printers, and parties, there can be little doubt that certain publishing houses were deeply identified with positions and causes; Quakers, Ranters, and Levellers had identifiable printing houses; it was in fact printers and publishers who created their communal identities, their public lives.[29] Less obviously, less tangibly, in his various editions of cavalier poets—Carew and Lovelace for example—Humphrey Moseley surely sought not only to form a literary canon but, while chasing a profit, to summon poetry and poets to the banner of ideology. The civil war rendered the literary edition a site of polemic and partisanship, and for the rest of this century the editing and publishing of literary as much as political lives was everywhere marked by ideology and difference. As Blair Worden demonstrated, John Toland's edition of the life of Edmund Ludlow erased religious radicalism to highlight republican sympathies in the service of Whig polemics.[30] Toland is more famous of course as one of the first editors and biographers of John Milton; but as Corns's survey of the early lives makes clear, Toland's design was to publicize a Milton of consistent republican commitments at the expense of the lives of spirit and scandal. Out of past political contest editors

---

[29] See e.g. Joad Raymond, *Pamphlets and Pamphleteering in Early Modern Britain* (Cambridge, 2003), 234–47; John Barnard, 'London Publishing, 1640–1660', *Book History* 4 (2001), 1–16; Keith L. Sprunger, *Trumpets from the Tower: English Puritan Printing in the Netherlands 1600–1640* (Leiden, 1994); and Katherine Van Eerde, 'Robert Waldegrave: The Printer as Agent and Link between Sixteenth-Century England and Scotland', *Renaissance Quarterly* 34 (1981).

[30] Edmund Ludlow, *A Voyce From the Watch Tower*, ed. A. B. Worden (London, 1978); and Blair Worden, *Roundhead Reputations: The English Civil War and the Passions of Posterity* (2001), 21–121.

such as Toland wrote and rewrote histories and lives as new models of exemplarity and for the new conditions of the politics of party. In these conditions of partisanship the acts of memorializing and commemorating lives were often written and likely to be read as polemic; acts of recollecting and re-presenting lives rewrote them in ways that often rendered the life quite other than originally written or lived. Elizabeth I, for example, might have happily embraced her Anglican afterlife, but surely would have been horrified by being memorialized as champion of international Calvinism, still more of Whig politics.[31] In the case of Charles I, from the moment of regicide and self-scripting the life was everywhere appropriated and rewritten; indeed, in serving myriad polemic ends the complexities of the life were subsumed in the typologies of saint and martyr, heretic and sinner.[32] Ironically, as rewritten by Restoration and revolutionary polemic, the lives of Charles I appear to have lost the intricacies of an interior life which was the essence of the *Eikon Basilike*.

We would not wish to argue, however, that the polemics of Restoration life writing are confined to the public and social, the external life. Nor was a Restoration fascination with the interior a business only of the lives of faith and spirit. In Restoration life writing as in Restoration culture, we can hardly avoid a contemporary fascination, an obsession, even a prurient engagement with the most intimate aspects of aristocratic and public lives. Lely's portraits of female aristocrats and courtiers disclose an interior and sexual life not obvious in the canvases of his great predecessor, Van Dyck.[33] No student can read *Poems on Affairs of State* without everywhere encountering the most intimate details of lives once veiled and proscribed as *arcana imperii*. Late seventeenth-century readers both demanded and secured an unprecedented access to the privacies and interiorities of lives of state and stage, even of the king himself. As mention of the king reminds us, Charles II responded to, even encouraged, such access to intimacy for his own purposes in

[31] See J. Watkins, *Representing Elizabeth in Stuart England: Literature, History, Sovereignty* (Cambridge, 2002); J. Walker, *The Elizabethan Icon, 1603–2003* (Basingstoke, 2004); M. Dobson and N. J. Watson, *England's Elizabeth: An Afterlife in Fame and Fantasy* (Oxford, 2002); J. Lynch, *The Age of Elizabeth in the Age of Johnson* (Cambridge, 2003).

[32] See See A. Lacey, *The Cult of King Charles the Martyr* (Woodbridge, 2003).

[33] See Catharine McLeod and Julia Marciari Alexander (eds.), *Painted Ladies* (New Haven and London, 2001).

the representation and scripting of his story. He was notorious for
the publicity and publication of the often lurid details of his private
affairs. As we have begun to appreciate, however, such acts of sexual
self-publication may have been tactical as well as self-indulgent; and in
the case of the narrations of his escape from the Battle of Worcester,
intimacy, humanity, even vulnerability were deployed and published
as personal virtues and qualities of rule.[34] Though unprecedented in
their preoccupation with Charles's vulnerability and humanity, early
narrations were popular not only as printed lives, but as songs, ballads,
and symbols. Charles II is by no means the only example of the inti-
macies and commonalities of the royal life. In the 1680s there was a
vogue for stories of Henry VIII as the companion of a humble cobbler
and for romances of Elizabeth's amorous and personal life, a vogue
which extends to the genre of the secret histories, which came into huge
popularity by the end of this century.[35] All these genres of lives gave
unprecedented access to arenas hitherto intimate and private; though
their relation to the broader stories of politics and ideology have yet to
be plotted, there can be little doubt that the publication of intimacy
was itself part of the narrative of revolutionary politics, and even of the
larger processes of demystification and democracy.

In Michael McKeon's formulation, we are presented with the exemplary life itself as it shifts from a focus on greatness to the celebration and

---

[34] K. Sharpe, ' "Thy Longing Country's Darling and Desire": Aesthetics, Sex and
Politics in the England of Charles II', in J. M. Alexander and C. Macleod (eds.), *Politics,
Transgression and Representation at the Court of Charles II* (New Haven and London,
2007); A. M. Broadley, *The Royal Miracle: A Collection of Rare Tracts, Broadsides, Letters,
Prints and Ballads Concerning the Wanderings of Charles II After the Battle of Worcester*
(1912); M. Williams (ed.), *Charles II's Escape from Worcester: A Collection of Narratives
Assembled by Samuel Pepys* (1967). See B. Weiser, 'Owning the King's Story: The Escape
from Worcester', *Seventeenth Century* 14 (1999), 43–62.

[35] *The Pleasant and Delightful History of King Henry 8th. and a Cobler Relating How
He Came Acquainted with the Cobler* (P2530, ?1670); *The Cobler Turned Courtier Being
a Pleasant Humour between King Henry the Eight and a Cobbler* (C4782, 1680). There
were many variant editions of *The History of the King and the Cobbler*, some in two parts,
published in the eighteenth century. For Elizabeth, see e.g. *The Novels of Elizabeth Queen
of England* (Wing A4221, 1680); *The History of the Most Renowned Queen Elizabeth,
and her Great Favourite, the Earl of Essex In two parts. A Romance* (Wing H2173, 1700);
The Secret History of the Duke of Alencon and Q. Elizabeth A True History (Wing S2341,
1691). For recent work on the 'secret history' genre, see McKeon, *The Secret History of
Domesticity*, 469–505, and Annabel Patterson, 'A Restoration Suetonius: A New Marvell
Text?' *MLQ* 61 (2000), 463–80.

publication of ordinariness, of the common man. McKeon finds in the rise of empiricism, the scientific revolution, and the 'sociological imagination'[36] the origins of new forms of imagining and writing lives—most signally the emergence of the novel with its new modes of virtual exemplarity and its new picaresque heroes and heroines. What we might also emphasize is the politics of these developments and transactions. 'The valorization of interiority'[37] in the figuring of all lives, the turn from greatness to common exemplarity, is unquestionably related to a Restoration unsettling of traditional structures of authority and hierarchy. Even aristocratic life, by the early eighteenth century, begins to be depicted less as removed greatness and privilege than as life lived not only within but across the socialities and social arrangements of order and class. The conversation piece—the favoured genre of aristocratic self-portraiture—was unquestionably a site of status and privilege, but status and privilege now presented not only as intimate and familiar but even accessible and inclusive. By the time of Queen Anne, the royal portrait—the very mode of iconicity and mystery—has become domestic, bourgeois, almost ordinary.[38] These demystified portraits have of course their own politics which in celebrating ordinariness and shared humanity construct new bonds of affectivity between rulers and subjects in ways that gesture to the familiar images of our own monarchs, prime ministers, and presidents. On canvas as in the novel, even the life of greatness has begun to be written as the ordinary life.

The common life identified by Michael McKeon is not only common in our sense of humble or lowly; it is common also in the sense of communal and shared. This may seem, if not a pious, a forlorn hope in an age that we have described as riven by difference and partisanship rather than defined by community and affinity. In fact rather than a disjuncture we identify a relation—a history—between the rage of party and quest for community and common humanity which fashioned the exemplary lives of the novel. It should not surprise us that after half a century of bitter conflict in which the discomforts of necessary allegiance troubled the careers and lives of so many public and literary

[36] See Ch. 16, p. 349.   [37] See Ch. 16, p. 341.
[38] Toni Bowers, *The Politics of Motherhood: British Literature and Culture* (Cambridge, 1996); S. Schama, 'The Domestication of Majesty: Royal Family Portraiture, 1500–1800', in R. Rotberg and T. Rabb (eds.), *Art and History: Images and their Meaning* (Cambridge, 1988), 155–83.

figures, contemporaries yearned for at least the illusion of community. That quest for harmonious coexistence has been told as the history of politeness and latterly as the forging of a common identity, that of Britons.[39] Do we not also detect the desire for pacification and community in new modes of life writing, and not only in the lives represented by fiction but as well in the new communities of readers fashioned by the form.[40] Whether written to underpin political causes and commitments or to deny or temper bitter partisanship, late seventeenth-century lives were formed by and within, and gave definition and expression to, human needs, social formations, and ideology.

Reflections on the end of our period inevitably lead us to review the processes and histories out of which biography emerged in late early modernity. We have briefly discussed within the broad and continuous category of exemplarity changes in the writing of lives as models of spirituality and civic virtue. We have argued—for all the continuing lability of the modes and forms of life writing—some increasing self-confidence within the form itself, a settling of locales and designs of the 'life'—that is a more clearly articulated sense of the project of biography. Unsurprisingly such emerging self-confidence and self-consciousness we have plotted in the history of genre: in the story of the clear publication and recognition of the life as a literary genre. In the case of a figure like John Dryden, the engagement with and the writing of biography is for the first time integral to the literary career, not only as a literary mode itself but for him a necessary site of self-reflection. The histories that we are tracing are not simply literary: the shifting forms of life writing and the emergence of biography must be told as part of economic and social history—of aristocratic patronage and clientage, of expanding literacy, of the commerce of print, of the development of urban and urbane lives. And finally we have urged the full situating of lives in all the high political narratives of early modern reformations and revolutions, in all ideological narratives. We would argue that the further exploration of such narratives—especially brought into conversation and play with one another—will unfold new perspectives and insights into the exchange between lives and histories. However, what most characterizes the essays

---

[39] See Colley, *Britons*.
[40] See Zwicker, 'The Constitution of Opinion and the Pacification of Reading', in Sharpe and Zwicker (eds.), *Reading, Society and Politics in Early Modern England* (Cambridge, 2003), 295–316.

in this collection, rather than grand narratives, is an engagement with, a celebration of, the local, the particular, the case study, the micro-historical. We discern here a congruence with broader historiographical scepticisms about master narratives and overarching explanatory models as well as with the de-centring moves of recent literary theory. In the case of writing early modern lives, many of our contributors argue that a full reinhabiting of the local and an embrace of the gaps and silences in the archive, of the fragmentary and the episodic, are crucial to comprehending and writing early modern lives.

What does such a reinhabiting of early modernity then teach us about our own writing of early modern lives? Whatever our addiction to narrative, coherence, and explanation, our contributors surely imply the historicity and ideology of the modern biographical project and consequently underline the risks of plotting pre-modern lives as Enlight-enment biography. Similarly our return to the fragmentary and episodic as well as to the condition of exemplarity point to the incongruence for early modern lives of a modernist model of developmental psychology with its profound teleologies.[41] To urge a scepticism about modernizing narratives and to reinhabit the fragmentary may seem to follow the turns, some might say raise the spectre, of the postmodern. And indeed it is not coincidental that some of the most interesting refigurings of the early modern have emerged from postmodern insistence on the historic-ity and ideologies of modernity and a disassembling of the modernist categories of the natural and normative. But as critics have increasingly objected, postmodernism has been less willing to accept the ideology and historicity of its own moves and moment—a moment which now appears itself transitory rather than exemplary.

How then might we conceive and write early modern lives in a time after postmodernity? For much of our period we have been talking about lives written for instruction, application, and polemic. Today biographies and lives seem far more obviously written for entertainment. Whether as books, bi-ops, or blogs, modern lives traverse all the media of the entertainment industry. What could appear more distant from early modern technology, spirituality, and exemplarity? And yet when we reflect on twenty-first-century modes of representing lives from an

---

[41] In her recent *The Sea Lady* (New York, 2006), one of Margaret Drabble's characters urges, 'The universe has shed the teleological fallacy' (p. 303).

early modern perspective we can identify some affinities. Though we are surely far removed from Renaissance scripts of exemplarity, we unquestionably take the lives of sporting celebrities and movie stars, even the ordinary figure raised to publicity through reality television, not only as cultural icons but as the very models of selfhood. And today the obsession with celebrity, the cult of the makeover, the ubiquitous desire to craft social identity out of fashion evoke and echo and speak to the impulses and desires of Renaissance self-fashioning. Despite the intense scepticism and secularism of our own time, do we not also discern in contemporary yearnings to find identity in popular icons some traces of the spiritual anxiety as well as psychological dislocations that we have identified in early modern lives? And for all our talk of entertainment and recreation, contemporary figurings of lives just as much as early modern representations are sites of ideology and contestation. In urging and explicating the exchanges among the early modern, the modern, and the contemporary we may find not only better ways of understanding and writing early modern lives but a greater willingness to historicize and critically read the scripts of our own life narratives—ourselves.

PART I
LIVES AND BORDERS

1

Biography and Modernity: Some Thoughts on Origins

Stella Tillyard

At the beginning of *Society and Sentiment*, his book about history writing in the eighteenth century, Mark Phillips tells a story about an angler who fishes all day.[1] He is watched, to his increasing annoyance, by a silent observer, a man who stands close to him hour after hour, looking at everything, saying nothing. At the end of the day, the angler, gritting his teeth to be civil, nods to the stranger as he leaves and says, 'Fish much yourself?' 'Oh no, not me,' the other man says, 'I'd never have the patience.'

Phillips uses this story to illustrate the sometimes tense relationship between those professional historians who cast their lines of enquiry into the past and those historiographers who watch them do it. But for me it stands equally for another, often uneasy, connection, that between academic historians and professional writers or even popular historians. In that scenario, the 'real' anglers are the professionals; the watchers, wonderers, and even enviers, are the writers who swim in the murky waters of commerce.

Changing places is hard, especially if one feels out of date with ichthian banter, rusty with the camaraderie of the river bank. So this assignment preyed on my mind, rising to the surface—if I can use that expression—at odd moments. One such, a few months ago, occurred for me at the Stadio Artemio Franchi in Florence, waiting for a match between Fiorentina and Empoli to begin. As the two teams ran onto the field an announcement was made that before the kick-off we would

---

[1] Mark Phillips, *Society and Sentiment* (Princeton, 2000).

remember two Italian soldiers killed in Iraq the previous week. The teams lined up opposite each other on either side of the centre circle and the whole ground fell silent. So far, so conventional, except that the solemn moment was slightly undercut by the referee blowing his whistle at the beginning and end. Two weeks later, though, we were back for the last match of the season, a very noisy affair between Fiorentina and Reggio Calabria. Over the chanting I caught the announcer saying something similar about remembering an ex-Fiorentina player who had just died. Again the players lined up; again the referee blew his whistle. But this time there was no silence. Instead everyone—players, coaches, Fiorentina and Reggio Calabria fans—applauded, clapping steadily until the minute was up. We were celebrating and not mourning a life—a life, I knew, from my reading of the local paper, that had latterly been spent in happy retirement, 'in the shadow of his beloved stadium', as the newspaper put it. A man who died at 89 years old and whose funeral had just been held in the church next door. His was a life to be celebrated with noise, not a death to be regretted in silence.

This distinction struck me at the time because I had been puzzled for years about another difference between the way death is recorded in Britain and in Italy, that is the lack of obituaries in Italian newspapers, or, to put it another way, the fact that there is, in Italy, no tradition of obituary writing as we know it in Britain. Since the obituary, as it has developed in the Anglo-Saxon world, is the most ubiquitous biographical form that we have, the complete absence in Italy of the obituary as a way of summing up and commemorating a life must say something about the Italian attitude towards death and life—but also asks the question why, as well as how, it ever developed in Britain at all.

Although I am loathe to use national identity or any idea about national character as a descriptive or explanatory category, the fact that this volume focuses on biographical writing in early modern England points to a nationally specific enquiry. This perhaps justifies the use of such generalizations if only as a foil or mirror in which to see more clearly.

In Italy, unlike Britain, there is, as the silence and clapping in the stadium showed, no uniform way of commemorating and remembering a life, either audibly or in print. A long life well lived will be applauded and then, if there is no mystery attached to it, left alone. Newspaper articles, published on the news pages rather than under any separate heading, will celebrate an individual's public achievements, mention his or her moral qualities and notice, probably, his attachment to his native town. Untimely deaths will be accompanied in print by interviews with relatives. In all cases, family and friends insert black-bordered death notices in newspapers, and in small towns, larger versions of these are displayed on public notice boards. Contrast this with Britain where, on the whole, grief remains a private affair, but all famous individuals will be given public cradle-to-grave obituaries. In these short essays—and here I think we approach explanations for the very existence as well as the resilience of the British biographical tradition—origins are described, character is at least in part ascribed to origins, and achievement is usually explained, indeed, with reference to character.

This difference, the relative lack of interest in the relationships between private and public, origins and achievement in Italy, and the overwhelming importance of the notion of character in all forms of writing in the British tradition, is, I think, usually ascribed to religion. Somewhere like Italy, the argument runs, was and remains an aural, confessional, and Catholic culture in which the story of a life—and its moral foibles—is told to a priest and atoned for daily before and after death. In prayer and in the confession box, sins are absolved, leaving the deeds to speak for the man. Protestant, literate cultures, on the other hand, in which men and women had to show their private worth by their public deeds, encouraged the writing of conversion narratives which emphasized and demonstrated moral reformation and lives well lived. It is out of saints' lives, moral narratives like *The Pilgrim's Progress* as well as their mirror images, the ubiquitous lives of highwaymen, pirates, or courtesans that the British biographical tradition is to have emerged. All such narratives rely on a notion of character already well developed by the end of the sixteenth century.

Think of the plots and themes of *1 Henry IV* (to select just one of many Shakespearian plays that fit the template). An extended revelation of true kingly character, the play's plot is the working out of the idea that a person's true character and origin—in this case those of the Prince of Wales—will in the end become manifest in public deeds, and that therefore, in the end, public deeds will reflect and describe the true private man.

Now it is obvious that such plots are far from absent in Catholic cultures. St Augustine's *Confessions* tell the story of just such a transformation. The emphasis, the balance, however, remains different, and perhaps mitigated against the development of a strong biographical tradition. In the first place, while origins are not denied in Italian culture, it is where a person arrives and what he does that is important, not where he started and how he arrived. Second—and this is perhaps because in a miraculous culture God himself can change your life and character in an instant—there is little interest in origin as the fount of character and thus of deeds.

It is here, however, that English biography was anchored from the beginning. The interest in origins so evident, for instance, in Aubrey, was compounded by Lockean notions of the importance of childhood to the creation and development of character that became current at the end of the seventeenth century. Samuel Johnson's *Account of the Life of Richard Savage*, often cited as the first great English biography, thus has at its heart and almost as its *raison d'être* both the search for aristocratic origin and Savage's mysterious and miserable childhood.[2] Amplified by Rousseau in the mid-eighteenth century, these beliefs in the importance of early experience were balefully confirmed by Freud at the beginning of the twentieth.

English biography then has been a genre centrally concerned with origin and character since its emergence in the late seventeenth century. But this idea of character, along with the concomitant interest in manners, habits and domesticity and private life, that goes along and perhaps grew out of it, is so ubiquitous in all forms of writing in the early eighteenth century that it may not make sense to talk of English biography at that time as a separate genre at all.

Eighteenth-century readers, it seems to me, existed until quite late on in the century and for the most part without comment or complaint, in a kind of genre soup. Letters, journals, biographies, history, the novel, what we can call, for want of a better word, journalism, memoirs, even poetry all had porous boundaries, often made claims to define themselves as something else, and were read equally in a spirit neither of belief nor scepticism but, perhaps, something in between.

Most readers seem to have been untroubled by taxonomic discretion. One of the eighteenth century's most enduringly popular works, never out of print before the French Revolution, was Anthony Hamilton's

---

[2] Johnson, *An Account of the Life of Mr Richard Savage* (London, 1744).

secret history of the Restoration court, translated into English and published in 1714 as *Memoirs of the Life of the Count de Grammont: containing, in particular, the amorous intrigues of the Court of England in the Reign of King Charles II.*[3] The text claimed to be a life—that is a biography—of the Count de Grammont written from his letters and journals and thus in some sense 'true'. But Grammont's *Memoirs* are not in any way autobiographical and he himself is neither the work's author nor its principal protagonist. The *Memoirs* are mostly taken up with Hamilton's brothers and sisters, and are part secret history and part fiction. Moreover, they contain within the narrated framework extensive passages of dialogue as well as poetry and letters, and thus slide about between scandalous history, a kind of picaresque fiction, and a pastoral romance. A decade after Hamilton, Defoe built a career on such ambiguities, publishing *Jonathan Wild* in 1725 as 'The True and Genuine Account of the Life and Actions of the Late Jonathan Wild; not made up of fiction and fable, but taken from his own mouth and collected from papers of his own writing'.

Exactly when biography becomes a distinct and recognizable genre, or when the different branches of writing peal away from one another, is one of the questions that this volume will try to address. But it is clear that it is not an overriding interest in character and private life that distinguishes it when it does, for these elements are common to the novel as it emerges, as well. What may distinguish biography, or run alongside its preoccupation with character and origin, may be something else entirely.

I have been struck, thinking about who in the seventeenth and early eighteenth century had tellable, telling, lives, by how many of them were products and agents of social change, of urban and imperial life: in short, of modernity. Modernity was (and is), of course more a state of mind than anything else. But the way in which, in the early eighteenth century, highwaymen's lives were told, or courtesans', merchants', or even writers', was as embodiments of the modern and thus of the present age. It was here, perhaps, that biography began to insist on a difference with history, for although history might have allegorical force it could never record and describe the modern age directly. The huge popularity

---

[3] Anthony Hamilton (trans.), *Mémoires de la vie du comte de Grammant* (London, 1714).

of lives of the recently dead, or even of the still living, suggests that they were read in part as a mirror to the modern.

The modernity that such biographies insisted on defined itself in two familiar ways, an insistence on a feeling of the separation and isolation of its subjects, and a belief that this feeling inheres in urban life, that is to say, in England, and in London life. London drew towards it more than a tenth of the population in the early decades of the century. If individuals began to think of themselves as isolated from others in the great city, where they acted a part, or could decide which part to act, then a branch of writing which came to concentrate on single subjects might seem to reflect, or come to reflect, contemporary experience. Biography could accommodate and describe new ways of life and new forms of fame. In narratives like those of Equiano or James Lackington, it could advertise and celebrate stories of arrival and transformation in the city.[4] But at the same time it could, in relating intimate life, offer individuals the sense that in the city, in the narrative, there were ways of being acquainted with those you might have seen, but would never know. Biography might thus describe and embody the conditions of modernity while simultaneously offering a consolation for their trials. It is no surprise then, that Boswell's *Life of Johnson*, the story of a provincial who came to London and made his mark in the modern metropolis, should have been immediately hailed as a masterwork. For Boswell remained true to English biography's interest in character, origins, private life, and transformation while at the same time offering a fable of success in the capital. Johnson's life, as Boswell told it, stood not only for modernity but also, in 1791, for a peculiarly English modernity, one that was pious, Anglican, monarchist, modest, anti-idealist and, above all, not French. Perhaps that is why, at that moment, English biography as a literary art seems, for the first time, to have come into its own.

[4] *The interesting narrative of the life of Olaudah Equiano, or Gustavus Vassa, the African. Written by himself* (London, 1789); *Memoirs of the first forty-five years of the life of James Lackington... In a series of letters to a friend...* (London, 1791).

2

An Irregular Life: Not a Biography of Constantijn Huygens

Lisa Jardine

Between early November 1670 and mid-September 1671, Sir Constantijn Huygens, 72-year-old secretary and adviser to the young William of Orange, was in London with his 20-year-old charge, attempting to retrieve monies owed to William by his uncle Charles II.[1] It was William's first visit to his mother Mary Stuart's country of birth. Strictly speaking he travelled as a commoner. He had not yet regained the position of stadholder of the Low Countries (of which he had been stripped as an infant, following his father's death in 1650), but now that he had declared himself 'of age', complex political manoeuvring by the Orange faction seemed likely to achieve that end.[2]

As far as Charles II was concerned, his young Dutch relative was a potential bit-part player in his complicated power-brokering negotiations with France and the Dutch Republic: 'According to the *Sommier Verhael* ("Summary Relation") of William's journey, Charles II had repeatedly kissed his nephew when he arrived in England in early November 1670.'[3] The king was particularly insistent that William be treated with all ceremony:

When the prince of Orange was to dine with the lord mayor in [January] 1671, there was much consideration of the seating arrangements; the king

---

[1] William returned to The Hague in late February 1671.

[2] William was made commander of the Northern Provinces Army by the States General in 1671, and stadholder in 1672, following the murder of the de Witt brothers and the fall of the Republic.

[3] W. Troost, *William III, the Stadholder-King: A Political Biography*, trans. J. C. Grayson (Aldershot, 2005), 63–4.

was consulted and he gave his ruling on the matter—that the prince should rank before the mayor. A 15th-century precedent was then unearthed which, showing Henry V's brothers had ceded place to the lord mayor, apparently contradicted Charles's decision on the matter, but 'notwithstanding the King kept his first opinion; alledging that forms of Ceremonies were changed in the world since that time; & that those Dukes were the Kings own brothers; yet they were his subjects; which the Prince of Orange was not.[4]

When the City of London refused to give way on the matter, the king simply declined to attend and the dinner was cancelled.

Still an 'ordinary' visitor, though a nephew of the king, William was fortunate to have with him the elder statesman who had served both his father and his grandfather as secretary—and someone as thoroughly conversant with English court ways as Huygens.

The debts owing to the House of Orange, which Huygens undertook to recover, included the dowry Charles I had contracted to pay William's grandfather when his father and mother were married (hastily, on the eve of the first English civil war, in 1642), and substantial sums later advanced to Queen Henrietta Maria for ships and weapons to assist the royalist cause.[5]

Among the Huygens letters in the Royal Collection at The Hague is a copy of the final letter from Charles II to William (who had returned to the Low Countries ahead of his old retainer), written during that residency:

Copie de ma derniere lettre de Residence du Roij de la Gr. Bretaigne à S. A. Whithall 13 Sept. 1671.

I am not a little ashamed that I have delayd Mon^r. de Zulichem from time to time wth. promise of a speedy dispatch, and according to what I haue written to y^u. in my former letters. The founds giuen me by the Parliament haue fallen infinitely short of their first computations which hath disturbed and made almost ineffectuall all mij orders; so that it were to abuse y^u. to giue y^u. any of them. The Treasurij tells me y^e. *haue y^e. first fourty thousand pounds orders: y^e.*

---

[4] PRO, LC5/2, pp. 29–31.

[5] 'The English King owed [William] 2,797,859 guilders, a debt which included the unpaid dowry of his mother, worth 900,000 guilders.... From the financial viewpoint William's journey had little result. The King and his nephew agreed to reduce the debt to 1,800,000 guilders, but the English King again proved to be a bad payer' (Troost, *William III, the Stadholder-King*, 62–3).

shall haue y^e. next before Christmas come twelf month and so from yeare to yeare,
till y^e. whole debt as it was stated at y^r. being here.

And this will be more effectuall then any orders I could giue y^u. This I will doe at the woorst, if mij condition inable me to doe better, and all other good turnes that can fall in mij way to do y^u. from mij kindnesse to y^r. person, as well as y^r. neare relation to me. I cannot finish this letter, wch. I meane to communicate to the bearer, before I seal it up, nor before I lett y^u. know how troublesome a sollicitor he hath been to me, though a most zealous one for y^u. and consequently how worthy he is of the continuance of y^r. esteem and good will. This is all I haue to saij to y^u. at present, but to assure y^u. that I am wth. all imaginable kindnesse yours.

Charles writes to William in English (a language he and Huygens spoke and wrote with almost native fluency); in his archive, Huygens heads it in French (the language of the Dutch elite). The exchange is clear evidence of Stuart–Orange understanding at a 'family' or domestic level, and of Huygens's pivotal role in crafting that relationship, vital to William's national and international political future.

The money, as I said, was never forthcoming (Charles II rarely settled his debts, and the 1670s were a particularly parlous time for his exchequer), but the sentiments expressed by the Stuart king towards Huygens may be taken to be sincere. Since the long-term result of this visit was the marriage alliance between James, Duke of York's daughter Mary (Charles's niece) and William, the anglophile Huygens's negotiations and bridge-building between the House of Orange and the Stuarts may be judged to have been overall a success. Indeed, I want to argue that Huygens's activities on either side of the Narrow Sea represent a version of Anglo-Dutch intellectual, cultural, and political accord in the seventeenth century which—whilst unfamiliar—actually sums up the age.

Quite recently, I came across another piece of epistolary evidence for the way the unexpected closeness of Anglo-Dutch accord—the almost cosy personal relations between William's circle and the Stuart court—had (or in this case, almost had) remarkable historical consequences, leeching away the national protocols separating English affairs from Dutch.

While in London, in December 1670, and presumably following an unspecified face-to-face encounter, Huygens wrote (in English) to

Sir Christopher Wren, the Royal Surveyor, responsible for the rebuilding
of London after the Great Fire, as follows:

The King hath been pleased to keepe a copie of this poor project, and would
doe me this morning the honour to commend it with the character of 'a very
good paper'. If it doe but chance to pass for half so good in your liking,
Sir, I will hold my paines happily bestowed. I pray you to peruse it, that we
may have occasion to conferre about [it], while I am here. It may be, one
time or other some relexion will be made upon the reasons of a simple autor,
who is . . . [6]

No further mention of this 'project' can be found in the Huygens
archives around this date, but in a letter of 18 February 1678 there is a
further, clarifying reference, this time in a letter in French to Monsieur
Oudart:

It matters little whether my inscriptions have been used for the Column or not.
I remain extremely well satisfied that so distinguished a person as Monsieur the
Surveyor [Wren] found them to be to his taste, to the point that he produced
them to the City officials, and thereby demonstrated to them my good will
towards their great and most noble City. I beg you to assure that most excellent
personage of my boundless esteem for his great talent and my most ardent
affection in his service. [7]

So, remarkably, the 'poor project', which both Wren and Charles II,
according to Huygens, found so much to their taste, was proposed
inscriptions for the plinth of the Monument to the Great Fire.

Sure enough, if we trawl through Constantijn Huygens's literary
works for this period (he was a prolific writer of poetry in four or
five languages), there we find the draft Latin inscriptions in question.
They are, as we might expect, carefully humanistic and classicizing, in a
distinguished tradition of erudite inscriptions. The second concludes, in
suitably ringing tones: 'Having been consumed as a city of wood, you

---

[6] J. A. Worp (ed.), *De briefwisseling van Constantijn Huygens 1608–1687*, 6 vols.
('s-Gravenhage, 1911–17), letter 6778.

[7] 'Il importe peu que mes inscriptions ayent esté employées à la colonne ou non. Je
demeure fort satisfaict de ce qu'une personne si entendue que Mr. le surveyor [Wren] y
ayt trouvé quelque gout, jusques à en faire part au magistrat, et leur ayt fait paroistre de
ma bonne volonté à l'endroict de leur grande et tres-noble Cité. Je vous supplie de bien
assurer cest excellent personnage de ma veritable estime de son grand merite et de ma
tres-ardente affection à son service' (Worp, *Briefwisseling*, letter 7077).

are resurrected in marble ... Nor should we doubt that restored, your glory will be even greater than before.'[8]

The Prince of Orange's arrival in London in late 1670 followed awkwardly on the heels of Charles II's signing of the secret Treaty of Dover with Louis XIV against the Dutch, in June of that year. Strictly speaking, England and Holland were on the brink of war (the third Anglo-Dutch war was eventually declared following France's invasion of Holland two years later). Yet here is William's most senior adviser, closely involved in discussions with the English king and his royal surveyor, concerning Dutch involvement in the memorial to England's most recent national calamity.

Neither Huygens's commemorative inscription, nor remarkably similar ones which Wren himself proposed, were in the end used as the inscriptions on the plinth of the Monument to the Great Fire.[9] On 4 October 1677 the Court of Aldermen of the City of London minuted their final decision as to the inscriptions:

This Court doth desire Dr Gale Master of the Schoole of St Paul to consider and devise a fitting inscription to be set on the new Pillar at Fishstreet Hill, and to consult therein with Sr Christopher Wren Knt his Matie's Surveyor Generall and Mr Hooke And then to present the same unto this court.[10]

Within three weeks of the first meeting of the inscription committee, the Court of Aldermen, having heard from the lord mayor that Charles II had 'very well approved' the inscriptions drafts, decreed that the inscriptions be carved 'forthwith'. On 25 October the Court rewarded Gale with 'a handsome peice [*sic*] of plate'.[11]

It is not entirely surprising that Huygens should have volunteered his services for the task of providing suitably imposing verses to commemorate London's providential deliverance from utter obliteration in the fire of 1666. In addition to his reputation as a cultivated diplomat, a

[8] *De Gedichten van Constantijn Huygens* online, University of Leiden website: http://www.let.leidenuniv.nl/Dutch/Huygens/index.html.

[9] For Wren's proposed inscriptions, see *Parentalia: or, memoirs of the family of the Wrens; viz. of Matthew Bishop of Ely, Christopher Dean of Windsor, &c. but chiefly of Sir Christopher Wren. In which is contained, beside his works, a great number of original papers and records ... Compiled by his son Christopher* (London, 1750), 323.

[10] CLRO, RCA 82, fo. 268ᵛ.

[11] See J. E. Moore, 'The Monument, or, Christopher Wren's Roman accent', *Art Bulletin* 80 (1998), 498–533. Gale was previously Regius Professor of Greek at Cambridge.

man of good taste, and a considerable musician, Huygens was internationally renowned as an accomplished poet (in Latin, Dutch, French, English, and Italian). The lines Huygens had proposed and crafted for the unbuilt Monument—the construction of which was being widely discussed during the period of his 1670 stay in London—were not the first he had been encouraged to propose for an internationally famous memorial.[12] Indeed, in all likelihood, it was his poetic involvement in an earlier memorial project which had led to the subject of the Monument inscription becoming a topic of conversation at the English court.

In 1620, the 22-year-old Huygens (with the support of his older poetic colleague Daniel Heinsius) had been given the task of composing the epitaph for the magnificent tomb of William the Silent (assassinated in 1584), erected in the New Church at Delft by the States General, designed and built by Hendrick de Keyser. That Latin inscription runs:

In honour of God Almighty and in eternal memory of William of Nassau, Prince of Orange, Father of the Fatherland, who valued the prosperity of the Netherlands higher than his own interests or those of his family; who twice, and largely at his own expense, gathered powerful armies and let them into battle under the command of the States; who averted the tyranny of Spain, brought back and restored the true religion and ancient laws; who finally bequeathed the almost fully regained liberty to be confirmed by his son Prince Maurice, heir to the virtues of his father; the truly pious, prudent and invincible hero whom King Philip II of Spain, the terror of Europe, feared, but could neither subdue nor intimidate, but killed with heinous perfidy by the hand of a hired assassin, the United Provinces have commissioned this to be erected as an eternal memorial to his virtues.[13]

---

[12] An Act of Parliament of 1667, related to the rebuilding after the Great Fire, already contained the instruction that: 'The better to preserve the memory of this dreadful visitation; Be it further enacted that a Columne or Pillar of Brase or Stone be erected on or as neare unto the place where the said Fire so unhappily began as Conveniently as may be, in perpetuall Remembrance thereof, with such Inscription thereon, as hereafter by the Mayor and Court of Aldermen in that behalfe be directed.' This early decision to erect a memorial Pillar was confirmed in the 1670 City Churches Rebuilding Act. There money was allocated for a memorial 'the better to preserve the memory of this dreadful visitation'. On 14 February 1671 the London Court of Common Council approved the 'Draught or Modell . . . of the Pillar'. Work excavating the foundations (to create that laboratory) was completed in November 1671, and construction must have commenced shortly thereafter.

[13] Concerning these lines, Huygens wrote to Heinsius: 'Fallor, amplissime domine, nisi ante discessum in Italiam de epitaphio mausolaeo Delphensi inscribendo tecum vel coram vel literis egi. Nondum adeo hac molestia perfunctus sum, quin ed reducem

The imposing monument to William the Silent was commissioned and built during the period 1618–23, as the inscription stresses, to commemorate the 'Father of the Fatherland', who had defended the Low Countries against the threat to freedom and Protestant religious practice. It became the key national monument to the House of Orange—a tourist destination for Netherlanders from all over the country. The monument was regularly depicted in fashionable 'church interior' paintings of the Neue Kirk in Delft, by a whole range of fashionable artists.

We might reflect on the fact that both William's tomb and the Monument to the Great Fire are conceived of as standing to posterity in remembrance of such a threat—and as focal points for a moderate Protestant faction's national fervour.

* * *

Huygens was certainly not exaggerating the warmth of his reception by Charles II. He had been on cordial terms with the English royal family since his early twenties, when he had visited London, and the court of James I, in the train of the Dutch ambassador.

On 10 June 1618 (new style) in the early hours of the morning, the 22-year-old Constantijn Huygens, son of the first secretary to the Dutch Stadholder, Maurits of Nassau, arrived in England for the first time in the entourage of the English Resident Ambassador to The Hague,

exceperint reliquiae. Ilustrissimus Princeps—quo jubente ac dirigente primum illud conamen meruisse videretur—totius denique rei curam parenti meo discedens mandavit atque ultimum exemplar potentissimis Ordinibus Generalibus exhibere jussit. Hic Hollandiae delegati negotium suo examine dignum praeter alias provincias censuere, ut quorum praecipue curae atque impensis haec fabrica constaret. Cum itaque eorum aliquos promovendi iudicii causa convenissem, indicavere tandem ad curatores et senatum academicum omnem causam devolutam esse. De curatoribus autem aliud heri ex D. Honerdo didici, qui sese de inscriptione ne fando quidem hactenus audjisse asserebat. Non restat nisi Academia. In ea quam tu pro merito personam sustineas, vir amplissime, nescis nescire nos. Adorior itaque nunc te et per illum candorem atque humanitatem quâ bene de me meisque mereri in usu habes, rogo et obtestor, ne diligentiam et, quod poteris, authoritatem tuam deesse patiaris mihi, quo brevem et expeditum judicij terminum haec mea quodammodo causa sortiatur. Adderem et benignum, nisi in sapientissimi Principis verba jurare, quam propriae imbecillitatis causam agere, satius longe crederem atque opportunius. Caetera tibi uni committo, iterum precatus, ut nos ab assidua operarum importunitate—gestiunt illi ultimam operi manum imponere—quam primum liberatos velis. 9° Cal. Septemb. (= 24 Aug.) 1620' (Worp, *Briefwisseling,* letter 90).

Sir Dudley Carleton.[14] The visitors disembarked, then waited at Gravesend until seven, when coaches were found to take them to King James I's palace at Greenwich. Arriving there shortly before noon, they discovered that the king had left at short notice, on a whim—they had missed his departure by just a few hours. The ambassador (whose first duty upon arrival was to present his credentials to his royal master) set off again in pursuit with his entourage.

As a result, the party spent their first week in England on the road, lodging each night at a different stately home and engaging in some enjoyable high-class tourism, before they eventually caught up with the king and his court at one of James's favourite royal residences, Theobalds ('Tibbalts') in Hertfordshire.[15] Here, on Saturday, 16 June, Carleton formally kissed the king's hand and received his royal instructions. Afterwards the party retraced its steps, arriving finally at the ambassador's London residence.[16]

For the rest of his long life, Constantijn Huygens recalled this first encounter with England, its topography and culture, and the lavish lifestyle of the English court with nostalgic delight. The magnificence of the parks and houses visited was in striking contrast to the way of life he had left behind him in the Low Countries—both because of the greater ostentation of English aristocratic life in the early decades of the seventeenth century, and because the fifty years since the beginning of the Dutch Revolt had scarred and depleted homes and countryside across the United Provinces.

A few days after that first encounter with King James, Constantijn left Carleton's household and took up more settled residence in London. As had been arranged by his father before he left, he went to lodge with the elderly Noel de Caron, Lord of Schoonewalle, Dutch Resident

---

[14] They had left The Hague on the evening of 7 June: 'En Angleterre aveq Carleton', 7 June 1618 (J. H. W. Unger, *Dagboek van Constantine Huygens: voor de eerste maal naar het afschrift van diens Klein zoon uitgegeven* (Amsterdam, 1884), 9).

[15] 'Depuis ma premiere que je vous envoyay de Gravesende je n'ay point eu nulle commodité pour vous faire entendre de mes nouvelles. De huit jour que j'ay esté en Angleterre à peine m'en suis-je trouvé trois à Londres, ayant continuellement suivi Mons.ʳ Carleton par le païs, ou il a esté trouver le Roy en une de ses maisons royals, dite Tibbalts, que est un des superbes palais de l'Angleterre, ou j'ay eu moyen de veoir le Roy et la court fort à mon aise' (6/16 June). Worp, *Briefwisseling,* i: (1608–1634) ('s-Gravenhage, 1911), 21.

[16] A. G. H. Bachrach, *Sir Constantine Huygens and Britain* (Leiden and Oxford, 1962), i. 113–17.

Ambassador in London, and long-term servant of the house of Orange, at Caron House on the south bank of the Thames. From this palatial residence the young Huygens proceeded to experience London life to the full, and to take advantage of Caron's excellent connections to further frequent the court circle (though in his letters home he complained to his parents about the distance from Caron House to central London, and the exorbitant cost of transport). He did some enthusiastic sightseeing, commenting expertly on elegant locations and new buildings in and around London, visited friends of his father and of his host across the city, dined and partied. He also made great strides with his English— the main purpose of the trip as far as his father (grooming him for a diplomatic career) was concerned. In Huygens's later reminiscing (some of it in elegant, celebratory Latin verses), one of the high points of his stay at Caron House was a private visit there by the king himself, accompanied only by his son Charles, Prince of Wales, and his closest favourites—the Earls of Arundel and Montgomery, and the Marquesses of Buckingham and Hamilton. The king was apparently anxious to spend some time in Caron's garden, picking and tasting recently ripened Dutch cherries (which James harvested himself by means of 'a ladder, specially carpeted for the purpose'). Afterwards the visitors stayed for a light meal, and a tour of Caron's picture gallery, 'to give serious attention to the paintings' ('à spéculer aux peintures').[17]

During the meal Huygens was presented to the king by his host, who especially drew attention to the young man's virtuosity on the lute (Constantijn may have been invited to provide the background music while the royal party ate). According to Huygens, proudly writing to keep his parents informed of his progress overseas, James was so impressed that he insisted that Caron must have Constantijn entertain him on the lute at length on a future occasion, at Bagshot (the grace-and-favour hunting lodge given by James to Caron for his use during his residence in England).[18]

That later occasion (towards the end of September 1618) made such an impression on Constantijn that he committed it to verse in a poem entitled, 'About to sing to the lute in the presence of the King of Britain':

[17] Bachrach, *Sir Constantine Huygens*, 139.
[18] Bachrach seems to suggest that this occasion followed immediately after the June encounter with King James, but that is not what is implied by the documents. See Bachrach, *Sir Constantine Huygens*, 139–40.

Thrice the greatest among Kings lends a majestic ear;
Grant, O skilful Thalia, more than my usual strains.
. . . .
Kingly glory, I admit, dazzles the eye.
In the Divine presence the tongue stiffens and is numb.[19]

'But shall he who speaks the Batavian [Dutch] language despair of pleasing the English Gods?' Huygens concludes.

On that second occasion, too, James engaged the young Dutchman in informal conversation. Although at the very moment they were talking together, the Dutch Stadholder Maurits of Nassau was in the process of effecting a very public coup in the United Provinces to take control of the States General (a power play in which Constantijn's father, a prominent official in the Dutch administration, was necessarily heavily involved), the exchange consisted entirely of social banter.

Nonetheless, Huygens was well pleased to have made a good impression on the English monarch. When he was dismissed from the royal presence he felt 'fairly delighted with the excellent success of my humble affairs'.[20] The delight was converted not long after into lasting benefit

---

[19] Bachrach, *Sir Constantine Huygens*, 218.

[20] 'une petite demie heure [je] m'acquitay si passablement bien que ce Prince, naturallement peu adonné à la Musique, fut tiré à interrompre par diverses fois son jeu à me donner audience, comme il fit fort débonnairement, sans espargner ses serments ordinaires, pour m'asseurer du contentement qu'il y prenoit, me faisant mesmes l'honneur de parler à moy avec un visage doux et soubsriant'. Huygens's second encounter with James also involved Buckingham, and suggests that Huygens was well placed to exploit his connections once he became secretary to the Dutch stadholder: 'It was Fortune which had provided the thunderstorm that kept the Royal hunting-party indoors [at Bagshot in late September] and, by interrupting the King's programme, favoured what Huygens did not hesitate to call his own designs. Caron had at once reminded His Majesty of the day when he had first presented his guest, and had added divers other good recommendations in his favour. . . . when the first showers broke as [the King] was about to drive off to the hunt—"desia il eut le pied dans la portière pour monter en Carosse"—he had retired to his apartments in order to have a game of cards with his "grand mignon", the Marquess of Buckingham, and another Gentleman of the Bedchamber. Then, some two hours later, the summons had come to Constantyn to appear with his lute in Caron's room, who again showed how greatly he was mindful of his youthful compatriot's honour by personally conducting him into the Presence—"volontièrement et sans que mesme h'en priasse"' (Bachrach, *Sir Constantine Huygens*, 179–80). Huygens also had a significant encounter with Charles, Prince of Wales (the future Charles I): 'In the case of [Prince Charles], Constantyn's good fortune had quite unexpectedly allowed him to join in a hunt in Richmond Park for an entire afternoon. The heir apparent had removed from Whitehall to his own palace at Richmond in the second half of July and from there begun "a little progress by himself". This was clearly a form of self-assertion on the part of the

for Huygens. On his third visit to England a few years later, he was personally knighted by the English monarch. The 'Sir' customarily prefixed to his name marked this leading member of an ostensibly democratic and republican-leaning nation out as one of its new, Orange aristocracy.

Still, what can have been the mentality of the Orange–Stuart accord, to have made it even a possibility that a senior Dutch diplomat, serving the House of Orange, should have come close—close enough to please the Stuart king and his loyal royal surveyor—to providing the inscription for the Monument to the Great Fire?

And there's another question we need to ask. We are clearly dealing here with a figure who functions freely and with some authority (cultural as well as political) in two nations separated by the Narrow Sea (as the Dutch called it). What is the impact of that upon any attempt to construct a coherent biographical picture of that person?

* * *

To try to advance this, for the moment tentative, argument, here is another episode of international cultural transaction with Constantijn Huygens at its fulcrum—the hasty assembling of a gift of suitably distinguished paintings by the States of Holland of the United Provinces, to present to the English king, Charles II, as he returned to his artistically depleted kingdom in 1660.

In spring 1660, as Charles II gathered his supporters and future ministers around him in the northern Netherlands prior to his return to England to lay claim to the throne, the Estates of Holland and West Friesland resolved to secure the favour of the new king by making him a fine and memorable diplomatic gift. Its centrepiece was a magnificent, highly decorated, carved bed, with bed-furnishings, and there was also the promise of a handsome ship, to be called the *Mary*. But the 'Dutch gift' also included a carefully selected group of paintings, by major, recognized artists, and a number of classically inspired sculptures.

Three years after his first visit to England, Constantijn had succeeded his father as personal secretary and artistic adviser to the Dutch

Prince, and Constantyn's introduction to Charles and his suite had become an adventure so dominated by youth and a carefree holiday spirit that it proved "le plus plaisant jour que j'aye eu en ce païs" ' (Bachrach, *Sir Constantine Huygens*, 161).

Stadholder Frederik Hendrik. That early visit was an important grounding influence on him, when he set about the task of acquiring art works
and exotica for Frederik Hendrik for his palaces in and near The Hague,
as part of a conscious effort to raise the profile of the Orange stadholders
to something like 'royal' status on the international scene.[21]

It was Huygens, too, who (in consultation with Jacob van Campen)
completed the carefully integrated programme of architecture and
painting for the Oranjezaal of the Huis ten Bosch on the outskirts
of The Hague (designed by Pieter Post), where an elaborate cycle of
paintings and decoration, entirely by Netherlandish artists, commemorated and glorified the achievements of Frederik Hendrik for his widow
Amalia van Solms, following Frederik Hendrik's death in 1647 (the
project was completed in 1652).[22]

By the late 1660s, Sir Constantijn Huygens was in his seventies, with
a career's worth of experience brokering art and culture for the house
of Orange. He occupied an unrivalled position in cultivated circles in
the Dutch Republic, as arbiter of taste in all things cultural, from music
and poetry to art and architecture. When it came to the delicate task of
selecting a few Dutch pieces to include in the 'Dutch Gift', he was the
obvious expert to consult.

Discreet enquiries had been made, and it had been determined that
Charles's taste, like his father's, was for Italian art and antique statuary. Accordingly, most of the works presented were by Italian masters,
beginning the process of reassembling a major collection for the English
monarch, to replace those sold off and dispersed by the Commonwealth
in 1650. Art connoisseurship at The Hague now tended towards modern, Dutch works—visiting the palace of Rijswijk some years earlier,
Evelyn had commented that 'nothing [is] more remarkable than the
delicious walks planted with lime trees, and the modern paintings
within'.

So the Italian paintings and sculptures for Charles's 'Dutch gift'
were acquired, conveniently, from the collection of art-collecting brothers, Gerrit and Jan Reynst, which had recently come on the market,

---

[21] See M. Keblusek and J. Zijlmans, *Princely Display: The Court of Frederik Hendrik
of Orange and Amalia van Solms* (Zwolle, 1997).
[22] Ibid. 121–5. See also J. Adamson (ed.), *The Princely Courts of Europe 1500–1750*
(London, 1999), 130.

following the death of Gerrit in 1658 (Jan had died in 1646).[23] This was, at the time, one of the most celebrated collections of Italian paintings of its time—though later the authenticity of a number of prominent works in it would become a very public matter of dispute.[24] The States of Holland approached Gerrit Reynst's widow, Anna, with the proposal that they should select from among her late husband's paintings and sculptures a group of the most outstanding. In September 1660, the sculptor Erasmus Quellinus and the dealer Gerrit Uylenburgh chose twenty-four pictures and twelve statues, which arrived in London at the beginning of November, where they were exhibited in the Banqueting House at Whitehall. Charles II ceremoniously visited the paintings to inspect them, and his evident delight caused a considerable stir.[25]

But in addition to the Italian art works, with their acknowledgement of the Stuart taste of Charles II's father, the Dutch Gift included four contemporary Dutch paintings. One of these was a classic near-contemporary Dutch work: Pieter Saenredam's *The large organ and nave of the St Bavokerk, Haarlem, from the choir* (1648), which was purchased from the Amsterdam burgomaster, Andries de Graeff. Three others were bought directly from the much-admired 'modern' artist, Gerrit Dou. One of these was a characteristic Dutch domestic interior (exquisitely detailed): Gerrit Dou's *The Young Mother* (1658), now in the Mauritshuis at The Hague.

In the case of Saenredam's *Large organ and nave of the St Bavokerk, Haarlem, from the choir*, the connection to Huygens's patronage can be documented, since we can identify the very painting acquired from de Graeff as one that Huygens had seen some years earlier, and considered purchasing himself. On 21 May 1648, Pieter Saenredam

---

[23] See full account in A.-M. S. Logan, *The 'Cabinet' of the Brothers Gerard and Jan Reynst* (Amsterdam, 1979), 75–86.

[24] For a concise account of this dispute, which involved Huygens's offering expert testimony in favour of the works' authenticity on behalf of the expert who had vouched for them (in which he was probably wrong), see John Michael Montias, *Vermeer and his Milieu: A Web of Social History* (Princeton, 1989), 207–9.

[25] See D. Mahon, 'Notes on the "Dutch Gift" to Charles II: I', *Burlington Magazine* 91 (1949), 303–5; 'Notes on the "Dutch Gift" to Charles II: II', *Burlington Magazine* 91 (1949), 349–50; 'Notes on the "Dutch Gift" to Charles II: III', *Burlington Magazine* 92 (1950), 12–18.

wrote a letter to Huygens, following up an approach by Huygens
on behalf of Stadholder Willem II concerning some newly completed
works:

My Lord van Zuylichem,

It pleases me very much to hear that His Highness has begun to take pleasure
in paintings, that he indeed desired to see my recently completed great church,
and that he wanted to have it shipped now, in which I foresee, on the basis of
continuous experience, difficulties of such magnitude, too long to relate, that
I do not dare ship it or take that risk. Nonetheless I cordially wished that His
Highness saw the same with his own eyes, as has happened with you, My Lord.
I have had this piece along with five more of the largest brought to Monsr
Vroons.

    As for the price of the church, I trust that Your Excellency still recalls our
oral discussion.[26]

Huygens had clearly been with Saenredam, seen the paintings, and
discussed purchase prices. Nothing, however, came of the stadholder's
interest in the St Bavokerk painting—Saenredam was never represented
in the collections of the House of Orange. But it is possible that the six
paintings were indeed sent via Vroom to The Hague, and five of them
purchased instead by Huygens himself, and thence into the art collections of members of his family. *Large organ and nave of the St Bavokerk,
Haarlem, from the choir* was sold to the Amsterdam burgomaster Andries
de Graeff, from whose collection it was acquired by the States of
Holland to give to Charles II.[27] It is a particularly appropriate piece
for the Protestant monarch, in a strongly symbolic moderate Protestant
Dutch tradition.[28]

    At the courts of The Hague, under Constantijn Huygens senior's
guidance, taste in painting had noticeably shifted away from the Italian

---

[26] See G. Schwartz and M. J. Bok, *Pieter Saenredam: The Painter and his Time*
(London, 1990), 206.

[27] 'Less speculative is the identification, now generally accepted, with the picture
described in the inventory of c. 1666/7 of Charles II's collection. Although neither
subject nor artist is mentioned in the documents relating to the so-called "Dutch Gift",
it is probably the painting purchased from the burgomaster of Amsterdam, Andries de
Graeff, by the States of Holland and West Friesland and presented with other pictures
and sculptures to the King in 1660.' H. Macandrew and K. Andrews, 'A Saenredam and
a Seurat for Edinburgh', *Burlington Magazine* 124 (1982), 752–5; 755.

[28] Schwartz and Bok, *Pieter Saenredam*, 128; 149–54.

pictures typical of the great collections in London and Paris. In their collections, heroic works by Dutch artists like Honthorst, van Everdingen, Poelenburgh, and Rembrandt took pride of place, together with comparable Flemish works by artists like Rubens, van Dyck, and Jordaens. Courtly taste still tended towards the large-scale and grandiose— by contrast with the typically Dutch landscapes, seascapes, still lifes and genre scenes produced in abundance for art-lovers from mercantile and professional backgrounds. But the emphasis was firmly on the Dutch 'moderns'.

Recent work on the art market in the northern Netherlands has stressed the fact that in the mid-seventeenth century, 'access to the latest artistic knowledge depended on personal introductions, from patrons to painters and painters to patrons. Even in the Dutch Republic, where painters sold their works through myriad channels, from auctions and dealers' shops to fairs and lotteries, some of the most innovative and expensive art remained primarily accessible through private élite channels.'[29] As well as his brokering of art acquisition for the house of Orange, Huygens also acted as just such a trusted facilitator, helping would-be collectors gain access to the already highly esteemed northern Netherlandish painters in the 1660s.

Gerrit Dou received his training as an artist alongside Jan Lievens, in Rembrandt's studio at Leiden. He entered Rembrandt's studio in February 1628, at the age of 14, and remained there for three years, until he became 'an excellent master'. Since Lievens painted Huygens's portrait at just around this time, and we may assume that he also made the acquaintance of Gerrit Dou (though Dou was too young to be included in Huygens's autobiographical fragment from this period, which included a celebration of the Rembrandt studio).

In 1669, Pieter Teding van Berckhout, a patrician of The Hague with family connections to both the Huygens and Paets families, was visiting Delft in the company of Huygens. He noted in his diary that he visited 'an excellent painter named Vermeer'. On a second visit to the 'celebrated painter named Vermeer' Van Berkchout saw several 'curious perspectives'. In assessing the value of Vermeer paintings currently on the market, he and Huygens compared these with prices for comparable

---

[29] Mariët Westermann, 'Vermeer and the Interior Imagination', in *Vermeer and the Dutch Interior* (Madrid, 2003), 225.

works by Gerrit Dou.[30] Here is somewhat more circumstantial evidence that Huygens probably played a part in selecting modern Dutch works to be included in Charles II's 'Dutch Gift'.

The arrival of the Dutch paintings in the Royal Collection made a tremendous impression on the English art-appreciating public, particularly after their public display at Whitehall, and may be credited with helping to consolidate a taste and a flourishing market for contemporary northern Netherlandish art in Britain. Evelyn saw the Dou (and another 'rustic' painting) at court, on 6 December 1660, and wrote with approval:

I waited on my Bro: & sister Evelyn to Court: Now were presented to his Majestie those two rare pieces of Drolerie, or rather a Dutch Kitchin, painted by Douce [Dou], so finely as hardly to be at all distinguished from Enamail.[31]

The king himself is supposed to have been so charmed by the exquisitely detailed painting that he offered Dou the post of court painter (Dou declined).[32]

* * *

Even from these fragments of cultural history, it is clear, I hope, that the life of Sir Constantijn Huygens is an object lesson in the dangers of life writing which does not cross national boundaries. Huygens has two separate 'lives', according to whether he is being looked at from one or other side of the Narrow Sea.

And yet, as we have seen, his life is inextricably intertwined with extremely important cultural moments, and whole movements in artistic taste, in both the Netherlands and in Britain. My task, in my next

---

[30] Ben Broos, 'Un celebre Peijntre nommè Verme(e)r', in *Vermeer and the Art of Painting* (New Haven, 1995), 49; Montias, *Vermeer and his Milieu*.

[31] *The Diary of John Evelyn*, ed. E. S. de Beer, 6 vols. (Oxford, 1955; repr. 2000), iii. 262.

[32] One of Dou's Dutch fellow artists protested at this English attempt to steal the services of yet another of the United Provinces' most distinguished sons, in verses which translate as follows: 'Thou paragon of painters, Dou | Shall Stuart spirit thee away? | Shall Whitehall's lures thy soul subdue? | Thyself wouldst surely rue the day! (...) | He who princes favour craves | Must join the ranks of sycophants and slaves.' See R. van Leeuwen (ed.), *Paintings from England: William III and the Royal Collections* (The Hague, 1988), 79.

book, will be to exemplify the fascinating 'irregular life' of Huygens—
the story one can tell of achievement spanning nations, binding them
together in ways we have failed to recognize. That has required me
to abandon traditional life writing—whether historical or literary—in
favour of entirely new strategies for weaving together the life stories of
outstanding individuals who shaped European culture. Hence my *Going
Dutch: How England Plundered Holland's Glory*, will be 'Not a Biography
of Sir Constantijn Huygens'.

PART II

LITERATURES AND LIVES

3

'Secrets and Lies': The Life of Edmund Spenser

Andrew Hadfield

A conservative instinct has paralysed Spenser scholars in the face of the problem of producing a modern biography and it is perhaps not surprising that the last attempt was published in 1945.[1] There are—broadly speaking—two sorts of early modern literary biography. There are biographies such as R. C. Bald's life of John Donne, or William Riley Parker's and Barbara Lewalski's long accounts of the life of John Milton, which are based on an extensive study of the mass of life writings and other evidence that survives.[2] More often than not, however, fewer traces of writers' lives exist, as is the case, most notoriously and frustratingly, with the life of William Shakespeare. Accordingly, biographers have to be more speculative, as the lives written

---

[1] Alexander C. Judson, *The Life of Edmund Spenser* (1945), in *The Works of Edmund Spenser: A Variorum Edition*, ed. Edwin Greenlaw et al., 11 vols. (Baltimore, 1932–49), p. xii. Recent work on Spenser's life includes: Ruth Mohl, 'Spenser, Edmund', in A. C. Hamilton (ed.), *The Spenser Encyclopedia* (London and Toronto, 1990), 668–71; Judith H. Anderson, Donald Cheney, and David A. Richardson (eds.), *Spenser's Life and the Subject of Biography* (Amherst, Mass., 1996). Overviews of work are provided in Richard Rambuss, 'Spenser's Life and Career', in Andrew Hadfield (ed.), *The Cambridge Companion to Spenser* (Cambridge, 2001), 13–36; Andrew Hadfield, 'Spenser, Edmund', *ODNB*; Patrick Cheney, 'Life', in Bart Van Es (ed.), *A Critical Companion to Spenser Studies* (Basingstoke, 2006), 18–41. Earlier versions of this chapter were given at the 'Writing Lives' conference at Queen Mary, and at the Universities of Cambridge, Essex and Exeter. The audiences raised very helpful issues on each occasion.

[2] R. C. Bald, *John Donne: A Life* (Oxford, 1970); William Riley Parker, *Milton: A Biography* (Oxford, 1968; rev. Gordon Campbell, 1996); Barbara K. Lewalski, *The Life of John Milton* (Oxford, 2000).

by Katherine Duncan-Jones, Stephen Greenblatt, and Peter Ackroyd demonstrate.[3]

Different life records often produce different biographies. When a substantial archive of letters survives, as in the case of Sir Philip Sidney or Sir Francis Bacon, such evidence would appear to preserve the thoughts and feelings of the subject in question, enabling the biographer to write an authentic life.[4] When nothing is left behind that preserves the opinions of the writer, then a new fact, new interpretation of a known piece of evidence, or even a new way of reading a once familiar context, bears a huge burden as a means of unlocking the mysteries of the psyche hidden from view. Did Shakespeare's leaving his second best bed to Anne Hathaway signal his contempt for her, his lasting affection, or was it simply a usual practice?[5] Was his grain hoarding during times of dearth and significant investment in land and property a sign that he was more interested in money than art, or are we reading too much into this stray fact?[6] Was Chaucer murdered, or was the timing of his death just a bit odd?[7] Was the fact that he was accused of rape significant, or are we fostering a modern meaning anachronistically on a rather more benign and less specific word?[8] Lives of Chaucer and Shakespeare invariably rely on a reading of the work to understand the personality behind the text, as well as an understanding of a variety of contextual details. Anyone writing the life of an early modern writer has to face this problem of the equivalence between lives and their relationship to life records. It is the task of the biographer to work out a reasonable series of questions to ask about the surviving evidence and an appropriate mode of narrating the resulting story.

[3] Katherine Duncan-Jones, *Ungentle Shakespeare: Scenes from his Life* (London, 2001); Stephen Greenblatt, *Will in the World: How Shakespeare became Shakespeare* (New York, 2004); Peter Ackroyd, *Shakespeare: The Biography* (London, 2005).

[4] Alan Stewart, 'Life Writing', in Donna B. Hamilton (ed.), *A Concise Companion to Renaissance Literature* (Oxford, 2006), 238–56.

[5] Park Honan, *Shakespeare: A Life* (Oxford, 1998), 396; Michael Wood, *In Search of Shakespeare* (London, 2003), 338.

[6] William Shakespeare, *Coriolanus*, ed. R. B. Parker (Oxford, 1994), introduction, 36; Honan, *Shakespeare: A Life*, 290–2.

[7] Terry Jones, with Robert Yeager, Terry Dolan, Alan Fletcher, and Juliette Dor, *Who Murdered Chaucer? A Medieval Murder Mystery* (London, 2004).

[8] Derek Pearsall, *The Life of Geoffrey Chaucer* (Oxford, 1992), 135–8.

I.

The problem of the lack of surviving evidence has inspired boldness in Shakespeare biographers, apparent timidity in would-be biographers of Spenser. Spenser's life is not especially well documented. However, there is a large amount of information relating to Spenser's life available in a variety of forms. There are a number of letters that he wrote out when working in the Irish civil service.[9] We are able to track Spenser's movements in Ireland to a certain extent through official documents (although some of these were destroyed when the Public Record Office in Dublin became embroiled in the fighting in the Irish civil war in 1922), and more scraps of information turn up from time to time.[10] Other pieces of evidence have also appeared, such as the Tresham letter detailing the hostile reactions of the authorities to the publication of *Mother Hubberds Tale* in 1591, and the only extant copy of a book that Spenser owned.[11] We know where Spenser went to school and university, who he married, what his children were called, some details of property he acquired, lawsuits in which he was engaged, where—but not how—he died. The bones of a life can be constructed, as Willy Maley has done so admirably, in his chronology of Spenser's life.

However, we do not know anything about his ancestry and family. Spenser claims, in the dedicatory letter to Lady Compton and Mountegle, prefacing *Mother Hubberds Tale*, that he is related to her in some capacity: '[I] am bound to beare to that House, from whence yee spring,' and that he hints that he is dedicating the poem to her from a sense of their shared ancestry.[12] Lady Compton and Monteagle was

[9] See the details collected in Willy Maley, *A Spenser Chronology* (Basingstoke, 1994); Christopher Burlinson and Andrew Zurcher, ' "Secretary to Lord Grey Lord Deputie here": Edmund Spenser's Irish Papers', *The Library*, 7th ser. 6 (2005), 30–75.

[10] See e.g. Andrew Hadfield and Raymond Gillespie, 'Two References to Edmund Spenser in Chancery Disputes', *Notes and Queries* 246 (Sept. 2001), 249–51.

[11] Richard S. Peterson, 'Laurel Crown and Ape's Tail: New Light on Spenser's Career from Sir Thomas Tresham', *Spenser Studies* 12 (1991), 1–35; Lee Piepho, '*The Shepheardes Calender* and Neo-Latin Pastoral: A Book Newly Discovered to Have Been Owned by Spenser', *Spenser Studies* 16 (2002), 77–103.

[12] *The Works of Edmund Spenser: A Variorum Edition*, ed. Edwin Greenlaw et al., 11 vols. (Baltimore, 1932–49), viii. 105. Works of Spenser cited from this edition unless otherwise noted. Relevant volume, page, or line numbers from the variorum [Var.] subsequently cited parenthetically in the text.

Anne Spenser, the fifth daughter of Sir John Spencer of Althorp. The claim is repeated in verse, in *Colin Clouts Come Home againe* (published 1595, but written in 1591, according to the dedicatory epistle to Sir Walter Raleigh):

> Ne lesse praiseworthy are the sisters three,
> The honor of the noble familie,
> Of which I meanest boast myself to be,
> And most that unto them I am so nie.
>
> (Var. vii. 162, ll. 536–9)

And, in case a few stray readers have not really got the point yet, Spenser boasts that he takes his name from 'An house of auncient fame' in *Prothalamion*, his poem on the marriage of the two daughters of Edward Somerset, the Earl of Worcester, published in 1596 (Var. xiii. 162, l. 131). Yet, there is no evidence of a connection between the families apart from their shared name. Nothing is known of Spenser's family, apart from the fact that his mother was called Elizabeth, as he tells us in *Amoretti* 74 (published 1595). Given that Spenser attended Merchant Taylors' School in London, the most likely candidate for his father is John Spenser, a cloth weaver from Hurstwood, Lancashire, who moved to London to join the Merchant Taylors' Company.[13] It may be of greater significance that by 1603 Sir John's heir, his grandson, Robert, was reputed to be the richest man in England (Var. vii. 476). Probably the only man in the British Isles who could rival the riches of the Spencers was Robert Boyle, first Earl of Cork, who acquired an enormous fortune in Ireland through his canny and relentless acquisition of land titles and estates.[14] Spenser married Elizabeth Boyle, his second wife, on 11 June 1594, a relative of Boyle's. Placed alongside Spenser's attempt to ingratiate himself with the Spencer family, such evidence suggests that Spenser was a man very much on the make, perhaps as keen on the acquisition of wealth as Shakespeare. But, of course, this is to read a great deal into two possibly unrelated pieces of information.

---

[13] Mohl, 'Spenser', 668.

[14] Nicholas Canny, *The Upstart Earl: A Study of the Social and Mental World of Richard Boyle, First Earl of Cork, 1566–1643* (Cambridge, 1982); Terence Ranger, 'Richard Boyle and the Making of an Irish Fortune, 1588–1641', *Irish Historical Studies* 10 (1957), 257–97.

More significantly still, there are no letters that survive, and no literary manuscripts in Spenser's hand, only legal documents and secretarial works. We know very little about Spenser's relationships with his patrons, friends or the social superiors to whom he was connected. It was assumed for a long time that he and Philip Sidney must have been intimate associates because they were both poets who had Irish connections but this is now thought unlikely, given their difference in class and status.[15] We do not know how close Spenser and Raleigh really were, especially if we bear in mind that their relationship survives principally in the form of literary works.[16] We do not know how close he was to Lord Grey, nor what his relationship was with Gabriel Harvey after he left for Ireland in 1580. In fact we do not know why Spenser left for Ireland in that year.[17] There are many people referred to in his poetry or related to his life, who may or may not really exist: Rosalind and E.K. in *The Shepheardes Calender*, the careless servant who supposedly lost the later books of *The Faerie Queene* in Wales.[18] We do not know how Spenser died.[19]

More gaps in the biographical record could be noted, but the key point to be made is that there is nothing of Spenser's opinions, comments, or even many details of his life outside his writings. This absence appears more glaring still if we include the paratexts (prefaces, printed letters, dedications, commentary, etc.) that surround the literary texts.[20]

[15] Donald Cheney, 'Spenser's Fortieth Birthday and Related Fictions', *Spenser Studies* 4 (1984), 3–31.

[16] Robert Lacey, *Sir Walter Raleigh* (London, 1975), 155–9; Judson, *Life of Spenser*, 135–42.

[17] One series of speculations is provided in Muriel Bradbrook, 'No Room at the Top: Spenser's Pursuit of Fame', in John Russell Brown and Bernhard Harris (eds.), *Elizabethan Poetry* (London, 1980), 90–109.

[18] On Rosalind, see Richard Mallette, 'Rosalind', in Hamilton, *The Spenser Encyclopaedia*, 622; Paul E. McLane, *Spenser's* Shepheardes Calender: *A Study in Elizabethan Allegory* (South Bend, Ind., 1961), ch. 3, 'Elizabeth as Rosalind'. On the servant, see Edmund Spenser, *A View of the State of Ireland*, ed. Andrew Hadfield and Willy Maley (Oxford, 1997), 5.

[19] Ray Heffner, 'Did Spenser Die in Poverty?', *Modern Language Notes* 48 (1933), 221–6; Josephine Water Bennett, 'Did Spenser Starve?', *Modern Language Notes* 52 (1937), 400–1.

[20] On the concept of the 'paratext', see Gerard Genette, *Paratexts: Thresholds of Interpretation*, trans. Jane E. Lewin (Cambridge, 1997); Wayne Erickson (contributing ed.), *The 1590* Faerie Queene: *Paratexts and Publishing, Studies in the Literary Imagination* 38/2 (2005).

These are often read as if they existed outside the text and served to root the fictions in a reality beyond it, a problematic assumption.[21] Biographies like to be able to anchor the work in a life outside the work, which is the ostensible purpose of the literary biography (although there are some people who would like to read a biography at least as much as a literary work). But with Spenser we cannot do this, as there is virtually no life outside the works, which raises a whole series of fundamental issues about the purpose of a biography.

We are presented with a fundamental dilemma: either take what appears in the literary works as evidence of the poet's life or abandon any quest for that life and declare that it is unwritable. This *might* be a coherent position to adopt, but it appears somewhat less tenable if we consider how much Spenser represents himself in his writings and how often he urges the reader to consider the work in terms of a life behind or beyond the printed page. There is a cat and mouse game established between author and reader about how much can be assumed, reconstructed, and what the text actually tells us. To take a first example: we know that Spenser went to Ireland in 1580 as secretary to Arthur, Lord Grey de Wilton, but in Spenser's prose dialogue, *A View of the Present State of Ireland* (*c.*1596), the character Irenius tells us that he witnessed the execution of the rebel Murrogh O'Brien, which took place in Limerick on 1 July 1577. The rhetoric of the 'I' witness lends credence to a point about the ancestors of the Irish (the Gauls), marking them out as a primitive people with ancient, barbarous urges: 'I saw an old woman, which was his foster mother, take up his head, whilst he was quartered, and sucked up all the blood that runne thereout, saying, that the earth was not worthy to drinke it, and therewith also steeped her face and breast, and tore her haire, crying out and shrieking most terribly.'[22] Why does this passage appear? Does it signal to us that Irenius is really Spenser and that his hard-line opinions about the inability of the Irish to reform themselves and adapt to English law and civility without the implementation of catastrophic violence is to be taken as true? Does it provide evidence that Spenser was in Ireland at this point? If so, is it meant to draw attention to this passage as true and

---

[21] For reflections on this problem, see Jacques Derrida, 'Tympan', in *Margins of Philosophy*, trans. Alan Bass (Brighton, 1982), pp. ix–xxix.

[22] Spenser, *A View*, 66.

of particular importance? Or is it just a strange, stray moment, a textual aberration?[23]

What is clear is that it is part of a pattern long established by Spenser in his writings. In the correspondence between Gabriel Harvey and Spenser published at the start of his career (1580), Spenser and Harvey are represented in bed together sharing verses. Spenser asks Harvey what he thinks of a new Anacreontic epigram with the insouciant comment that seems designed for a third party, 'Seeme they comparable to those two, which I translated you *ex tempore* in bed, the last time we lay together in Westminster?' (Var. x. 16). The detail might simply be without any particular significance, as, according to many social historians, men often shared beds before they were married as they were keen to ward off the cold and save heating bills, as well as space in crowded London.[24] But placed in a published letter, an unusual genre in 1580, especially for a relatively young, unknown writer, and immediately after an indented stanza, Spenser's question surely draws the reader's attention to the comment and demands further investigation.[25]

Spenser's words assume an even greater significance if read against the first eclogue of *The Shepheardes Calender*, published a year earlier. Colin Clout (Spenser) rejects the advances of Hobbinol (Gabriel Harvey) in favour of Rosalind, explaining to the reader:

> It is not *Hobbinol*, wherefore I plaine,
> Albee my love he seeke with dayly suit:
> His clowinish gifts and curtsies I disdaine,
> His kiddes, his cracknelles, and his early fruit.
> Ah foolish *Hobbinol*, thy gifts bene vayne:
> *Colin* them gives to *Rosalind* againe.
>
> ('Januarie', ll. 55–60; Var. vii. 17)

[23] For discussion, see Willy Maley, *Salvaging Spenser: Colonialism, Culture and Identity* (Basingstoke, 1997), 10, 30, 42.

[24] Alexandra Shepard, *Meanings of Manhood in Early Modern England* (Oxford, 2003), 121–2. For a discussion of the poem in the light of such issues, see Jonathan Goldberg, *Sodometries: Renaissance Texts, Modern Sexualities* (Palo Alto, Calif., 1992), 63–101.

[25] Judith Rice Henderson notes the pioneering importance of the Spenser–Harvey correspondence, an experiment that 'made possible' 'The aristocratic revival of the classical familiar letter': 'letter as genre' in Hamilton, *The Spenser Encyclopaedia*, 434.

Harvey not only refers to himself as Hobbinol in letters to Spenser, but uses the name when signing his commendatory verse to *The Faerie Queene*.[26] So, if we read the texts biographically, then we have a clear case of Spenser rejecting Harvey in favour of heterosexual love, suggesting that his early attachment to another man disappeared when he discovered girls. Again, this is a narrative that social historians can support.[27] An innocent reading is undercut, however, by the very odd note that appears on the same page as the text by E.K. that draws attention to the exact nature of the relationship between Colin and Hobbinol, which is worth quoting at length:

> In thys place seemeth to be some savour of discorderly love, which the learned call paederastice: but it is *gathered beside his meaning*. For who that hath read Plato his dialogue called Alcybides, Xenophon and Maximus Tyrius of Socrates opinions, may easily perceive, that such love is muche to be alowed and liked of, specially so meant, as Socrates used it: who sayth, that in deede he loved Alcybiades extremely, yet not Alcybiades person, but hys soule, which is Alcybiades owne selfe. And so is paederastice much to be praeferred before gynerastice, that is the love whiche enflameth men with lust toward woman kind. But yet let no man thinke, that herein I stand with Lucian or hys develish disciple Unico Aretino, in defence of execrable and horrible sinnes of forbidden and unlawful fleshlinesse. Whose abominable errour is fully confuted of Perionius, and others. [my emphasis]

In denying any untoward sexual relationship between the two men, the note emphasizes its possibility. The fact that the commentary raises the ability of a reader to work against the grain ('gathered beside his meaning') indicates that this principle might apply to the text itself, especially when it is realized that the sexual meaning is, in fact, the obvious one and the platonic reading the counter-intuitive explanation.

These two passages constitute a nightmare for biographers. Is Spenser advertising the fact that he and Harvey had a homosexual relationship? Or is he confuting rumours that they might have done? Or, most likely perhaps, is he teasing an audience by appearing to reveal certain things that may or may not be true, and leaving the reader to decide how to relate the text to the life? Is he telling us that Rosalind, the ostensible

---

[26] Virginia F. Stern, 'Harvey, Gabriel', in Hamilton, *The Spenser Encyclopaedia*, 347–8; McLane, *Spenser's* Shepheardes Calender, 237–61, 'Gabriel Harvey as Hobbinol'.
[27] Alan Bray, *Homosexuality in Renaissance England* (London, 1982), ch. 2.

object of Colin's affections, does not really exist, contrasting her to the real presence of Harvey/Hobbinol? Signalling, in a manner that may or may not be facetious, that men are better off without women? Or, do these passages actually tell us very little at all, being either partially true or wholly fictitious?

There is a second problem, which indicates the intricate levels of fiction that envelop these passages. Who is E.K.? If you read the old *Dictionary of National Biography* you will discover that he was Edward Kirk, a friend of Spenser's at Pembroke College, who was part of the Spenser–Harvey intellectual axis, later disappearing from view to become an obscure clergyman. His notes to *The Shepheardes Calender* are a strange mixture of the profound and the rather ignorant. A key part of the evidence is that Spenser visited a woman who might have been his mother, as he records in the first letter to Harvey, 'Thus muche was written at Westminster yesternight: but comming this morning, beeyng the sixteenth of October, to Mystresse *Kerkes*, to have it delivered by carrier, I receuyued youre letter' (Var. x. 7). The banality of the detail would appear to confer an authenticity, and, as Henry Wouduysen has commented, 'the correspondence is the most important, at times the only, source for Spenser's biography at this crucial time'.[28] The two texts, the *Calender* and the letters, when taken together seem to be deliberately constructing a life relating to the text, one in which Spenser is a friend of Edward Kirk.

But can we actually believe that Edward Kirk wrote the notes? They have the appearance of being comments made as the commentator is reading the text along with the reader. In a gloss to line 176 of 'September', E.K. notes of 'Colin Clout':

Nowe I thinke no man doubteth but by Colin is ever meante the Authore selfe, whose especiall good friend Hobbinall sayth he is, or more rightly Master Gabriel Harvey: of whose speciall commendation, aswell in Poetry as Rhetoricke and other choyce learning, we have lately had a sufficient tryall in diverse of his workes, but specially in his Musarum Lachrymae, and his later Gratulationum Valdinensium which boke in the progresse at Audley in Essex, he dedicated in writing to her Majestie. (Var. vii. 93)

---

[28] Henry Woudhuysen, 'letters, Spenser's and Harvey's', in Hamilton, *The Spenser Encyclopaedia*, 435. See also Jon A. Quitsland, 'Questionable Evidence in the *Letters* of 1580 between Gabriel Harvey and Edmund Spenser', in Anderson et al. (eds.), *Spenser's Life*, 81–98.

This comment surely cannot be serious and meant to be taken at face value. The wealth of detail indicates that the author of the note cannot be who he says he is. If he knows this much about Harvey then how could he possibly only have realized at this stage that Hobbinol was Harvey? And why the sense of discovery in the notes, as if E.K. was reading them for the first time? The more likely explanation is that Harvey and Spenser wrote the notes—possibly with the help of the relatively anonymous Kirk—constructing the *Calender* as a humanist book which resembled the great classical editions produced by leading European scholars, as a means of self-promotion but also as a huge, self-regarding joke.[29] It is up to us as readers to work out how clever the author of the text and his associates are, what is fiction, and what is fact. The life is used as a game to promote the poetry, a splendid example of the literary text coming first. As many critics have noted in the wake of Richard Helgerson, Spenser saw the dizzying excitement of promoting himself and his writing through the new medium of print, which in the 1590s held out the possibility of providing a career and an audience for the poet, freeing him of the need for an absolute dependence on patrons.[30] It was vital that poets who could not depend absolutely on the favours of the rich and powerful saw other ways of making their mark. Spenser's disciple, Michael Drayton, went much further and was actively rude to patrons who failed to support him as he felt was his due, using his prefaces to attack patrons and readers alike (the readers failed to buy *PolyOlbion*).[31] Drayton left no estate when he died but appears to have had a good career as a poet, exploiting the opportunity of constructing an audience in print, a path that Spenser had pioneered.

It is worth noting that Spenser published his work in two distinct phases: in 1579–80, when he attempted to take the London literary world by storm by promoting himself as the great new English poet; and then after 1590, just after he had acquired the house and estate in

[29] On the relationship between the *Calender* and humanist editions, see Michael McCanles, '*The Shepheardes Calender* as Document and Monument', *Studies in English Literature, 1500–1900* 22 (1982), 5–19. On the problem of who wrote the notes, see Andrew Hadfield, 'Kirk, Edward', *ODNB* (2004).

[30] Richard Helgerson, *Self-Crowned Laureates: Spenser, Jonson, Milton and the Literary System* (Berkeley, 1983); Stephen B. Dobranski, *Readers and Authorship in Early Modern England* (Cambridge, 2005).

[31] Andrew Hadfield, 'Michael Drayton's Brilliant Career', *Proceedings of the British Academy* 125 (2004), 119–47.

Kilcolman that accorded him the rank of gentleman.[32] He published the bulk of his works in a frenetic outpouring of six years: part one of *The Faerie Queene* appeared in 1590, as did the *Complaints*; *Daphnaida* and *Colin Clouts Come Home Againe* in 1591; the *Amoretti* and *Epithalamion* in 1594; and part two of *The Faerie Queene*, the *Fowre Hymns*, and the *Prothalamion* in 1596, an astonishing amount. It is hard to account for this long and strange hiatus which is odd for a man who announced himself in such confident and grand terms in 1579/80. One answer might be that there was a fear of getting himself into more trouble after the early problems with Burghley when *Mother Hubberds Tale* circulated in manuscript. This is a plausible explanation, but the trouble is that we do not know if this story is actually true, as there is no evidence that the poem was widely read in manuscript before it was published in 1591.[33] It might still have been the case that now that Spenser had an estate he felt freer to write, no longer constrained by his employment in a variety of jobs within the Irish civil service. Clearly much had been written before, as no one could have produced work at this rate (and we know that a version of *The Faerie Queene* existed in the early 1580s).[34] The publication record does suggest that Spenser thought really carefully about how he used the medium of print to promote himself, but also how he used it to represent himself to a public readership. He did not just write what he thought was good poetry in a vacuum. The life and the art are intertwined in ways that are not easy to separate. Such evidence indicates that we simply cannot take the life out of the art because it no longer exists independently. But we cannot take the art away from the life because the work depends so much on us having a conception of the author who appears within the work. We have to play this guessing game if we want to read Spenser seriously, which is why we should not avoid the problem of the biography and its relationship to the literary text.

---

[32] Maley, *Spenser Chronology*, 55. It is instructive to compare Spenser's productivity once he had acquired an estate and reached the rank of gentleman with the change many have detected in Shakespeare's writing in 1599 once he became a shareholder in the Globe: see James Shapiro, *1599: A Year in the Life of William Shakespeare* (London, 2005), 369.

[33] The claim was first made by Edwin Greenlaw, 'Spenser and the Earl of Leicester', *PMLA* 25 (1910), 535–61.

[34] Thomas E. Wright, 'Bryskett, Lodovick', in Hamilton, *The Spenser Encyclopaedia*, 119.

II.

So, how does Spenser represent himself in his work? In his early days, he appears as a cheeky and cocksure young man, delighted to inform everyone that he is the future of English poetry. In his later years, he is a forlorn and embittered figure, invariably telling readers that he should have been the future of English poetry. Spenser most frequently casts himself as the plain spoken man of the people, Colin Clout, making use of the well-known satirical mask adopted by John Skelton, one of the few English poets taken seriously by English writers in Elizabeth's reign.[35] Towards the end of the final book of the published *Faerie Queene* Spenser poses the rhetorical question, 'Who knowes not *Colin Clout?*'[36] The obvious answer he is expecting the reader to produce is 'Colin Who?'[37] This is a long way from the bravura performance in the letters and the *Calender*. The audience of these works is expected to expand, readers to take notice and help establish Spenser as the major figure in the English literary world. The audience of the later work is imagined as contracting, Colin Clout having become an obscure and isolated figure to whom no one listens. Spenser reminds us frequently enough that he has been scandalously treated by those who rule in England.[38] The *Faerie Queene* ends with a lament for past misreadings and a plea for a sympathetic audience so that the author's verse will not become the target of the venomous Blatant Beast who misreads and slanders everything that comes his way:

> Ne may this homely verse, of many meanest,
> Hope to escape his venomous despite,
> More then my former writs, all were they clearest
> From blamefull blot, and free from all that wite,
> With which some wicked tongues did it backbite,
> And bring into a mighty Peres displeasure,
> That neuer so deserued to endite.

(VI. xii. 41)

---

[35] Anthony S. G. Edwards, *Skelton: The Critical Heritage* (London, 1981), 56–66.

[36] Edmund Spenser, *The Faerie Queene*, ed. A. C. Hamilton, rev. edn. (London, 2001), VI. x. 16. All subsequent references to this edition in parentheses in the text.

[37] Andrew Hadfield, *Literature, Politics and National Identity: Reformation to Renaissance* (Cambridge, 1994), 170–1.

[38] See e.g. John D. Bernard, *Ceremonies of Innocence: Pastoralism in the Poetry of Edmund Spencer* (Cambridge, 1989); Thomas H. Cain, *Praise in* The Faerie Queene (Lincoln, Nebr., 1978).

Spenser is probably referring to the fact that his satire of William Cecil, Lord Burghley in *Mother Hubberds Tale* (published 1590), in which he represented the queen's first minister as a crafty and self-seeking fox, came to the attention of the peer in question, who was not amused.[39] Spenser had ample reason to be paranoid. The second edition of *The Faerie Queene* was read by James VI of Scotland, who took particular exception to Spenser's representation of the execution of his mother, Mary Queen of Scots. James wrote a series of furious letters to Elizabeth demanding that she punish the poet. Given that Spenser had portrayed Mary as Duessa, who elsewhere in the poem appears as the Whore of Babylon, James clearly had reason to be angry.[40]

Given this history, and the relationship between the personal and the political in Spenser's poetry, we should be wary of *not* reading Spenser's poetry in terms of his life and opinions, a reversal of the ways in which critics generally approach the relationship between life and art. The verse cited above establishes a complicated and tense relationship between author, intention, reader, and interpretation, teasing the reader to read the verse rightly or wrongly. The idea that *Mother Hubberds Tale*—assuming this is the work to which the lines refer—was 'clearest | From blamefull blot' is absurd, as it was clearly designed to wound its target, making the author's profession of innocence disingenuous. If so, this would suggest that Spenser wants his reader to be aware of who is writing, alerting us to the fact that he is likely to appear in the text himself at any given moment. The works contain, as might be expected, a number of key moments when either the author in persona does appear, or the passage in question adopts a register of truthful sincerity at odds with the fictional nature of the poem.

Spenser habitually relates the metaphysical nature of the universe, and the geopolitical situation of England, Britain, and Ireland to his own life, establishing his authority as a poet to pass judgement on the world. Perhaps the most spectacular example of this occurs in the 'Two Cantos of Mutabilitie', apparently a fragment of *The Faerie Queene*,

---

[39] For recent comment, see James Norhnberg, 'Britomart's Gone Abroad to Brute-Land, Colin Clout's Come Courting from the Salvage Ire-land: Exile and Kingdom in Some of Spenser's Fictions for "Crossing Over"', in J. D. Lethbridge (ed.), *Edmund Spenser: New and Renewed Directions* (Madison, Wisc., 2006), 214–85 at 262–6.

[40] Richard A. McCabe, 'The Masks of Duessa: Spenser, Mary Queen of Scots and James VI', *ELR* 17 (1987), 224–42.

Book VII, which the poet did not publish in his lifetime. The cantos describe the challenge that the Titaness Mutabilitie makes to Jove, who is the current ruler of the universe. Mutabilitie argues that the world is really chaotic and constantly changing so that she should be its rightful sovereign. Jove, who stands for the stability brought about by the right of conquest, resists her claims and the two agree to be judged by Nature on Arlo Hill, just by Spenser's house, in front of the assembled gods.[41] Here the personal does indeed meet the political.

Nature awards victory to Jove. However, his triumph is undercut in a number of ways. His representative on earth is the goddess Cynthia, and we are given a graphic picture of the changes that she is undergoing. As Mutabilitie points out, rather cruelly:

> Then is she mortall borne, how-so ye crake;
> Besides, her face and countenance euery day
> We changed see, and sundry forms partake,
> Now hornd, now round, now bright, now brown & gray:
> So that *as changefull as the Moone* men vse to say.
>
> (VII. vii. 50. 5–9)

Cynthia, as Spenser makes clear elsewhere in the poem, is a representation of Elizabeth, the virgin queen, now coming to the end of her life and reign.[42] The lines point out that not merely was Elizabeth thought to be capricious and inconsistent, but that she was dying. In 1598, when these lines were probably written, Elizabeth was 65, which made her the oldest reigning English monarch for over 400 years, since Henry II, who died in 1189 (aged 56). Her subjects were unsure who would replace her as the succession had not been sorted out and it was an offence to discuss it.[43] The most likely candidate was actually James VI of Scotland, the son of Mary Stuart, Mary Queen of Scots, whom Elizabeth had had executed in 1587.[44] Mary was killed because of her apparent

---

[41] The locations are represented in A. C. Judson, *Spenser in Southern Ireland* (Bloomington, Ind., 1933).

[42] For comment, see David Norbrook, *Poetry and Politics in the English Renaissance*, rev. edn. (Oxford, 2002), 134–9.

[43] Cyndia Susan Clegg, *Press Censorship in Elizabethan England* (Cambridge, 1997), 81–9.

[44] For discussion and analysis, see 'Revenge Her Foul and Most Unnatural Murder? The Impact of Mary Stewart's Execution on Anglo-Scottish Relations', *History* 85 (2000), 589–612; 'Gender, Religion, and Early Modern Nationalism: Elizabeth I, Mary Queen of Scots, and the Genesis of English Anti-Catholicism', *AHR* 107 (2002), 739–67.

complicity in plots against Elizabeth that would place her on the throne, but now she would be triumphing posthumously as she had produced an heir whereas Elizabeth had not, which was indeed a change. Spenser had justified the execution in trenchant terms in *The Faerie Queene*, much to the chagrin of James. Now it looked as if Elizabeth had undone all the good work of the Protestants and allowed the son of an evil Catholic to rule England, her changeable nature proving Mutabilitie's point, and demonstrating that Cynthia/Elizabeth was no longer really fit to rule. Mutabilitie's challenge to Cynthia makes her sound rather like Mary, given that she is a queen challenging another queen's right to rule, so Spenser's poem represents the battle between the two queens living in the British Isles.[45]

But how does this relate to Spenser's life? What part does Spenser himself play in these events? The 'Two Cantos' contain an allegory of Ireland, the setting for the debate over the fate of the universe, which in itself shows how important Spenser thought his adopted homeland was and that its vulnerability to a Catholic revolt against English rule was likely to spell the end of English Protestantism. Ireland was once the fairest of the British Isles where the goddess Diana—another name for Cynthia—would visit for her private pleasure (VII. vi. 38). The cheeky god Faunus had an overwhelming desire to see her naked. He persuaded one of her nymphs, Molanna, to lead him to her favourite bathing spot, hid in the bushes and was able to possess his heart's desire:

> There *Faunus* saw that pleased much his eye,
> And made his hart to tickle in his brest,
> That for great ioy of some-what he did spy,
> He could him not containe in silent rest;
> But breaking forth in laughter, loud profest
> His foolish thought. A foolish *Faune* indeed,
> That couldst not hold thy selfe so hidden blest,
> But wouldest needs thine owne conceit areed.
> Babblers vnworthy been of so diuine a meed.
>
> (VII. vi. 46)

Who is Faunus? Faunus is another name for the god Pan, the god of flocks and shepherds who was always represented with his

---

pipe.[46] Given Spenser's representation of himself as Colin Clout—always with his pipe—it is hard not to think that Faunus is a version of the poet himself. Like Spenser he is loquacious and in trouble with the authorities. Spenser would appear to be saying that he is the one who has seen the queen naked, seen her for the fool that she really is, unable and unwilling to protect her true subjects from the ravages of time and mutability, a problem exposed most cruelly and dangerously in Ireland. But perhaps he is the real fool, for when exposed she flees and leaves the land to its unhappy fate. This may, of course, be a problematic reading of the passage, but the crucial point is that the reader is asked to make the connection between the poet's life and the serious issues represented in the works.

Spenser represents himself in a variety of ways in his works, inviting the reader to make connections between the two, whether we see him as a sage of political wisdom, as he is cast in the 'Letter to Raleigh' appended to the first edition of *The Faerie Queene*; or the faithful husband and lover in the *Amoretti*. Indeed, in an extraordinary moment Spenser merges the personal and the political as his marriage is consummated in the *Epithalamion*. Spenser, in a pointed, discordant moment, imagines the queen peering through the windows in envy as she perceives the joy of the lovers:

> Who is the same, which at my window peepes?
> Or whose is that faire face, that shines so bright?
> Is it not Cinthia, she that never sleepes,
> But walkes about high heaven al the night?
> O fayreset goddesse, do thou not envy
> My love with me to spy:
> For thou likewise didst love, though now unthought,
> And for a fleece of woll, which privily,
> The Latmian shephard once unto thee brought,
> His pleasures with thee wrought.
> Therefore to us be favourable now;
> And sith of wemens labours thou hast charge,
> And generation goodly dost enlarge,
> Encline thy will t'effect our wishfull vow.

---

[46] On Faunus and Pan, see Jane Davidson Reid (ed.), *The Oxford Guide to Classical Mythology in the Arts, 1300–1990s* (Oxford, 1993), 802. Patricia Merivale, in her entry, 'Pan', fails to mention this vital link: in Hamilton, *The Spenser Encyclopaedia*, 527.

And the chast wombe informe with timely seed,
That may our comfort breed:
Till which we cease our hopefull hap to sing,
Ne let the woods us answere, nor our Eccho ring.

(Var. xiii. 251, ll. 372–89)

This can be read as an extraordinarily offensive stanza, especially given Spenser's track record, designed to insult the queen—should she read it—and out of place in a marriage hymn.[47] The key word is 'envy', given Elizabeth's virginity, and the reminder that she once loved (*The Shepheardes Calender* makes a number of references to the projected Alençon match).[48] The queen is cast as a voyeur, peeping through the curtains, jealous of the joy of the lovers, an image that repeats the closing lines of the first edition of *The Faerie Queene* with Britomart gazing enviously at the joy of the hermaphrodite created by the lovers Amoret and Scudamore.[49] The narrative had already made it clear that Britomort would have her time when she married Artegall. Here we are told that Cynthia/Elizabeth has had hers, and needs to bless the lovers and stop her envy. Spenser would—again—appear to be commenting on her failures as a ruler in Ireland, and her failure as a ruler of men and women who have sexual desires (Elizabeth was a notoriously jealous queen who could not bear her courtiers getting married, as Sir Walter Raleigh discovered to his cost when he secretly married Elizabeth Throckmorton, Elizabeth's maid-of-honour, in 1592, as *The Faerie Queene*, Book IV, canto vii, narrates in considerable detail).[50] The stanza is yet another memento mori, an attack on Elizabeth for failing to marry and produce an heir. Spenser has linked his own life and situation with that of the monarch, skilfully drawing together his main concerns. His personal life is seen at odds with, and more ordered than, the larger political state of affairs. Perhaps we might even speculate that the passage can be read as a more accurate representation of the

---

[47] For a splendid reading of the complex politics of the poem, see Christopher Warley, *Sonnet Sequences and Social Distinction in Renaissance England* (Cambridge, 2005), 116–22.

[48] McLane, *Spenser's* Shepheardes Calender, ch. 2.

[49] See Lauren Silberman, *Transforming Desire: Erotic Knowledge in Books III and IV of* The Faerie Queene (Berkeley, 1995), ch. 3.

[50] James P. Bednarz, 'Ralegh in Spenser's Historical Allegory', *Spenser Studies* 4 (1983), 49–70.

poet's life than the passages in the Harvey letters and the paratexts in the *Calender*, which may be mediated by other concerns. The more literary may, paradoxically, be the more truthful work.

III.

I want to conclude with a further piece of speculation. Usually Spenser signals when we are to read his life in the text, but there is one passage which might be related to his life without any such obvious signs, one in which he may have been telling the truth about his life without signalling his intention. At the start of *The Faerie Queene*, Book III, canto vi, the epicentre of the poem, as numerological studies have pointed out, Spenser gives us a description of a painless birth granted to Chrysogenee, the virginal nymph and mother of the twins Amoret and Belphoebe:

> Her berth was of the wombe of Morning dew,
> And her conception of the ioyous Prime,
> And all her whole creation did her shew
> Pure and vnspotted from all loathly crime,
> That is ingenerate in fleshly slime.
> So was this virgin borne, so was she bred,
> So was she trayned vp from time to time,
> In all chast vertue, and true bounti-hed
> Till to her dew perfection she was ripened.
>
> (III. vi. 3)[51]

The stanza is an affectionate and moving moment in the poem that seems to recognize the pains and perils that women went through when giving birth. The Garden of Adonis serves a key function in Book III, the book of chastity (married sexuality). As the later cantos demonstrate, especially when Amoret is trapped in the Castle of Busiraine, adult sexuality is a dangerous and very painful game, albeit sometimes comically so. The Garden of Adonis is a fantasy within fairyland, a place where, for a brief moment, this sexuality is suspended, nature is fecund and reproduces without problem. It is, as the name implies, unstable and doomed, just as Venus's boy will be painfully taken from her before he

---

[51] On the numerological significance of the canto, see Michael Baybak, Paul Delaney, and A. Kent Hieatt, 'Placement "In the Middest" in *The Faerie Queene*', *Papers in Language and Literature* 5 (1969), 227–34.

has a chance to reach maturity. But the real victims of sexual behaviour were generally women. The most dangerous years for women were those of sexual maturity and childbirth when a huge percentage of women died. As Sara Mendelson and Patricia Crawford point out, 'During every pregnancy, each woman feared her own death'.[52] If women survived these trying times, they had a good chance of living to a ripe old age; most did not. Spenser would appear to recognize this through his description of the lucky escape of Chrysogenee.

What happened to the first Mrs Spenser, Maccabaeus Chylde? She married Edmund on 27 October 1579 and they had two children, Sylvanus and Catherine. Spenser got married again, to Elizabeth Boyle, on 11 June 1594, as he announced in his own poetry. At some point in that fifteen-year period, Maccabaeus died. Spenser was between 25 and 27 in 1579 (again, this is evidence largely derived from his own literary writings, as the *Amoretti* 60 records). It is likely that Maccabaeus was somewhat younger, as women usually married older men, probably between 18 and about 24.[53] This means that she died at the earliest in 1582 (as she had two children), and at the latest in 1593, probably at some point in between. So she was 21 to 36 when she died, precisely the years when women were likely to die after complications relating to childbirth. Is that what the poem is telling us happened to the first Mrs Spenser?

[52] Sarah Mendelson and Patricia Crawford, *Women in Early Modern England* (Oxford, 1998), 152.

[53] See the discussion in Mendelson and Crawford, *Women in Early Modern England*, 108–23. Peter Laslett, *The World We Have Lost*, 2nd edn. (London, 1971), claims that the average age of men when they married was nearly 28, and women were about 24.

4

The Early Lives of John Milton

Thomas N. Corns

This is an account of the earliest lives of John Milton. I shall be considering five rather diverse but interconnected texts:

1. John Aubrey, *Minutes of the Life of Mr John Milton* (manuscript, *c.*1681)
2. Cyriack Skinner (attrib.), *The Life of Mr John Milton* (manuscript; n.d., but on internal evidence dated between 1676 and 1691)[1] (sometimes termed 'the anonymous biography'; formerly attributed to John Phillips)
3. Anthony Wood, *Athenae Oxonienses... to which is added The Fasti or Annals of the said University* (London, 1691)
4. Edward Phillips (ed.), *Letters of State, Written by Mr John Milton... To which is added, An Account of his Life* (London, 1694)
5. John Toland (ed.), *A Complete Collection of the Historical, Political and Miscellaneous Works of John Milton... to which is prefix'd the life of the author* (Amsterdam, 1698)

All are helpfully available in *The Early Lives of John Milton*, edited by Helen Darbishire and published in 1932.[2] Darbishire also included 'The Life of Milton, and a Discourse on *Paradise Lost*', written by Jonathan Richardson to accompany the edition of 1734. She included it because it seems to be the last biographical essay to have drawn directly on the testimony of people who actually knew Milton, and

---

[1] William Riley Parker, *Milton: A Biography*, 2nd edn., rev. Gordon Campell (Oxford, 1996), i, p. xiii.
[2] *The Early Lives of Milton*, ed. Helen Darbishire (London, 1932).

it does contain from what we may hypothesize are such sources a couple of details missing from the other lives. I exclude it from consideration because it falls outside the cultural era of the other lives. They are all products of the fascination in the late Restoration and the Williamite period with that persistently notorious figure whom Sir Joseph Williamson, the civil servant who hunted out and suppressed some of his posthumous writing, called 'that late Villain Milton'.[3] Over the last two decades of the century, Milton's reputation and status were both disputed and sufficiently prominent to render him almost a test case for an emerging cultural ideology. In terms of his poetic idiom, he offered a radical alternative to Dryden in the role of founding father of English literary neoclassicism. Moreover, in political terms, he embodied either values that anticipated those of, successively, proto-whigs, whigs, and apologists for the Williamite revolution, or else exemplified in extreme form the social and political destructiveness of those movements. Not till Joseph Addison's calming influence, in his eighteen essays on *Paradise Lost* (1712, 1719), did a relatively non-partisan view of Milton's life and works become prevalent (though Addison, of course, evades biographical issues, while producing a perspective which is subtly whiggish).[4]

In genre terms and in terms of the circumstances of production, there are important differences between the early lives. Aubrey's notes are just that: a working document and a rather messy, composite manuscript that allows the reader to trace the stages and the process by which Aubrey accumulated evidence. He poses himself questions which subsequently he answers. He records the taking of evidence from Milton's widow and includes a list of his prose works in the hand of Edward Phillips, to whom we turn shortly. The document also contains the occasional rather grumpy note from Anthony Wood: 'Why do ye not set downe where Joh. Milton was borne?'[5]

Aubrey, of course, was functioning in effect as Wood's research assistant. Wood, in turn, was prompted to work on Milton as part of his massive antiquarian project of documenting the lives of writers and

[3] National Archives, SP 104/66, fo. 120.

[4] Joseph Addison, *Notes Upon the Twelve Books of Paradise Lost* (London, 1719), a reprint of the eighteen papers on *Paradise Lost* published in *The Spectator* between 5 January 1712 and 3 May 1712.

[5] Darbishire, *Early Lives*, 12.

bishops educated at the University of Oxford after 1500, his *Athenae Oxonienses*. But Milton was a Cambridge graduate. However, under the *Fasti* or *Annals* section Wood noted that in 1635 'This year was incorporated Master of Arts *John Milton*, not that it appears so in the Register...'.[6] We may reasonably surmise on Wood's own account that a personal contact pointed out to him that Milton could legitimately be included in the Oxford annals and that he then set Aubrey to work to put together the necessary information. Quite why Milton should have sought incorporation, which in a reciprocal arrangement bestowed on Cambridge graduates the privileges enjoyed by Oxford graduates, remained unexplored by Wood and remains uncertain today, though modern biographers usually assume Milton, who was anticipating a move to live in rural retirement about forty miles away, may have wanted to travel over to Oxford to use the Bodleian. Given Milton's later care in placing his prose works in that library, the hypothesis sounds plausible. He evidently understood the scope and status of the Bodleian in the mid-seventeenth century.

Wood had another important resource besides Aubrey's notes, though Aubrey may well have been the channel by which it reached Wood. Indeed Darbishire confidently believed that she had identified its author as John Phillips, brother of Edward, whom Aubrey certainly knew and drew on, and the younger nephew of Milton himself. William Riley Parker's subsequent research identified the author, not as John Phillips, but as Cyriack Skinner.[7] Skinner moved for the most part in the same circles as Edward Phillips. Like Phillips, he had been a pupil of Milton, and, like Phillips, he was part of the support network that formed around Milton in his blindness. He would have known much that was also known to both the Phillips brothers.

Edward Phillips's life, like Toland's, is part of the prefatory material to an edition, though in this case a relatively modest one, a translation of Milton's state letters. They had first been published in the face of the vigorous attempts of Sir Joseph Williamson to suppress them, and one manuscript of them was among the papers Williamson had succeeded in confiscating, along with the text of what we know as *De Doctrina Christiana*. Phillips evidenced a discernible edginess when he published his edition in 1694. Though contemporaries recognized his part in it, it

---

[6] Ibid. 35.   [7] Parker, *Milton: A Biography*, ii, p. xiv.

did not carry his name. Nor does the title page bear the name of printer or bookseller, and the volume thus carries a frisson of transgression. Toland's edition and life are part of a rather more energetic project in which leading Whigs commissioned him to prepare biographies and editions 'to show how Commonwealthsmen Algernon Sidney, Denzil Holles, Edmund Ludlow, John Milton and James Harrington were models of public religion and civic virtue'.[8] Again the imprint—in this case Amsterdam—implies that this, too, is a publication on the edge of legality.

That the early lives share considerable common ground is scarcely surprising. Wood drew directly on Aubrey and Skinner and had access in manuscript to some notes from Phillips, who had in part supplied Aubrey and had very similar exposure to Milton to Skinner's own experiences, as both pupil and later aide. Toland had access to Wood's synthesis of the others and to Edward Phillips's printed life. But two other influences shaped the early lives and determined their convergence: the nature of earlier hostile representation of Milton, and the effect of Milton's own prose writings, which in turn was, in part, shaped to meet the accusations of his enemies.

All the lives are to an extraordinary degree concerned with a small number of topics while silent on issues of massive significance. The narratives cluster around a handful of incidents. They are fascinated with his sex life, and especially with the circumstances of his first marriage. Milton was by then nearly 34. The question of quite where his sexual urge had hitherto led him rises inevitably in the curiosity of casual readers across the centuries, and the disparity in ages between Milton and his 17-year-old bride adds a certain prurient fascination. All the accounts attempt in some detail to establish the sequence of events that led to the marriage, separation, and reconciliation of the couple.

Milton in the late 1630s made an extended visit to Italy, with briefer sojourns en route in France and Geneva. The early lives cover it, in some cases with an obsessive attention to detail: whom he met in Paris (John Scudamore, Viscount Sligo, Charles I's ambassador to the French court; and Hugo Grotius, ambassador from the Swedish queen); how he moved on through Genoa, Pisa, Florence; whom he met there; how he moved on to Rome; whom he met there, and Naples—and whom he

---

[8] Stephen H. Daniel, *ODNB*.

met there; then back to Rome; then Venice and Verona and Milan; then Lombardy and across the Alps; then Geneva and whom he met there; then France and home. The fine-grained accounts stand out sharply from the vagueness of much of the rest of the narratives. Even Wood, whose version is comparatively brief about it, spends 500 words on his continental experiences.

Again, the period he taught a few pupils in a limited way, among them his nephews, produces a wealth of detail. Some narratives capture the names of some of the pupils and some accounts are almost obsessive in their particulars. Edward Phillips ushers in a two-page reading list with 'I judge it not impertinent to mention the many Authors both of the Latin and Greek, which through his excellent judgment and way of teaching, far above the Pedantry of common publick Schools...were run over within no greater compass of time, then from Ten to Fifteen or Sixteen Years of Age'. Phillips seems to bethink himself, and resumes his narration with 'But to return to the Thread of our Discourse'.[9]

Finally—and this pervades all accounts—there is obsessive attention both to the aetiology of his blindness and to his coping strategies. We are told that he overworked by poor light from his childhood; that 'his hard nightly study in his youth had first occasion'd an eye problem; that the sight in one eye had started to deteriorate and the second eye was adversely affected by the medical procedures adopted; that he remained cheerful; that he had people to read to him; that he used amanuenses; and so on.[10]

Alongside this welter of detail, we find some extraordinary silences, especially at the level of motivation. All the biographers tell us something about Milton's father and about the household he grew up in, but not about its ideological orientation. Modern biographers, with some honourable exceptions, have read the familial evidence of the early lives as an explanation of the making of the puritan revolutionary. Milton's father, on all the early accounts, appears as a sort of anti-Catholic Dick Whittington, expelled from his papist parental home to earn his fortune in London. But those accounts speak only of his anti-Catholic sentiments; they do not call him a puritan, nor do they hint at any involvement in any of the oppositional activities of English

---

[9] Darbishire, *Early Lives*, 60, 62.
[10] See e.g. Cyriack Skinner in Darbishire, *Early Lives*, 28.

puritans in the early Stuart period. They speak also of his hiring several tutors for his children. Thomas Young, the one whose name we know, happens to have been a Scot of Presbyterian orientation, and is perhaps distinguished because Milton later addressed a Latin elegy to him or because Milton wrote to support the puritan writing consortium, Smectymnuus, of which he was a member in the early 1640s. The other tutors have passed into obscurity. These fragments, to luminaries as diverse as John Shawcross and Barbara Lewalski, add up to a rabidly puritanical background that nurtured the alleged early radicalism of John Milton. Yet what limited archival evidence has been unearthed suggests, rather, that John Milton senior was simply a communicant of the Church of England, showing no apparent resentment of the Laudian ascendancy; indeed, he served as a church warden of the chapel of ease at Hammersmith, which was a Laudian foundation dominated by Laudian enthusiasts.

The stages in Milton's radicalism are never satisfactorily explained. The early lives offer no plausible explanation of why, when the church was riven in the early 1640s he so vehemently justified the execution of the king. They simply stress that he was headhunted by the republican Council of State, and that he had not applied for the office. There is no real explanation of how he escaped so lightly at the Restoration when contemporaries confidently expected his execution.

Of course, Aubrey, who appears relatively unpartisan about Milton's politics—he is, after all, assembling research notes to be used by another author—and Wood, who is explicitly hostile, relied on those who knew him directly, and the knowledge of their sources was inevitably partial, in both senses of that word; nor, necessarily, would Skinner or Edward Phillips have recognized much advantage in a detailed exploration, were they capable, of the rationale for regicide or, for that matter, of the horse-trading surrounding the Restoration and its immediate aftermath. From their point of view, it made more sense to glide over the republican commitment of Milton, rather than to explore the arguments that drove both Milton and his republican colleagues to the abolition of monarchy and the execution of the king. Even to supporters of the Williamite revolution, these were issues too inconvenient to examine, and the constitutional fudges of the late 1680s and early 1690s fortunately made such examination supererogatory. Such points can explain the silences; but what of the elements selected for emphasis?

Milton's notoriety and the hostility he had aroused surely played a huge part. Milton was successively assailed by three waves of opponents: by defenders of the prelacy, by what Ann Hughes has recently termed 'the presbyterian mobilization',[11] and by royalist apologists. Those attacks cumulatively had defined a negative representation that the information pushed forward by Phillips and Skinner in the early lives meets with some precision. The first group were responding to his contributions, over 1641–2, to the Smectymnuan debate and especially his attack on Bishop Joseph Hall, the episcopalian apologist whom the Smectymnuans were attempting to confute. The second group fell upon Milton in the mid-1640s as a result of his publication of tracts advocating a radical revision of divorce laws. The final group began their assault with his regicidal tracts, both English and Latin, and continued beyond the Restoration.

His opponents had tried three versions of his sex life. The earliest printed attack, and a view that in the event did not really stick, is to be found in an anonymous work of 1642, *A Modest Confutation of A Slanderous and Scurrilous Libell, entituled, Animadversions upon the Remonstrants Defense against Smectymnuus*: that is, an attack on Milton's attack on Joseph Hall's attack on Smectymnuus's attack on Joseph Hall. This is at quite a late stage of the controversy. The pamphlet is usually attributed to Hall's son. Milton is represented as a young, recent graduate on the make and something of a roisterer, to be traced to '*the* Play-Houses, *or the* Bordelli'; '*it is like hee spent his youth, in loytering, bezelling, and harlotting.*'[12] The Presbyterians and their allies played a different game, wholly based on a tendentious misrepresentation of his first divorce tract as a 'tractate of divorce in which the bonds are let loose to inordinate lust'.[13] The book-length attack on *The Doctrine and Discipline of Divorce, An Answer to a Booke, Intituled, The Doctrine and Discipline of Divorce* (1644) developed a rather different tack. The author repeats the concern that divorce reform would lead to a situation

---

[11] Ann Hughes, Gangraena *and the Struggle for the English Revolution* (Oxford, 2004), esp. ch. 5.

[12] Anon., *A Modest Confutation of A Slanderous and Scurrilous Libell, entituled, Animadversions upon the Remonstrants Defense against Smectymnuus* (London, 1642), sigs. A3^v, A3^r.

[13] Ephraim Pagitt, *Heresiography: or, A description of the Heretickes and Sectaries of these latter times* (London, 1645); quoted in *The Life Records of John Milton*, ed. J. Milton French (New Brunswick, NJ, 1949–58), ii. 127.

where 'many thousands of lustfull and libidinous men wold be parting
from their Wives every week and marrying others'. But he combines
that with a concern for deserted wives and children, some left 'in their
Wives bellies'.[14] Indeed, Pagitt's thesis also left some room for the image
of the brutal divorcer, thrusting away his abandoned spouse, and the
equation of the 'divorcer', presumably exemplarily Milton, and the wife-
abuser plainly stuck. It features as a detail of the anti-Independent and
anti-sectary broadside, *A Catalogue of Several Sects and Opinions* (1646)
and was incorporated into the illuminated title page of later editions of
Heresiography. The divorcer in one case pushes his wife from him; in the
other, he actually cudgels her.

Royalist apologists played a different game, offering, in place of the
lustfully heterosexual Milton, a Milton with a shady past, expelled from
Cambridge for some homosexual scandal, and driven to Italy where on
one account he worked as a male prostitute. John Bramhall in 1654 in
private correspondence had certainly noted the possibilities of putting
into play against him the charge that he was thrown out of university,
'turned . . . as he well deserved to have been both out of the University
and out of the society of men. If Salmasius his friends knew as much
of him as I, they would make him go near to hang himself.'[15] Milton's
circle had attributed to Bramhall the 1651 Latin attack, *Pro Rege et Pop-
ulo Anglicano Apologia* (Antwerp), which had been confuted in turn by
Milton's younger nephew, John Phillips. Bramhall almost certainly knew
Milton's old tutor, William Chappell, who, like himself, held an Irish see
in the years before they both fled Ireland for continental exile. Aubrey
claimed that Chappell had whipped the undergraduate Milton for an
unspecified offence. It can scarcely have been for slacking at his studies.
Salmasius and his friends believed themselves to have turned up a similar
rumour: they certainly toyed with making a claim that in Italy he was
'selling his buttocks for a few pence'.[16] Royalist diehards included in
their ranks at least one other person who had known Milton fairly well
at Cambridge, Michael Honywood, a Laudian clergyman who had gone
into exile, but who had been both a fellow of Milton's college and a

---

[14] Anon., *An Answer to a Booke, Intituled, The Doctrine and Discipline of Divorce*
(London, 1644), 8–9.

[15] Gordon Campbell, *A Milton Chronology* (London and New York, 1997), 153.

[16] Gordon Campbell, 'The Life Records', in Thomas N. Corns (ed.), *A Companion
to Milton* (Oxford, 2001), 489; Campbell, *Chronology*, 146.

moving force behind the commemorative volume which first included Milton's 'Lycidas'. And certainly there were rumours of effeminate appearance or behaviour in Milton's undergraduate days. In Prolusion 6, written when he was 19, he acknowledges his college nickname as 'the Lady of Christ's'. The Prolusion is a 'salting' in which Milton played the role of a sort of lord of misrule. As he assails his contemporaries, he remarks, with no hint of embarrassment or resistance to the sobriquet, 'some have recently called me "Lady". But why do I seem unmanly to them? . . . I suppose they do it because I have . . . not proved my manhood in the way these debauchees do. I wish they could as easily stop being asses as I could stop being a woman!' (Literally, 'as I [could give up] whatsoever is of woman'; 'quam ego quicquid est feminae'.)[17] In the event, perhaps driven by some uncertainty or even a residual sense of decorum, the author of *Regii Sanguinis Clamor* (1652) settled for the loftily vague but darkly suggestive, 'They say that the man was expelled from his college at Cambridge because of some disgrace, that he fled shame and his country and migrated to Italy.'[18]

Blindness, inevitably, had been identified as God's punishment for Milton for his justification of the regicide. The theme was much rehearsed in *Regii Sanguinis Clamor* and plainly the charge adhered to Milton through the rest of his life. Roger L'Estrange's jeering attack in April 1660 made nothing of his blindness in the text but certainly alluded to it in its unlovely title: *No Blind Guides*. By the Restoration the political nation knew Milton primarily as the defender of regicide and the republic and as a Cromwellian apologist; the other fact they knew about him was that he was blind.

Among the early biographies two hold a privileged position: that by his nephew Edward Phillips and that attributed currently to Cyriack Skinner. They do so because they were written by men who knew him, who had been often in his household in the 1640s, and with whom he retained an extended acquaintance, indeed a friendship, probably through the rest of his life. Quite simply, Phillips and Skinner write into the biographical tradition a Miltonic version of events. Milton as an undergraduate roisterer is countered by an image of what Skinner calls

[17] John Milton, *Latin Writings: A Selection*, ed. and trans. John K. Hale (Assen and Tempe, Ariz., 1998), 90–1.
[18] *The Complete Prose Works of John Milton*, ed. Don M. Wolfe et al. (New Haven, 1953–82), iv. 1050.

'his virtuous and sober life'.[19] The image of Milton as abusive husband is met by the detailed narrative of his first marriage. Its proximity with the account of his divorce tracts in both Skinner's and Edward Phillips's lives ties the postulated answer to the implied criticism. Milton as deserted husband had thought through the issues and come up with a humane solution to an apparent breakdown in marital relations—a peaceful settlement rather than a brutal cudgelling. Before that, though, we get a brief depiction of Milton, as romantic lover, a man who 'courted, married, and brought home' in a mere month his young bride.[20] (Skinner immediately rather spoils the account of emotional impetuosity by adding that Milton was completely preoccupied with writing anti-prelatical pamphlets and could not spare the time for anything more protracted.) Phillips offers the fullest account of the eventual reconciliation between Milton and his wife in which 'his own generous nature, more inclinable to Reconciliation than to perseverance in Anger and Revenge' plays a crucial part; and soon they are happily engaged in what in *Paradise Lost* he would call 'the rites | Mysterious of connubial love:'[21] 'The first fruits of her return . . . was a brave Girl, born within a year after.'[22]

If Skinner and Phillips laid the ghost of the brutal Milton in this way, they still faced the problem of Milton the scandalous homosexual. But their accounts engage with the issue in concerted fashion. Milton's gait, we are told, was 'erect & Manly, bespeaking Courage and undauntness. . . . On which account hee wore a Sword while hee had his Sight, and was skill'd in using it.'[23] Milton may have been a non-combatant in the civil turmoil of the mid-century, but not out of cowardice or physical indisposition. The leaving of Cambridge is addressed with care. Phillips emphasizes his academic success and attributes his departure to 'having no design to take upon him any of the particular learned Professions',[24] preferring instead a life of scholarship in genteel retirement at his father's expense. Indeed, Phillips is generally quick to stress Milton's propertied background, to pre-empt the assumption that his political choices and partisan writing were determined by motives of

---

[19] Darbishire, *Early Lives*, 19.   [20] Ibid. 22.
[21] *Paradise Lost*, ed. Alastair Fowler, 2nd edn. (London and New York, 1998), iv. 743–4, p. 264.
[22] Darbishire, *Early Lives*, 67.   [23] Skinner in Darbishire, *Early Lives*, 32.
[24] Ibid. 19.

personal gain: his Milton is a rich man's son, who enjoys the freedom of choice and action that financial independence affords. Similarly, Phillips explicitly picks up on the allegations in *Regii Sanguinis Clamor*, stressing that his 'Fellow-Collegiates' were 'in general' sorry to see him go.[25] Once more, the choice, here to leave Cambridge and not pursue a formal academic career, is represented as Milton's.

Both Phillips and Skinner then launch into one of the two most detailed parts of their account, the travels around Italy. To those who have read Milton's Latin defences much of the account seems familiar. There a passage of sustained autobiography meets the charges against him. He asserts his family's wealth and his commitment to liberal scholarship. After a glittering Cambridge career (on his own account) he leaves 'to the regret of the fellows of the college, who bestowed on me no little honor'.[26] He retreats to his father's country estate. He goes to Italy, after visiting Sir Henry Wotton, and the details thereafter, of whom he meets, what he does, how he conducts himself and how he defends the Protestant faith, accord very closely with the accounts of Skinner and Edward Phillips. Far from peddling his sexual services in the alleys of Naples, Milton of course is meeting with the leading intellects, reading his own poetry at the academies, receiving the members' compliments, and outwitting and eluding 'plots laid against me by the English Jesuits'.[27] Of course, it is possible that Skinner and Edwards may be thinking back on happy conversations with Milton perhaps many years before, in which he expatiated on his expatriate experiences. Alternatively, they could have had the *Defensio Secunda* open before them as they wrote.

The *Defensio Secunda* also anticipated their account of Milton's blindness, offering a detailed aetiology. Studying till midnight from the age of 12 'was the first cause of injury to my eyes, whose natural weakness was augmented by frequent headaches'.[28] He talks through the stages of his blindness. He was already blind in one eye before the task of writing the *Defensio Prima* was assigned to him and 'the doctors were making learned predictions that if I should undertake this task, I would shortly lose both eyes, I was not in the least deterred by the warnings'.[29] In any

---

[25] Ibid. 55.   [26] Milton, *Complete Prose*, iv. 613.   [27] Ibid. 619.
[28] Ibid. 612.   [29] Ibid. 588.

case, total blindness was a sacrifice he elected to make, not a punishment divinely inflicted.

Skinner and Edward Phillips in all probability took their direction from Milton's own apologia, though, more certainly than in the case of the Italian travels, which occurred when they were still children, there could well be personal recollection as well. Both have details of his blindness missing from *Defensio Secunda* that have a plausibility. Skinner writes of 'the Issues and Seatons' used to save the first eye to be afflicted as 'hasten[ing] the loss of the other', though immediately he ties the account to the thesis of elective sacrifice made in *Defensio Secunda*. Edward Phillips writes of the damage caused over twelve years by his 'perpetual tampering with Physick to preserve [the first afflicted eye]'.[30] All the circumstantial details stack up against any resort to divine retribution as an explanation of the chronic illness.

A printed source could also rest near the surface of another surprisingly prominent element in especially the narrative of Edward Phillips: the curriculum of his private educational establishment. Indeed, both he and Skinner were his pupils. Skinner opts for a relatively light touch. He notes that Milton set out a pedagogic method in *Of Education* and 'it seem'd he design'd *in some measure* to put this in practise'.[31] Phillips, however, favours the production of a two-page reading list. Possibly his memory does indeed stretch back fifty years to recollection of what he read when he was a 10 year old. Likelier, however, he turned to the printed text in *Of Education* to refresh and inform his personal recollection. Interestingly, both stress that Milton taught children out of conviction and charity, not out of any necessity of securing an income. Once more, a negative image, that of the hireling schoolmaster, is tacitly countered. (Richard Perrinchief, for example, had pilloried him in 1662, in the introduction to his edition of the works of Charles I, as a 'needy pedagogue'.)[32]

Toland followed Phillips closely.[33] Indeed, Toland and Wood depended heavily on the biographers who actually knew Milton in ways that shaped the narratives they produced. They come at their subject from ideologically polarized positions. For Wood, Milton embodied the subversive and destructive spirit of English republicanism, and the

---

[30] Darbishire, *Early Lives*, 72.   [31] Ibid. 24; my emphasis.
[32] Campbell, *Chronology*, 196.   [33] Darbishire, *Early Lives*, 98.

talents that he documents were appallingly misdirected. Darbishire, whose own impartiality may perhaps merit a moment's pause, observes that Wood 'began the evil work of twisting facts and misinterpreting motives'. In support, she notes, for example, that Wood 'says...that [Milton] "did great matters to obtain a name and wealth." The anonymous biographer [i.e. Cyriack Skinner] had insisted that Milton's "labours for the glory of God and some public good" were wholly disinterested.'[34] Yet Wood's account nevertheless shows an antiquarian's reluctance to suppress information that has come to him, even down to repeating the account of Milton the erect and manly swordsman. Similarly, Toland revels in using Milton's writing as a means of articulating proto-whig arguments of a dangerously radical kind; but the concerns laid down in the sources on which he draws still shape his writing.

Darbishire concluded the preface to her immensely helpful edition with this sentence: 'If the book brings its readers a little nearer to Milton himself, I shall be content.'[35] Poignantly, it brings us, I would suggest, rather closer to Milton than she realized, in that the most significant contribution to the early biographical tradition comes from writers for whom the imperatives were set by the polemical exigencies confronting Milton in his own lifetime and whose responses were largely fashioned by the ways in which Milton himself had fashioned his own image to meet them. The early lives that ultimately shape the version of Milton that has come down to us are the early lives he wrote himself.

* * *

What value do the early lives really have for a modern biographer of Milton? Certainly, they contain some information not available elsewhere in the life records. There are details about Milton's wider circle of acquaintance not captured, for example, in the extant correspondence, though sometimes they are of a riddling kind. Edward Phillips tell us his uncle was wont in the time immediately after his return to London every month or so 'to keep a Gawdy-day' with 'Mr. *Alphry*, and Mr. *Miller*, two Gentlemen of *Gray's*-Inn, the *Beau's* of those Times'.[36] The friends remain unidentified, nor is it at all clear what these gaudies involved, though Phillips suggests these beaux were 'nothing near so bad as those now-a-days'. Drinking, rather than whoring, we assume.

[34] Ibid., p. x.   [35] Ibid., p. iv.   [36] Ibid. 62.

There are occasional descriptions of an almost endearing kind, though even here literary mediation plays a part. He may indeed have met his morning amanuensis with the cry that '*hee wanted to bee milked*' of the verses he had composed overnight, though that anecdote is also told of Virgil in his own early lives.[37] Milton probably was, consciously or unconsciously, imitating Virgil (rather than the biographers imitating Virgil's biographers). Nevertheless, once the literary antecedent to the anecdote is recognized, it seems less a comment on his charmingly whimsical conduct and more a disclosure of a concern with mannered self-representation.

More positively, Edward Phillips's narrative traces Milton to the various addresses he occupied in London after 1639, with illuminating descriptions of the properties concerned, greatly facilitating at least that part of the modern biographer's task. Both he and Skinner are particularly helpful in describing the support network which developed around Milton after the onset of blindness, and which made practicable the composition of his late works. Indeed, their accounts, and especially Phillips's, suggests working practices that accord with and corroborate the recent work on the composition of *De Doctrina Christiana*.[38]

In general, however, the early lives, at least before Toland's, show an imperfect engagement with Milton's writing, and none systematically connects biography and even the most rudimentary critical insight. The discourse of criticism was still too underdeveloped to make even the kinds of connections that came easily enough to Dr Johnson. It is the sensational and notorious figure of Milton the ideologue which is variously debated, and that controversy proceeds along lines that are both tendentious and predictable. Indeed, why would it not, since it marks the revival in the late seventeenth century of the earlier, often vituperative exchanges between Milton's enemies and the man himself? The exigencies of those debates had shaped the Miltonic defence. Moreover, since Milton wrote so much about himself, his earliest biographers had a store of material to hand at a time when primary archival research, as it is now understood, was at best difficult and at worst impossible. Scholars sometimes complain that Kew, the home of the

---

[37] Skinner in Darbishire, *Early Lives*, 33; Gordon Campbell, 'Milton and the Lives of the Ancients', *Journal of the Warburg and Courtauld Institutes* 47 (1984), 234–8.

[38] Gordon Campbell, Thomas N. Corns, John K. Hale, and Fiona Tweedie, *John Milton and the Manuscript of* De Doctrina Christiana (Oxford, 2007).

National Archives, which holds numerous pertinent documents about Milton, is difficult to get to, but that minor inconvenience compares very favourably with the impossibility of research access to state papers in the early modern period. In the early lives, we have versions of a Milton the author himself had produced to serve his needs, refracted through the changed assumptions of friends and foes, each of whom offered a partial Milton, in both senses of that term, that transformed into a continuing site of controversy.

5

Gossip and Biography

Harold Love

Between 1661 and 1684 a small British community huddled on the Atlantic shore of Morocco in the storm-beaten citadel of Tangier. Cut off from local travel by the encircling Moors, the town's elite filled their days with conversation:

Gossip and scandal throve apace in the narrow circle of Tangerine society; social jealousy was acute. It can be gathered from John Luke's 'Journal' that almost every look and word was noticed and commented upon. He himself took a deep interest in the affairs and intrigues of his neighbours; even the Governor and the chief officers of the staff did not despise the diversion of an hour's gossip.[1]

On one such occasion in 1671 'Major Fitzgerald recounted to his Excellency the carriage of all the ladyes last night at his house, a pleasant discourse wee had concerning Mistress Legg'. No doubt at the same time Mistress Legg and her women friends were engaged in a parallel discussion of the males: there was probably not much else to talk about. John Luke himself underwent the experience of being looked at 'something strangely' when he attended a wedding reception organized by his social betters. While such mutual scrutiny was understandable among the inhabitants of an isolated garrison town, even a passing acquaintance with Restoration comedy and the clandestine satire of the period will indicate that it was also a defining activity of leisured, upper-class life in the metropolis. Participants in this life nourished their days with a highly seasoned diet of oral personal narratives, which as well as providing precautionary models of how to avoid ridicule were

---

[1] E. M. G. Routh, *Tangier: England's Lost Atlantic Outpost* (London, 1912), 287.

also their main form of entertainment, promulgated through coffee-house conversations, the incessant 'visits', and other occasions of Town sociability.

Gossip was a subset of the wider category of news, whose circulation through Britain during the seventeenth century has been anatomized by Adam Fox.[2] The first greeting to a stranger met on the road or arriving in a town or village was likely to be 'What newes?' (p. 341). Certain classes of traveller had a special role as news transmitters: these might include professional carriers, petty chapmen, pedlars and vagabonds, or a poor woman 'who goeth abroad to sell sope and candels from towne to towne to get her lyving and she useth to carrie tales betwene neighbours'.[3] At London, Paul's Walk, the Royal and New Exchanges, and the theatre auditoria acted as clearing houses for oral information flowing in from the country and out to it again. Thames watermen were another source of topical news, in this resembling taxi-drivers today. In the country a news hub function was performed by fairs, markets, inns, especially those standing on well-travelled roads, and by churches and conventicles on sermon days. On 8 June 1651 Ralph Josselin recorded an occasion on which yearning after godliness and hunger for news mingle discordantly:

a hearer at Halsted, the sermon very spirituall and profitable, lord blesse the towne and contry in the labours of that man, heard as if the Scots were neare Carlisle, the lord our god stand up for our helpe in whom I putt my trust: the great rumours of this weeke came to nothing, Cromwell recovers apace for which gods name bee praised.[4]

Tangier was a news hub in its own right, regularly supplied with homeland news by travellers and mail but also a listening point for happenings around the Mediterranean. Its news from Spain, southern France, Italy, and the Ottoman dominions would have been better and more timely than that received at Whitehall. Its leading inhabitants—traders, officials, diplomats, naval and military officers, and contractors working on a gigantic breakwater—were professionals for whom accurate information was vital and who would spare no pains to secure it.

---

[2] Adam Fox, *Oral and Literate Culture in England 1500–1700* (Oxford, 2000), 335–405.

[3] Ibid. 343–5, 341.

[4] *The Diary of Ralph Josselin 1616–1683*, ed. Alan Macfarlane (Oxford, 1976), 247.

But gossip was something different, and it is gossip that concerns us here. We need then to ask how gossip differed and still differs from other forms of orally circulated narrative.

A distinction which, while it should not be forced, is certainly in conformity with our own experience is that gossip arises from a concern with personalities rather than bare happenings. The whereabouts of the Scots army was news but whether the king of England was a papist and when he might have become so and the sayings and foibles of prominent courtiers belong with gossip. Individuals most commonly become the focus of gossip when their behaviour departs in a singular way from accepted norms; and yet, because gossip is essentially a narrative art and draws on a repertoire of proven, pre-existing story types, it will often elaborate on what was directly observed in ways dictated by those types. A good story may attach itself to new protagonists as old ones drop from memory. Often—indeed, almost always—gossip sets out to erode personal dignity. It is the enemy of pretensions to virtue whether fraudulent or perfectly justified. A further distinction, already implied, is that gossip has to entertain. This becomes evident when we compare Pepys, a diligent searcher after usable information, with Aubrey, an anecdotalist. While Aubrey will sometimes hunt down informants in order to verify claims, he is primarily interested in telling a good story. His lives frequently turn their subject into a species of monster. He is capable of admitting ancient jests (for example, the 'switter swatter' story about Raleigh) as biographical materials. Pepys will sometimes record gossip of this kind but his primary aim in conversation is to obtain information about people with whom he may have to deal pro-fessionally. Fabulous or inaccurate data might be positively dangerous to him. He also had to assess his informants carefully. Consider him on that saltwater pyromaniac, Sir Robert Holmes:

He seems to be very well acquainted with the King's mind and with all the several faccions at Court, and spoke all with so much franknesse that I do take him to be my Lord's good friend, and one able to do him great service, being a cunning fellow, and one (by his own confession to me) that canne put on two several faces and look his enemies in the face with as much love as his friends. But good God, what an age is this and what a world this is, that a man cannot live without playing the knave and dissimulacion.[5]

---

[5] Entry for 1 Sept. 1661, *The Diary of Samuel Pepys*, ed. Robert Latham and William Mathews (London, 1970–83), ii. 169.

The gossips of Tangier, as well no doubt as angling in Pepysian style for the *utile*, were entertaining each other in an Aubrey-like way and helping to make the city itself a place of interest and excitement. They probably did this by discovering a great deal more deviant behaviour in the lives of their fellow citizens than they were ever guilty of.

In order to be entertaining the good gossip has to be a performer, even something of a stand-up comedian. In my *English Clandestine Satire* I explore a negative symmetry between gossip and the verse lampoon, arguing that the lampoon was a form of gossip in writing and gossip, in sufficiently skilled hands, a form of oral lampoon.[6] Interestingly, the best-known lampoon writers were all male while the virtuoso gossips like Catherine Sedley, Penelope Osbourne, and Mrs St John were generally female. A satirist of 1698 has left an account of Sedley in full flight:

> A wither'd Countess next, who rails aloud
> At the most reigning vices of the Croud,
> And with the product of that ill turn'd brain,
> Does all her Guests at Visits entertain,
> Thinks it a Crime for any one to be,
> Either ill natur'd or as leud as she,
> A Soveraign Judge over her sex does sitt,
> Giving full scope to that injurious witt,
> Too old for Lust and prove against all shame,
> Her only business now is to defame . . . [7]

Here we have a lampooner attacking a gossip. No doubt the compliment was often returned but, while the verses remain, the more dazzling art of the countess is preserved only imperfectly in her correspondence. A letter from Ireland of 1686 conveys something of her deixis:

The match you writ off concerning the Lord Arron I believe true, for some people love to propagaite ffools. I doupt the pretty little widdow will come in at that toe, for her choyse is not very good. I thought she would have bin true toe love, and have married Tolmedge; sure she has Royall blood in her, she is soe fickle. Pray write toe mee offen, for letters from England are the only things that make this place supportable. Send the news true or false, I care not. I love an English lye . . . [8]

[6] Harold Love, *English Clandestine Satire 1660–1702* (Oxford, 2004), 191–217.

[7] 'An answer to J. Poultney's Letter' (1698), Leeds University Library, Brotherton MS Lt. q. 38, p. 207.

[8] V. de Sola Pinto, *Sir Charles Sedley 1639–1701: A Study in the Life and Literature of the Restoration* (New York, 1927), 347–8.

Clearly this was something different, and much more in-your-face, than her father's affable charm that so amused Pepys in the theatre.[9] Sedley *père* is sometimes represented as a gossip (as for instance when he appears as Medley in Etherege's *The Man of Mode*) but what can be determined of his real-life conversation suggests that his actual line was non-stop wit, smart similes, and quick replies. The gossip fascinated through a gift for storytelling rather than sprightliness of manner.

It should be stressed here that, despite Sedley *fille*'s declared preference for an 'English lye', gossip cannot be entirely careless of accuracy. Its attractiveness lies in the possibility that the outrageous proposal might just conceivably be true. Whenever that possibility is wholly lost, the standing of the deliverer of the gossip is undermined. This applies even in the case of present-day newspaper gossip columns. Practitioners have variously defined the difference between a salacious rumour and a usable item as lying between 'half a dozen phone calls' and 'close to 100 emails a day'.[10] In earlier times this might involve having spies at work.[11] A gossip is assumed to embroider but will be the more appreciated to the extent that she appears to be preternaturally informed. The *vero* comes with much more force to the listener than the *ben* (or *mal*) *trovato*, as well as being a compliment, since no one wants to think they are seen by their informant as credulous. In addition, the gossip of the Town was very often based on a direct acquaintance by both speaker and hearers with the persons concerned, allowing a knowledgeable estimate of the plausibility of an accusation. Where actual social closeness was lacking, behaviour and deportment could be assessed as part of the licensed voyeurism of the theatres or the park. Even the king's body language was open to analysis as he lolled in the royal box among his favourites.[12] However, there is a significant difference between gossip and legend. Left to petrify, gossip quickly mutates into myth. Alan Macfarlane, having compiled his detailed, document-based account of the doings of two Restoration highwaymen named Smorthwait, found that their names had become incorporated into a regional folk tale

---

[9] See e.g. *Diary*, v. 288; viii. 72.

[10] 'Careless whispers', *The Age (Melbourne) Magazine* (February 2005), 36–8.

[11] See on this Love, *Clandestine Satire*, 163–4, 167, and Burnet's story of Rochester disguising a spy as a sentinel in order to obtain information about court intrigues.

[12] Decorum dictated that the other spectators should not turn their backs on the monarch, which might require pit attenders to adopt a twisted, side-on position. It was equally forbidden to establish direct eye-contact with the monarch; however, Pepys's accounts are evidence that this did not inhibit careful, indeed often fascinated, scrutiny.

that had virtually nothing to do with their actual deeds.[13] Despite the tendency of gossipers to reapply old stories, good gossip is always of the week, the day, even the hour. Hearers have no wish to rehear what they have already heard and might just as well have been uttering themselves. Good gossip is also fluid in the sense that it can be contested by those with different views and information, making it a stimulus to conversation.

What has been said will suggest something of the operations of gossip in Restoration England in an age when there was no rival public source of information about other people's personal lives. While at one level an almost universal pastime, it was one that at London had its recognized virtuosi, performing their art at visits and salons, and through this determining both the content and the governing inflections of what was passed down the informational food chain. The 'visit', as it has been anatomized in the case of the Verneys by Susan E. Whyman, was a key institution of gossip.[14] Members of the landed ruling class in town for the winter, consolidating themselves into a new, dominant urban demographic, spent a good deal of their time on highly ritualized observance of each others' nominated visiting days.[15] Gossip was the primary activity of these meetings. 'Where I was visiting the other night' narrates Rochester's Artemiza, before launching into an unforgettable portrait of a bad, because overbearing and untrustworthy, gossip seizing the floor and refusing to stop until she was totally out of breath.[16] In passages from Southerne's *The Wives Excuse* (1692) and Congreve's *The Way of the World* (1700), we learn of regular club-like cabals convened solely for the purpose of exchanging gossip—a leisured-class counterpart to the meetings of godmothers at a christening, which were the etymological origin of the term.[17] Such gatherings had a more oligarchic function in the gossip economy than the salons of Katherine Sedley or Penelope Verney. New gossip would certainly be transmitted and stale

---

[13] Alan Macfarlane, *The Justice and the Mare's Ale* (Oxford, 1981), 160–72.

[14] In Susan E. Whyman, *Sociability and Power in Late-Stuart England: The Cultural Worlds of the Verneys 1660–1720* (Oxford, 1999), 87–109.

[15] On this social phenomenon, see also Love, *Clandestine Satire*, 66–79.

[16] *The Works of John Wilmot, Earl of Rochester*, ed. Harold Love (Oxford, 1999), 65.

[17] *The Plays of William Congreve*, ed. Herbert Davis (Chicago, 1967), 396; *The Works of Thomas Southerne*, ed. R. J. Jordan and Harold Love (Oxford, 1989), i. 289. Discussed in Love, *Clandestine Satire*, 70–1. On lying-in as an occasion of gossip see Laura Gowing, *Common Bodies: Women, Touch and Power in Seventeenth-century England* (New Haven, 2003), 172–6.

gossip laughed out of court, but we should also assume an editorial or reviewing function by which stories were shaped and approved for the further circulation that would take place once the participants were returned to their regular domestic networks.

Gossip owes its power to its capacity to expose the subject to ridicule, either open or dissembled—the suppressed smile or the muffled laugh behind the back, whether actually observed or only imagined. But this power is not exercised solely for its own sake. Here we need to acknowledge what makes gossip so fascinating to social anthropologists, which is as a way of defining norms for behaviour and encoding practical morality.[18] The prospect of being gossipped about with the same freedom as one gossips about others is so unpleasant that one can hardly not pay attention to the lessons gossip teaches about what is acceptable and what unacceptable. Not in Tangier in this case but Tripoli, three Christians caught with prostitutes had to pay a huge fine and 'were well drubbed into the Bargaine... Twas a deere bout! But they would take noe Warning!'[19] They had failed to learn from gossip. There is, admittedly, a sub-class of individuals for whom gossip, whatever its content, is not resented because it provides reassurance that they are still reigning celebrities. Thomas Campion's Latin epigram I. 23 'Ad Calum' describes a great man who collects lampoons written against himself and enjoys reading them because they prove that he is still feared.[20] Gossip also constructed boundaries around desirable social formations. In order to be admitted to a circle one might have to pass a trial by gossip, or a bad run at the hand of the town gossips might lead to one's exclusion. A process of enrolment is described in a Restoration lampoon in which the narrative of a duchess's misdoings is agreed by a gossip circle to qualify her for being 'sworn of the Gang'.[21] The gossip of the Restoration Town was also an element in its most important and most eagerly scrutinized form of commerce—that of the marriage market. Members of gentry families came to London to seek spouses in what,

[18] A subject more fully considered in Love, *Clandestine Satire*, 193–8, and Patricia Meyer Spacks, *Gossip* (New York, 1985), 34 and n. 24.

[19] C. R. Pennell (ed.), *Piracy and Diplomacy in Seventeenth-century North Africa: The Journal of Thomas Baker, English Consul in Tripoli, 1677–1685* (London and Toronto, 1989), 141.

[20] *Campion's Works*, ed. Percival Vivian (Oxford, 1909), 240.

[21] BL, Harl. 7315, fo. 211ᵛ; more fully quoted in Love, *Clandestine Satire*, 206.

in the case of the Verneys, was always primarily a financial transaction. (Like most of their class, caught in a downward trend of agricultural prices, they could not afford for it to be otherwise.) The social side of the activity was usually managed by their female town relatives, the business side by a trusted agent who would haggle, often for months on end, over settlements, dowries, and jointures. These negotiations were in turn the object of intense, curious inspection by the Town at large. The value of the commodified human property under offer was very much at the mercy of gossip. 'Reputation' as Patricia Meyer Spacks has remarked 'is social currency'.[22] Rumours of unchastity in females or venereal disease in males might shave thousands from an estimate. By contrast, as Whyman records, approving gossip 'drove up prices and produced financial offers'.[23] We know of no case in which an attack through gossip on a woman's chastity was deliberately implemented in order to improve an intending husband's chances in the market, but it would be rash to say that it never happened. One heiress found her value as a matrimonial property enhanced by gossip that she was so badly infected with syphilis that she could not live long.[24]

GOSSIP AND BIOGRAPHY

Having obtained at least an imperfect sense of gossip as a phenomenon in early modern Britain and its dependencies, we now need to look more closely at the nature of its relationship to biography. In one significant case, that of Aubrey, the question has already been posed and the answer given that he showed little interest in discriminating between gossip and other sources of usable narratives. He is always primarily the storyteller. Biography in its modern, print-mediated sense rests primarily on records, correspondence, and newspapers. For the early modern period we also have the court depositions which have been so effectively used by Alan Macfarlane and Laura Gowing.[25] Anthony

---

[22] Spacks, *Gossip*, 31.   [23] Whyman, *Sociability and Power*, 142.

[24] See *The Surviving Works of Anne Wharton*, ed. G. Greer and S. Hastings (Stump Cross, 1997), 100–3.

[25] Macfarlane, *The Justice and the Mare's Ale*; Gowing, *Domestic Dangers* and *Common Bodies: Women, Touch and Power in Seventeenth-century England* (New Haven, 2003). On gossip, see ibid. 120–3.

Wood was much more resourceful than Aubrey in his use of documentary sources and comes closer to the modern ideal of biographical practice but shows little interest in the personal as opposed to the public lives of his subjects. As Alan Pritchard has shown, given a juicy anecdote by Aubrey he might well ruin it in his retelling.[26] Pritchard's other important point is that most seventeenth-century biographers saw their role as one of providing exemplary models of vice or virtue from which private occurrences were rigorously excluded. Thomas Sprat suppressed, or possibly even destroyed, Cowley's diverting letters to his friends on the grounds that they were too personal for the world at large. That Swift, in the following century, was the subject of a long series of biographical treatments is chiefly due to the preservation of large bodies of correspondence, including the diary-like *Journal to Stella*, but also reflects a massive shift of interest on the part of readers of biographies towards the private person. Roger North, important both as a theoretician and practitioner of biography, illustrates the same shift. He had little time for biography composed solely on the basis of public documents (notoriously subject to the distortions of party), preferring that it should rest on close living acquaintance. A revisionist before his time, his preferred form of life writing was not of great men at all but of figures whose lives provided a meaningful conformity to those of the educated reading public. Most ancient biography was valueless for him because it was constructed around a bare record of actions and required to be padded out with fiction. Exemplary biography was not biography at all but a form of rhetoric. The authority he claimed for his own biographies rested on a lifelong intimate knowledge of their subjects. As a legal adviser to members of the royal family and witness of Privy Council meetings he had also been a close enough observer of the political leaders of his day to reject assessments in White Kennett's *Compleat History of England* (1706) made solely on the basis of written and second-hand oral sources.[27] Izaak Walton could have made a similar claim of intimacy with his subjects and was respected by North for that reason.[28] It was appreciated, of course, that social

[26] Alan Pritchard, *English Biography in the Seventeenth Century* (Toronto, 2005), 167.
[27] In his *Examen: or, an Enquiry into the Credit and Veracity of a Pretended Complete History* (London, 1740).
[28] Roger North, *General Preface and Life of Dr. John North*, ed. Peter Millard (Toronto, 1984), 64.

behaviour was governed by insincerity and self-disguise and that the art of interpersonal negotiation was one of concealing one's real motivations (not only recognized by Pepys in the passage quoted earlier but an incessant theme of Restoration comedy). The good Northian biographer, like the good gossip, must also be a skilled decoder of pretence and reader of disguised intentions. Only intimate knowledge could ensure this.

Yet a concern for the personal does not imply approval of gossip as a means to supplying this. Gossip is made unreliable as a way of representing individuality by its norm-enforcing function. On one hand it is stimulated by the unusual and eccentric as departures from the norm that deserve to be subjected to ridicule. This process may convey a vivid sense of individuality, though one that is always on the edge of caricature. But at the secondary level where it delves for the hidden meanings of observed actions, it consistently seeks to activate a small repertoire of reductive story-types, in the sense that a chance meeting between two individuals might be turned into a liaison or a choice of dress into an occasion for treason. This process works to erase the real complexity of individual selves and their social relationships by accommodating them to stereotypes. North deeply resented the power by which gossip, especially once hardened into legend, might be used to project false and distorted images. His *Examen: or an Enquiry into the Credit and Veracity of a Pretended Complete History*, published posthumously in 1740, was written in response to the Whig Kennett's negative view of the characters of Charles II and James II and those who, like North himself and two of his brothers, had conscientiously served them. North's response was to stigmatize the work as '*a continual Libel, or rather Cloaca of Libels*' (A1ᵛ). In one key passage, he upbraids Kennett for a malicious and uncritical use of gossip:

His general Method of working up this fine Portraiture, is as gross as the Design, for he deals in the very Language, and useth, almost, the very Words which, at the Time, were current at Clubs, Cofee-houses, and factious Assemblies of the Party-Men. And he culls out of Libels, and Lampoons of the Town, choise Relations, Sentences and Flowers, which together with the factious Calumniations, Lyes and Raileries then in Vogue, he applies to the like Purposes, for which they were at first coined; that is to render the King little, and odious to the People, and his Government contemptible. (pp. 17–18)

These oral sources are seen as disingenuously manipulated. On the belief that the Popish Plot Martyr, Sir Edmund Berry Godfrey, had been murdered by Catholics he writes:

Those who first launched such a Rumour, had Reason for what they sent forth. As for the Progress of it, we knew it depended on the idle Coffee-House Company, with whom certain Hints and Nods, of a few choise Persons, went for Inspiration. (p. 201)

Kennett's key accusation, that Charles II had been a papist even before his Restoration, is instanced by Fox as a perennial item of gossip.[29] Yet, while rejecting vulgar and malicious gossip (the kind mostly considered in this chapter), North in his own approach to both his subjects and his reader is very close to what Spacks has described as 'serious gossip . . . the kind that involves two people, leisure, intimate revelation and commentary, ease and confidence' and affords an opportunity for 'emotional speculation'.[30] It would be good to have a different word for this kind of gossip.

North's method, presented by him as empirical rather than intersubjective, did not, paradoxically, lead to an assertion of the coherence of the individual life. In the cases of both his beloved elder brothers, Francis, Lord Guilford, Keeper of the Privy Seal, and John, Master of Trinity College, Cambridge, he had to confront the emergence of a submerged personality as each approached death. Francis suddenly became uncharacteristically 'rigid', suspicious, and parsimonious and, what wounded Roger most, lost his pleasure in music.[31] John, following a severe stroke, was transformed from a pious dedicated scholar into a layabout who delighted in buffoonery and risqué stories, devoting his formerly brilliant mind to 'low concerns and reptile conceits that scarce rose from the ground'.[32] North's method of exact observation ('the profession I make of truth, for better or worse') (p. 155) required him to record these things, much as Boswell did with Johnson's many oddities and inconsistencies, while lacking or not

---

[29] Fox, *Oral and Literate Culture*, 357.   [30] Spacks, *Gossip*, 3.

[31] *The Life of the Lord Keeper North*, ed. Mary Chan (Lewiston, NY, 1995), 129. In this he differed from George Herbert, whose calling for his lute the Sunday before his death is represented by Walton as a prefiguration of his entry into heaven.

[32] North, *General Preface and Life of Dr. John North*, ed. Millard, 156.

desiring Boswell's capacity to assimilate these to an aesthetically integrated characterization.

As Pritchard has pointed out, even to admit such matters to a biography was a radical break from reigning traditions of life writing. It
would be possible to interpret the move from Walton, say, via Aubrey
and North to Boswell as reflecting a progression from biography as a
philosophically or theologically grounded practice firmly located within
the parameters of print culture to biography as a written-down deriv-
ative of gossip, conversation, and oral legend. Spacks sees the change,
I believe anachronistically, as an effect of biography's negotiations with
the novel.[33] The point remains, however, that biography's new concern
with fabrications of the intimate rests directly or mediatedly on oral
sources, premier among which was gossip. Even in Swift's case, literary
sources and correspondence were largely valued as a means of inter-
rogating questions that had become the matter of gossip, such as the
nature of his relationships with Stella and Vanessa. The understanding
of historic lives existed as oral legend prior to its being recorded in
documentary form and the nature of the documentation was likely to
be heavily influenced by the pressure of legend. Gilbert Burnet's *Some
Passages of the Life and Death of the Right Honourable John, Earl of
Rochester*, so admired by Johnson, is at least based on acquaintance with
Rochester and a series of interviews with him in the period prior to his
death; but the assessment of his subject that the biographer brought to
those interviews came from orally circulated stories of his subject's wild
freaks and mocking of religion. North, having himself known Rochester,
regarded Burnet's portrait as 'mere froth, whipped up to serve a turn'.[34]
That this does not seem to have bothered Burnet's contemporaries arises
from their lacking any other notion of how a contemporary life might
be made the subject of a personal as opposed to an exemplary narrative.
The moment the insufficiency of gossip as a ground for biography began
to be recognized is marked by a sudden impatience over exactly this theoretical problem, only then perceived to be a problem. Not surprisingly
it was the losers in the biographical stakes, such as North, who first
became acutely aware of it. His own writings are an attempt to rescue

---

[33] Spacks, *Gossip*, 92–120. Anachronistically, because it involves a reading backwards
from the novel in its achieved form to earlier life writing.
[34] North, *General Preface and Life of Dr. John North*, ed. Millard, 77.

individuals he respected from misrepresentation through gossip, using both a scrupulous record of his first-hand recollection of every aspect of their living selves and a critical analysis of the disputational practices of the misrepresenters.

Yet even today biographers, however scholarly and scientific their methodology, and however subtle their theorization of their practice, are likely to be drawn to a subject by a sense of presence that is a product of social repute. Once research begins, the problems of testimony that so worried North will be found to be just as present as they were for him. As Jean Cocteau once warned:

Our opinions are based on matter which in us and in others gets deformed. Our readiness to mythify and accept myths is incredible. A falsified truth is soon gospel to us. To it we add something of our own brew, and little by little a likeness is formed which bears no relation to the original.[35]

Mythification, whose natural medium is gossip and which so soon hardens into legend, continues to invade the core of the biographical project, serving as a standing temptation to biographers to become storytellers, holding their audience through the vibrancy of narrative, rather than historians sceptically processing documentary traces, or philosophers reflecting on the strange alchemy by which flesh is transmuted into text. Most readers of contemporary biography clearly prefer it that way. The withered countess's salon has always been a more diverting place than Roger North's sober study.

As for Restoration Tangier, it remains, as it always was, a city without biography. A survey of its quarter-century under British rule reveals stirring stories of military and naval heroism, engineering genius and mercantile enterprise to set against others of chicanery, betrayal, and neglect; but the individuals whose acts gave rise to these stories remain little more than names on muster-rolls, ships' manifests, and treasury dockets. In so far as any of the day-to-day human agents are still comprehensible to us as living presences it is only through the journals of John Luke and the peripatetic Henry Tonge, both of them arrant gossips. Otherwise oblivion has scattered her poppy over all. Peter Millard has argued that it was the fear of a similar oblivion overtaking his brothers

---

[35] Jean Cocteau, 'Of the Pre-eminence of Fables', *The Hand of a Stranger (Journal d'un inconnu)*, trans. Alec Brown (London, 1956), 107.

and himself that inspired Roger North's biographical project. While he planted trees that he knew would last for many generations 'he was aware always of the terrible impermanence of things, especially of people' (p. 13). Again, the rarely examined impulse that moves a biographer to negotiate the mysteries of another life, whatsoever the means, the methodology, or the theory, will often have bubbled up from the undertow of the personal or its lingering, duplicitous, presence in gossip.

6

Considering the Ancients: Dryden and the Uses of Biography

Steven N. Zwicker

In a career that included the writing of more than two dozen plays; a raft of prologues and epilogues; odes, elegies, and satires; literary criticism and literary history; and a huge amount of translation from the ancients, Dryden also found time to become something of a biographer: to write the lives of Plutarch, Polybius, and Lucian, to complete a character of St Evremond, and to sketch the lives of Ovid, Horace, Juvenal, Persius, and Virgil in the prefaces and dedications that he wrote for his translations.[1] Indeed, Dryden is the only major writer of the early modern period to have both written and to have written about biography.[2] This is not of course to say that he is the only major writer to have thought biographically or indeed, under some generic guise or other, to have written life histories, nor is it even to suggest that formal biography was an important concern for Dryden; but Dryden's relation to biography was not adventitious. He practised a form of life writing that is perfectly recognizable to us as biography; he reflected on the form, seems to have introduced the term into vernacular use, and fashioned biographical texts that link him to contemporary practice but that also point forward to Johnson's forging a biographical mode for literary criticism in the *Lives of the Poets*. What is paramount in all

---

[1] To this list we should also add Dryden's 1688 translation of Dominic Bouhours's *La Vie de S. François Xavier.*

[2] Dryden's most explicit remarks on biography come in the course of his *Life of Plutarch, The Works of John Dryden*, ed. H. T. Swedenberg et al., 20 vols. (Berkeley and Los Angeles, 1956–2000), xvii. 273–7; all further citations to and quotations from Dryden are to the California edition and will be included parenthetically within the text.

this work is the use Dryden made of life writing to reflect on literary identity and inheritance and on politics and literary imagination—his own and those whom he wrote about. That this should be so is not very surprising for a professional writer who knew how to make economical use of whatever came to hand. But in the instance of a set of minor exercises that were merely occasional and commissioned, biography got him surprisingly far in thinking through the relations between life and art and in thinking about himself as artist. Of course Dryden used the occasion of writing about the lives of others to reflect on his own circumstance; but rather than a distraction from critical thinking, the approximation of others, especially the ancients, to himself provided Dryden with a way to explore the complex, at times troubled, and always productive relations among writing, society, and politics, and to do so by cultivating an unusual degree of disinterestedness as a biographer. My aim in this chapter is to trace the development of that biographical disinterestedness, to identify its relation to other aspects of Dryden's work, and to suggest the role of disinterestedness within the greater domain of subjectivity.

From the beginning of his career Dryden was considering the ancients, and early on what is striking about Dryden and antiquity is his ability to think of ancient writers in terms of distance and difference.[3] They were not simply a series of contemporary models for imitation who happened to live a long time ago, but a set of figures who had distinct and distinctly foreign identities. Tucked into his early triumph, the *Essay of Dramatic Poesy* (1667), is a striking passage where Dryden remarks the difficulty of acquiring proper intimacy with the languages and aesthetics of the past. The passage is so casual that it has gone almost unnoticed,[4] though in it Dryden strikes a remarkable pose of archeological sophistication and literary disinterestedness. The ancients are often difficult to know for we lack philological sophistication and historical understanding. That Dryden would spend much of his career in their company, translating their poets, acquiring them, indeed possessing them, is also true, but we ought not to take too lightly the position from which he begins to meditate on that relationship, the

---

[3] As Dryden wrote in the Preface to *Sylvae*, 'Virgil, Homer, and some others, whose beauties I have been endeavouring all my Life to imitate', *Works*, iii. 4.

[4] But see Michael Gelber, *The Just and the Lively: The Literary Criticism of John Dryden* (Manchester, 1999), 201.

true disinterestedness that informs his understanding of ancient writers and that forms an important basis for his practice of biography, perhaps that makes it possible for Dryden to write biographically about the ancients. It is true that the *Essay* is variously inflected by arguments and ideals and by the pleasures and challenges of representation and indeed self-representation, but that said we should also remind ourselves that Dryden made up all the words in the *Essay*, he occupied every position in the piece whether or not he is writing in the character of Neander— the name under which Dryden represented himself. I want to return to this perhaps too self-evident point in a moment, but first the passage itself:

So long as Aristophanes and Plautus are extant; while the Tragedies of Euripides, Sophocles, and Seneca are in our hands, I can never see one of those Plays which are now written, but it encreases my admiration of the Ancients; and yet I must acknowledge further, that to admire them as we ought, we should understand them better than we do. Doubtless many things appear flat to us, the wit of which depended on some custome or story which never came to our knowledge, or perhaps on some Criticism in their language, which being so long dead, and onely remaining in their Books, 'tis not possible they should make us understand perfectly. To read Macrobius, explaining the propriety and elegancy of many words in Virgil, which I had before pass'd over without consideration, as common things, is enough to assure me that I ought to think the same of Terence; and that in the purity of his style (which Tully so much valued that he ever carried his works about him) there is yet left great room for admiration, if I knew but where to put it. (*Works*, xvii. 20–1)[5]

Dryden is here extraordinarily sensitive to the past, to the ways in which we will always hear Virgil's or Terence's words but at a distance whether we read them behind the scrim of translation or with a complete fluency in ancient languages. He knows that the accidents of usage and custom and the passage of time render some things unrecoverable, and he repeated this argument when he wrote of Plutarch's distance from some 'Idiotism of that Language in which [a jest] was spoken; and where the

---

[5] Eugenius answers Crites's argument: 'But though I grant that here and there we may miss the application of a Proverb or Custom, yet a thing well said will be wit in all Languages; and though it may lose something in the Translation, yet, to him who reads it in the Original, 'tis still the same[;] He has an Idea of its excellency, though it cannot pass from his mind into any other expression or words then those in which he finds it', *Works*, xvii. 28.

conceit is couch'd in a single word, if all the significations of it are not critically understood, the grace and the pleasantry are lost' (*Works*, xvii. 276).[6] Dryden has an archaeologist's sense of the fragility of cultural inheritance and of the possibility of recovering the past by following hints and clues, by piecing things together, by a kind of linguistic and intellectual patchwork, as he says of his use of the sources for Plutarch's life.[7]

On the other hand, and not infrequently, Dryden also claims intimacy with the ancients, 'One Poet may judge of another by himself' (*Works*, v. 283).[8] In this language—and it is a position he more than once claimed—Dryden defends his idea, despite the silence of learned commentary, that Virgil carefully shaded his representations of figures in the *Aeneid* so that he could compliment his patrons and settle scores with his enemies. This was clearly some business that Dryden had in mind for himself as he went about translating Virgil in the 1690s when he was more dependent than ever on patrons and had perhaps more enemies than ever because of his conversion to Rome and his Jacobitism. But Dryden's reading of book 6 of the *Aeneid*, however singular, was not simply opportunistic. He had by the 1690s come into possession not only of Virgil's poem but also of the poet's life and circumstances; he had a sense, that is, of the obligations and debts and complicities that marked the life of a poet writing for an aristocratic court and that shaped the production of even so exalted a genre as epic poetry, perhaps especially of that exalted genre. He had, that is, a fully developed understanding of the biographical underpinning and social contexture of art. And Dryden makes similar moves when he writes of Horace, that 'mild Admonisher', who was 'bred...in the best School, and with the best Company of young Noblemen', and formed 'by the Conversation of Great Men' (*Works*, iv. 57)—he was a courtier who could not help but comply 'with the Interest of his Master' (*Works*, iv. 68). He had

---

[6] See also, *Works*, xvii. 270, and 243–4, for Dryden's sensitivity to differences in language and custom.

[7] See Dryden as Plutarch's biographer, 'I pretend not to an exactness of method in this Life, which I am forc'd to collect by patches from several Authors', *Works*, xvii. 257.

[8] Cf. Dryden's Preface to *Sylvae* (1685), 'Perhaps, in such particular passages, I have thought that I discover'd some beauty yet undiscover'd by those Pedants [Dutch commentators], which none but a Poet cou'd have found', *Works*, iii. 4, and 'I may seem sometimes to have varied from his sence; but I think the greatest variations may be fairly deduc'd from him; and where I leave his Commentators, it may be I understand him better', *Works*, iii. 9.

earlier made such observations on Ovid whose extraction, inheritance, literary sociability, and intimacy with the Augustan court marked his verse epistles;[9] and so it was in his portrait of Juvenal, or in his wonderful remarks on personal fear and literary style in Persius who was not 'sometimes, but generally obscure . . . an apt Scholar [who] . . . when he was bidden to be obscure, in some places, where his Life and Safety were in question, took the same Counsel for all his Book; and never afterwards Wrote ten Lines together clearly' (*Works*, iv. 53).

Dryden writes of birth, education, social hierarchy, personal attributes, and politics as determinants of style and form, of the ways in which the fabric of a poem is woven out of the circumstances of a life and might be unravelled by understanding how poems are fashioned by fears and ambitions, by the hunting after favour, by dependency on the great, by the need for admiration and the sense of obligation. Summarized in this way, such a reciprocity of life and letters may seem reductive, but in the performance of these readings Dryden's social acuity and psychological subtlety, his historical understanding (gathered, he readily admits, second hand) and not least his wit, guard against simplification. Further, and more importantly, Dryden's real capacity for disinterestedness steadily weighs against the too easy acquisition of others to himself, though his enemies and antagonists were loath to acknowledge such objectivity.

And here I want to return to Dryden's capacity for disinterestedness and its relation to the creation of dramatic character, and to return to the *Essay of Dramatic Poesy*. On the one hand it is clear that Dryden shapes the characters of the *Essay* with an attentiveness both to problems of representation and issues of argument. He wants to characterize, even at points gently to caricature, the figures who take part in the debate over the merits of the ancients and moderns and so give weight and shading to what might seem abstractions by anchoring them within personalities, and historical personalities at that. This is especially true of the ways in which Crites's personality—arch and self-important as Sir Robert Howard was reputed, and often reported, to have been—may slightly embarrass the presentation of the ancients.[10] And there is

---

[9] See Dryden's 'Preface' to *Ovid's Epistles* (1680), *Works*, i. 109–19.

[10] The most familiar of these is Shadwell's characterization of Howard as 'Sir Positive At-All', *The Sullen Lovers* (1668); but see as well Dryden's characterization of Howard as a know-it-all in his *Defence of an Essay of Dramatique Poesie* (1668), 'one who has the reputation of understanding all things', *Works*, ix. 5.

something winning in the diffidence and fluency that Dryden fashions for Neander who is of course none other than Dryden himself. But while he has an eye, and more than an eye, on character and characterization in the *Essay*, Dryden also allows ideas to occupy an importantly different space, a realm of disinterestedness, a site of intellectual debate that floats free of opinion and idiosyncrasy. Yes, Dryden arranges for Neander to have the last word, the 'new man' and the 'new theatre' emerge victorious, but just barely, and it is rather with a touch of self-embarrassment than triumphalism that Dryden closes Neander's speech.

At the end of the *Essay* it is Dryden the writer and omniscient narrator who backs slightly away from Neander to observe (and to stage) a young man's enthusiasm overriding his sense of place and decorum, 'Neander was pursuing this Discourse so eagerly, that Eugenius had call'd to him twice or thrice ere he took notice that the Barge stood still, and that they were at the foot of Somerset Stairs, where they had appointed to land' (*Works*, xvii. 80). Neander's modest self-absorption and intellectual engagement are a calculation; but this slight and rather lovely theatrical move also announces something more important: Dryden's understanding of himself as a character, a figure fit for representation. This is not exactly what we now refer to as a performative self though there is clearly an element of the performative in Dryden's decision to cast himself as a character. Rather it is the simultaneous creation and observation of the self that I want to note here. What is at stake is not simply a capacity to create theatre from the self, from one's own personality and ideas, but the rarer and more important capacity for disinterestedness, a writerly impartiality that allowed Dryden distance on himself and distance on others. He knew where advantage lay, the rhetorical edge that objectivity lent, but he also understood the intellectual and aesthetic and ethical meanings of disinterestedness, and the theatre and the capacity to imagine his own theatricality were sites where Dryden developed this capacity for disinterestedness.

How did Dryden reconcile the different positions that he took on the language and lives of ancients: were they his intimates or was the past a different country? Perhaps he had by the 1690s simply forgotten the youthful diffidence with which he faced the Old Comedy or confronted Terence and Virgil. He had travelled a very long way over the thirty years that separated the *Essay* from the *Dedication of the Aeneis*. But perhaps he was also capable of holding both positions, of acknowledging the many things that were for him unknown and unknowable and quite distant about antiquity, and at the same time claiming intimacy with the spirit of Ovid or Horace or Homer and especially Virgil. The fulcrum on which Dryden balanced these positions was his sense of the life of the poet, the shape of a literary career, and a hard-won understanding of the circumstances that rule a writing life and of the psychology of writing that allowed intimacy without denying difference. As he said of Plutarch's ability to withhold judgement, 'We ought not to measure possibilities or impossibilities by our own standard' (*Works*, xvii. 280). This was not an easy negotiation for Dryden who, after all, made a good deal of fuss over his own literary lineage and his intimacy with the ancients; but in different ways both the archaeologist and the dramatist in him, his various capacity for disinterestedness and for theatrical representation, allowed Dryden to imagine another life without denying kinship and understanding.

To use Dryden's words, his critical intelligence allowed him to 'go out of himself', to see otherness without interest, to own, as it were, without the penalties of possessiveness; it was, in a way, the theatricality of a man who was in his own person awkward, shy, quite un-theatrical,[11] and who used the theatre as a place where he could observe and display the practices and passions of others in a most detached fashion. Dryden writes wonderfully of the ways in which pride and possession spoil critical intelligence, of interest compromising judgement, and he puts his finger on exactly the right place when—generously including himself— he writes of critics choosing a favourite among Horace, Juvenal, and Persius and 'falling in love with our labours':

Every Commentator, as he has taken pains with any of them, thinks himself oblig'd to prefer his Author to the other two: To find out their Failings, and decry them, that he may make room for his own Darling. Such is the partiality of Mankind, to set up that Interest which they have once espous'd, though it be to the prejudice of Truth, Morality, and common Justice: And especially in the productions of the Brain. As Authors generally think themselves the best Poets, because they cannot go out of themselves, to judge sincerely of their Betters: So it is with Critiques, who, having first taken a liking to one of these Poets, proceed to Comment on him, and to Illustrate him; after which they fall in

---

[11] See Harold Love, 'Roger L'Estrange's Criticism of Dryden's Elocution', *Notes and Queries*, 48 (2001), 398–400; and see also Love's citations of other references to Dryden's lack of theatrical presence.

love with their own Labours, to that degree of blind fondness, that at length
they defend and exalt their Author, not so much for his sake as for their own.
(*Works*, iv. 49)

Swift would accuse Dryden of exactly such self-love, but what distinguishes both Dryden's criticism and his self-understanding is the
capacity he had for going out of himself. Not that an awareness of the
faults of self-love is ever really prophylactic, but Dryden's understanding of the ways that life conditioned letters—the great lesson for him
of biography—allowed him to acquire self-understanding even while
identifying with others. It did not take the exercise of writing biography
to teach this lesson; he understood that by the time he had written the
Essay of Dramatic Poesy. But the formal occasion of biography developed
his sense of the life as a school for studying letters, and it was after
the biographies of the 1680s and early 1690s that he wrote his deepest
appreciation of this lesson in his study of Virgil's complaisance: here
was a poet who knew how to caress and compliment his master while
yet warning him of the dangers of elective monarchy, who had both a
deep sense of the needs of the Roman public as his readers and the care
he ought to take over the common good.[12]

   It is certainly true that in the *Dedication of the Aeneis* Dryden measured himself and his circumstance against Virgil's. The language, for
example, in which he imagines Virgil troubling himself over elective
monarchy not only seems to say more about Dryden (and William
III) than about Virgil (and Augustus Caesar) but surely as well spoke
to Dryden's own sense of public responsibilities, of the care the now
deposed laureate ought himself to take—and to be seen to be taking—
over the common good. That said, Dryden also displays a wonderfully
detailed sense of Virgil's situation as client in the Augustan court, of the
intricacies of Roman history and court intrigue, and, throughout, of the
ways in which Virgil's ethical sensibility was subject to the circumstances
and times in which he lived. The moral of Virgil's poem is not so exalted
as that of his model; Homer had argued 'the necessity of Union . . . he

---

   [12] See the *Dedication of the Aeneis, Works*, v. 298–9: 'But he knew the Romans were
to be his Readers, and them he brib'd, perhaps at the expence of his Heroe's honesty, but
he gain'd his Cause however; his Pleading before Corrupt Judges. They were content to
see their Founder false to Love, for still he had the advantage of the Amour: It was their
Enemy whom he forsook, and she might have forsaken him, if he had not got the start
of her.'

sets forth the ruinous Effects of Discord' and urged the preservation of freedom 'from an encroaching Enemy. Such was his Moral, which all Criticks have allow'd to be more Noble than that of Virgil: though not adapted to the times in which the Roman Poet liv'd' (*Works*, v. 278). No doubt, Virgil would have urged the same exalted public good had he flourished in another age and written under the patronage of a different court. But Virgil owed 'Obligations' (*Works*, v. 280) to Caesar; despite his own 'Republican Principles' (*Works*, v. 280), he was bound to defer to Caesar, to study his patron's temper, to consider the condition of the times, and to acknowledge, at least to himself, that 'an entire Liberty was not to be retriv'd' (*Works*, v. 281). Virgil was dependent on Caesar's bounty and as a Roman he owed him political allegiance; he shaped his poem in such a way that he might counsel and caress his patron as well as promote the common good. He knew that he addressed a public that valued its Trojan ancestry, and he was willing to indulge their beliefs despite his own opinions:

These things, I say, being consider'd by the Poet, he concluded it to be the Interest of his Country to be so Govern'd: To infuse an awful Respect into the People, towards such a Prince: By that respect to confirm their Obedience to him; and by that Obedience to make them Happy. This was the Moral of his Divine Poem: Honest in the Poet: Honourable to the Emperor, whom he derives from a Divine Extraction; and reflecting part of that Honour on the Roman People, whom he derives also from the Trojans; and not only profitable, but necessary to the present Age; and likely to be such to their Posterity. That it was the receiv'd Opinion, that the Romans were descended form the Trojans, and Julius Caesar from Julius the Son of Aeneas, was enough for Virgil; tho' perhaps he thought not so himself. (*Works*, v. 281–2)

This is a wonderful portrait of that web of compromising circumstances and beliefs in which the poet found himself as he shaped his poem. Dryden underscores Virgil's superior morals and ethics—his principled republicanism, his clear-sighted understanding of history, his sense of public obligation—and at the same time he points to the ways in which Virgil sacrificed convictions both because he was indebted to Caesar—'he held his Paternal Estate from the Bounty of the Conqueror, by whom he was likewise enrich'd, esteeme'd, and cherish'd' (*Works*, v. 281), obligated in quite material ways—and because he understood the value of public mythologies. Even in the creation of his hero, Virgil had to shadow the person of Aeneis with the figure of Augustus, complimenting Caesar by figuring piety as Aeneis' principal virtue,[13] for in that term is comprehended 'the whole Duty of Man towards the Gods; towards his Country, and towards his Relations' (*Works*, v. 288).

Using a myriad of details Dryden spins out a wonderful reading of Virgil's aesthetics; he has a deep conviction about the ways in which Virgil's poem was implicated in Roman history both as the product of aristocratic patronage and as a public performance before an audience in whom he would cultivate political values that ensured the stability of the commonweal. It is true that Dryden cribbed information from a number of sources, that he worked with what was easy to hand— that was always his way. Yet there is no question that he shaped the historical material as a narrative, that he understood biography as a series of threads, accidents, and circumstances to be 'drawn together in a single story' (*Works*, xvii. 274), and that he fashioned a coherent sense of Virgil's person in a way that is distinct from his sources. Dryden was interested in conveying his appreciation of the *Aeneid* as the masterpiece of the most exalted of literary genres—that was after all a commonplace of Renaissance poetics, and the *Dedication* is filled with commonplaces (they seem in fact a waiting room for Dryden as he warmed up to do more complicated things). But he also situated the poem historically and politically and most especially biographically with a detailed sense of the life and person and circumstances and psychology of its poet. Whatever we make of this reading of Virgil, Dryden has fashioned a figure of the poet who hovers over the creation of the entire poem, who animates a particular way of using history and mythology, and who can be traced throughout in his images, his diction, his particular turns of speech, and in the structure he provided for the whole.

The life of the poet that emerges from the *Dedication of the Aeneis* is Dryden's most interesting achievement in biography but it is not his only exercise in life writing and I want to turn now to the biographies to observe Dryden's practices in the genre when his attention is more explicitly on the form. The first of these exercises was a life of Plutarch, the master biographer of the ancients. It would be nice to think that Dryden chose to begin his own career in biography with that pioneer

---

[13] Cf. Dryden in the 'Character' of St Evremond' (1692), where he writes of Virgil's 'chiefest aim [to make] a nearer Resemblance betwixt *Aeneas* and his Patron *Augustus Caesar*, who, above all things, lov'd to be flatter'd for being Pious, both to the Gods and his Relations', *Works*, xx. 9.

of the genre, but the origins of the project are not certain and more likely Tonson's idea than Dryden's, and more likely determined by occasion and opportunity than by careful planning—a category that seldom applies to Dryden's literary or indeed his political or spiritual life. What we know of Dryden's contribution to Tonson's Plutarch is that he was commissioned to do the *Life of Plutarch* that prefaces the whole and that he took the occasion to dedicate *Plutarch's Lives* to one of his great patrons, James Butler, first Duke of Ormond. His relations with the Ormonds are part of another set of stories and negotiations;[14] suffice it here to say that in the Dedication and *Life of Plutarch* Dryden discovered ways of using biography and history that both compliment the sensibility and reputation of his patron and engage the proper uses and partisan misuses of history that had defined Ormond's exactly contemporary controversy with Arthur Annesley, Earl of Anglesey.[15]

But as so often in Dryden's career, once the project was under way he made multiple uses of the occasion and there emerge from Dryden's *Life of Plutarch* a number of insights into his understanding of biography. First, and perhaps most obvious, Dryden knew that biography, through allusion and innuendo, might allow a set of reflections on the present, and that biography gave space and occasion for the biographer to discover himself within the images of the past. He performed in this fashion almost every time he turned his hand to life writing; drawing the figure of Plutarch was no exception, and he was to do the same in the *Character of Polybius* (written 1692, published 1693) and in the *Life of Lucian* (written *c*.1696, published 1711). In what he portrayed as Plutarch's disinterestedness—the ancient's lack of dogmatism and detestation of arrogance—surely there emerges more than a hint of Dryden's own distaste for imposing judgement and opinion, of what he identified, early on, as his own sceptical temperament, and Dryden returns to this theme in the sketches of Polybius and Lucian.[16] Further,

[14] See Steven N. Zwicker with Jane Ohlmeyer, 'John Dryden, the House of Ormond, and the Politics of Anglo-Irish Patronage', *Historical Journal* 49 (2006), 677–706.

[15] See especially Dryden's attack on historians who pleaded their cases like partisan lawyers, *Works*, xvii. 235–6: 'These Authors are for obscuring truth, because truth would discover them. They are not Historians of an Action, but Lawyers for a party: They are retain'd by their principles, and brib'd by their interests: Their narrations are an opening of their cause; and in the front of their Histories, there ought to be written the Prologue of a pleading, *I am for the Plaintiff,* or *I am for the Defendant.*'

[16] On Dryden's scepticism see *Works*, xvii. 348.

he renders the refusal of dogmatism an important element in a broader rationality, a sensibility that makes a universal virtue out of common sense in matters of the spirit, 'I have ever thought, that the Wise-men in all Ages, have not much differ'd in their opinions of Religion; I mean as it is grounded on human Reason' (*Works*, xvii. 250). Dryden had outlined this position in the Preface to *Religio Laici* (1682),[17] but in the biography of Plutarch, written one year later, he would aim not only to discover salvation for the ancients but for all like-minded sceptics and rationalists. That Dryden is a bit nervous in collapsing all religions into one is evident from the speed with which he qualifies the main clause: 'I mean as it is grounded on human Reason: for Reason, as far as it is right, must be the same in all Men' (*Works*, xvii. 250), but there is a daring piece of self-portraiture in this passage.

At the same time, the biography of Plutarch offered Dryden an occasion to turn historian, to admire Plutarch's diligence as an archivist, to compliment him as a scholar who understood the necessity of compiling and collating diverse sources, who searched among 'Records and publick Instruments' (*Works*, xvii. 247), and who knew when to depend on primary and secondary sources and when to mark his distance even from those who might know better. What emerges from this admiration is Dryden's own sophisticated sense of biographical argument, his appreciation of the varied archive of historical knowledge—not only the written record, but also statues, medals, inscriptions, paintings, proverbial sayings, epigrams, and epitaphs, and as well oral history.[18] Dryden's grasp of the cultural dimensions of the historical record opened

---

[17] See *Works*, ii. 99: 'It has always been my thought, that Heathens, who never did, nor without Miracle cou'd hear of the name of Christ were yet in a possibility of Salvation. Neither will it enter easily into my belief, that before the coming of the Saviour, the whole World, exception only the Jewish Nation, shou'd lye under the inevitable necessity of everlasting Punishment, for want of that Revelation, which was confin'd to so small a spot of ground as that of Palaestine . . . it seems unaccountable to me, why so many Generations of the same Offspring, as preceeded our Saviour in the Flesh, shou'd be all involved in one common condemnation, and yet that their Posterity shou'd be Intitled to the hopes of Salvation: As if a Bill of Exclusion had passed only on the Fathers, which debar'd not the Sons from their Succession: or that so many Ages had be deliverer'd over to Hell, and so many reserv'd for Heaven, and that the Devil had the first choice, and God the next.'

[18] *Works*, xvii. 248: 'To these [Plutarch] added a curious Collection of Ancient Statues, Medals, Inscriptions, and Paintings, as also of proverbial sayings, Epigrams, Epitaphs, Apothegemes, and other Ornaments of History, that he might leave nothing unswept behind him.'

him to an understanding of the ways in which culture is continuous but also to differences and distinctions. He asserts this repeatedly as a truth of social behaviour and of language—its universality which can be measured by translation and the inevitable and obscuring changes to which all language is subject.[19] Dryden admires Plutarch's assiduity as archivist, an ancient who was himself aware that the past was a different country, and Dryden practices this negative capability himself, 'I cannot but wonder that every one, who has hitherto written Plutarchs Life, and particularly Rualdus, the most knowing of them all, should so confidently affirm that these Oracles, were given by bad Spirits according to Plutarch; As Christians, indeed we may think them so; but that Plutarch so thought, is a most apparent falsehood' (*Works*, xvii. 254).

Dryden's capacity to use biography as mirror and as perspective-glass, to arrange ancient lives according to his own interests while at the same time retaining an ability to see the past if not in its own terms— whatever that might have meant in the late seventeenth century—then at least to recognize that its terms were not simply his own may not be a singular achievement among his contemporaries, but in a world where biography was insistently deployed as polemic, his disinterestedness is unusual, and it is unusually pointed in the Plutarch life. In the Dedication to which *The Life of Plutarch* was attached, Dryden scorned the polemical misuses of history that marked Angelsey's performance in his controversy with Ormond. These concerns mark Dryden's own *Life of Plutarch*, and in a more modest and casual register they are also to be found in the poet's biographies of Polybius and Lucian. Like the *Life of Plutarch*, the lives of Polybius and Lucian preface collaborative translations, and they are thoroughly occasional pieces done at the request of editors or publishers who sought to attach Dryden's prestige to new translations of the ancients. That said, these texts confirm much of what we have seen in the Plutarch biography and in Dryden's biographical interpolations in his preface to the *Sylvae*, the *Discourse concerning Satire*, and the *Dedication of the Aeneis*: a sensitivity to the qualities that identify and distinguish the ancient life but as well a sense of those places where the figure might be drawn close to himself. *The Character of Polybius and his Writings* gestures towards birth, education, social

---

[19] On the inevitable decays to which the written word is subject, see also *The Hind and the Panther*, part 2, ll. 314–88, *Works*, iii. 149–51.

circumstance, and political expertise—Polybius's experience as courtier, counsellor, and companion to the great—as they determined life and writing. Like Plutarch, Polybius is a diligent archivist: he is immersed in his materials, weighing, collating, and correcting his sources, disdaining legends, superstitions, prodigies, and miracles. Such is the character of the virtuous historian, and Dryden traces the principles of honesty and disinterestedness across the life.

But there is another story that also emerges in *The Character of Polybius*, and while it may not quite contradict probity and plain-dealing (*Works*, xx. 22), it does not follow exactly from those ideals. For what seems more to catch Dryden's interest than Polybius's virtue is the historian's prudence and practicality, his 'dexterous management' (*Works*, xx. 15) of his materials towards the ends of expedience and obligation, his aim to instruct his countrymen on the necessity of yielding in a timely and compliant manner to the Romans 'to make it easie to them, by a cheerful compliance with their commands, rather than unprofitably to oppose them' (*Works*, xx. 19). It is not plain-dealing that here attracts Dryden but Polybius's arts of management, his complaisance, his understanding of interest and obligation. This is Polybius the courtier, the friend of the great, the wise manager of opinion who writes that 'it would be happy for History, if those who undertake, to write it, were Men conversant in Political Affairs . . . [who] have form'd themselves before-hand to their undertaking, by prudence, and long experience of Affairs' (*Works*, xx. 33–4). This aspect of Polybius may remind us more of Dryden's Virgil masterfully playing upon the desires and uncertainties of his patron and the taste and dependencies of his readers than of Plutarch the scrupulous historian and moralist, and it speaks less of Dryden's efforts to discover the past than it does of his efforts at self-understanding. For what he creates in these images of the ancient lives is an appreciation of how complaisance and compliance might discover sanctuary in the precincts of poetry or philosophy or history. This is not anything quite so simple or obvious or indeed self-serving as apologetics—Dryden finding an exculpatory version of himself when he looks to the past, returning to and refiguring qualities that he may not have admired in himself or in his own career, or qualities that he had ruefully to acknowledge as his own after they had been mercilessly publicized by his enemies. For in examining compliance in Polybius or, as we shall see, religious scepticism in Lucian, the ancient life seems less a model for public display than matter for a more private form of self-understanding.

Of Lucian, Dryden cheerfully admits that he has almost no historical knowledge. Generally, he confesses, the lives of the learned lack action which is the heart of narrative. But what is one to do with a subject about which almost nothing is known? Lucian 'has left so little of his own Affairs on Record, that there is scarce sufficient to fill a Page from his Birth to his Death' (*Works*, xx. 208). There is a touch of biographical or pseudo-biographical information—and Dryden is not certain of the category—and he fashions from that a sketch of Lucian's learning, independence, and wit, his interest in and wide knowledge of 'Men, Manners and Arts' (*Works*, xx. 211). The phrase has about it the air of a slightly worn formula, and indeed Dryden has little interest in the limited information that he has to hand. Mostly he is dismissive of what others have made of the life story, but Dryden does engage with Lucian's spiritual life. Here he is not hampered by lack of information; indeed, rather than a problem, the lack of such is an advantage for the work that he wants to do which is not independent of the person but true to Lucian's writing rather than to the meagre life record, true to the spirit that emerges from Lucian's work, to 'the Genius of the Man, whose Image we may clearly see in the Glass, which he holds before us of his Writings, which reflects him to our Sight' (*Works*, xx. 215). From Lucian's spiritual life Dryden fashions not a self-portrait but an ahistorical ideal, a figure of toleration and scepticism, of spiritual diffidence, charity, and doubtfulness, even to the point of fluid self-definition. Whether Lucian is stoic or epicurean, Dryden cannot say; he is 'in one half of his Book, a Stoic, in the other an Epicurean, never constant to himself in any Scheme of Divinity' (*Works*, xx. 216). One might have thought that Dryden had been often enough accused of pliancy and opportunism to steer clear of those qualities as he portrayed the spiritual ideals and itinerary of Lucian. Others had made of that spiritual journey a movement from paganism to Christian belief, but Dryden ridicules that easy formula. He goes out of his way to berate the failure of Christian charity when faced with pagan beliefs; indeed, Dryden is far more caustic on the failures of Christian charity than he is on heathen error. He allows that Lucian the satirist 'lashes his own false Gods with more severity than the true'; but when he has Lucian portray the early Christians 'with their cropt

Hair, their whining Voices, melancholy Faces, mournful Discourses, and
nasty Habits' (*Works*, xx. 213), Dryden punishes the ill temper of his
co-religionists. Smiling, he adds that Lucian has rendered them 'with
a greater air of Calvinists or Quakers, than of Roman Catholicks or
Church of England men' (*Works*, xx. 213). What Dryden concludes of
Lucian's beliefs is very little certainty indeed: 'He might as well believe in
none, as in many Gods. And on the other side, he might believe in many,
as Julian did, and not in one. For my own part, I think it is not prov'd
that either of them were Apostates; though one of them, in hopes of an
Empire, might temporize, while Christianity was the Mode at Court'
(*Works*, xx. 215). Spiritual opportunism is raised to a principle; either
Lucian was an 'Eclectic' fashioning his own body of beliefs out of several
opinions and dogmas or he was a 'Sceptic' (*Works*, xx. 215), doubting
of everything: 'he weigh'd all Opinions, and adher'd to none of them;
only us'd them as they serv'd his occasion for the present Dialogue; and
perhaps rejected them in the next. And indeed, this last opinion is the
more probable of the two, if we consider the Genius of the Man, whose
Image we may clearly see in the Glass, which he holds before us of his
Writings.'

There are two important issues here. First, writing itself most clearly
and deeply discovers the truth of a life; biography is a form of literary
criticism, or literary criticism is a variant, perhaps the highest variant,
of biography. Dryden knows this as he goes about discovering certain
qualities and convictions, even eccentricities, among the ancients even
against the superior scholarship of a Casaubon or a Scaliger. He is a
better student of the ancients because he is a more knowing and intuitive
reader. The second issue is 'occasion and opportunity'; opportunism
had long been a charge levelled at Dryden, crudely, if effectively, when
his loyalties or religions were in question—mourning Cromwell one
year, celebrating the return of Stuart kingship the next; defending the
Anglican faith under Charles II, then turning Roman Catholic apologist
after James ascended the throne; and perhaps more subtly when climb-
ing and opportunism were in view as Dryden grasped for success at the
fringes of the court or thrived in the theatre with entertainments for
his betters. There is a rich archive of such abuse,[20] but what surprises

---

[20] See Hugh Macdonald's *John Dryden: A Bibliography of Early Editions and of Drydeniana* (Oxford, 1939), 'Drydeniana', 187–315.

when Dryden writes of Polybius and Lucian, even of Virgil, is his way
of hovering over the issue of opportunity, indeed of opportunism, not
so much to discover allies in the ancients, to take cover among the
shades of Polybius and Lucian or Horace and Persius, as to explore
the mechanisms of compliance, to understand how it was that writers
repeatedly discovered themselves and were to be discovered within structures of dependency and obligation. Dryden understood that character
and integrity were at stake when his enemies ridiculed his turning from
one principle to another, and of course he defended himself against
such attack, often giving as good as he got. But he was also capable
of sufficient distance to explore the structural circumstances that made
compliance and opportunism professional hazards for a writer. It did
not hurt that Virgil, the greatest of the ancients, might be discovered
within the precincts of Dryden's own discomforts, but surely Dryden
was not so naive as to think it rhetorically persuasive to display his own
dilemmas as Virgil's. He understood the rules of the game when it came
to polemics, and he could not have thought of biography merely as
a form of vindication in the skirmishes over character. He had noted
in the Preface to *Sylvae*, 'This exact propriety of Virgil, I particularly
regarded, as a great part of his Character' (*Works*, iii. 7). Virgil's person
was to be recovered from his writings; his poetry was bound to his
person. For Dryden, writing the life of others was an historical practice,
a form of literary understanding but as well an opportunity for self-
understanding.

'Never constant to himself in any Scheme of Divinity' (*Works*,
xx. 216); so Dryden had written of Lucian, emphasizing writerly
mobility, fluidity of character. He had arraigned Buckingham on such
charges—'everything by starts, and nothing long'—understanding fully
the relations between public loyalties and private convictions. For a
politician, mobility was not a skill worth advertising. But it is also
clear that Dryden himself prized mobility, that there was a kind of
alliance between mobility and the more elevated intellectual, rhetorical,
and aesthetic forms to which he was attracted: scepticism as a spiritual
stance, dialectic as an argumentative form, theatre as an aesthetic, and a
pervasive sense of irony that more or less defined Dryden as he looked
towards the world. Perhaps then we ought to consider the *Life of Lucian*
(1696) simply as a self-portrait, Dryden construing the past with a kind
of careless indifference to historical distance, willing to indulge a look

into the mirror of history so long as it reflected his own concerns, more self-absorbed than in his earlier biographical projects. Yes, the *Life of Lucian*—like the sketch of Polybius—is work of the left hand, Dryden now writing quickly and for a bit of cash in the midst of the great Virgil translation, hardly something to absorb much attention. That is so, but neither speed nor commerce should obscure the ways in which the late examples of life writing are part of a more continuous project that throughout claimed Dryden's interest. Early on he had developed a sense of the writing life as a product of birth and education but more importantly of social position and political circumstance, of a network of dependencies, allegiances, and obligations from which emerged the special genius and the particular vulnerabilities of a poet. He worked this out most fully in writing of Virgil at the Augustan court, but the idea that style and design, even 'imperfect Sense, or at the least Obscurity' (*Works*, iv. 10), might be traced to the character and circumstance of a writer repeatedly drew his attention and his historical sympathy and imagination, so that he might say, whatever the achievements of scholarship, that he had an intimate, indeed a writerly understanding of the ancients.

An early modern life, or an ancient life read in early modernity, might stand as a model for imitation, an instance of piety, a gathering of social markers, a polemical argument, a form of political identity, an example or a warning. But the life rendered disinterestedly as a whole, the life seen on its own terms, or the life seen as the interplay of circumstance, psychology, and genius—such notions lay in the future, pointing more to Enlightenment ideals or to modern or modernist notions about the sources of identity than to early modern convictions. Dryden's biographical writings do not wholly break with early modern forms, but they are also scenes of disinterested appraisal and of self-understanding that cannot be simply conflated with contemporary practices and that surely drew from Dryden's energies and convictions and dependencies as a writer. In the various modes of Dryden's life writings—the prefaces, the biographical sketches, the dedications that form sustained essays in literary criticism—there emerges an ideal of the authorial life in which a coherent, even an organic, sense of the self can be discerned. Such a self gives shape to and a rationale for the qualities of ancient writers. Dryden is interested in fashioning a form of life writing that explains what is Ovidian in Ovid, what makes Virgil, Virgilian—what animates the style, the temperament, and the historical character of the ancients.

At the same time he often extends the psychology until we can feel it touching his own circumstance, his own sense of self. Here biography as mirror of the self comes directly into play with and perhaps into conflict with biography as history, and I want to close by addressing these contradictory impulses. What does it mean for Dryden to have simultaneously understood biography as self-imagining and as historical difference, and how is it possible simultaneously to do both?

Early in these remarks I made the obvious point that the positions that Dryden mapped in *The Essay of Dramatic Poesy* all belonged to him; he was the inventor of every point of view in the *Essay*, and his work was not a transcription but an artistic creation, and if we properly appreciate Dryden's capacity to create a series of contradictory positions and to hold these as equally valuable, that is equally dramatized, we might discover at their root his capacity for disinterestedness. Dryden's ability to dramatize different points of view so that they might emerge from persons and personalities was not a decorative impulse, a way of making aesthetic debate more entertaining, but an achievement of remarkable objectivity, especially obvious when we consider Dryden creating himself as a character in the *Essay* and then pointing to the gap between himself as its writer and as a character within its fiction. Perhaps it is also an obvious point, but one that bears repeating as we attempt to tease out the qualities of Dryden's achievements as biographer, that what we are dealing with when we read Dryden's biographies is the work of an artist. I use a slightly quaint term to emphasize Dryden's work within the domain of the imagination. What we might expect from an artist turned biographer is a performance of the self, biography as mirror, an occasion for self-inspection, self-understanding, self-admiration. This is true of Dryden and in some cases—as in the portrait of Virgil trapped within the contingencies of an aristocratic court or in the portrait of Lucian's scepticism—quite interestingly true; introspection and self-admiration are one of the privileges of art though we may not always feel—and certainly Dryden's contemporaries did not feel—obliged to admire narcissism, even within the precincts of art.[21] What is less obvious and less expected but I think no less important about Dryden's impulses

---

[21] See the contemporary manuscript annotations on the Folger Library copy (from the Dobell Collection, D2212.3) of the Preface to *Absalom and Achitophel*, the first page of which is reproduced in *John Dryden: Selected Poems*, ed. Steven N. Zwicker and David Bywaters (Harmondsworth, 2001), 112; Swift made a brilliant attack on Dryden's self-regarding prefaces and dedications in *The Battle of the Books*.

to understand the biographical subject is the determined objectivity of which he was also capable, certainly with respect to the ancients, but also and as importantly with respect to himself. Self-inspection or self-admiration and historical objectivity belong together, they inhabit without contradiction the same intellectual and artistic impulses. In his capacity as artist Dryden had a determination to go out of himself, to put himself, and others, at arm's length, to consider himself, and others, as objective creations. In order to achieve this with the ancients Dryden had to turn archivist or archaeologist and historian, and he understood that even with the best will and most scrupulous effort the past might always escape an immediate and intimate and intuitive understanding. In order to achieve objectivity with and of the self he also had to become its student, he had to inspect the self as it might be observed when he looked at others—when he looked at the ancients—and so we often feel the image of Horace or Juvenal or Virgil somewhat occluded by the figure of the poet seeing himself in the past. But the otherness of others and the otherness of the self were not different creations for Dryden; they were aspects of the same kind of artistic objectivity, the same imaginative capacity. We may find it more attractive, more diffident, to make of the ancients figures for admiration and understanding, but Dryden knew that it was also necessary to make of himself such a figure, and in his practice as biographer he moved fluently between these projects. It may feel counter-intuitive to think of them as the same, but as an artist Dryden knew that they were but aspects of the same kind of understanding. Biography gave Dryden an occasion for such work and in it he went to some of the same places as his contemporaries; but in fashioning biography into an instrument for self-understanding he moved towards a very different and what feels to us a modern, or perhaps more accurately modernist, notion of the objectivity of art— at the best moments in these biographies Dryden achieved exactly that disinterestedness, the artist standing apart from his own creation even as he seems most deeply to peer into it.

PART III

PAINTING LIVES

7

'Naught But Illusion'? Buckingham's Painted Selves

Alastair Bellany

Ben Jonson and Inigo Jones's masque for Twelfth Night 1618, 'Pleasure Reconciled to Virtue', had reached an awkward moment. The revels had begun but the aristocratic dancers were tiring, the masque was beginning to drag, and King James I was getting annoyed. Orazio Busoni, chaplain to the Venetian ambassador, described what ensued. 'Being well nigh tired they began to lag,' he reported, 'whereupon the king, who is naturally choleric, got impatient and shouted aloud "Why don't they dance? What did they make me come here for? Devil take you all, dance!"' Disaster was averted, however, by the king's favourite, George Villiers, the newly created Marquis of Buckingham, who 'immediately sprang forward, cutting a score of lofty and very minute capers [*capriole*], with so much grace [*gratia*] and agility that he not only appeased the ire of his angry lord, but rendered himself the admiration and delight of everybody.' Inspired by Buckingham, the other courtly masquers danced with renewed energy, 'but none', Busoni thought, 'came up to the exquisite manner [*maniera*] of the marquis'. The evening saved and the masque concluded, Prince Charles, whose much-anticipated debut performance this was, 'went in triumph to kiss his father's hands', and was embraced and kissed by the king. James then

This essay has been much helped by the audience comments at the QMC conference 'Writing Lives' and at the Ohio State Early Modern Europe Seminar, and by the provision of advice and references by Julia Alexander, Tom Cogswell, Barbara Haeger, and Peter Lake.

'honoured' Buckingham 'with marks of extraordinary affection, patting his face'.[1]

Roger Lockyer's 1981 biography of Buckingham narrates these events to illustrate the homoerotic dynamics underpinning the favourite's relationship with the king—he notes, in particular, the display of 'Buckingham's physical charms, and his capacity to soften the King's ill humour'.[2] I, however, want to draw attention to another feature of this incident: its intense theatricality. Buckingham's capers constituted an improvised performance addressed to and admired by not only the king but also the six hundred or so other courtiers and visiting dignitaries— including the Venetian and Spanish ambassadors and their entourages— crammed into the room for the show. Here was a theatrical assertion and presentation of self, a performance that departed from—but nevertheless was clearly linked to—the more scripted masque it interrupted, a masque in which courtly dance was presented as a form of moral pedagogy.[3] Buckingham's solo performance also conformed remarkably to the ideals of courtly *sprezzatura* discussed by Castiglione—the capers were a display of seemingly spontaneous, effortless and unaffected 'grace' designed to win the prince's favour. But, of course, these capers were not effortless—Buckingham drew from the dancing lessons he probably had taken in France and elsewhere, lessons that taught him to move and display his body in an elegant, controlled, and spectacular fashion. Indeed Busoni's comment on Buckingham's exquisite 'manner' was as much a technical as an aesthetic evaluation: in Italian choreographic theory, the dancer's 'maniera' referred to the correct relation between the upper and lower body.[4]

---

[1] *Calendar of State Papers: Venetian (1617–19)* (London, 1909), xv. 110–14, esp. 113–14 (trans.); C. H. Herford and Percy and Evelyn Simpson (eds.), *Ben Jonson* (Oxford, 1950), x. 580–4 (original).

[2] Roger Lockyer, *Buckingham: The Life and Political Career of George Villiers, First Duke of Buckingham 1592–1628* (London, 1981), 33. Lockyer (incorrectly, I think) states that James's kiss and embrace were given to Buckingham.

[3] Stephen Orgel (ed.), *Ben Jonson: Selected Masques* (New Haven and London, 1970), 170–2; Skiles Howard, *The Politics of Courtly Dancing in Early Modern England* (Amherst, Mass., 1998), 129–32.

[4] Howard, *Politics*, 16 (on *maniera*) and 33, 66, 74 (on the caper). On Buckingham's dance lessons and on his career as what she calls 'arguably the most famous aristocratic dancer of his time', see Barbara Ravelhofer, *The Early Stuart Masque: Dance, Costume, and Music* (Oxford, 2006), 54–6, and esp. 107–8; see too Lockyer, *Buckingham*, 11.

This chapter wonders what happens to the writing of early modern lives when we write them through the paradigm of the spectacular presentation and fashioning of the courtly self.[5] I want to take as my example George Villiers, and as my main focus the theatrical 'presentation of the self' not in dance, but in the parallel dramaturgical medium of court portraiture.[6] The remarkable history of George Villiers's transformation from the younger son of a decayed gentry family into the all-powerful royal favourite with a dukedom and unparalleled influence over domestic, military, and diplomatic affairs, is, as Lockyer's biography makes clear, fundamentally grounded in the personal relationships he forged with two successive English kings. But it is also in part a story of an energetic and ongoing fashioning of the self. Buckingham's life was marked by the highly politicized performance of a multiplicity of selves, presented and fashioned through multiple forms of media, on multiple stages and to multiple audiences.[7] Portraiture was one

[5] For stimulating theoretical and trans-disciplinary reflections on self-fashioning and self-presentation, see Erving Goffman, *The Presentation of Self in Everyday Life* (New York, 1959); Stephen Greenblatt, *Renaissance Self-Fashioning: From More to Shakespeare* (Chicago, 1980); Michel Foucault, 'What is Enlightenment?', 'On the Genealogy of Ethics', and 'Technologies of the Self', in Paul Rabinow and Nikolas Rose (eds.), *The Essential Foucault* (New York, 2003).

[6] My approach to court portraiture has been shaped by Roy Strong, *Van Dyck: Charles I on Horseback* (New York, 1972), and Kevin Sharpe's appropriation of Strong's approach in *The Personal Rule of Charles I* (New Haven and London, 1992), 183–8. My sense of the theatricality of seventeenth-century painting owes much to a reading of Simon Schama, *Rembrandt's Eyes* (New York, 1999).

[7] I hope to write at greater length about these processes at a later date. Any fuller study would also need to explore the presentation and fashioning of the self in intimate and daily life, in Buckingham's modes of interaction with peers, with inferiors, with masters, lovers, and relatives. The best work on Buckingham's self-presentation and self-fashioning has thus far focused on his participation in court masques and on his appeals to the public in the later 1620s. See James Knowles, 'The "Running Masque" Recovered: A Masque for the Marquess of Buckingham (c.1619–20)', *English Manuscript Studies 1100–1700* 8 (2000); ' "Songs of baser alloy": Jonson's *Gypsies Metamorphosed* and the Circulation of Manuscript Libels', *Huntington Library Quarterly* 69 (2006), esp. 162, 165; Thomas Cogswell, 'The People's Love: The Duke of Buckingham and Popularity', in Thomas Cogswell, Richard Cust, and Peter Lake (eds.), *Politics, Religion and Popularity: Early Stuart Essays in Honour of Conrad Russell* (Cambridge, 2002); ' "Published by Authoritie": Newsbooks and the Duke of Buckingham's Expedition to the Île de Ré', *Huntington Library Quarterly* 67 (2004); and Thomas Cogswell and Peter Lake, ' "Full of State and Woe": Shakespeare, the Duke of Buckingham and the "Politics of Popularity" in the 1620s' (forthcoming).

key site and medium for this performance and self-fashioning. Paintings of the favourite displayed potent idealized images not only to important elite audiences, but also to Buckingham himself: they could thus not only work to fashion and display a version of the self, but also become an aesthetic instrument for the constitution of the self, modelling, like a panegyric poem, ideals and virtues for emulation.[8] Paintings of Buckingham—like other sites of his performance of self— were also intensely politicized.[9] Paintings of Buckingham reflected on the origins and legitimacy of his political power, and in so doing they helped construct political and social authority for a man without the stable inherited aristocratic identity—the 'blood'—so many of his fellow courtiers took for granted. These visual images were also embedded in political contexts, reflecting and responding to shifting events, to courtly factional strife and competition, and to a broader political culture of public debate and dissent in which images of Buckingham played an increasingly central role. Portraits of the duke, I will argue, constituted one side of an implicit and explicit dialogue with proliferating 'public' counter-images of Buckingham circulating in the literary underground of illicit tracts and verse libels.[10]

I want to explore the politicized presentation of the self in court portraiture by looking closely at one picture (Fig. 1), a massive equestrian portrait of the duke commissioned at a cost of £500 from Peter Paul Rubens when Buckingham met him in Paris in May 1625.[11] We do

[8] For suggestive comments on the didactic and ethical function of paintings, see R. Malcolm Smuts, *Court Culture and the Origins of a Royalist Tradition in Early Stuart England* (Philadelphia, 1987), 159–62; and Philip McEvansoneya, 'Italian Paintings in the Buckingham Collection', in Edward Chaney (ed.), *The Evolution of English Collecting: Receptions of Italian Art in the Tudor and Stuart Periods* (New Haven and London, 2003), 326.

[9] Greenblatt (channelling mid-1970s Foucault) situates Renaissance self-fashioning within the matrices of Power; my focus on politics operates at a different, though not necessarily theoretically incompatible, level of analysis.

[10] On libels, the literary underground and the 'public', see Alastair Bellany, ' "Rayling e Rymes and Vaunting Verse": Libellous Politics in Early Stuart England, 1603–1628', in Kevin Sharpe and Peter Lake (eds.), *Culture and Politics in Early Stuart England* (Basingstoke, 1994); Bellany, *The Politics of Court Scandal in Early Modern England: News Culture and the Overbury Affair, 1603–1660* (Cambridge, 2002); and Andrew McRae, *Literature, Satire and the Early Stuart State* (Cambridge, 2004).

[11] The key documentary and interpretive art-historical works on this painting are: Frances Huemer, *Portraits Volume One*, part xix.1 of the *Corpus Rubenianum Ludwig Burchard* (London, 1977), 57–61; Julius S. Held, *The Oil Sketches of Peter Paul Rubens*

Fig. 1. Peter Paul Rubens, *Buckingham on Horseback*, c.1625–27.

not know when the picture was finished and delivered—some scholars argue that it may not have been shipped until as late as September 1627—but the window of its production and initial display, 1625–7, coincides with one of the must tumultuous periods of Buckingham's

(Princeton, 1980), i. 392–4; Hans Vlieghe, *Rubens Portraits of Identified Sitters*, part xix. 2 of the *Corpus Rubenianum* (London and New York, 1987), 64–7; Christopher White, *Peter Paul Rubens: Man and Artist* (New Haven and London, 1987), 188–91; Walter Liedtke, *The Royal Horse and Rider: Painting, Sculpture, and Horsemanship 1500–1800* (New York, 1989), 24–5, 260–1; and Peter C. Sutton, Marjorie E. Wieseman, and Nico van Hout, *Drawn by the Brush: Oil Sketches by Peter Paul Rubens* (New Haven and London, 2004), 142–6. See too Graham Parry, *The Golden Age Restor'd: The Culture of the Stuart Court, 1603–42* (Manchester, 1981), 142–3; and Smuts, *Court Culture*, 206–8.

career.[12] As we shall see, the equestrian portrait communicated multiple images of the self in a number of ways and we will have to deploy an appropriately diverse range of techniques and contextual sources to read the performance and its politics properly.

YORK HOUSE, AESTHETICS, AND
THE COURTLY CONNOISSEUR

Something of the self the equestrian portrait projected can be deduced from the most likely site of its original display—the Great Chamber of Buckingham's Thames-side residence at York House, a large paved room added to the mansion by Buckingham's agent and chief art buyer, Balthazar Gerbier.[13] This was perhaps the most public space in the house, the likely site of a regular cycle of feasts, masques, and ambassadorial receptions, and thus a space in which the duke routinely presented himself to a courtly, aristocratic, and international audience.[14] It was

[12] For the case for a September 1627 dating, see Gregory Martin, 'Rubens and Buckingham's "fayrie ile"', *Burlington Magazine*, 108/765 (1966), 614. The case depends, however, on the assumption that Rubens's news that 'The pictures for my Lord the Duke are all ready' in a letter of 8/18 Sept. 1627 to Gerbier refers to portraits *of* the duke rather than to a consignment of paintings *for* the duke. See Ruth Saunders Magurn (trans. and ed.), *The Letters of Peter Paul Rubens* (Evanston, Ill.,1991), 204; and Jeffrey M. Muller, *Rubens: The Artist as Collector* (Princeton, 1989), 78. For other discussions of the dating issue, see Julius S. Held, 'Rubens's Sketch of Buckingham Rediscovered', *Burlington Magazine*, 118/881 (1976), 548; and Vlieghe, *Rubens Portraits*, 65. The painting was destroyed in a 1949 fire and thus can only be studied from photographs, but a much smaller (and iconographically far less busy) oil sketch for the portrait survives in the Kimbell Art Museum in Texas.

[13] Philip McEvansoneya, 'Some Documents Concerning the Patronage and Collections of the Duke of Buckingham', *Rutgers Art Review* 8 (1987), 30; John S. Brewer (ed.), *The Court of King James the First by Dr. Godfrey Goodman* (London, 1839), ii. 360; Balthazar Gerbier, *A Brief Discourse Concerning the Three chief Principles of Magnificent Building* (London, 1662), 42 (which gives the dimensions of a room at York House used for masques—perhaps the Great Chamber—as 35 × 35 feet); P. H. Hulton, 'Drawings of England in the Seventeenth Century by Willem Schellinks, Jacob Esselens and Lambert Doomer', *Walpole Society* 35, parts 1 and 2 (1954–6), part 1, 31–2, and part 2, plate 28a.

[14] Gerbier, *Brief Discourse*, 27–8, 42; John Orrell, 'Buckingham's Patronage of the Dramatic Arts: the Crowe Accounts', *Records of Early English Drama Newsletter* (1980: issue 2). Helen Andrews Kaufman, *Conscientious Cavalier: Colonel Bullen Reymes, M.P., F.R.S. 1613–1672: The Man and his Times* (London, 1962), 28–9, describes the room, but probably conflates the inventory entries for York House and Chelsey House.

to this elite (and, during the political, diplomatic, and military crises of the later 1620s, potentially restive and sceptical) audience that the Rubens portrait was primarily addressed. But others from outside the courtly and aristocratic elite may have seen the picture too. Although explicit evidence about access to York House is sketchy, we can assume that men and women of lower social rank worked or visited there as servants, messengers, or purveyors. Petitioners and clients also had access. Edmund Howes, for instance, records that Buckingham entertained a party of over two hundred Cambridge scholars in the Gallery at York House in 1626, and that his 'table was accessible for any gent[leman] and his Bedchamber for any poore man that had bussines with him'.[15]

All that remains of York House today is the splendid stone water gate built in 1626 where the Thames once met the bank, a miniature triumphal arch providing a spectacular entrance to the gardens and mansion house beyond. A handful of contemporary drawings give some impression of the mansion's exterior and fragments of evidence suggest the splendour of the gardens, perhaps designed and planted by John Tradescant, fitted with fountains and waterworks by Cornelius Drebbel, and featuring a spectacular sculpture of Samson slaying a Philistine, carved 'bigger than the life' by Giambologna.[16] Without contemporary drawings, however, it is hard to get a real sense of the mansion's interior. An inventory drawn up for the duke's widow shortly before her remarriage in 1635 does give some sense of the spectacle, however— the luxurious furnishings, the collections of jewels and antiquities, and, above all, the hundreds of paintings that hung on the walls.[17] Rubens's

[15] BL, Egerton MS 2533, fos. 63^r, 63^v.

[16] Randall Davies, *The Greatest House at Chelsey* (London, 1914), 154–7, quotation at 156; Lita-Rose Betcherman, 'The York House Collection and its Keeper', *Apollo* 92/104 (NS) (1970), 252; Philip McEvansoneya, 'A Note on Cornelius Drebbel', *Journal of Garden History* 6/1 (1986), 20; Kaufman, *Conscientious Cavalier*, 27; Gerbier, *Brief Discourse*, 25; Henry Peacham, *The Compleat Gentleman* (London, 1634), 108; Arthur MacGregor, 'The Tradescants: Gardeners and Botanists', in MacGregor (ed.), *Tradescant's Rarities: Essays on the Foundation of the Ashmolean Museum* (Oxford, 1983), 8–9.

[17] The inventory is in Bodleian Library, MS Rawlinson A 341, fos. 30^r–41^r, and is transcribed (minus the preamble) in Simon Jervis, 'Furniture for the First Duke of Buckingham', *Furniture History* 33 (1997), 57–74. Supplementary material has been discovered by Philip McEvansoneya, see e.g. 'A Note on the Duke of Buckingham's Inventory', *Burlington Magazine* 128/1001 (1986), 607. An incomplete transcription was published by Randall Davies, 'An Inventory of the Duke of Buckingham's Pictures, etc., at York House in 1635', *Burlington Magazine* 10/48 (1906–7), 376, 379–82.

equestrian portrait hung within this spectacular space at York House, another dazzling object in a world of dazzling objects exemplifying the power and taste of the house's master.

Traditionally, family portraits hung in rooms full of other family portraits, but, as John Peacock has noted, by the 1620s, the most sophisticated courtly collectors had begun to display portraits as works of art whose cultural and social status derived not only from their formal aesthetic qualities but also from their creator's reputation.[18] If we can assume that the 1635 inventory records an arrangement of works essentially similar to the display at the time of the duke's death in 1628, then it appears that the Great Chamber at York House was in part an arena of aesthetic display. The Rubens equestrian portrait was one of nineteen paintings the inventory listed on the walls of the Great Chamber; other evidence indicates the presence of a twentieth, a ceiling mural of the Nine Muses by Orazio Gentilischi, whom Buckingham and Gerbier had recruited from France in 1624–5, though it is not clear whether this had been finished by the time of the duke's death.[19] Eleven of these paintings were by Rubens. One was a second image of the duke, 'A great peice' intended for 'the Ceiling of my Lords Closett' that shared a number of iconographic features with the equestrian portrait (Fig. 2). The rest—many of which had been bought directly from the artist in 1626–7—were of other subjects.[20] Three were portraits, including images of the general Spinola and of the Archduchess of Brabant. Of the remaining six, four were landscapes, and two were religious works, including a crucifixion that may be the one presented to Buckingham by the Catholic secretary of state, George Calvert.[21] The only family portrait in the room was an unattributed full-length of Buckingham's brother-in-law, William Feilding, Lord Denbigh. The two Rubens images of Buckingham were clearly displayed not primarily as part of a

[18] John Peacock, 'The Politics of Portraiture', in Sharpe and Lake, *Culture and Politics*, 211 ff.

[19] Inventory, fo. 30ᵛ (Jervis transcription, 57–8); Betcherman, 'York House Collection', 255; Jeremy Wood, 'Orazio Gentileschi and Some Netherlandish Artists in London: The Patronage of the Duke of Buckingham, Charles I and Henrietta-Maria', *Simiolus* 28 (2000–1), 111–13, 113 n. 51.

[20] On the sale of Rubens's collection to Buckingham, see Muller, *Rubens*, 57–8, 78, 84–7.

[21] A. J. Loomie, 'A Lost Crucifixion by Rubens', *Burlington Magazine* 138/1124 (1996), esp. 737–8.

Fig. 2. Peter Paul Rubens, *Apotheosis of Buckingham*, c.1625–27.

pageant of Villiers family connections and history, but as two Rubenses among other Rubenses, objects that derived their prestige from the immense fame, continental courtly connections and bravura baroque style of the Flemish artist who produced them.[22] The other paintings in the room reinforced the equestrian portrait's status as a work of art, as an aesthetic object betokening the patron's connoisseurship and sophistication: they were all high-status works by eminently

---

[22] On Rubens's fame, see e.g. Schama, *Rembrandt's Eyes*; and C. V. Wedgwood et al., *The World of Rubens 1577–1640* (Alexandria, Va., 1967), 80–1, 97.

collectable painters—Guido Reni's *Four Seasons* bought by Gerbier for
Buckingham in Italy in 1621; one, or perhaps two, Titians; and a
Manfredi which, like the Reni, suggested Buckingham's interest not only
in the sixteenth-century Venetian masters, but also in the cutting-edge
Italian schools of the Carravagists and 'tenebrists'.[23] As if to underline
the room's commitment to art and the artist, one of the remaining
paintings was a Flemish depiction of the paradigmatic classical artist
Apelles 'drawing Venus naked'.

Some scholars of Buckingham's picture collection doubt that the
duke had a true connoisseur's learned interest in or understanding of
art. Instead, they argue the collection is much better read as a mirror of Balthazar Gerbier's aesthetic tastes and of the duke's desire for
brilliantly conspicuous consumption.[24] But Buckingham undoubtedly
understood the importance of at least playing the role of virtuoso
connoisseur to fit the new English fashion for the courtier-collector of
paintings, sculptures, jewels, antiquities, and exotic 'rarities', and thus to
emulate and compete with a number of important contemporaries: his
predecessor as favourite, Robert Carr; his periodic political rival, the Earl
of Arundel; the late Prince Henry; the young Charles I; and the continental exemplars of courtly art collectors he encountered in Madrid and
Paris in the 1620s.[25] The sheer size of his collection clearly had weight

[23] McEvansoneya, 'Italian Paintings', 323; I. G. Philip, 'Balthazar Gerbier and the
Duke of Buckingham's Pictures', *Burlington Magazine* 99/650 (1957), 155–6; and L.-R.
Betcherman, 'Balthazar Gerbier in Seventeenth-Century Italy', *History Today* 11 (1961),
325–31; Betcherman, 'York House Collection', 251–2.

[24] On Buckingham's collecting activities, see Betcherman, 'York House Collection';
Parry, *Golden Age*, ch. 6; Jonathan Brown, *Kings and Connoisseurs: Collecting Art in
Seventeenth-Century Europe* (Princeton, 1995), 23–33; Wendy Hefford, 'The Duke of
Buckingham's Mortlake Tapestries of 1623', *Bulletin du CIETA* 76 (1999); McEvan-
soneya, 'Some Documents', e.g. 31 and 32 on the duke's lack of interest; McEvansoneya,
'Italian Paintings'; and Jerry Brotton, *The Sale of the Late King's Goods: Charles I and his
Art Collection* (London, 2006), chs. 2–4. On Buckingham's collection of exotic 'rarities'
(particularly flora, fauna, and cultural artefacts from the Americas, Africa, and Asia), see
Arthur MacGregor, 'The Tradescants as Collectors of Rarities', in *Tradescant's Rarities*,
19–20; and John Tradescant (the younger), *Musaeum Tradescantianum: Or, A Collection
of Rarities* (London, 1656), 179.

[25] McEvansoneya, 'Italian Paintings', 319–20; Roy Strong, *Henry, Prince of Wales and
England's Lost Renaissance* (London, 1986); A. R. Braunmuller, 'Robert Carr, Earl of
Somerset, as Collector and Patron', in Linda Levy Peck (ed.), *The Mental World of the
Jacobean Court* (Cambridge, 1991); Timothy Wilks, 'The Picture Collection of Robert
Carr, Earl of Somerset (*c*.1587–1645) Reconsidered', *Journal of the History of Collections*

in the competition for prestige: in 1625, Gerbier wrote to Buckingham that, 'out of all the amateurs and Princes and Kings, there is not one who has collected in forty years as many pictures as your Excellency has collected in five'.[26] But in this status competition, the quality and rarity of the content mattered too—it mattered that Buckingham had two Honthorsts and Arundel only one, and that the purchase of Titian's *Ecce Homo* gave Buckingham the largest and most prestigious Titian yet brought to England.[27] Other motives were also at play. Gerbier assumed his master might experience a range of responses to his art collection: pictures, Gerbier wrote to the duke, were not 'bobles and schadows' but 'noble ornaments', 'delightful amusement[s]', 'histories that one may read without fatigue', and great long-term financial investments.[28] Buckingham may also have understood and appreciated the iconographic and the aesthetic elements of his paintings. In addition to Gerbier, he had many scholarly clients to advise him on iconographic schemes.[29] Letters exchanged with his agents reveal the role of aesthetic criteria in his collecting activities. In 1626, Buckingham told one agent that he had insufficient scholarly interest in classical statuary 'to court it in a deformed or misshapen stone, but where you shall meet beauty with antiquity in a statue, I shall not stand upon any cost your judgment shall value it'.[30] Some agents assumed that Buckingham had at least some familiarity with basic standards of art appreciation as well as a taste for

---

1 (1989); David Howarth, *Lord Arundel and his Circle* (New Haven and London, 1985); Smuts, *Court Culture*, ch. 5; Pauline Croft (ed.), *Patronage, Culture and Power: The Early Cecils* (New Haven and London, 2002); Linda Levy Peck, *Consuming Splendor: Society and Culture in Seventeenth-Century England* (Cambridge, 2005), ch. 4; Brotton, *Sale*.

[26] Brewer, *Court of King James*, ii. 369–70.

[27] McEvansoneya, 'Italian Paintings', 323, 327; on competition, see Peck, *Consuming Splendor*, 171.

[28] Brewer, *Court of King James*, ii. 370–1. Peacham's chapter on the collection and display of antiquities (*Compleat*, esp. 104–11) offers a similarly broad range of meanings and functions: their beauty produces pleasure, delight, wonder; they create knowledge of the past; their rarity, expense and beauty all add to their renown; their display symbolizes princely magnificence, liberality, greatness, and honour; they produce ennoblement; the connoisseur's study of them is a mark of gentility.

[29] See e.g. Pamela Gordon, 'The Duke of Buckingham and van Dyck's *Continence of Scipio*', in *Essays on van Dyck* (Ottowa, 1983), 54; John Peacock, 'Looking at Van Dyck's *Scipio* in its Contexts', *Art History* 23 (2000), 269; Cogswell and Lake, ' "Full of State and Woe" '.

[30] Brown, *Kings and Connoisseurs*, 32.

the depiction of naked female flesh. Gerbier's mouth-watering report to the duke concerning works of art in France, for instance, dwelled on fine drawing, the perfection of a crucifixion 'la plus divine chose du monde', or the beauty of a Tintoretto painting of Danäe with 'un corps tout nud, le plus beau' that could inspire amorous thoughts in even the coldest heart.[31] In December 1622, Sir Henry Wotton wrote to Buckingham concerning a shipment of paintings he had sent from Venice, noting of a Titian that 'the least figure . . . is alone worth the price of your expense for all four, being so round, that I know not whether I shall call it a piece of sculpture, or picture, and so lively, that a man would be tempted to doubt whether nature or art had made it'. A second picture, he noted, would give Buckingham an occasion to judge whether the Italians were as good at still lifes as the Flemish.[32] Wotton later offered Buckingham a painting as a gift, noting both the skill in the picture's 'handling' and the contribution it might make to the duke's nobility and delight.[33] Dudley Carleton's nephew opined that the duke was 'the most earnest lover of paintings (I thinck) in the world', while Gerbier told Rubens in 1626 that 'all the machinations of the Duke's enemies have never struck so near his heart as to divert his taste for pictures and other objects of art'.[34] Rubens himself was impressed by the duke's collection when he saw it for the first time, nearly a year after Buckingham's death. He was surprised to find in England 'none of the crudeness which one might expect from a place so remote from Italian elegance. And I must admit that when it comes to fine pictures by the hands of first-class masters, I have never seen such a large number in one place as in the royal palace and in the gallery of the late Duke of Buckingham.'[35]

Circumstantial evidence might also suggest that Buckingham (or Gerbier at least) took an active role in dictating the iconographic content of the Rubens equestrian portrait. The surviving oil sketch, for instance, is relatively free of iconographic business. If this represents the artist's original conception of the portrait, then it may well

---

[31] Brewer, *Court of King James*, ii. 338–9.

[32] Logan Pearsall Smith (ed.), *The Life and Letters of Sir Henry Wotton* (Oxford, 1907), ii. 257–8.

[33] Ibid. ii. 282.

[34] Robert Hill and Roger Lockyer, ' "Carleton and Buckingham: The Quest for Office" Revisited', *History* 88/289 (2003), 29; Mogurn, *Letters of Rubens*, 138.

[35] Ibid. 322.

have been the duke who urged Rubens to add the extra symbolic elements that eventually graced the finished painting.[36] It is possible Buckingham always had in mind an image that would match the hyperbolic splendour of Rubens's allegory-laden cycle on the life of Marie de Medici that the duke might have seen during his 1625 week in Paris.[37]

Wotton's letters indicate another significance to Buckingham's collection beyond its purely aesthetic qualities and its value as a conspicuous display of splendour and connoisseurship: paintings and statues were important currency in the patronage and gift relationships that structured court hierarchies and bound the domestic and international courtly elite together. Buckingham purchased most of his collection but some works were gifts: the Giambologna statue in the garden was a gift from Philip IV of Spain to Prince Charles who in turn gave it to the duke, the doubly royal origins of the gift enhancing the statue's meaning and value; the duc de Montmorency gave Buckingham a Tintoretto in 1624; Henry Wotton, Dudley Carleton, and George Calvert all used gifts of art as ways to solicit, seek, or solidify patronage and favours from the duke.[38] Even the works bought or commissioned from Rubens could signify a political relationship: the Flemish painter was deeply involved in international diplomacy during the 1620s and the duke used their art dealings as cover for back-channel discussions on a possible reconciliation with Spain.[39] The Rubens portrait thus hung amidst an art collection that spoke to the duke's social

[36] Julius S. Held, who considers the design of the sketch artistically preferable to the over-busy finished product, speculates Buckingham was to blame. See, 'Rubens's Sketch', 551. Held's opinion is seconded by White, *Peter Paul Rubens*, 190.

[37] The cycle includes an equestrian portrait of Marie in the panel on the 'Victory at Jülich'. Buckingham's visit to Paris coincided with the formal opening of the gallery containing the cycle: see the chronology in Ronald Forsyth Millen and Robert Erich Wolf, *Heroic Deeds and Mystic Figures: A New Reading of Rubens' Life of Maria de' Medici* (Princeton, 1989), 18.

[38] Peacham, *Compleat*, 108; Brotton, *Sale*, 102, 105–6; Betcherman, 'York House Collection', 252; McEvansoneya, 'Italian Paintings', 322; Brown, *Kings and Connoisseurs*, 32, 37; Hill and Lockyer, ' "Carleton and Buckingham" '; Loomie, 'Lost Crucifixion'; Brewer, *Court of King James*, ii. 326–45. On ambassadors as art brokers, see Brotton, *Sale*; and Peck, *Consuming Splendor*, 174–6.

[39] For an elegant overview of these activities, see C. V. Wedgwood, *The Political Career of Peter Paul Rubens* (London, 1975).

and political authority as a patron and as a courtly and international
power-broker.

MILITARY COMMAND, COURTLINESS, AND CHIVALRY

Hanging among the Rubenses and Titians in the Great Chamber, the
equestrian portrait radiated a variety of meanings, projected various
courtly selves: it was a large (10 by 11 feet) luxury object placed
among other luxury objects, painted by the most fashionable and best-
connected artist of the day, a status symbol that constructed and presented status not simply through its material splendour but also through
the prestige of the artist and the picture's place in a broader collection
that symbolized courtly connoisseurship, wealth, and political power.
But the equestrian portrait also uses pictorial, iconographic, and stylistic
elements to fashion and project a persona for Buckingham. To begin
decoding this persona, we can leave the Great Chamber of York House
for another of the building's major, essentially public spaces—the hall,
in which, the 1635 inventory records, two large canvases hung: 'One
great Peice being Scipio' by Van Dyck, and a second painting that
mirrors the equestrian motif of the Rubens: 'One great Peice of the
Emperor Charles, a copy call'd Titian's Glory being the Principall in
Spaine now in the Escuriall'.[40] This was probably a copy of one of
Titian's most famous paintings, and one of the most influential monar-
chical representations of the early modern era, the equestrian portrait
celebrating Charles V's triumph at the battle of Mühlberg.[41] Titian presented the emperor as the Christian warrior prince, utilizing the classical
motif of the royal rider on horseback as a symbol of imperial power.
By the 1620s, early modern artists and patrons everywhere recognized
the equestrian portrait as a paradigmatic image of military and political
authority. Rubens himself produced a number of such images during
his career, depicting both royal favourites—the Duke of Lerma in

[40] Inventory, fo. 30ʳ (Jervis transcription, 57).
[41] Betcherman, 'York House Collection', 252; on Titian's original, see Liedtke, *Royal
Horse*, 40–1, 188–9.

1603—and monarchs—Marie de Medici in 1625 and Philip IV in 1628.[42] Buckingham himself probably knew of the English royal icono-graphic precedents—the equestrian images of the monarch on the reverse of the Great Seal; Robert Peake's equestrian portrait of Prince Henry; or any number of Jacobean engravings of the royal family.[43] He probably knew too of English precedents for depicting aristocratic military commanders on horseback, whether Thomas Cockson's series of late Elizabethan engravings of the earls of Devonshire, Cumberland, Nottingham, and Essex or the more recent anonymously produced engravings of English commanders fighting in Germany, like the double portrait of the Earls of Oxford and Southampton.[44] Most pertinently, by the time Rubens completed his commission, Buckingham himself had been depicted in the equestrian pose on at least two earlier occa-sions. Gerbier had painted a miniature image of the favourite on horse-back shortly after Buckingham's elevation to Lord Admiral in 1618–19; and in 1625 Willem van de Passe had published an engraving of the duke on horseback quite similar in composition to the Rubens portrait.[45]

Like Cockson's engravings of Elizabethan commanders, the van de Passe and Rubens images from the mid-1620s had a topical signifi-cance: they celebrated the favourite's fitness for military command at the moment that the inexperienced Lord Admiral was spearheading Eng-land's controversial military intervention in the continent's confessional wars. Earlier images had evoked the duke's military competence in a less pressing context—Gerbier's miniature of the newly minted Lord Admiral celebrated potentialities not likely to be immediately tested, and the same might be said of Van Dyck's imposing *Continence of Scipio*,

[42] Liedtke, *Royal Horse*, 228–9, 234, 236–7, 248–9. Buckingham appears to be the first contemporary Rubens painted sideways on in the equestrian pose. He depicts Lerma, Giancarlo Doria, and Marie head-on. On the Lerma portrait, which Buckingham may have seen in Spain in 1623, see Schama, *Rembrandt's Eyes*, 112–13.

[43] Liedtke, *Royal Horse*, 255; Strong, *Van Dyck*, 49–54. For the range of royal eques-trian engravings in Jacobean England, see Arthur M. Hind, *Engraving in England in the Sixteenth and Seventeenth Centuries* (Cambridge, 1955), part 2 (James I), plates 26(b), 30, 90, 91, 94, 95, 120, 127, 145, 165(f).

[44] Liedtke, *Royal Horse*, 222; Hind, *Engraving*, plates 191(a), 234(b), 241(b), and 241(c); Richard C. McCoy, *The Rites of Knighthood: The Literature and Politics of Eliza-bethan Chivalry* (Berkeley, 1989), 96–8.

[45] Liedtke, *Royal Horse*, 222–3; McEvansoneya, 'Italian Paintings', 315; Betcherman, 'York House Collection', 250.

Fig. 3. Anthony Van Dyck, *The Continence of Scipio*, 1620–21.

the painting that hung alongside Titian's Charles V in the Hall of York House (Fig. 3). This canvas, which Van Dyck probably painted for Buckingham in 1620–1, depicts the victorious Roman general Scipio at his most magnanimous, one of two characters in the picture who represent and model the favourite's governing virtues.[46] The Rubens

[46] This is a controversial painting, and the argument (which I endorse) that Buckingham is to be identified with both Scipio and the bridegroom Allucius has been contested. I follow Peacock, 'Looking', 266; Gordon, 'Duke of Buckingham', 54; and Alan McNairn, *The Young van Dyck/Le Jeune van Dyck* (Ottowa, 1980), 137–40 (cat. 64). For other readings, see Gregory Martin, ' "The Age of Charles I" at the Tate', *Burlington Magazine* 115/838 (1973), 59; Ron Harvie, 'A Present from "Dear Dad"? Van Dyck's *The Continence of Scipio*', *Apollo* 138/380 (NS) (1993), 224; Jeremy Wood, 'Van Dyck's Pictures for the Duke of Buckingham: The Elephant in the Carpet and the Dead Tree

equestrian portrait is, however, very much a wartime image, one element in the favourite's high-stakes programme of self-presentation and self-fashioning in the run-up to and during the course of English military engagements with Spain and France between 1624 and 1628. As such it can be read alongside the martial images of the duke in the printed newsbooks covering the 1627 Île de Ré expedition and in the masques he staged to 'inflame the king's ardour' shortly before the expedition's departure.[47]

Because we cannot pinpoint when exactly the painting was finished and hung in York House, we cannot tie its production and initial display as closely as we might like to the constantly shifting political and diplomatic circumstances of 1625–7. When the portrait was commissioned, England was mobilizing for war with Spain; perhaps by the time of its completion, England was also at war with France. Events must also have shifted the painting's meaning after completion: the painting would have seemed very different in early 1627, before the Ré debacle, than it would in the expedition's aftermath. Despite these uncertainties, we can identify certain prominent martial themes. Rubens presents the duke poised for triumph. The central flamboyant figures of horse and rider are surrounded by a host of allegorical deities. In front of the horse floats a goddess of Victory, a laurel wreath held out in her right hand, a cornucopia tucked in the crook of her left arm, her backward glance urging Buckingham onward to claim the spoils and crown of triumph. Beside her, a small seraph blows the wind ahead, projecting the movement of the horse and rider onward towards the laurel wreath. In the foreground, beneath the horse's rearing hooves, lie two sea deities

with Ivy', *Apollo* 136/365 (NS) (1992), 39, 46 n. 44; and David Kunzle, 'Van Dyck's *Continence of Scipio* as a Metaphor of Statecraft at the Early Stuart Court', in John Onians (ed.), *Sight and Insight: Essays on Art and Culture in Honour of E. H. Gombrich at 85* (London, 1994). See too Oliver Millar, *Van Dyck in England* (London, 1982), 43–4 (cat. 3); David Howarth, 'The Arrival of Van Dyck in England', *Burlington Magazine* 132/1051 (1990); and Christopher White, *Anthony Van Dyck: Thomas Howard, the Earl of Arundel* (Malibu, 1995), ch. 4. For the now mostly rejected thesis that Arundel commissioned the painting as a wedding gift for Buckingham, see e.g. Parry, *Golden Age*, 139–40.

[47] Cogswell, 'The People's Love' and ' "Published by Authoritie" '; Lake and Cogswell, ' "Full of State and Woe" '; and Orrell, 'Buckingham's Patronage', 16. Cogswell tracks shifts in the duke's military image between 1625 and 1628, and his difficulties sustaining a martial image before he actually commanded in the field.

staring in awe at the duke, their submissive postures beneath the arc of
the rearing horse acknowledging Buckingham's mastery over the seas.
In the background, partially obscured by reeds, the duke's fleet flying
the flag of St George engages in broadside battles with an unidentified
enemy.

Atop his horse, the baton of command grasped in his right hand,
the painting's dynamic right to left movement reinforcing the allegorical predictions of triumph, Buckingham exudes military authority
and power. The naval battle in the background evokes and taps into
nostalgia for the Elizabethan glory days of successful and lucrative naval
struggle with the Spanish. The image also fuses military and courtly
imagery: the duke is very much a courtly warrior. In part this courtliness
is suggested by the painting's attention to luxury objects symbolizing
courtly wealth and status. The duke's clothing—the delicate white lace
collar, the billowing dark cloak and rich blue sash, the elegant off-
white gloves and riding boots, the gleaming black armour edged in
gold, the golden hangers supporting the golden-hilted sword—and his
equestrian gear—the ornamented bit and bridle, the golden spurs, the
fine gold thread and bejewelled surface of the embroidered saddle—
all speak to the viewer in the language of courtly magnificence.[48] The
rider's head, with its finely barbered beard, and hair newly curled by
a Parisian hairdresser, signified courtly sophistication, French fashion,
and aristocratic cosmopolitanism.[49] In Rubens's image, virile military
power and the kind of fashionable elegance captured in Miereveldt's
contemporaneous portrait of Buckingham drenched in pearls are not in
tension.[50]

The equestrian portrait uses chivalric imagery to further forge this
seamless connection between courtliness and military power. Hanging
low on the rider's breastplate is a cross-shaped jewel attached to a
medallion that seems to depict the Lesser George, the badge of the
Knights of the Order of the Garter. Garter imagery was a recurrent
feature in the duke's portraiture, as it was supposed to be for all members

[48] I have relied in this paragraph on the low-quality colour reproductions of this picture in Charles Richard Cammell, 'George Villiers First Duke of Buckingham: Portraits
of a Great Connoisseur', *The Connoisseur* 98 (Sept. 1936), 126; and Simon Schama, *A
History of Britain: The Wars of the British* (New York, 2001), ii. 62.

[49] On Buckingham's hair, see Wood, 'Van Dyck's Pictures', 43; Lockyer, *Buckingham*,
239.

[50] Buckingham also cultivated a more military wardrobe for public appearances in
this period—see Cogswell, ' "Published by Authoritie" ', 2, 7.

of this elite group of courtly knights, and several artists depicted him sporting the Lesser George medallion, the garter badge on the cloak and the leg garter itself. As Roy Strong has noted, the garter-knight image resonated in complex ways, fusing the martial with the courtly arts; and it clearly marked the duke as the servant of the king who was the chief of the Garter Knights and the font of chivalry.[51] Garter-knight imagery could also resonate in more topically political ways. It could assert Buckingham's claim to aristocratic status, and to the possession of honour defined by military prowess and service to the crown—particularly important claims for a man whose lack of noble 'blood' was a focal point for contemporary criticism. In the war years of the 1620s, chivalric imagery could also have a popular, neo-Elizabethan, anti-Spanish hue.[52] Buckingham himself was certainly capable of rhetorically manipulating the chivalric idiom so that it encompassed both romantic and confessionalized—militantly anti-Spanish—modes. In a 1626 speech to Parliament, Buckingham alluded to machinations against him two years earlier by the Spanish ambassadors 'who would have had my head when you thought me worthy of a statue', insisting on his status as a Protestant victim of Spanish malignity. But he also urged MPs to fund a war they had begun for honour and religion's sake, a war he framed in neo-chivalric, romantic terms: 'You that are young men may in these active times gain honor and reputation, which is almost sunk, and gain the ancient glory of our predecessors. And remember,' he added, 'it is for restoring to her [Elizabeth of Bohemia] the inheritance of the most virtuous lady, I think, in the world.'[53]

HORSEMANSHIP AND GOVERNMENT

Rubens thus presented Buckingham as a courtly, chivalric military hero, riding off to seize fame and tame the seas. The painting is noticeably reticent about the warrior's religious identity—it fashions Buckingham

---

[51] Strong, *Van Dyck*, ch. 4.

[52] See e.g. William Hunt, 'Civic Chivalry and the English Civil War', in Anthony Grafton and Ann Blair (eds.), *The Transmission of Culture in Early Modern Europe* (Philadelphia, 1990); and J. S. A. Adamson, 'Chivalry and Political Culture in Caroline England', in Sharpe and Lake, *Politics and Culture*.

[53] William B. Bidwell and Maija Jansson (eds.), *Proceedings in Parliament 1626* (New Haven and London, 1992), ii. 409.

a persona that, while not fundamentally incompatible with, did not explicitly endorse contemporary understanding of the wars of the later 1620s as Protestant crusades against an Antichristian Catholic foe. But the image is profoundly concerned with questions of virtue. Buckingham appears as an exemplar of virtuous government and legitimate authority—and here what matters is the horse. As Walter Liedtke notes, modern viewers of baroque equestrian portraits have difficulty grasping the centrality of horses and horsemanship to early modern aristocratic and courtly cultures.[54] We do not see horses the way the intended audience for this image did—recognizing their breeding, appreciating their movements and conformation, assessing their riders' skill. Many contemporary viewers of the painting, for instance, would have considered the horse itself a luxury object, an aesthetic spectacle projecting the status of its rider.[55] Horsemanship was an essential gentle, aristocratic, and courtly activity, and from the mid-sixteenth century onwards, numerous widely and closely read manuals brought the continental 'cult of horsemanship' (as Joan Thirsk puts it) to an English-reading audience.[56] Rubens's Buckingham rides his mount with consummate skill: as Liedtke notes, the horse is captured in a position midway between the highly controlled *levade* taught in the continental riding schools (and soon to become standard in Velázquez's images of the Spanish royal family) and the more precipitous natural rearing of a startled beast.[57] With his taste for theatrical dynamism, Rubens presents the horse in what might be described as a controlled rear, the animal's energy contrasted with and balanced by the perfect poise of its rider, whose left hand loosely and effortlessly handles the reins.[58] This was skilled riding

[54] Liedtke, *Royal Horse*, introduction and *passim*. See too Karen Raber and Treva J. Tucker (eds.), *The Culture of the Horse: Status, Discipline, and Identity in the Early Modern World* (Basingstoke and New York, 2005), 2–4 and *passim*; Lisa Jardine and Jerry Brotton, *Global Interests: Renaissance Art between East and West* (London, 2000), ch. 3; and Peter Edwards, *Horse and Man in Early Modern England* (London, 2007).

[55] On the Renaissance horse as luxury object, see Jardine and Brotton, *Global Interests*, ch. 3. On the English horse trade, see Peter Edwards, *The Horse Trade of Tudor and Stuart England* (Cambridge, 1988).

[56] Joan Thirsk, 'Horses in Early Modern England: For Service, For Pleasure, For Power', in *The Rural Economy of England: Collected Essays* (Hambledon, 1984), 388, 389–93; see too Edwards, *Horse and Man*, 82–4.

[57] Liedtke, *Royal Horse*, 25.

[58] Rubens produced numerous images of rearing horses in dynamic motion: see the examples in Wedgwood, *World of Rubens*, 40–9, 158; and Liedtke, *Royal Horse*, 230–3.

as aesthetic spectacle, an object of delight and connoisseurly appreciation, 'proof', as the Italian horsemanship expert Corte wrote, 'of the rider's excellency'.[59] Such a sight was assumed to generate awe in social inferiors. Sir Thomas Elyot thought that 'the moste honorable exercise' fit for the status of 'every noble persone' is to ride the 'great horse' well, which 'importeth a maiestie & drede to inferiour persones beholding him above the common course of other men dauntyng a fierce and cruell beaste'.[60] And if (as Castiglione had insisted) horsemanship was an essential skill for the courtier—'our Courtyer' should be 'a perfecte horseman for everye saddle'—Rubens also presents a dazzling image of the *sprezzatura* of the perfect courtier: Buckingham's horsemanship (like his Twelfth Night capers) was an example of effortlessly brilliant aristocratic bodily control.[61]

Of course, the image of the skilled rider also reinforced the military meanings of the painting: equestrian skill was necessary for the soldier.[62] But the military resonances also work on a less prosaic level: in Graeco-Roman myth, the god Neptune was believed to have created the horse from the tumultuous energy of the seas and to have tamed it just as he tamed the waters. Thus in Rubens's painting, Buckingham's control of the horse duplicates and mirrors the control of the waves suggested by the sea deities beneath the horse's hooves, auguring victory in the naval battles anticipated in the painting's backdrop.

As the ubiquity of the symbolism in royal iconography implied (and as the Neptune myth also suggested), contemporaries also drew an analogy between the rider's skill and the art of government: control over the animal, and thus over the forces of nature, represented control

[59] Thirsk, 'Horses', 390.

[60] Thomas Elyot, *The boke named the Governour* (London, 1531), sig. J3ᵛ; Edwards, *Horse and Man*, 28.

[61] Baldassare Castiglione, *The Book of the Courtier*, trans. Sir Thomas Hoby (Everyman edn.: London, 1994), 48. Buckingham had probably studied riding as a young man in France; he appears to have been an energetic Master of the Horse for James, purchasing horses to improve the stock of the royal stable; he kept and bred horses of his own; and received them as gifts: see Lockyer, *Buckingham*, 11, 25–6, 152, 197; Hill and Lockyer, ' "Carleton and Buckingham" ', 22; G. P. V. Akrigg (ed.), *Letters of King James VI & I* (Berkeley, 1984), 409, 414, 437; and Edwards, *Horse and Man*, 8, 83, 111. On horsemanship and aristocratic identities more generally, see Raber and Tucker, 'Introduction', in *Culture of the Horse*, 7–11, 22–4. On dance and bodily control, see Howard, *Politics of Courtly Dancing*.

[62] See e.g. Elyot, *Governour*, sigs. J3ᵛ–J4ᵛ; Edwards, *Horse and Man*, ch. 6.

over a potentially turbulent populace (and could also, through the logic of patriarchy, represent masculine and adult control over women and children).[63] The equestrian metaphor also implied a particular style of good government. Under the influence of Italian and French experts, the widely read English manuals on horsemanship increasingly argued that horses were better trained by gentle persuasion than by brute force: in this context, the skilled rider represented a very specific type of ruler, one who governed through skill and persuasion and not through the crude, wilful exertion of power that might veer into tyranny.[64] As Michaell Baret argued in a 1618 manual on horsemanship partially dedicated to Buckingham, the true horseman steered a middle way as he worked to curb the 'rebellious disposition' of the horse: Baret's skilled horseman epitomized the virtues of firm government, based on an initial and foundational subjection, but exercised by the rational application of moderation, and the avoidance of the excesses of cruelty and lenity. 'Horsemanship may be resembled to Warre', he writes, 'for it is sooner gained by pollicy and reason, then by strength and will'.[65]

But the horse had another meaning; it could stand not only for the potentially unruly people, but also for the potentially ungovernable passions. Thus the skilled rider could represent the government of the self through the taming and control of the natural passions.[66] Reading Nicholas Morgan's 1609 treatise on horsemanship, Kevin Sharpe concludes, 'The emperor on horseback depicts the man fitted to rule because he has tamed his own nature and learnt to order the wildness of nature herself. His mastery of the great horse expressed his

---

[63] Keith Thomas, *Man and the Natural World: Changing Attitudes in England 1500–1800* (Harmondsworth, 1984), 29, 45–50; Edwards, *Horse and Man*, 84–7.

[64] Thirsk, 'Horses', 389–91; Thomas, *Man and the Natural World*, 101; Raber and Tucker, 'Introduction', 2, 14–22; Pia F. Cuneo, 'Just a Bit of Control: The Historical Significance of Sixteenth- and Seventeenth-Century German Bit-Books', 161–3; and Elisabeth LeGuin, 'Man and Horse in Harmony', all in Raber and Tucker, *Culture of the Horse*; Edwards, *Horse and Man*, ch. 3.

[65] Michaell Baret, *An Hipponomie or The Vineyard of Horsemanship* (London, 1618), e.g. 12–13, 26–7, 33–4, 36–40; quotations at 10, 51. The analogy could also work to critique bad government: see e.g. Kevin De Ornellas, ' "Faith, Say a Man Should Steal Ye—and Feed ye Fatter": Equine Hunger and Theft in *Woodstock*', in Raber and Tucker, *Culture of the Horse*.

[66] Stephen Orgel, *The Illusion of Power: Political Theater in the English Renaissance* (Berkeley, 1975), 75–7.

virtue.'[67] In Baret's manual, the rider's mental and bodily self-government and self-control were prerequisites for the successful government of the horse: the skilled rider curbed his will and passions by reason and deliberation, and closely controlled the disposition and gesture of his own body for 'the least disorder in the gesture of the man, causeth a greater in the horse'.[68] The good horseman, his passions and body under his control, becomes a joy to behold: 'his Horse and hee both must make but one body and will, and then they shall make such a delight-full consonant, both to himselfe for feeling, and to others for seeing.'[69]

Buckingham on horseback, effortlessly controlling his tumultuous beast as it rears, was thus an image of Buckingham's aristocratic virtue, his ability to tame his own passions and control his own body. The image was thus a projection of his authority to govern, for the government of the self was a prerequisite for the government of others. Similar images of self-control, of the taming of the passions, can be found in other portraits of the favourite. If we turn from the martial to the marital, we can track this motif in at least two of the major canvases Buckingham commissioned of himself with his wife and children. Van Dyck's *Continence of Scipio* (Fig. 3), which suggested Buckingham's potential military skill by portraying the favourite as the great Roman general, was almost certainly commissioned to mark Buckingham's marriage to Katherine Manners, daughter of the Earl of Rutland, in the spring of 1620. Although John Peacock finds a vein of playful theatricality in the painting, its major moral points are still securely made. The painting celebrates a famous act of sexual self-control, Scipio's renunciation of his conqueror's right to take sexual advantage of a beautiful captive, and his subsequent restoration of the woman

---

[67] Kevin Sharpe, 'A Commonwealth of Meanings: Languages, Analogues, Ideas and Politics', in *Politics and Ideas in Early Stuart England: Essays and Studies* (London, 1989), 51–2, quotation at 52. See too Cuneo, 'German Bit-Books', 155–7.

[68] Baret, *Hipponomie*, 41. See too the summary statement on the duty and office of the horseman on 26–7, chs.7–11 on the will and passions, and chs. 12ff. on the body.

[69] Baret, *Hipponomie*, 27–8. For broader context on early modern aristocratic concerns with posture and self-control, see Georges Vigarello, 'The Upward Training of the Body from the Age of Chivalry to Courtly Civility', in Michel Feher (ed.), *Fragments for a History of the Human Body*, pt. 2 (New York, 1989). For another example of the horsemanship/government metaphor, see the image from Geoffrey Whitney's 1586 book of emblems reproduced (but not analysed) in Jardine and Brotton, *Global Interests*, 171 (illus. 76).

(along with a ransom paid on her behalf) to her betrothed, Allucius. Scipio embodies—and models for Buckingham—the virtues of self-control, restraint, and magnanimity, virtues underpinning success as a ruler.[70] The picture also links Buckingham to the bridegroom Allucius: as Jeremy Wood has pointed out, Allucius and his bride-to-be stand on a carpet embroidered with a picture of a rather startled-looking elephant, an image of sexual temperance and marital chastity. The elephant may have been a deliberate retort to Katherine Manners's father, who suspected some sexual impropriety before the match was made, but it is also an image of the favourite as the possessor of ordered, controlled passions.[71]

Gerrit Van Honthorst deploys a very different visual language of marital harmony and self-control in his 1628 portrait of the duke and duchess with their children, Mary and George (Fig. 4). By the late 1630s, this portrait was hanging 'above the chimney' in the King's Bedchamber in the Privy Lodgings at Whitehall, an intimate companion piece to the 1626 Mytens portrait of the duke in the public Bear Gallery, and to Van Dyck's painting of the duke's sons in the gallery at St James's.[72] Catherine Belsey, struck by the familial affection in the picture, suggests it anticipates the modern 'naturalized affective family'.[73] The painting does depict a playful and affectionate interaction between the two children and between the mother and the baby standing up on her lap, and it is tempting to project onto this image some of the affection documented in the surviving letters between the duke

[70] He also models wise statecraft—Machiavelli, for instance, glossed Livy's account of Scipio's actions not as a story about morality but about the political advantages of a calculated gesture of magnanimity.

[71] Wood, 'Van Dyck's pictures', 37–42.

[72] Peacock, 'Politics of Portraiture', 218–19; Oliver Millar (ed.), 'Abraham van der Doort's Catalogue of the Collections of Charles I', *Walpole Society* 37 (1958–60), 6, 36, 226. On the significance of the chimney location as perhaps the most important in the room, see Brewer, *Court of King James*, ii. 343–4. Several copies were made of this group portrait as a whole and many more of just the duke. See J. Richard Judson and Rudolf E. O. Ekkart, *Gerrit Van Honthorst 1592–1656* (Doornspijk, 1999), 284 (cat. 385 and plate 281); Christopher White, *The Dutch Pictures in the Collection of Her Majesty the Queen* (Cambridge, 1982), 56–7 (cat. 75).

[73] Catherine Belsey, 'Disrupting Sexual Difference: Meaning and Gender in the Comedies', in John Drakakis (ed.), *Alternative Shakespeares* (London and New York, 1985), 173–5.

Fig. 4. Copy of Gerrit Van Honthorst, *The Duke of Buckingham and his Family*, 1628.

and duchess.[74] But familial affection is subsumed within the image's depiction of the loving yet patriarchal control and self-control that order the family unit into a successful miniature commonwealth. This family painting, like the *Continence of Scipio* and like Rubens's equestrian portrait, is an image of the duke as governor.[75] As striking as the children's playfulness is the calm and elegant poise of Buckingham the father, who is depicted in both private/familial and public/official guise—the cloak over his shoulder bears the badge of the Order of the Garter, symbol of Buckingham's chivalric service to the crown, and, on his lap, his right hand holds a letter signifying another side of his public responsibilities as a royal councillor. His posture is relaxed yet controlled, courtly and

[74] See e.g. Brewer, *Court of King James*, ii. 277–86.
[75] On affective and patriarchal marital and familial imagery as images of government and order see Sharpe, *Personal Rule*, 183–8; and Jonathan Goldberg, *James I and the Politics of Literature: Jonson, Shakespeare, Donne, and Their Contemporaries* (Palo Alto, Calif., 1989), 85ff.

commanding; his silver and black attire is fashionable and elegant but not extravagant; and the stylishly thin cane in his left hand (a fashion accessory that appears in contemporary and later images of Charles I) symbolizes both status and courtly refinement.[76]

Rubens's image of Buckingham on horseback is thus a complicated and highly charged piece of self-presentation and self-fashioning. The armour-clad duke on the rearing horse plays a series of overlapping roles: he is the chivalric military commander, servant of his king, master of the seas, posed in the guise of kings and emperors; he is the Master of the Horse who is a master of the courtly and aristocratic arts of horsemanship, effortlessly maintaining perfect control over his superb mount; he is the equestrian whose control of the animal reveals his ability to govern others, and to master his own unruly passions, a self-mastery that suggests not only his ability to rule but also his moral authority to do so. And it is not only the iconographical content of the image that communicates a vision of Buckingham's self: as a luxury object in a house crammed with expensive paintings, statues, furniture, tapestries, jewels, mirrors, and curiosities, the painting asserts aristocratic status through the spectacular consumption of splendour; as an aesthetic object—a stylistically innovative, beautiful work by the most famous and fashionable courtly artist of the day, displayed in a room full of other masterworks—the portrait constructs an image of Buckingham as a man not only of wealth, but also of educated taste and sophistication. Martial skill is not in tension with courtliness or even with a certain degree of sartorial flamboyance. The painting presents Buckingham as the embodiment of aristocratic and courtly virtue, honour, and status, all essential attributes for a man lacking noble blood whose meteoric rise left him vulnerable to accusations of transgressive ambition.

ENVY AND VIRTUE

The selves projected by this painting echo the role Ben Jonson gave Buckingham in the never-performed January 1624 masque *Neptune's*

---

[76] Julius S. Held, '*Le Roi à la Ciasse*', in *Rubens and his Circle* (Princeton, 1982), 74–5. I plan to write elsewhere about the one atypical marital image of the duke—Van Dyck's 1620–1 portrait of Buckingham and his wife as Adonis and Venus.

Triumph for the Return of Albion, an entertainment that attempted to rewrite Buckingham and Charles's ill-fated 1623 journey to Madrid. The poet gives Buckingham two guises. He is 'loyal Hippius,' the horse tamer, the 'powerful Manager of Horse' for Neptune/James, here presented not as god of the seas but as 'chief in the art of riding'. Through this persona, Jonson connects Buckingham's court office as Master of the Horse to the neoplatonic idea of horsemanship as analogous to the taming of the passions and thus as a badge of authority. Buckingham is also 'Haliclyon', 'renowned at sea', the famed Lord Admiral, who on royal orders protected the prince (Albion) during his perilous journey. Yet while elevating his courtly protagonists to mythical status, Jonson is acutely aware of the politically dangerous alternative perceptions of the Spanish voyage and of Buckingham's part in it. Jonson alludes comically to the artistically and socially coarse popular celebrations of the prince's return, and to the lower orders' ignorant desire for political news. He alludes too to the popular anxiety and criticism that the journey inspired, and in particular to criticism of Buckingham. Hippius/ Haliclyon, we are told, is the victim of Envy, a vice over which the favourite triumphs through the virtue exemplified in his loyal service to the king: with Albion, 'loyal Hippius is returned', the poet intones, 'Who for it, under so much envy, burned | With his own brightness, till her starved snakes saw | What Neptune did impose to him was law'.[77]

Rubens's canvas, too, is conscious of divergent, critical perspectives on the duke, and Rubens also diagnoses this hostility as Envy destined to be dispelled by the favourite's virtue. To the right of the duke, floating above the rear of the horse, the curves and gestures of her voluptuous body mimicking the beast's arching back, is another goddess accompanied by a second seraph blowing on Buckingham's head a small cascade of flowers signifying hope and the virtuous, pleasant life. In the goddess's upraised left hand sits a flaming heart, suggesting that she is a symbol of divine love and Charity.[78] But Charity's attention, as well as her right hand and left foot, is preoccupied, not with praising the duke, but with repelling a hideously ugly demon lurking on the margin of the canvas. The snake curling up from the demon's head marks her as a figure of

---

[77] Orgel (ed.), *Ben Jonson*, 259–74, quotations at 263, 270 and n.
[78] Huemer, *Portraits*, 59, 60.

Envy.[79] Frances Huemer glosses this iconography as a demonstration
of the strength of Buckingham's virtue: 'Masculine virtue, or *Fortezza*,
is epitomized by the Duke. Envy, who is devoid of Charity and Love
(the flaming heart), forms his ever-present female counterpart, who
constantly tries to deprive virtue of his strength, but is here suppressed
by the Duke's own spirit of charity.'[80]

Buckingham's battle with Envy preoccupied the duke's artistic clients
in 1626–8. The other major allegorical painting delivered by Rubens
in 1627 also gives the struggle iconographical prominence (Fig. 2).
This work, intended for the ceiling of the duke's 'closett' at York
House but apparently kept in the Great Chamber, represented Buckingham in neoclassical military guise carried by Minerva and Mercury—
emanations of his moral qualities—away from the grasp of Envy and
other monsters up to where Honour and Virtue sit on the steps of a
classical temple.[81] Honthorst's 1628 masque-like image of the duke in
the guise of Mercury presenting the seven liberal arts to Apollo and
Diana (Charles and Henrietta-Maria) depicts Envy being cast into a pit
in the lower left of the canvas.[82] The battle with Envy was also the
theme of a masque Buckingham presented before the king and queen
at York House in May 1627—possibly the same masque in which the
duke attempted to excite the king about the forthcoming expedition to
Ré—'wherein,' one reporter commented, 'first comes forth the duke,
after him Envy, with divers open-mouthed dogs' heads representing the
people's barking; next came Fame; then Truth'.[83] These depictions of
Envy as monstrous, bestial, and—in the masque especially—as dangerously 'popular' are highly politicized. The dispelling of Envy not
only suggests the duke's virtuous ability to withstand and overcome
other's scorn, but also rewrites and contains contemporary critiques
of Buckingham—whether court-factional, parliamentary, or popular—
as manifestations not of legitimate grievances or authorized counsel
but as manifestations of the sin of Envy, understood as the resentment the low-born and second-rate inevitably feel towards their betters.

---

[79] Martin, 'Rubens', 614; Huemer, *Portraits*, 58–9; Held, 'Rubens's Sketch', 551,
tentatively labels the figure 'Discord'.

[80] Huemer, *Portraits*, 59.

[81] On this picture, see Martin, 'Rubens'; and Held, *Oil Sketches*, 390–3.

[82] Judson and Ekkart, *Honthorst*, 107–8; White, *Dutch Pictures*, 54.

[83] Thomas Birch (comp.), *Court and Times of Charles I* (London, 1848), i. 226.

The existence of Envy thus becomes proof of the victim's virtue and worth.[84]

AND ART RETURN'D?

The figure of Envy pushed to the margins of Rubens's equestrian portrait alluded to—and, as we have seen, challenged—an image of Buckingham very different from that presented in the painting. Beginning in 1625, and accelerating over the course of 1626 and 1627, attacks on Buckingham's military pretensions and competence had steadily mounted. For a fuller sense of the politicized nature of the self presented in the Rubens equestrian portrait, we can turn to one of the most widely read indictments of Buckingham's military capabilities, the libel 'And art return'd againe with all thy Faults'.[85] This rich and complex poem, which survives in at least twenty-five contemporary copies, is a perfect inversion of Rubens's image, savagely critiquing the duke's handling of the 1627 expedition to Ré, and dismantling the links the painting forges among courtliness, self-control, authority, and chivalric heroism. The libeller's Buckingham is conquered by his sinful passions—he is jealous, lustful, tyrannical, oppressive, raging, vengeful, ambitious, and murderous; he is a patron of witches and theologically suspect clerics, and the son of a popish sorceress. His sins are so great, that his defeat was inevitable:

> To those that wilbee vitious,
> Praie who will praie, Heaven will not bee propitious.
> God's deafe to those that will not hear the cries
> Of their oppressed Subjects Injuries.
> Happie successe then great attempts attends
> When those commaunds vertue and skill commends.
> Thy Sinne, Gods Justice, and the Kingdomes curse,
> Makes mee admire thy Fortunes were noe worse.

---

[84] See, too, my 'The Embarrassment of Libels', in P. Lake and S. Pincus (eds.), *The Politics of the Public Sphere in Early Modern England* (Manchester, 2007).

[85] I use the copy in British Library Sloane MS 826, fos. 161ᵛ–164ʳ, now published in Alastair Bellany and Andrew McRae (eds.), 'Early Stuart Libels: An Edition of Poetry from Manuscript Sources', *Early Modern Literary Studies*, Text Series I (2005), Oii12 (http://purl.oclc.org.emls/texts/libels/).

'Vertue and skill' were prerequisites for military success; Buckingham had neither. The libel depicts Buckingham as a military incompetent and, more tellingly, as a coward, his cowardice undercutting any claims to nobility. The duke was 'heedlesse' and thus the army 'headlesse'; in the heat of battle, the duke retreated to cowardly safety:

> What Men or Angels can devise
> T''excuse thy base ignoble cowardise,
> That brunt of dangers could soe little bide,
> The very bruite would allwaies make thee hide;
> And when the bloodie Die of Warr was throwne,
> And each Mans valour should bee chiefly showne,
> Was't not a noble part, and bravely playd,
> To send a shadowe [i.e. a double] in thy Arms array'd,
> To personate thee in the battaile, while
> Thou sat'st environ'd with a cable coyle
> Discharging sugar pelletts?

The poet immediately contrasts the frightened, cowardly duke with the patriot heroes and 'valient leaders' Sir Charles Rich and Sir Alexander Brett, who bled 'brave English blood'. And the poet strikingly diagnoses Buckingham's courtliness as one source of his military incapacity: had the duke returned, the poet asked, because his 'queasie stomach', 'gorg'd with sweet-meates', could not take 'the surging and distemper'd Seas'? By the libel's end, the poet urges 'upstart Greatnes' to stay at court, and distinguishes between an effeminate courtliness, marked by sexual licence, sartorial luxury, and foreign dance, and the kind of 'manly' martial ardour that is the only means to recapture English might and honour:

> Stay, stay at court then, and at Tennys play,
> Measure French Galliards out, or Kil-a-gray.
> Venus Pavilions doe befitt thee best:
> Perwiggs with Helmetts use not to bee prest.
> To o're-run Spaine, winne Cales, and conquer France,
> Requires a Soldier's March, noe Courtiers daunce.

Rubens's courtly warrior is portrayed here as an impossibility, a contradiction in terms: the courtly favourite, ruled by the passions, softened and effeminated by sexuality and luxury, cannot control the self and cannot govern men—from the libellers' perspective, the horse has thrown the rider.[86]

CONCLUSION

On 23 August 1628, Buckingham was assassinated in Portsmouth as he readied a second expedition against the French. On 27 November 1628, his assassin John Felton was tried for murder, convicted, and condemned to hang. In his 'Annals' entry for that day, James Balfour recorded that,

At this tyme, one Mr. [Richard] James, ane attender one Sir Robert Cotton, a grate lover of his countrey, and a hatter of all suche as he supposed enimes to the same, was called in question for wretting some lynes, wich he named a statue to the memorey of that vorthey patriot S. Johne Feltone.[87]

Whether Richard James—Cotton's librarian—had in fact written the lines in question cannot at this distance be established; in fact, no other evidence corroborates Balfour's report that James or anyone else was ever questioned about the poem. Yet it is clear why the authorities might have been concerned with lines like these.[88] Like many libels celebrating the murder, this one dwells at some length on Buckingham's sins and untamed passions—his proud dominion over 'Nobles, Gentles, Commons'; his wilful, impetuous conduct of foreign policy, striking 'Peace and Warr at pleasure'; his exhaustion of the treasury

---

[86] On politicized anxieties about effeminacy in the 1620s, see Michael B. Young, *James VI and I and the History of Homosexuality* (Basingstoke, 2000); for the broader cultural context, see Ian Moulton, *Before Pornography: Erotic Writing in Early Modern England* (Oxford and New York, 2000). Moulton (166) notes that the 'galliard' was thought to be an effeminating dance, and that a galliard was also a synonym for fop and sodomite. Howard, *Politics*, 65–6, 74, 101–2 notes that in courtly theory the 'galliard' was very much a display of masculine power over women. This reading is modified somewhat by Ravelhofer, *Court Masque*, 115–16, who also (p. 69) includes evidence for the emergence of English stereotyping of 'figures who danced very well as effeminate, theatrical, or foreign'.

[87] *The Historical Works of Sir James Balfour* (Edinburgh, 1824), ii. 174.

[88] I quote from the version of the poem in British Library MS Sloane 826, fos. 191ᵛ–192ʳ published in Bellany and McRae, 'Early Stuart Libels', Pii8. See too the brief comments in Knowles, ' "Songs of baser alloy" ', 166.

on 'Panders, Minions, Pimpes, and Whores'; his betrayal of the exiled Elector and Electress Palatine, and thus of the Protestant cause and the Elizabethan legacy of English anti-Spanish militancy; his corruption of the law courts and 'auntient English Libertie'; his calamitous military adventures in Spain and France, wasteful 'Illiads of greife'.

The libel suggests that Buckingham's rule was a kind of illusionary enchantment, holding the nation in 'Magique thralldome'. Buckingham was a false idol, destroying 'all | That to his Idoll Greatnes would not fall | With groveling adoration'. He clung to illusion even after military disaster, when he nevertheless 'bore | Himselfe triumphant'. The poet explicitly links Buckingham's 'Magique thralldome' to his use of the visual arts. After his military failures, Buckingham, 'neither trayn'd in lore | Of Arts or Armes',

> yet in a hautie vast
> Debordment of Ambition, now in haste
> The cunning Houndhurst must transported bee
> To make him the Restorer Mercurie
> In an heroick painting, when before
> Antwerpian Rubens best skill made him soare,
> Ravisht by heavenly powers, unto the skie
> Opening, and ready him to deifie
> In a bright blissfull Pallace, Fayrie Ile.

The poet then addresses the assassin, earlier hailed as the 'Immortall Man of glorie, whose brave hand | Hath once begun to disinchaunt our land | From Magique thralldome':

> Naught but illusion were we, till this guile
> Was by thy hand cut off, stout Machabee;
> Nor they, nor Rome, nor did Greece ever see
> A greater glorie to the Neighbour Flood.
> Then sinke all Fables of old Brute and Ludd,
> And give thy Statues place. In spight of charme
> Of Witch or Wizard, thy more mighty Arme,
> With Zeale and Justice arm'd hath in truth wonne
> The prize of Patriott to a British Sonne.

Thus the last section of the poem establishes a stark contrast between assassin and victim. Felton is the patriot hero, a Macabee excelling the deeds of classical and mythical British forebears; his 'mighty Arme', driven by 'Zeale and Justice', has 'cut off' Buckingham's transgressive domination, disenchanting the nation from his spell.

Most interesting for our purposes is the poet's decision to focus his critique of Buckingham's politics of 'illusion' on the commissioning of two identifiable works of art: Honthorst's early 1628 painting of Buckingham as Mercury presenting the Seven Liberal Arts to Apollo and Diana, and Rubens's image of Buckingham's triumphal ascent to the temple of Virtue and Honour (Fig. 2). The poet presents these images as products of Buckingham's 'hautie vast / Debordment of Ambition', ambition being the sin at the root of the duke's transgression of his natural social status. At the heart of these images, the libeller finds only illusions: Buckingham as Mercury restoring the arts implies a commitment to learning that, the poet claims, Buckingham did not possess; the Rubens image heroizes Buckingham's non-existent military virtues. The poet captures the excessiveness of Buckingham's desire for self-glorification by having the duke transport Honthorst into England 'in haste'; and the poet destroys the illusions at the heart of Rubens's grand baroque concoction by dismissing the Temple of Honour and Virtue as a mere 'Fayrie Ile'. In this poem, the 'best skill' of 'Antwerpian Rubens' and the 'cunning' of Honthorst are not the objects of the connoisseur's assessing eye, but weapons to manufacture Buckingham's illusory 'Idoll Greatnes', to enchant and enslave the nation like the 'charme | Of Witch or Wizard'. Drawing from rich Protestant strains of iconoclastic and iconophobic anxiety about the visual arts, the poet here yokes court portraits to more sinister modes of manufacturing illusion, the sins of witchcraft and idolatry: thus, the adjectives applied to the two painters take on a sinister hue, with 'Antwerpian' reeking of popery, and 'cunning' of witchcraft. At the end of the poem, Felton's violence dispels these illusions, and the reader's gaze is drawn from the idolatrous deceits of the court artist, towards Felton's 'Statue', carved in words and deeds, a monument to 'Zeale and Justice' and to 'truth'.

In this poem then, lies not only a profound critique of an individual embodiment of court corruption, but also a devastating reinterpretation of the meaning of court art: vehicles of power, agents of authority and symbols of sophistication are here rewritten as vehicles of illusion, agents of political and social transgression, symbols of idolatry. The 'idealization' that Renaissance and courtly theorists of portraiture argued was essential to the socio-political and moral success of such paintings, is here glossed as dangerous deceit, as 'naught but illusion'.[89] In the painted images of the duke of Buckingham, and in contemporary responses to them, we can, I think, glimpse the deeper cultural strains that made early Stuart English politics so catastrophically combustible.[90]

But I do not want to end by invoking the distant thunder of cataclysmic political breakdown. I want instead to return briefly to the question of the relation between a traditional biographical approach to Buckingham's life story and an approach focused on Buckingham's performance and fashioning of self. In his recent work on the ways in which successive issues of a short-lived officially sponsored news book crafted a potent image of Buckingham's military heroism during the earlier stages of the Ré expedition, Thomas Cogswell has suggested that the duke himself was, in a sense, trapped by his own image makers: after the humiliating retreat from Ré, Buckingham felt compelled by his own 'PR', as it were, to persist in the military conflict with France, not simply to relieve the suffering of the Huguenots, but also to redeem himself, to live up to his image. What then, we might ask, did George Villiers see and feel when he gazed upon Rubens's equestrian portrait after the return from Ré? Was it an embarrassment, a rebuke, an inspiration? Did he seek to fashion himself into the ideal shape modelled in the portrait? Did Rubens's 'best skill' not merely represent but impinge upon the favourite's 'self', inflecting his subjectivity and motivating his behaviour? Where do we draw the line between the supposedly authentic, autonomous self and the outward presentations of the self, the performative masks the self wears? Can we ever fully disentangle the dancer from the dance, the courtly actor from his act, the favourite from his fictions?

[89] On idealization and portraiture, see Peacock, 'Politics of Portraiture', 207–11.

[90] It is time to revisit P. W. Thomas, 'Two Cultures? Court and Country Under Charles I', in Conrad Russell (ed.), *The Origins of the English Civil War* (London, 1973); see, too, the theme of cultural schism in Brotton, *Sale*. For a critique of courtly art appreciation as an effeminating distraction from military duty, see the English version of Crispijn de Passe's Dutch satirical print 'The Kingly Cocke', discussed in *Catalogue of Prints and Drawings in the British Museum* (London, 1870), i. 83–4 (no. 133); and Peck, *Consuming Splendor*, 184–5.

8

Painting a Life: The Case of Barbara Villiers, Duchess of Cleveland

Julia Marciari Alexander

From the late years of the Commonwealth until today, Barbara Villiers Palmer, Countess of Castlemaine, Duchess of Cleveland (1641–1709), has remained a figure of fascination for all types of historians of Britain: social, art historical, and amateur. Along with her two main rivals, Nell Gwyn and Louise de Kéroualle, Duchess of Portsmouth, Barbara Villiers (Fig. 5) is the best known among Charles II's numerous mistresses, and was so both to her contemporaries and to ours. In her day, she was called everything from 'pretty',[1] to 'enormously vicious and ravenous: foolish but imperious',[2] to a woman 'whose Lust was insatiable . . . so infamous in her Amours, that she made no Scruple of owning her Lovers'.[3] Political giants, such as Edward Hyde, Earl of Clarendon, noted the 'Power and Interest She had with the King'.[4] Eighteenth- and nineteenth-century writers seem to have adopted a more condescending tone: even the most sympathetic emphasize her 'shrewish' temper and note, in a voyeuristic tone, what they deemed her uncommon sexual prowess. Modern scholars, as well, fall into this trap; one went so far

---

[1] *The Diary of Samuel Pepys*, ed. R. Latham and W. Matthews, 11 vols. (London, 1970–83; repr. with additional notes, 1995), i. 199 (13 July 1660).

[2] Gilbert Burnet, *Bishop Burnet's History of His Own Time: from The Restoration of Charles II. To the Treaty of Peace at Utrecht, in the Reign of Queen Anne. A New Edition, with historical and biographical notes* (London, 1839), 62.

[3] John Oldmixon, *The History of England, During the Reigns of the Royal House of Stuart . . .* (London, 1730), 577.

[4] Edward Hyde, Earl of Clarendon, *The Life of the Earl of Clarendon*, 3 vols. (London, 1759), ii. 324.

Fig. 5. Sir Peter Lely, *Barbara Villiers, Countess of Castlemaine (1640–1709)*, *c.*1662. Oil on canvas, 1880 × 1282 mm. Private Collection.

as to dub her 'a teeming mistress, a strong personality before bedtime and an omniscient witch afterwards, a woman [whose] only ecstasy was avarice'.[5]

This chapter presents a particular case study of two portraits of Barbara Villiers, Countess of Castlemaine, painted between 1660 and 1668 by Sir Peter Lely, who was made Principal Painter to King Charles in 1661. This examination aims to demonstrate that painted portraiture must be considered one of the central sites for early modern self-presentation (a case that I have made elsewhere).[6] More particularly, the study of portraiture should be considered as one among the most critical tools we have for the recovery of the stories of early modern *women's* lives. More so than the lives of their male counterparts, early modern women's lives have been occluded by the conventions of traditional 'biography'.[7]

Before turning to my specific subject, it is critical to define my goal within the context of this volume, and to locate it precisely in the larger project of early modern 'life writing'. In discussing the paintings and visual objects at the core of my study, my own rhetoric intentionally avoids the terms 'reading' and 'writing' because, as an historian of the visual, I feel it is imperative that one must try to understand the mechanisms of visual images outside the boundaries that the rhetoric of 'reading' imposes upon them. When possible, the deciphering of an image's *visual rhetoric* can reveal more than when images are thought of as visual texts. Indeed, disentangling the visual from the verbal is not only appropriate to this project, but also necessary, given that the culture which this chapter explores was one in which only part of the viewers, even among the elites, could have been considered highly 'literate'. This is particularly appropriate when one considers the specific issue of early modern *women's* lives; many women, even elites, were considerably less

---

[5] Allan Andrews, *The Royal Whore: Barbara Villiers, Countess of Castlemaine* (Philadelphia, 1970), 108.

[6] See particularly, Catharine MacLeod and Julia Marciari Alexander, *Painted Ladies: Women at the Court of Charles II, 1660–1685* (exhibition cat.: National Portrait Gallery, London, 2001); and Julia Marciari Alexander, 'Self-fashioning and Portraits of Women at the Restoration Court; The Case of Peter Lely and Barbara Villiers, Countess of Castlemaine, 1660–1668', unpublished Ph.D. thesis, Yale University (1999).

[7] It is interesting to note that the *Oxford English Dictionary* gives as the first definition of the word 'biography' (coming from John Dryden's 1683 *Biographia*) as 'The history of the lives of individual men, as a branch of literature'.

literate—or at the very least *differently* literate—than their male peers. Examining the ways these paintings function as images as opposed to texts, therefore, gives twenty-first-century scholars and viewers a better method of understanding the unique contributions of the rhetoric of the image to the creation and perception of self and society in the early modern world.

More numerous than suggested by the selection of images analysed here, Barbara Villiers's portraits as a group present one of the more straightforward and enlightening cases for a study of a Restoration sitter.[8] Two factors determine this assertion: (i) she was without question the woman most often represented in painted portraits during the first decade of the Restoration; and (ii) the greatest number of her portraits came out of the studio of one artist, Sir Peter Lely (1618–80). The face patterns and the poses in which they are found, as painted by Lely, are both numerous and various. Indeed, Lady Castlemaine's various portraits by Lely expose a special painter–sitter relationship that reflects artistic, political, and personal ambition on the part of both portrayer and portrayed. Furthermore, as a group, her portraits document on the one hand, Lely's campaign to establish himself as a painter through the patronage and depiction of the most beautiful and important woman at court and, on the other, Lady Castlemaine's own role in the creation of a visual campaign to establish herself as the visual and virtual consort to the King.[9] Consequently, a study of her portraits demonstrates the ways in which the portrait as a genre functioned as an integral component in the fashioning and performance of the lives of early modern elite women.

The earliest contemporary remarks about Barbara Villiers and her activities at the newly restored court come, not surprisingly, from Samuel Pepys, who saw Barbara, young wife of the royalist supporter Roger Palmer, for the first time on 13 July 1660: '[there were] great doings of Musique at the next house... the King and Dukes

---

[8] See Marciari Alexander, 'Self-fashioning and Portraits of Women'.

[9] For the purposes of this chapter, I have limited my discussion of Villiers's iconography to those painted by Sir Peter Lely, although during her lifetime, she was also frequently painted, among others, by John Michael Wright (?1617–94), by the French painter Henri Gascar (*c*.1635–1701), and, later, by Sir Godfrey Kneller (1646–1723). Most of the portraits of her by other artists, however, derive or respond to portraits by Lely.

[of York and Gloucester were] there with Madam Palmer, a pretty woman that they have a fancy to ... make her husband a cuckold.'[10] He traced Barbara's movements throughout the first year of the Restoration, remarking whenever he laid eyes on her. He spotted her at Whitehall Chapel in October 1660 and commented on what he considered her inappropriate attitude during the service: 'Here I also observed how the Duke of Yorke and Mrs. Palmer did talke to one another very wantonly through the hangings that parts the King's closet and the closet where the ladies sit.'[11] He again noted her presence with the royal brothers in April 1661, only three days before the coronation, observing that the king and Mrs Palmer 'doth discover a good deal of familiarity'.[12] On 23 July 1661, Pepys reported that he 'sat before Mrs. Palmer ... [and] filled my eyes with her',[13] and it was that night that he designated her for the first time as 'the King's mistress'. Pepys's report—which we must remember remained unpublished until the nineteenth century and was written as a personal record of his life ostensibly not meant for publication during his lifetime—indicates that she was openly acknowledged as the king's lover by her contemporaries in the summer of 1661, and, indeed, confirms his observation of the previous year that the king had hoped to make a 'cuckold' of her husband.

Sir Peter Lely's first portrait of Barbara Villiers (Fig. 5) attests to the complex relationship between Charles and his mistress, and represents the first in a series of paintings that document Lady Castlemaine's attempts to construct a public persona. This portrait type lies at the heart of Lely's iconography of this sitter, and I have called it elsewhere 'her signature image'.[14]

This composition came to be particularly associated with the young Barbara, probably due to both the numerous studio versions and copies that were produced during her lifetime and to William Faithorne's 1666 engraving after it (Fig. 6). The version of the painting that is now at Knole in Kent (Fig. 5) is almost certainly the prime version of the composition, but a number of good contemporary versions in varying formats still exist. Based on style, this work must be dated to *c*.1662.

---

[10] Pepys, *Diary*, i. 199 (13 July 1661).   [11] Ibid. 265–66 (14 Oct. 1660).
[12] Ibid. ii. 80 (20 April 1661).   [13] Ibid. 139 (23 July 1661).
[14] MacLeod and Marciari Alexander, *Painted Ladies*, cat. 33, pp. 118–20.

Fig. 6. William Faithorne after Sir Peter Lely, *Barbara Villiers, Countess of Castlemaine (1640–1709)*, 1666. Line engraving, 354 × 276 mm, trimmed. British Museum, Department of Prints and Drawings.

Given its date and its grandeur, Lely's full-length portrait was probably made to commemorate Barbara's new title, Countess of Castlemaine, her husband Roger Palmer having been made earl by Charles II in December 1661.[15] Charles and Barbara had openly flaunted their flourishing relationship in the very early 1660s, and there is some evidence that the king may have owned the prime version of this image—possibly even commissioned it.

Although it is impossible to determine definitively whether this portrait was painted to honour Lady Castlemaine's new status at court, it is certain that her new title was a hot topic of discussion at the time the work was in progress. Not surprisingly, we can gauge the court's interest through Pepys's report in which he, upon spying the patent for Palmer's elevation in the Privy Seal Office, noted that the document held the stipulation that the Castlemaine titles could pass only to the male children who were, in his words, 'got on the body of this wife, the Lady Barbary'. To this the diarist added wryly 'the reason whereof everybody knows'.[16] Apparently, Mr Palmer's elevation to the peerage, in spite of his personal service to the crown before and after the Restoration, was generally perceived as being—and likely was—due solely to his wife's relationship with the king.

Ostensibly a straightforward court portrait, this image of the king's young mistress seated with her head on hand is, however, laden with artistic and allegorical allusions that are only slightly veiled. The most potent of these allusions depended on the pose of the sitter. As discussed elsewhere, this pose had its origins in the iconography associated with depictions of Melancholia, and in Jacobean and Caroline England, it had been especially popular in portraits of young, philosophically minded men.[17] The pose was not, however, solely used for male portraits in the seventeenth century. In women's portraits it appears to have carried more varied implications, ranging from prudence to piety. In the sixteenth and seventeenth centuries, it was often used in representations of the reformed and penitent prostitute, St Mary Magdalen, and Lely based Barbara's pose on these well-known images. Most especially, his

[15] Ibid.   [16] Pepys, *Diary*, ii. 229 (7 Dec. 1661).
[17] Much of this discussion is taken from my doctoral dissertation and my catalogue entry on the Knole portrait in MacLeod and Marciari Alexander, *Painted Ladies*, cat. 33, pp. 118–20.

painting recalls the Magdalens painted by the Italian Bolognese artist Guido Reni (Fig. 7).

By the 1660s, Reni's were the most famous and admired images of the Magdalen in Europe, and through distribution in painted and engraved copies Reni's works had become the archetypal depictions of the so-called penitent whore. Given his reputation, Guido Reni and his work were well known in England, and his signature full-length depiction of the Magdalen in the wilderness is a certain source for Lely's portrait of Barbara Villiers. In fact, there were a number of paintings by Reni in Charles I's own collection. Clearly, Lely was hoping to have comparisons made between his portrait of the king's mistress and Reni's images of the penitent Magdalen.

Given the highly erudite culture of viewing art so prevalent at the Restoration court, viewers of Lely's portrait would have recognized Lady Castlemaine's pose and long, loose tresses as an intended evocation of the Magdalen's. Indeed, the Magdalen theme was and would have been regarded as particularly appropriate to Barbara Villiers at the time when this portrait was painted: in 1661, at the time of the portrait, she was patently the most reputed beauty of her day; she led the life of an openly sexual sinner; and she was openly revelling in her role as the king's acknowledged favourite. Moreover, the role of repentant was one that suited her political purposes.

In 1662, just as Lady Castlemaine was preparing to give birth to her second child by the king, he took as his bride a shy, devoutly Catholic, Portuguese princess, Catherine of Braganza. Given the extreme affection the king had publicly lavished on Lady Castlemaine for over two years, it is not surprising that on her arrival Charles II's bride took an immediate dislike to the king's mistress. An open rivalry between the two women began even before the young bride stepped ashore at Portsmouth in May 1662. The night of the queen's landing in Portsmouth Pepys reported:

The King dined at my Lady Castemayne and supped [there] every day and night the last week ... the night that the bonefires were made for joy of the Queenes arrival, the King was there; but there was no fire at her door ... which was much observed. And that [night] the King and she did send for a pair of scales and weighed one another; and she, being with child, was said to be heavyest.[18]

[18] Pepys, *Diary*, iii. 87 (21 May 1662).

Fig. 7. Guido Reni, *The Penitent Magdalen*, *c.*1631–2. Oil on canvas, 2310 × 1520 cm. Galleria Nazionale d'Arte Antica, Rome.

After his marriage, the king felt it imperative that his mistress become a Lady of the Queen's bedchamber, one of the most important positions for women at court and one made newly possible by the arrival at court of his bride.[19] As a result of his desire to see his mistress ensconced in one of the most visible official posts at court, an open battle of king, queen, and mistress ensued. The king continually put his lover's name on the list of 'Ladies of the Bedchamber' to be approved by the queen; she, in turn, consistently 'pricked' Lady Castlemaine's name off the list and refused to meet her rival. Ultimately, it was through both the king's authority (he was reported as threatening his bride with treason), and, according to contemporary 'histories', his downright trickery that Catherine was made to capitulate to her husband's demand.

Among the most descriptive—and unquestionably biased—contemporary accounts of this Bedchamber incident is that of Lord Clarendon. In his memoirs, he described the final reconciliation of queen and mistress thus, '[the king] . . . brought [Lady Castlemaine] into the Queen's Presence Chamber . . .' and

> presented [his mistress] to the Queen, who received her with the same Grace as She had done the rest . . . But whether her Majesty in the Instant knew who She was, or upon Recollection found it afterwards, She was no sooner sate in her Chair, but her Colour changed, and Tears gushed out of her Eyes, and her Nose bled, and She fainted . . . [20]

In the context of this battle and the ensuing forced public (should I say 'sanguine'?) reconciliation between queen and mistress, Lely's portrait represented Lady Castlemaine's visible—if ironic—effort to 'right' her reputation as a rival to the queen. Her implied 'penitence' was not necessarily moral, but more importantly, political. In fact, the suitability and usefulness to Lady Castlemaine of marking similarities between the Magdalen and the mistress was not lost on court wits and critics, who closely monitored the mistress's status within court circles, and particularly within the queen's household.

---

[19] On the Bedchamber politics and their role in the lives of elite women, see Sonya Wynne, ' "The Brightest Glories of the British Sphere": Women at the Court of Charles II', in MacLeod and Marciari Alexander, *Painted Ladies*, 36–49, and her unpublished D.Phil. thesis, 'The Mistresses of Charles II and Restoration Court Politics, 1660–1685', University of Cambridge (1997).

[20] Edward Hyde, Earl of Clarendon, *The Life of Edward Earl of Clarendon* (Oxford, 1759), 168–9.

One satire, entitled *The Chimney's Scuffle* (sometimes attributed to Samuel Butler and published in or around June 1662) highlighted the rocky relationship between wife and lover. It proclaimed Barbara:

> —a Convert and a Mirrour now
> Both in her Carriage and Profession too;
> Divorc'd from strange Embraces: as my pen
> May justly style her Englands Magdalen.
> Wherein She's to be held of more esteem
> In being fam'd a Convert of the Queen.
> And from relapse that She secur'd might be,
> She wisely daigns to keep her Companie.

Not only did this satire lampoon Lady Castlemaine's penitence in her own sexual behaviour, but also that of her political and religious attitudes. Indeed, in looking from the poem to the painted image, one might speculate that the poem's author was writing with Lely's portrait in mind or vice versa. Like the satirist's subject, Lely's sitter appears as an 'English'—that is, Protestant—version of the saint. Unlike her catholic model (Fig. 7), she bears no overt symbols to denote her role (there is neither cross, nor skull nor, most tellingly, ointment jar, the particular symbol of the Magdalen who anointed Christ's feet). Whether or not the writer used the painting as his inspiration, that he dubbed Barbara Villiers 'Englands Magdalen' provides evidence that Restoration readers and viewers were eager to see and make links between the mistress and the Magdalen in a variety of contexts, and provides corroboration as to how this portrait's pictorial ambiguities would have evoked multiple aesthetic and symbolic associations for its viewers.

Kevin Sharpe and others have postulated that the ambiguities of implied meaning in the arts of the Commonwealth and Restoration is precisely what differentiates the visual culture of the later periods from the earlier conflations of visual and political objectives at the Elizabethan, Jacobean, and Caroline courts.[21] Although certainly pictorial meaning was portrayed and relayed in more complex (and, perhaps, more obtuse) ways following the Restoration, such relationships were directly linked to earlier Caroline strategies of visual culture. If such links became more and more obvious over the course of Charles II's

---

[21] Kevin Sharpe, 'Remapping Early Modern England', a lecture given at Yale University, 25 March 1997, and author's on-going discussion with Sharpe.

reign, at the beginning, they were necessarily veiled and ambiguous so as to allow for various interpretations by the factions tenuously brought together by the Restoration settlements.[22]

While these English precedents for role-play and disguise in painted portraiture were clearly at the root of the Restoration visual culture, it must also be remembered that the majority of Restoration courtiers (most notably the king and his family) were steeped in the artistic conventions of continental Europe, as many of them had spent some time 'travelling' in Europe during the 1650s. There, and especially at the court of Louis XIV during the troubled 1650s, they would have seen the myriad portraits of men as modern adaptations of ancient heroes and of women as fashionable goddesses like Minerva and Diana.[23] These light allegories-cum-portraits are the visual analogues to the *historiettes, portraits littéraires,* and grand novels of Bussy-Rabutin, La Grande Mademoiselle, and Mademoiselle de Scudéry—the backdrops, if you will, to the verbal portraits and *romans à clef* that so amused mid-century French nobles.[24]

Barbara's 1661 portrait, then, with its allegorical allusions wrapped in a fashionable package, its multivalent potential political meanings, and its worthy aesthetic pretensions, stands squarely within the broad context of continental pictorial practices of the *portrait historié* and, most especially, within the specificity of the English courtly traditions that

[22] Katharine Gibson points out that although Charles II's personal iconography was virtually void of any kind of symbolism which smacked of absolutism, as his reign progressed his personal iconography became almost unabashedly absolutist. See ' "Best Belov'd of Kings": The Iconography of Charles II', unpublished D.Phil. thesis, University of London, Courtauld Institute of Art (1997), 88 and 199.

[23] On the participation of Charles and James in French ballets and masques during the 1650s, see Andrew R. Walkling, 'Court, Culture, and Politics in Restoration England: Charles II, James II and the Performance of Monarchy', unpublished Ph.D. thesis, Cornell University (1997), 80–3.

[24] For the parlour-game aspect of portraiture within mid-century French aristocratic culture, see Jacqueline Plantié, *La Mode du portrait littéraire en France, 1641–1681* (Paris, 1994); and Erica Harth, *Ideology and Culture in Seventeenth-Century France* (Ithaca, NY, 1983), esp. ch. 3. For a more specific discussion of the *portrait historié,* see Emmanuel Coquery (ed.), *Visages du Grand Siècle: Le Portrait français sous le règne de Louis XIV 1660–1715* (exhibition cat., Musée des Beaux Arts de Nantes, 1997), esp. chs. 3 and 4; and for a related study of the practice of creating and discerning meaning with regard mainly to history pictures, from the point of view of French academic practice, see Jennifer Montagu, 'The Painted Enigma and French Seventeenth-Century Art', *Journal of the Warburg and Courtauld Institutes* 31 (1968), 307–35.

exploited images for political ends.[25] Lely's full-length 1662 portrait of Barbara clearly was constructed from the outset as an elite image, one to be seen and recognized by an 'educated' courtly viewer with extensive knowledge of high-art traditions: it was primarily in the context of the inner circles (political and social) of Whitehall in 1662 that its whole range of potential meanings would have been most fully understood.

In effect, by creating a complex web of allusions—aesthetic, political, religious, and even satirical—both artist and sitter cleverly manipulated viewers by multiplying rather than circumscribing the potential meanings of the portrait. Indeed, by avoiding specificity, Lely and Barbara together fashioned an image of the king's mistress which itself allowed for—even demanded—the viewer to map onto the image his or her understanding of the particularities of the sitter. In so doing, artist and sitter created a portrait that broke free of iconographic constrictions. For Lely the allusive nature of this portrait aligned him not only with the best artists of his own time but also with those of previous generations, foremost among them Anthony Van Dyck and Guido Reni; for Barbara, the painting (as well as the many versions of it produced by Lely and his studio in the early years of the Restoration) introduced her image and her body visually to a broad courtly audience as the embodiment of ideal beauty and—however ironic—exemplary conduct.

Despite this space for interpretation left by the allusive nature of the image as constructed originally, the visual narrative of the painting necessarily became more circumscribed as time passed, which J. Enghels's 1667 engraving of the portrait demonstrates (Fig. 8). In this print, of which there are only two still extant examples, Barbara holds a cross and is surrounded by the overt symbols of the Magdalen, books, skulls, and an ointment jar. In the space of five years, then, Barbara's portrait had diminished from a richly veiled *portrait historié*, in which interpretation was demanded from the viewer, to a narrative allegory, in which interpretation was dictated: by 1667 England's Magdalen had been returned to the strictures of the 'Catholic' and 'continental'.

Were Lely's 1662 portrait of Lady Castlemaine as the Magdalen exceptional in his portrayals of her made during the years of her ascendancy at court, it might have been possible to accept critics' assertions that the artist's use of allegory was more often than not trite and

---

[25] See also Ch. 7 by Alistair Bellany on the Duke of Buckingham's portraits.

Fig. 8. J. Enghels after Sir Peter Lely, *Barbara Villiers, Countess of Castlemaine (1640–1709), as the Magdalen*, 1667. Etching, 280 × 202 mm, trimmed. British Museum, Department of Prints and Drawings.

'primitive' and that the choice of pose was largely driven by artist's choice rather than sitter's agency. But, this first portrait of Barbara by Lely was just the most important and pervasive of a series of canvases in which and through which Barbara's personal and political status was created, portrayed, projected, and promoted. In other words, it is one in a series of markers that display her efforts to create a visual 'life'.

Perhaps the most audacious of the images that Barbara and Lely collaborated on was his painting of her from 1663 (Fig. 9). Numerous copies of this painting exist, but the prime version was recently purchased by the National Portrait Gallery by a national subscription campaign. Stylistically, the portrait type belongs squarely within the earliest period of Lely's production shortly after the Restoration, that is, *c.*1660–5. I and my colleagues have dated this work to 1663 based on the probability that the child represented is Charles Fitzroy, later Duke of Cleveland and Southampton, the first-born son of Barbara Villiers and Charles II. There are, unfortunately, no contemporary records that provide certain identification of the child. The earliest records in which the child is named date from the eighteenth century and describe its sitters alternatively as Barbara Villiers with her daughter Charlotte Fitzroy, later Countess of Lichfield (born 5 September 1664)[26] or with her second son, Henry, later Duke of Grafton (born 20 September 1663).[27] Because the stylistic reasons for identifying the child as Barbara Villiers's first son, Charles Fitzroy, who was baptized on 16 June 1662, are discussed elsewhere, the following examination will focus on the conceptual reasons for this identification.[28]

The most striking feature of this portrait is its clever—and quite obvious—reference to depictions of the Madonna and Child. The pose of the sitters relies on pictorial traditions that variously show Mary with the Christ Child in her lap, at her side, or held out to the viewers for adoration. Here, Barbara Villiers's loose-fitting red and blue robes, which have little in common with any style of ordinary, contemporary dress, clearly allude to the Virgin's traditional attire, the

---

[26] First noted in the collection of Lichfield and Dillon at Ditchley by Hearne in 1718, as noted in David Piper, *Catalogue of the Seventeenth-Century Portraits in the National Portrait Gallery, 1625–1714* (Cambridge, 1963), 74–5.

[27] Horace Walpole, *Aedes Walpolianae*, 1748, p. xvi.

[28] Marciari Alexander, in MacLeod and Marciari Alexander, *Painted Ladies*, cat. 37, pp. 124–5.

Fig. 9. Sir Peter Lely, *Barbara Villiers, Countess of Castlemaine (1640–1709) and her son Charles Fitzroy (1662–1730)*, c.1663–4. Oil on canvas, 1247 × 1020 mm. National Portrait Gallery.

red robe and blue cloak symbolizing the Virgin's passion as well as her role as Queen of Heaven. That the visually erudite Restoration court audiences, steeped in aesthetics of Christian traditions, would have immediately made the obvious pictorial connections between the sitters depicted here and the other holy pair is proven by a commentator who, in 1677, commented on a version of this picture as the 'Dutches of Cleveland being as a Madonna & a babe'.[29]

As does the earlier portrait of Barbara as 'England's Magdalen', this portrait openly complicates the visual conventions of its subject matter: it subverts its subjects' implied piety, flaunting the very preposterousness of mistress and bastard as Madonna and Child. The composition's ironic, and arguably humorous, meanings are intensified by Barbara's noticeable girth: under her robes she appears to be pregnant (a condition in which she found herself almost constantly from 1661 until 1665, during which time she gave birth to four of the king's children).

Pregnancy had long been used in female portraits to emphasize the continued succession of a dynastic line, as had portraits showing children in the arms of their mothers. The use of these visual indicators in this image emphatically asserts the place of both mistress and child in the succession of the Stuart dynasty. In fact, although her second son, Henry, was eventually acknowledged by the king, his paternity was hotly discussed in the months shortly before and after his birth in September 1663. When considered within this context, the allusion to her pregnancy may well have been meant to create—and would likely have been considered as doing so—a link of clear and equal kinship between the first-born son and the unborn child.

Even without certain identification of the child, this painting holds up Barbara Villiers, acknowledged mistress of the English king, as 'England's Madonna', in contrast to the full-length portrait of the previous year in which she posed as 'England's Magdalen'. As in that portrait, the role she dons here conveniently—if ironically—flatters Charles II: if she and her child are Mary and the infant Christ, the absent father/king is implicitly and necessarily conflated with God. While certainly verging on the blasphemous, Barbara Villiers's assumption of the guise of the Madonna is strangely appropriate: hers was a child not begotten by

---

[29] George Vertue, *Note Books*, in *Walpole Society*, 6 vols. (Oxford: The Walpole Society, 1930–47), iv. 173.

her lawful husband but, rather, was the son of one more powerful; in Barbara's case, the father was not only her religious leader (Charles, of course, was Head of the Church of England) but her secular leader as well.

Not surprisingly, subsequent generations did consider this composition as a conscious send-up of those very Catholic pictorial traditions it immediately invoked—and one engineered by Barbara Villiers herself. Most famously, in his *Aedes Walpolianae* of 1748 (p. xvi), Horace Walpole reported that:

Sir Peter Lely was employ'd by the Dutchess of Cleveland to draw Her and her Son . . . for a Madonna and a little Jesus, which she sent for an Altar-piece to a Convent of Nuns in France. It staid there for two years, when the Nuns discovering whose Portrait it was, return'd it.

When considered independently, each of the two portraits of Barbara Villiers as Magdalen and Madonna is rich in its own right. Yet, when considered in the context of their creation and reception, however, they become a kind of diptych that enriches and emboldens their meanings. In both the roles of Madonna and Magdalen the mistress is visually posited as physical and spiritual consort to the king, so that the two pictures might be thought of part of an implied triptych that places each notionally on either side of a missing image of Charles II. Just two of the numerous role portraits Lely painted of Lady Castlemaine when she was at the height of her power and influence at court during the 1660s, these works collectively suggest that both Barbara Villiers and the artist Lely devised her portraits as cunning visual tools in her bid to create a vision of herself as the consort of the king, who was her spiritual leader and bodily possessor.

As his practice developed in the late 1660s and 1670s, Lely's portraits—of Barbara and other sitters alike—were no longer replete with multi-layered meanings pertinent to the sitter's personal 'history' that could be deciphered variously depending on each viewer's personal 'access' to the woman depicted. Instead, Lely's portraits increasingly featured the women in numbered poses and guises that reflected neither the aspirations, the actual events of their lives, nor the desires of the sitters. These later paintings presented mere formulaic tropes of identity (i.e. women in pastoral settings were considered modern-day incarnations of

Flora; riding costumes signalled warrior amazons; and Cleopatras were recognized by the pearls they held).[30]

It could be argued that the more formulaic approach to Lely's painted portrait in the late 1660s and 1670s was actually necessitated by Barbara Villiers's augmented visibility. Indeed, by 1667 her increasing notoriety rendered nearly impossible any further pictorial ambiguity as the decade progressed. Her 'stories' enveloped her portraits even as she may have continued to try to manipulate their possible interpretations. By the late 1660s her body had become too available to a broad audience— literally, visually, and notionally—for her to maintain control over her appearance. An example of this is, no doubt, Andrew Marvell's unpublished but widely circulated *Last Instructions to a Painter*, in which he lampooned both Lady Castlemaine's status at court and her sexual appetites.[31] Also, and even more widely circulated, was a group of satirical broadsheets that took as their subject the brothel riots of 1668; foremost among them, the so-called 'Poor-Whores' petition asked Lady Castlemaine, who was dubbed 'the most Splendid, Illustrious, Serene and Eminent Lady of Pleasure' for her help in restoring prostitutes' ability to ply their trade. They claimed Barbara's sponsorship on the basis that she had 'great Experience [with the trade], and for your diligence therein, [you] have arrived to high and Eminent Advancement for these late years'.[32] These satirical 'pleas' to the perceived 'Pope' of London's church of prostitution,[33] ended with a fictional 'response', purportedly from Lady Castlemaine herself, in which she proclaimed

[30] See Susan Shifrin's doctoral thesis for a complete discussion of these tropes and their relevance to theories of portraiture in England from the 1620s to the 1690s and to the practice of portraiture in the 1670s, especially in the case of Hortense Mancini, Duchess of Mazarin. Susan Shifrin, ' "A Copy of my Countenance": Biography, Iconography, and Likeness in the Portraits of the Duchess of Mazarin and her Circle', unpublished Ph.D. thesis, Bryn Mawr College (1998).

[31] Andrew Marvell, *Last Instructions to a Painter*, in *The Complete Poems*, ed. Elizabeth Story Donno (Harmondsworth, 1972; repr. 1985), 159. See also Zwicker above, 123–38.

[32] Mrs Cresswell and Damaris Page, *The Poor-Whores Petition to the most Splendid, Illustrious, Serene and Eminent Lady of Pleasure, the Countess of Castlemayne, &c., The Humble Petition to the Undone Company of poore distressed Whores, Bawds, Pimps, and Panders, &c.* (London, 25 March 1668), n.p.

[33] Creswell and Page; the writers of the petition suggest they will 'Contribute to Your Ladyship, (as our Sisters do at Rome ad Venice to his Holiness the Pope), that we may have your Protection in the Exercise of all our Venerial Pleasures'.

her rightful status as a 'Famous Lady... satisfied... with the Delights of *Venus*,[34] and in which she pledged her aid in their misfortunes. Such satirical poems and broadsheets, which appeared with much more frequency as the decade progressed, demonstrate the extent to which Lady Castlemaine's identity had become notorious even outside court circles and, therefore, how it necessarily was beginning to be perceived in ways she could no longer control.[35]

Lady Castlemaine's body by the late 1660s had, in fact, become itself a site of ill-repute, no longer one of beauty. Lorenzo Magalotti in his *Relazione d'Inghilterra* noted her declining beauty, remarking that 'Presentemente questa dama non è molto bella, benchè se gli riconoscono i vestigi d'una bellezza maravigliosa'.[36] Her body, therefore, was seen as a deteriorating 'sight' and 'site' of beauty, one that was increasingly defined as visual proof of the licences and lasciviousness of all women at the Restoration court. Inevitably, the control she may have wished to maintain through her portraiture was becoming subsumed and even negated.

Ultimately, the use of enigmatic, non-symbol-driven allegory like that used in her Magdalen portrait necessarily failed as a satisfactory pictorial tool since it inherently created a temporally specific genre that inevitably led to a loss of control over interpretations of those meanings as time passed and as the schism between real woman and sitter became irreparable. In fact, the ambiguously emblematic role portrait, like her Magdalen portrait, which allowed for multiple levels of decipherability on the part of each viewer ultimately itself permitted and encouraged a total mapping of 'notorious identity' onto a painting at the expense of the original, self-fashioned one. For later generations, such allusive portraits, at best, prompted viewers to infer from the 'guise' that the portrait might have once made obvious references to the actualities of the sitter's experience; but, at worst (and more often) it trapped the sitter in her role, leaving space only for the 'stories' imposed upon her

---

[34] Anonymous, *The Gracious Answer of the most Illustrious Lady of Pleasure, the Countess of Castlem—To the Poor Whores Petition* (London, 24 April 1668).

[35] For an analysis of these poems and broadsheets, see William Pritchard, 'Outward Appearances: The Display of Women in Restoration London', unpublished Ph.D. thesis, University of Chicago (1998), esp. 182–7.

[36] 'Presently this lady is no longer pretty, although one can see the vestiges of a wondrous beauty'. *Lorenzo Magalotti, Relazioni d'Inghilterra 1668 e 1688*, ed. Anna Maria Crinò (Florence, 1972), 83.

by her audiences. In other words, it contained the seeds of its own subversion.[37]

Whatever the ultimately negative effects of allegorical guise—or, in other words, whatever the inevitable 'loss' therein—for many there was distinct potential for empowerment inherent in symbolic role-play. Gill Perry has observed that 'despite the negative or prurient possibilities in ... readings ... of the [various] myth[s], the connotations [of role-play] ... could ... carry more positive and (relevant) social meanings'.[38] Whatever those connotations would devolve into over the course of the 1660s, Barbara's portraits clearly manifest an attempt (both on her part and on Lely's) to manipulate from the outset these more positive aspects of the mythic and religious figures in whose guise she posed. Consequently, her portraits stand as the instruments of a conscious 'fashioning' or performance/presentation of her own image, one that prohibited the viewer's complete access to her since it necessarily presented her as multifaceted and polyvalent.[39] Indeed, in posing 'as' many various women, Barbara effectively both promoted herself as all-powerful and denied viewers access to a single, exclusive, and final definition of her 'self'.[40]

---

[37] This reflects what Stephen Greenblatt has demonstrated in the literary context: 'self-fashioning occurs at the point of encounter between authority and an alien, that what is produced in this encounter partakes of both the authority and the alien that is marked for attack, and hence that any achieved identity always contains within itself the signs of its own subversion or loss.' Stephen Greenblatt, *Renaissance Self-Fashioning from More to Shakespeare* (Chicago, 1980), 9.

[38] Gill Perry, ' "The British Sappho": Borrowed Identities and the Representation of Women Artists in late Eighteenth-Century British Art', *Oxford Art Journal* 18 (1995), 56.

[39] Joel Weinsheimer has summarized the necessary integration between portraiture and pose, stating that the former 'is neither objective nor academic precisely because *as* takes center stage: it is the point of tangency between history and the present that cannot be reduced to a simple past or present, identity or non-identity ... The two [past and present] interpenetrate in the word *as*, the point of tangency fusing two temporal horizons.' Joel Weinsheimer, 'Mrs. Siddons, The Tragic Muse, and the Problem of *As*', *Journal of Aesthetics and Art Criticism* 36 (1978), 317–28; 318.

[40] Marcia Pointon has remarked on the perceived appropriateness of ambiguity in young women's portraits since marriageable women had to be seen as blank pages to be 'formed' as opposed to 'already' formed in their opinions and nature. See Marcia Pointon, *Hanging the Head: Portraiture and Social Formation in Eighteenth-Century England* (London, 1997), 60.

Lady Castlemaine's project of allusive portrayal confirms pictorially what some have documented through studies of the verbal displays of women in Restoration London. They have characterized the period of Charles II's reign as a moment in which society—in other words men— saw an increasing need to categorize and to control women's appearances (real and notional), and this was prompted by the perception that women were ably evading and frustrating any such controls.[41] They assert that after the Restoration the increased efforts to create a codification of ways of describing and viewing women (evidenced in literary texts, conduct manuals, and the like) was actually fuelled by a growing discomfort with the physical autonomy and visual availability of women in Restoration London. This observation is directly corroborated by Barbara's willing and complex self-display in her portraiture by Lely.[42]

As objects that literally show and direct her gaze, her portraits demonstrate the extent to which women attempted to control their own appearances through the return of their gaze. To characterize the Restoration actress—of which Barbara was one who lived her life on the court stage—as primarily scenic 'simplifies their effect on the spectator'.[43] Like actresses who looked out from the stage, Barbara's images at once promote her as an object to be viewed but at the same time they attempt to control her viewer's reactions and interpretations through her own gaze and the ambiguity of the various roles she assumes.

Self-display is always effectively a conscious masking of the self, at once inviting and frustrating the viewer's knowledge of the subject; as was the case of an actress donning a role on stage, Lady Castlemaine

[41] See Pritchard, 'Outward Appearances'. Pritchard cites as his goal: 'to describe and account for this cultural preoccupation with women's exteriors and to chart its progress through these three exterior locales [playhouse, park, and New Exchange]' (p. 12). His introduction is especially helpful in its overall discussion of the impulses behind and results of this 'preoccupation' during the Restoration in particular, and his examination of 'the evidence to which men appealed in their efforts to counter doubts as to female authenticity and legibility' (p. 51).

[42] Pritchard states that 'the claim that "[w]omen were not supposed to enter the public world in any form" needs . . . to be modified. Certainly women were prized if they possessed certain virtues to which the "public world" was presumed to be inimical, but they were encouraged to make those virtues outwardly, publicly apparent. The wish to keep women private, in order to encourage or safeguard their good qualities, coexisted with a wish to make them public, so that those good qualities might be appreciated and tested, verified and ratified' (p. 41).

[43] Pritchard, 'Outward Appearances', 97; he stresses that 'unlike a film actress, for instance, a player on the Restoration stage could return the spectator's gaze' (p. 96).

'could be seen, and perhaps had, but not known'.[44] Lady Castlemaine's portraits achieve the simultaneous revelation and masking inherent in any portrait, but when considered together they are at best a conglomerate portrait of the personae she and Lely devised for us to see. In fact, they are *never* a representation of an unmediated 'self'.[45] As such, they require to be approached and understood well outside not only the now-dated physiognomic theory of portraiture but also the confines of teleological, biographical interpretation.

As Marcia Pointon has pointed out, 'the portrait [is] ... one component in a wider and encompassing practice of delineation through which women are constructed in that world but within which women also construct a position, a voice, and an identity through their own acts of portrayal and delineation'.[46] Restoration female portraits, especially those of elite women in highly visible and politically charged roles, should be considered precisely as such 'constructions of position, a voice, and an identity' and not the mere visual clichés they have so often been assumed to be.[47]

An examination of this particular, focused group of portraits demonstrates, at best, how looking to these works as visual evidence (which itself must be considered within a tapestry of other sources) can help us elucidate the various ways a woman's portrait played and depended upon the circumstances pertinent to her situation at the time of an image's execution. This model should provide a useful method by which we, modern scholars, might better comprehend the meanings and

---

[44] Ibid. 114.

[45] On women and masquerade as a mode of wilful and deceitful presentation in Restoration London, see ibid. 120; more generally, see Joan Riviere, 'Womanliness as Masquerade', reprinted in Hendrik M. Ruitenbeek (ed.), *Psychoanalysis and Female Sexuality* (New Haven, 1966), 209–20; Judith Butler, *Gender Trouble: Feminism and the Subversion of Identity* (New York, 1990); and Terry Castle, *Masquerade and Civilization: The Carnivalesque in Eighteenth-Century English Culture and Fiction* (Palo Alto, Calif., 1986).

[46] Pointon, *Hanging the Head*, 7.

[47] Catharine MacLeod has previously proposed that the portraits of Frances Teresa Stuart, Duchess of Richmond display an analogous case to that of Barbara's portraits, in which allegorical symbolism does contain meaning beyond that of pure aesthetic quotation. Catharine MacLeod, 'Paradigms of Beauty: Portraits of Frances Teresa Stuart, Duchess of Richmond', paper given at the 21st annual conference of the Northeast Association for the Society of Eighteenth Century Studies, Boston, 12 Dec. 1997.

possible impetuses behind modes of display in all Restoration female portraits, and, further, in the genre of early modern female portraits as a whole.[48] These efforts are not made in the service of 'writing' lives, but rather in order to help us recover the various non-verbal—but, nonetheless permanent—ways in which early modern women might have constructed their public personae.

Like Pointon's work on female portraiture and representation in eighteenth-century England, my study of Lady Castlemaine's early role-portraits attempts 'not to discover the "real" people behind the paintings or to tell a life-story, but rather to understand the processes whereby these subjects—through a relatively mundane act of sitting for a portrait—are woven into a complex web of discourses'.[49] My work does not aim to recover either a 'real' Barbara or one who came to be seen through later interpretations of her portraits. Rather, my method tries to expose the ways in which the sitter/subject herself could be considered as an active agent in the construction and manipulation of the creation of her persona, one that would be seen by her contemporaries as multifaceted and polyvalent. It is precisely in its fragmentary nature that the tandem performances of Lady Castlemaine and Lely in painting her 'life' become so potent. To try to localize her power within the bounds of any narrative trajectory would betray the very tools of her power, which depended upon the slippery nature of her existence outside sexual, social, or political convention. Any biographical enterprise undertaken by twenty-first-century scholars must engage with the fact that this woman's power rested precisely on her vital liminality. It is precisely that elusiveness which she and Lely capture so eloquently in these paintings.

---

[48] This method would greatly benefit from more knowledge about pictures' early provenance history and original display. Especially in cases where portrait-types seem to be unique, information about where these portraits hung and who had access to them would aid in determining the extent to which they, as objects, affected the sitter's broad, public 'reputation'.

[49] Pointon, *Hanging the Head*, 12.

PART IV

MATERIALS AND MONARCHS

9

Two Queens, One Inventory:
The Lives of Mary and Elizabeth Tudor

Paulina Kewes

Early modern royal biography was seldom generically pure or conceived as a self-contained narrative that would circulate on its own, whether in manuscript or print. Rather, lives of princes were located at the intersection of chronicle, politic history, panegyric, martyrology, hagiography, confessional polemic, and other more ephemeral forms such as ballads, poems, sermons, pageants, and plays. John Foxe's 'lyfe and story of Queen Elizabeth' well illustrates the busy traffic between and across genres. Appearing in the *Actes and Monuments* (1563), a book that was itself an encyclopedic compendium of forms and styles, the life of Elizabeth was not only incorporated verbatim into the second edition of Holinshed's chronicle, recycled in a series of abridgements, and utilized in a classroom exercise—in the 1570s Eton schoolboys, Sir John Harington among them, turned Foxe's tale of Elizabeth's tribulations into Latin and presented a copy to the queen—but it also furnished plots for early Stuart plays and prose narratives retailing Elizabeth's near-martyrdom.[1]

The work on this essay was made possible by the generosity of several institutions: the British Academy which awarded me a Visiting Fellowship at the Huntington Library, California; the Arts and Humanities Research Council which granted me a term's leave in spring 2006; and Jesus College and the English Faculty at Oxford both of which provided much-needed travel grants. I am grateful to Tom Freeman, Helen Hackett, Diarmaid MacCulloch, Thomas F. Mayer, and Rob Hume for valuable comments on earlier drafts, and to the staff of the Huntington Library for their unfailing efficiency and courtesy.

[1] Daniel Woolf, 'The Rhetoric of Martyrdom: Generic Contradiction and Narrative Strategy in John Foxe's *Acts and Monuments*', in Daniel R. Woolf and Thomas F. Mayer (eds.), *The Rhetorics of Life-Writing in Early Modern Europe: Forms of Biography from*

'I am not ignoraunt howe hard a matter it is to intermedle with princes lyues them selues yet being aliue,' noted Foxe in the preamble to his account of Elizabeth, 'least either for flattery a man shall seme to saye to much, or saying no more then truth, to saye to litle'. 'Best for good princes to haue their stories set forth in their lyfe, for yl princes after their death,' announced the corresponding marginal gloss. Foxe's comments were patently self-serving. 'The comparison betwene the ii. raygnes of Quene Mary and quene Elizabeth' made crystal clear that Elizabeth was a good prince, Mary an evil, or, rather, a misguided one who did evil things at the instigation of wicked popish prelates. Rhetorically, the contrast between the two Tudor queens could not have been sharper. The very transition from Mary to Elizabeth was said to have afforded 'ease', 'gladnes', and 'delectacion' to the chronicler wearied by recounting 'the bitter and sorowfull matters of such terrible burning, imprisoning, murdering, famishing, racking, and tormenting... of the pitifull bodies of Christes blessed saintes'. Now his task is a joyful one: to tell of the 'blessed preseruation' and 'the florishing, and long wished for reigne... of this our drede and souereigne mistres and gouernesse Quene Elizabeth'.[2]

Once taken as an expression of unadulterated praise, Foxe's sketch of Elizabeth's 'princelye life' is now recognized as a canny application of the principle of *laudando praecipere*. In a series of illuminating articles, Thomas S. Freeman has reconstructed the providential thrust of Foxe's account and explained the function of revisions Foxe made to it in the two subsequent editions of the *Actes and Monuments* published in his lifetime, to wit, obliquely to impugn the queen's lack of progress with reforming the English church. Freeman has also documented the extraordinary range of sources on which Foxe had relied and has assessed

Cassandra Fedele to Louis XIV (Ann Arbor, 1995), 243–82; Raphael Holinshed et al., *The Third volume of Chronicles* (London, 1587), 1151–60 (based on the 4th edn. of Foxe of 1583); Jason Scott Warren's *ODNB* article on Sir John Harington; Thomas Heywood's history play of *c.*1604–5, *If you know not me, You know no bodie: Or, The troubles of Queene Elizabeth* (London, 1606); Heywood's prose narrative *Englands Elizabeth: Her Life and Troubles, During Her Minoritie, from the Cradle to the Crowne* (London, 1631); and briefer accounts in *Gunaikeion: or, Nine Bookes of Various History Concerninge Women* (London, 1624) and *The Exemplary Lives and Memorable Acts of Nine the Most Worthy Women of the World* (London, 1640).

[2] *Actes and Monuments of these Latter and Perillous Dayes, Touching Matters of the Church* (London, 1563), 1720, 1719, available at http://www.hrionline.ac.uk/johnfoxe/.

the veracity of the resulting text.[3] So far, however, the similarity of Foxe's narrative of Elizabeth's preservation to countless descriptions of the miraculous survival and God-given victory of Mary Tudor published at the start of *her* reign has gone unnoticed. Much has been made of Foxe's debt to the writings of Marian exiles such as John Aylmer. Yet it was the precedent of Elizabeth's Catholic half-sister that furnished the principal model for Foxe, Aylmer, and other Elizabethan divines, poets, pageant-makers, and pamphleteers celebrating the advent of the Protestant queen.

PROVIDENCE AND EXAMPLE

Elizabeth was greeted as a providentially ordained monarch and complimented as a latter-day Deborah, Judith, Esther, Daniel, David, Josiah, and Time's Daughter Truth.[4] Her survival under Mary and triumphant ascent to the throne were seen as the work of God and a sign of His care for His people. With the late Queen Mary vilified as a tyrant in the mould of Jezebel, Athaliah, Caligula, Nero, Herod, Domitian, and Diocletian, her younger sister was urged to prove herself a worthy recipient of divine grace by restoring the Protestant religion and continuing the reforms inaugurated by her brother. In a congratulatory address

[3] Thomas S. Freeman, 'Providence and Prescription: The Account of Elizabeth in Foxe's 'Book of Martyrs', in Susan Doran and Thomas S. Freeman (eds.), *The Myth of Elizabeth* (Basingstoke, 2003), 27–55; ' "As True a Subiect being Prysoner": John Foxe's Notes on the Imprisonment of Princess Elizabeth, 1554–5', *English Historical Review* 470 (2002), 104–16; 'Fate, Faction, and Fiction in Foxe's *Book of Martyrs*', *Historical Journal* 43 (2000), 601–23. See also Tom Betteridge, 'From Prophetic to Apocalyptic: John Foxe and the Writing of History', in David Loades (ed.), *John Foxe and the English Reformation* (Aldershot, 1997), 210–32.

[4] John N. King, 'The Godly Woman in Elizabethan Iconography', *Renaissance Quarterly* 38 (1985), 41–84; *idem, Tudor Royal Iconography: Literature and Art in an Age of Religious Crisis* (Princeton, 1989), 182–266; *idem*, 'Queen Elizabeth I: Representations of the Virgin Queen', *Renaissance Quarterly* 43 (1990), 30–74; Helen Hackett, *Virgin Mother, Maiden Queen: Elizabeth I and the Cult of the Virgin Mary* (Basingstoke, 1995; repr. 1996), 39ff.; Alexandra Walsham, ' "A Very Deborah?" The Myth of Elizabeth as a Providential Monarch', in Susan Doran and Thomas S. Freeman (eds.), *The Myth of Elizabeth* (Basingstoke, 2003), 143–68; Dale Hoak, 'A Tudor Deborah? The Coronation of Elizabeth I, Parliament, and the Problem of Female Rule', in Christopher Highley and John N. King (eds.), *John Foxe and his World* (Aldershot, 2002), 73–88.

presented to Elizabeth some time in winter 1558–9, one of the returning exiles, John Hales, hailed her as a type of Deborah, David, and Solomon even as he warned that unless she repay God's favour, she will suffer the fate of Saul.[5] Foxe sounded a similar note in his Latin *Gratulatio* printed in Basle and despatched to the queen on 21 January 1559. If less stridently than Hales, he too mixed praise with admonition, insisting that 'she has nothing which she has not received from the gift of God'.[6] So did other former exiles, John Aylmer in his apology for Elizabethan queenship published in late April 1559 and Lawrence Humphrey in a treatise issued in Latin in 1560 and English in 1563. Figuring the queen as Deborah, Judith, and mother of the nation, Aylmer emphasized that God had chosen to save his people 'by the hande of a weake woman'.[7] Humphrey, who also likened the queen to a series of biblical worthies, both male and female, stressed her 'weakenes & infirmitye' even as he extolled 'the bountye & mercy of God. To whose becke, worde, and providence, all and whole this wondrous facte . . . must freely and wholly be imputed.'[8] Similar scriptural iconography and providential rhetoric shaped popular ballads and poems, finding potent visual expression in the sequence of pageants mounted by the City of London for the queen's coronation progress on 14 January 1559.

Elizabeth's sufferings at the hands of Marian henchmen were endlessly retold to highlight the miraculous nature of God's intervention and the magnitude of her debt to him. 'I was tombled and tost, | From piller to post | And prisoner in the Towre', Elizabeth's alter ego, Bessy, complained in William Birch's *Songe betweene the Quene's Majestie and Englande*.[9] '[I]n this horrible tiranny and most cruell persecution', Hales

---

[5] *An Oration of Iohn Hales, to the Queenes Maiestie, and deliuered to her Maiestye by a certayne Noble man, at her first entrance to her reigne* was first printed by Foxe in the 3rd edition of *Actes and Monuments* in 1576. See Freeman, 'Providence and Prescription', 42–3. I quote from the online version of the fourth edition of 1583 available at http://www.hrionline.ac.uk/johnfoxe/main/12_1583_2115.jsp.

[6] John Foxe, *Germaniae ad Angliam, de Restituta euangelii luce, Gratulatio* (Basle, 1559), trans. John S. Wade, in Wade, 'Thanksgiving from Germany in 1559: An Analysis of the Content, Sources and Style of John Foxe's *Germaniae ad Angliam Gratulatio*', in David Loades (ed.), *John Foxe at Home and Abroad* (Aldershot, 2004), 157–222; 202.

[7] *An Harborowe for Faithfvll and Trewe Svbiectes* (Strasburg [1559]), sig. B3ᵛ.

[8] Dedication to Elizabeth in *Optimates sive de nobilitate* (Basle, 1560), trans. verbatim for the English version, *The Nobles or of Nobilitye* (London, 1563), sig. A2ᵛ.

[9] William Birch, *A Songe betweene the Quene's Majestie and Englande, The Harleian Miscellany*, ed. William Oldys and Thomas Park, x (1813), 260–2; Hackett, *Virgin*

stressed, 'your grace hath bene more hunted for, then any other.'[10] '[T]rust thou in God, since He hath helped thy smart | That as His promise is, so He will make thee strong', the child-actor exhorted the queen in front of the coronation tableau of 'The eight beatitudes' set up at Soper Lane.[11] The point of the display was to remind Elizabeth of her personal suffering and subsequent deliverance. For all the praise of her meekness, mildness, mercy, purity of heart, and so on, the crux is not that those qualities ensured her preservation but that she owes both them and her eventual rescue to God's mercy. In this respect the pageant foreshadowed Foxe's narrative that also dwelt on her passivity and helplessness in the face of popish cruelty so as to underline her obligation to the Lord. Another early forerunner of Foxe's relation of Elizabeth's— and the nation's—trials included Robert Crowley's updating of Thomas Lanquet's chronicle printed in 1559.[12]

Elizabeth was not unmindful of the benefits of claiming that Providence was on her side. In a prayer she allegedly said in the Tower before the start of her coronation progress, the queen compared herself to that prototypical recipient of divine aid, Daniel: 'I acknowledge that thou hast dealt as wonderfully and as mercifully with me as thou did with thy true and faithful servant Daniel, thy prophet, whom thou delivered out of the den from the cruelty of the greedy and raging lions; even so was I overwhelmed and only by thee delivered.' Protestant publicists seized upon the prayer as a mark of the queen's piety and gratitude. First published in Richard Mulcaster's commemorative booklet, the *Queens Maiesties Passage*, it was reprinted in Grafton's *An abridgement of the Chronicles*, and eagerly exploited by preachers, poets, and pamphleteers.[13]

Mother, 57. On this and other early Elizabethan ballads, see Elkin Calhoun Wilson, *England's Eliza* (Cambridge, Mass., 1939, repr. New York, 1966), 3ff.

[10] *Oration*, in Foxe's *Actes and Monuments* (1583), 2117.

[11] *The Queen's Majesty's Passage and Related Documents*, ed. G. Warkentin (Toronto, 2004), 85.

[12] Crowley, *An epitome of cronicles* (London, 1559). In contrast to Crowley and Foxe, Thomas Brice's versified martyrology did not dwell on Elizabeth's sufferings. See his *A compendiou[s regi]ster in metre contei[ning the] names, and pacient suffry[ngs of the] membres of Iesus Christ, a[nd the tor]mented; and cruelly burned [within] Englande, since the death o[f our] famous kyng, of immortal me[mory] Edvvarde the sixte* (London, 1559).

[13] *The Queen's Majesty's Passage*, 98; Grafton, *An abridgement of the Chronicles of England* (London, 1563), fo. 166ᵛ. On the prayer's authenticity and resemblance to Elizabeth's other addresses to God, see William P. Haugaard, 'Elizabeth Tudor's *Book*

How original were the queen and her publicists in their use of biblical tropes and in declaring as providential the recent revolution in English affairs? The genesis of early Elizabethan iconography has been traced to the writings of continental Protestants such as Bullinger and Calvin and of Marian exiles. Continuities with Edwardian depictions of godly kingship too have been noted.[14] The scope of the Elizabethans' debt to Marian apologists, however, has gone largely unnoticed and underestimated. Yet to commandeer for Elizabeth the images of biblical heroines, prophets, and monarchs—Deborah, Judith, Esther, David, Solomon, and Joshua, and portray her as Truth, was first and foremost a conscious attempt to appropriate, and variously to transform, refute, or cancel out, the tropes popularized by the encomiasts of the Catholic Mary Tudor.[15] So too was the persistent harping on Elizabeth's—and England's—providential delivery from popish thraldom.

The parallels are striking. Within days of the suppression of the Duke of Northumberland's coup on behalf of Lady Jane Grey, Mary's accession was hailed as providential, and the new queen compared to a host of biblical and classical worthies. In a sermon delivered in Luton church on 23 July 1553, the Roman Catholic priest, composer, and publicist John Gwynneth emphasized 'the myghtye operation of god' in placing Mary on the throne and paid tribute to her as the new

of Devotions: A Neglected Clue to the Queen's Life and Character', *Sixteenth-Century Journal* 12 (1981), 79–106; 94. Cf. a strikingly similar passage on Mary in John Christopherson's *An exhortation to all menne to take hede and beware of rebellion*: 'hauing god on her syde, as both she most earnestly prayeth to haue, and also it plainly appeareth, that she hath, she shalbe alwayes able to gyue her enemies an ouerthrow, & saye wyth the holy prophete Dauid, myne enemyes that troubled me are discomfited, and hath catched a fall' (London, 1554), sigs. O3ᵛ–O4ʳ.

[14] King, *Tudor Royal Iconography*, 182–266; David Norbrook, 'Panegyric of the Monarch and its Social Context under Elizabeth I and James I', D. Phil. thesis, University of Oxford (1978), 20ff.; Robert M. Healey, 'Waiting for Deborah: John Knox and Four Ruling Queens', *Sixteenth-Century Journal* 25 (1994), 371–86; Stephen Alford, *Kingship and Politics in the Reign of Edward VI* (Cambridge, 2002), 179ff.

[15] A few instances of the reuse of Marian tropes by Elizabethan publicists have been noted by earlier scholars: on biblical typology, see Jennifer Loach, 'The Marian Establishment and the Printing Press', *English Historical Review* 101 (1986), 135–48; 140; and King, *Tudor Royal Iconography*, 183ff.; on the image of the Virgin Mary and Time's Daughter Truth, see Hackett, *Virgin Mother, Maiden Queen*. Neither the scope nor the function of the appropriation of Marian iconography by Elizabethan publicists, however, has been properly explained. For discussion, see Paulina Kewes, *Drama, History, and Politics in Elizabethan England* (forthcoming).

Judith and Virgin Mary.[16] Soon Mary's divinely assisted victory was celebrated in popular ballads, *A ninvectyve agaynst Treason* by one Thomas Wateroune and *A new ballade of the Marigolde* by William Forrest, a priest who in 1555 would be appointed one of the queen's chaplains.[17] The Florentine pageant prepared for her coronation entry into London on 30 September 1553 invoked comparisons with Judith, Thomyris, Pallas Athena, and Veritas.[18] John Harpsfield, a formidable Catholic writer whom John Bale would denounce as 'Dr Sweetlips', praised Mary as a latter-day Judith, Esther, Deborah, Martha, and Virgin Mary in a Latin sermon given at St Paul's on 26 October 1553.[19] Another of Mary's clerical supporters, James Brooks, recycled the analogies with Judith, Esther, and the Virgin Mary in the open-air pulpit at Paul's Cross on 12 November 1553. To that list, Brooks added the mother

[16] *A Briefe Declaration of the Victory of Quene Marye in her Accession to the Throne* (London, 1553). On the uses of Mariological iconography for Mary Tudor, see Hackett, *Virgin Mother*, 34–7; King, *Tudor Royal Iconography*, 197–9; William Wizeman, SJ, 'The Virgin Mary in the Reign of Mary Tudor', in R. N. Swanson (ed.), *The Church and Mary*, Studies in Church History 39 (Woodbridge, 2004), 239–48; and *idem*, 'The Pope, the Saints, and the Dead: Uniformity of Doctrine in Carranza's *Catechismo* and the Printed Works of the Marian Theologians', in John Edwards and Ronald Truman (eds.), *Reforming Catholicism in the England of Mary Tudor: The Achievement of Friar Bartolomé Carranza* (Aldershot, 2005), 115–38; 127–8; Glyn Redworth, ' "Matters Impertinent to Women": Male and Female Monarchy under Philip and Mary', *English Historical Review* 112 (1997), 597–613; 599–600.

[17] *A ninvectyve agaynst Treason* (London, 1553), in *Old English Ballads 1553–1625, Chiefly from Manuscripts*, ed. Hyder E. Rollins (Cambridge, 1920), 2–7; 5; *A new ballade of the Marigolde*, ibid. 8–12.

[18] *Two London Chronicles from the Collections of John Stowe*, ed. C. L. Kingsford, *Camden Miscellany* 12 (London, 1910), 29–30; *The Chronicle of Queen Jane, and of Two Years of Queen Mary*, ed. J. G. Nichols (London, 1850), 27–30; *The Diary of Henry Machyn*, ed. J. G. Nichols (London, 1848), 43–5; and *The Accession, Coronation, and Marriage of Mary Tudor as Related in four Manuscripts of the Escorial*, trans. C. V. Malfatti (Barcelona, 1956), 31–2. For discussion, see Sydney Anglo, *Spectacle, Pageantry, and Early Tudor Policy* (Oxford, 1969, repr. 1997), 320–1; Judith M. Richards, 'Mary Tudor as "sole queen"?: Gendering Tudor Monarchy', *Historical Journal* 40 (1997), 895–924; 899. On Mary as Truth, see Fritz Saxl, 'Veritas Filia Temporis', in Raymond Klibansky and H. J. Paton (eds.), *Philosophy and History: Essays Presented to Ernst Cassirer* (Oxford, 1936), 197–222; 206–8; D. J. Gordon ' "Veritas filia temporis": Hadrianus Junius and Geoffrey Whitney', *Journal of the Warburg and Courtauld Institutes* 3 (1939–40), 228–40.

[19] John Strype, *Ecclesiastical memorials: relating chiefly to religion, and the reformation of it, and the emergencies of the Church of England* (Oxford, 1822), iii. 175; Harpsfield, *Concio quædam admodum elegans, docta, salubris, & pia* (London, 1553), sigs. A2ᵛ–A3ᵛ. See Loach, 'The Marian Establishment and the Printing Press', 139–40; William Wizeman, *ODNB* article on Harpsfield.

of Emperor Constantine, 'Helena, as shoulde be an ernest restorer of the crucifixe of Christe, and a speedy redresser of all thinges amisse, touching bothe faithe, and manners, in every condicion'.[20] Before the year was out, Leonard Stopes, a Catholic priest-turned-versifier, eulogized Mary as 'Judeth doutlesse', 'Hester, that virtuous Quene', 'princely Mynerue', and Virgin Mary in *An Ave Maria in Commendation of our most Vertuous Queene*. She was also figured as Judith in a set of Latin encomia collected by John Seton, an acclaimed logician and Roman Catholic priest closely associated with Gardiner, who was to suffer for his beliefs under Elizabeth. Commonly attributed to Nicholas Udall, the interlude *Respublica*, which may have been performed at court during the Christmas Revels in December 1553, portrayed Mary as Veritas and the Goddess Nemesis.[21] Elizabeth's erstwhile tutor Roger Ascham, now angling for Mary's patronage and employment, hailed the queen as the new Helena in a fulsome Latin eulogy he proffered to Gardiner on 1 January 1554 alongside a golden coin with the image of the empress.[22]

The following two years brought fresh applications of these and other images in the work of George Marshall, Miles Huggarde, John Christopherson, John Heywood, Leonard Gorecki, Hadrianus Junius, John Standish, Richard Smith, Robert Wingfield of Brantham, George Cavendish, Robert Parkyn, John Proctor, John Angel, John Elder, and James Cancellar.[23] The analogy with the queen's namesake and

---

[20] *A Sermon very notable, fruictefull, and Godlie* (London, 1553), sigs. J6ʳ–J7ʳ.

[21] Stopes, *An Ave Maria in Commendation of our most Vertuous Queene* (London, 1553), in *Old English Ballads*, ed. Rollins, 13–18; 14–17; *Trivmphus Mariae...de Ionne Dudlaeo duce Northumbriae*, in John Seton, *Panegyrici in Victoriam...Mariæ, Angliæ...Reginæ* (London, 1553), sig. B3ʳ; Udall, *Respublica: An Interlude for Christmas 1553*, ed. W. W. Greg (London, 1952).

[22] Ascham to Gardiner, 1 Jan. 1554, in *The Whole Works of Roger Ascham*, ed. J. A. Giles, 3 vols. (London, 1864–65), i: 400–2. Ascham's bid succeeded: he was appointed the queen's Latin secretary in May 1554. See Rosemary O'Day's *ODNB* article on Ascham.

[23] Huggarde, *A treatise declaring howe Christ by perverse preachyng was banished out of this realme* (London, 1554); id., *The assault of the sacrament of the altar* (London, 1554); Marshall, *A compendious treatise in metre* (London, 1554); Christopherson, *An exhortation*; Heywood, *A balade specifienge partly the maner, partly the matter, in the most excellent meeting and lyke marriage between our Sovereigne Lord and our Sovereigne Lady, the Kynges and Queenes highnes* (London, 1554); *Oratio pia, & erudita* (London, [1554]); Gorecki, *Oratio Leonhardi Goretii* (London, 1554); Hadrianus Junius, *Philippeis*

patroness the Virgin Mary was the encomiasts' stock in trade. Other tropes such as the comparison to Judith gained a new lease of life after the suppression of Wyatt's rebellion in February 1554. The restoration of papal supremacy in November and ongoing campaign for a Catholic reformation reinforced the efficacy of depicting Mary as Truth, Lady Faith, Helena, Handmaid of God, and His chosen instrument of England's delivery from schism and heresy. Her status as a godly monarch was bolstered by references to Old Testament rulers—Joshua, Esdras, and Judas Machabeus, and her learning and wisdom extolled by analogy with Roman noblewomen (Cornelia and Hortensia), early Christians (Paula and Blesilla), and King Solomon. The queen's marriage to Philip of Spain and her supposed pregnancy prompted references to biblical examples of late maternity, Sarah, Elizabeth, and Anna.

Princess Elizabeth would have been well aware of the emergent iconography of her sister's reign. Having accompanied Mary on her inaugural progress through East Anglia, and having entered the City of London in her entourage, she rode in Mary's coronation procession, attended her coronation feast at Westminster Hall, and listened to sermons in which the queen was praised as a type of Deborah, Judith, and Esther. Imprisoned and interrogated in the aftermath of the Wyatt rebellion, Elizabeth would have known that Mary's defeat of the insurgents was publicized as yet another token of God's providential care as was England's official return to the papal fold the following autumn. And she would doubtless have been familiar with the gist, and perhaps even the text, of Cardinal Reginald Pole's address delivered to the queen, her

(London, 1554); Standish, *A discourse wherin is debated whether it be expedient that the scripture should be in English for al men to reade that wyll* (London, 1554); Smith, *A bouclier of the catholike fayth* (London, 1554); Wingfield, *The Vita Mariae Angliae Reginae of Robert Wingfield of Brantham*, ed. Diarmaid MacCulloch, Camden Miscellany, xxviii (1984), 181–301; Cavendish, 'In laudem regine Mariae', in *The Life of Cardinal Wolsey...and Metrical Visions*, ed. Samuel Weller Singer, 2 vols. (London, 1825), ii; 'Robert Parkyn's Narrative of the Reformation', ed. A. G. Dickens, *English Historical Review* 62 (1947), 58–83; Proctor, *The historie of Wyates rebellion* (London, 1554); Elder, *The Copie of a letter sent in to Scotlande* (London, [1555]); Angel, *The agreement of the holye Fathers and Doctores of the churche* (London, [1555?]); Proctor, *The waie home to Christ and truth leadinge from Antichrist and errour*, trans. of St Vincent of Lerins, *Pro Catholicæ fidei antiquitate...liber* (London, 1556); Cancellar, *The Pathe of Obedience* (London, [1556?]).

Spanish consort, and the three estates on 27 November 1554. In it, Pole eloquently dwelt on the continued workings of divine Providence in the country's affairs. 'And see howe miraculouslye GOD of hys goodness preserued her hyghenes', he stressed, 'contrarye to the expectacyon of manne. That when numbers conspired agaynste her, and policies were deuised to disinherit hir, and armed power prepared to destroye hir, yet she being a Virgin, helpless, naked and unarmed, preuailed, & had the victorye ouer tyrauntes, which is not to be ascribed to any pollici of man, but to the almighty greate goodness & prouidence of God.'[24] Ever a confident manipulator of scriptural typology, Elizabeth found it expedient to appear to subscribe to the providential reading of Mary's various triumphs. 'I most humbly thank Him', she assured her sister in a letter of 2 August 1556, 'that He hath ever thus preserved your majesty through His aid (much like a lamb from the horns of these Bashan bulls).'[25] The parenthetic allusion to Psalm 22 served to strengthen the point.

The spectrum of genres and forms in which and through which Marian iconography and the providential view of recent history were disseminated, or at least recorded, is staggering. Among them, we find pulpit oratory, parliamentary speeches, panegyric, religious polemic, political pamphlets, narrative histories, royal proclamations, commonplace books, diplomatic dispatches, private letters, songs, ballads, and plays in English, Latin, Italian, and Spanish. Some of those were communicated viva voce, others circulated in print or manuscript, at home and abroad. However diverse their immediate aims and preoccupations, all drew on a common fund of images and all presented Mary as a powerful queen whom heaven had made its special charge.

---

[24] Elder, *Copie of a letter*, sig. E6ʳ⁻ᵛ; see also Philip's and Pole's respective accounts of the occasion in letters to Pope Julius III both of which Foxe reproduced in *Actes and Monumentes* (1563), 1011–14. On the parliamentary context of the speech, see Jennifer Loach, *Parliament and the Crown in the Reign of Mary Tudor* (Oxford, 1986), 40–1, 105–27; for a reassessment of Mary's achievement in re-Catholicizing England, see John Edwards and Truman (eds.), *Reforming Catholicism in the England of Mary Tudor*; and David Loades and Eamon Duffy (eds.), *The Church of Mary Tudor* (Aldershot, 2006).

[25] *Elizabeth I: Collected Works*, ed. Leah S. Marcus, Janel Mueller, and Mary Beth Rose (Chicago, 2000), 43.

MARY THE MARTYR?

Mary's troubles and triumphs since her ultimately successful bid for the throne in July 1553 were extensively described and commemorated. What about her painful experiences under Henry and Edward? Catholic publicists could easily have produced affecting narratives of Mary's sufferings at the hands of her father and brother. Yet although they fashioned her as an innocent victim of religious persecution, for the most part they chose to chronicle that period in her life with the utmost circumspection. A miniature poetic biography of the queen, Forrest's *A new ballade of the Marigolde* (1553) stressed her virtuous education, resilience, and piety. The closest hint of the harassment visited on Mary by the reformers came in the lines retailing 'her enduring paciently | The stormes of such as list to scolde | At her dooynges, with cause why, | Loth to see spring this Marigolde'.[26] If the metaphoric 'stormes' were apposite in the context of natural imagery suffusing Forrest's poem, the 'stormye showers' in Cavendish's 'In laudem regine Marie' seem merely banal: 'our Lord of his benygne goodness | Hathe preserved [Mary] from many stormye showers, | Or ells had she persyhed in great disresse'. The lines vaguely recall Mary's trials up to and including the Northumberland conspiracy.

The Spaniard Antonio de Guaras was more explicit than English versifiers in chronicling Mary's persecution by her confessional enemies. Even so, he strategically placed the blame on the by then safely dead Northumberland whom Protestants and Catholics alike held in utter contempt. Completed by 1 September 1553, his *Relacion muy verdadera* provided a vivid account of Mary's accession. De Guaras witnessed the mixed reaction of Londoners to the proclamation of Lady Jane Grey and the public rejoicing at the news that Mary's succession was secured. The people's love for the queen borders on idolatry, de Guaras reflected, yet their adulation is understandable given her admirable patience 'in her

---

[26] In *Old English Ballads*, ed. Rollins, 10. Forrest produced another, somewhat fictionalized and also more pessimistic version of Mary's past in his versified life of her mother, Catherine of Aragon, which he presented to the queen in 1557–8: *The History of Grisild the Second*, ed. W. D. Macray (London, 1875). See Tom Betteridge, 'Gender and Mary Tudor', in Susan Doran and Thomas S. Freeman (eds.), *Mary Tudor: New Perspectives* (forthcoming). I am grateful to Dr Betteridge for sending me a copy of his essay in advance of publication.

many and long-continued troubles' and seeing that 'her life has been so exemplary and catholic'. Like so many others, she had fallen prey to that arch-villain Northumberland who 'under pretext that such was the will of the King, persecuted her Highness with great oppression because she heard mass publicly in her house, as she did as long as she could'. De Guaras was concerned to establish Mary's religious orthodoxy, resilience, and bold defiance of her tormentors. Her chaplains languishing in prison, he related, 'her Highness has been about two years without hearing mass in public. Yet, notwithstanding this, being so good a Catholic...she has always had mass in secret, unknown to more than three of the most confidential persons at the utmost, by reason of the great danger that she might have incurred thereby.'[27] Mary, he insisted, had daily risked her life to remain true to her God.

Designed for public consumption, de Guaras's narrative was respectful of English royalty irrespective of their confessional complexion. By contrast, the confidential report of the Italian envoy Monsignor G. F. Commendone openly vilified Henry and Edward and sneered at Elizabeth. Commendone recorded with satisfaction the recent reversal in the fortunes of the two sisters, Queen Mary now being paid 'reverence by her to whom in times gone by she had carried the train of the robe'. That humiliation had been imposed on her 'under threat of heavy punishment' by her father, who had preferred the Protestant Elizabeth. Henry

endeavoured by such abuses to compel Mary to alter her opinions, nor did he fail to find every day new ways and means of disfavouring her, being given, as he was, to the devil. But that was of no avail either to the father or to the brother, in spite of the many ill treatments they inflicted upon her, as she was constantly growing more zealous in the love of God and of the true Christian religion bearing with great constancy the ill fortune, putting her whole trust in our Lord from whom she has got in the end such a high reward.[28]

[27] *Relacion muy verdadera* (1553), in *The Accession of Queen Mary being the Contemporary Narrative of Antonio de Guaras*, ed. Richard Garnett (London, 1892), 97, 100–1. Foxe reproduced letters from the Council and from Edward urging Mary to conform. The object was to cast her as unnatural sister, rebellious subject, and blind follower of a false religion.

[28] 'Events of the Kingdom of England Beginning with King Edward VI until the Wedding of the Most Serene Prince Philip of Spain and the Most Serene Queen Mary as Related by Monsignor G. F. Commendone' (an Italian Manuscript in the Library of the Monasterio de San Lorenzo el Real del Escorial X-III-8; fos. 133–240), printed in

Unlike Commendone, early Marian publicists tended not to voice overt hostility to their queen's father and brother. Written in the aftermath of Wyatt's rising and published on the eve of Mary and Philip's nuptials, Christopherson's *An exhortation to all menne to take hede and beware of rebellion* is a case in point. The opposition to the Spanish match, Christopherson argued, had had its roots in the heretics' resentment of the true Catholic faith 'confirmed with the bloude of all holy martyrs'. That faith the queen had ever professed and 'would not forsake ... if she knewe certaynly, yt she shulde loose the crowne of this realme therfore, and her life to'. Even as he memorialized her zeal and courage during that latest ordeal, Christopherson lashed out violently at Wyatt and his schismatic associates. When he looked back to Mary's near-martyrdom prior to ascending the throne, however, he carefully avoided naming names and apportioning blame:

For whensoeuer she was eyther by gentle exhortation, by fayre promyses, yea or by threatenyng (as sometyme she was) moued to forsake the catholike fayth, & to leaue of the godly ordinaunces of the churche, she neuer wolde relent, but settynge all worldly thynges at noughte, and carynge nothynge for the malice of men, mynded rather to dye for the defence of her fayth, then to lyue in honoure wyth the forsakynge thereof. And this hath her grace done not of her selfe onelye, but by thassistence of Goddes grace, who hath alwaies ayded her.[29]

Focusing squarely on the hapless object of persecution, Christopherson cast his brief retrospective on Mary's plight during the previous two reigns entirely in the passive voice. We find more explicitly derogatory references to Henry at the end of Mary's reign than at the beginning. One reason for this is the death, in 1555, of Stephen Gardiner; an attack on Henry was, to a degree, an attack on him. The second, and more important reason, is the growing influence of Pole, who had been outspokenly hostile to Henry for twenty years.[30]

Accession, trans. Malfatti, p. 23. Commendone deliberately exaggerates the indignities Mary had to endure: after Anne Boleyn's execution, she always preceded Elizabeth in status and in the order of succession.

[29] *An exhortation,* sigs. P3^{r-v}, P4^{v}–P5^{r}. Other commentators were even more circumspect: see Huggarde *The Assault*; Proctor, *The historie of Wyates rebellion*; Smith, *Bouclier*.

[30] A number of Marian works were fairly hostile to Henry: Nicholas Harpsfield's life of More (admittedly not published), Harpsfield's *Treatise on the Pretended Divorce* (again not published) and by obvious implication, Rastell's *Complete Works of More*. Henry also

Both foreigners and Englishmen depicted Princess Mary as a saint in the making. She might well have achieved the crown of martyrdom, they implied, had not the timely intervention of Providence elevated her to the crown of England. Here was a template that Foxe and others adapted for Elizabeth.

ROBERT WINGFIELD'S *VITAE MARIAE ANGLIAE REGINAE*

With the exception of Robert Wingfield of Brantham, none of Mary's apologists produced a substantial biographical account comparable to Foxe's life of Elizabeth. Wingfield called his Latin tract 'Commentariolus': little commentary or notebook. By choosing so unprepossessing a title, he signalled his intention, made explicit in the dedication to Sir Edward Waldegrave, that his account should provide raw materials for more skilled historians. That is also presumably why he refrained from printing it. An unnamed reader who acquired a copy of Wingfield's work some decades later recognized its biographical slant and rechristened it accordingly. The leather binding of the single surviving manuscript copy now housed in the British Library is inscribed 'Vitae Mariae Angliae Reginae' in a late sixteenth- or early seventeenth-century hand.[31]

Ever since the appearance in 1984 of Professor Diarmaid MacCulloch's masterful translation and edition, Wingfield's treatise has been extensively mined for information about the chronology of Mary's bloodless victory over the supporters of Lady Jane Grey, the places she passed, and the names of those who joined her during the dramatic days in July 1553.[32] Yet no attempt has been made to analyse its depiction of

comes in for some very pointed public comments at Cranmer's trial. I am grateful to Dr Thomas S. Freeman for drawing my attention to these.

[31] Wingfield, *Vita Mariae*, 182–3. I am grateful to Professor MacCulloch for confirming this point in a private communication.

[32] For recent accounts of the abortive *coup*, see Anna Whitelock and Diarmaid MacCulloch, 'Princess Mary's Household and the Succession Crisis, July 1553', *Historical Journal* 50 (2007), 265–87; Dale Hoak, 'The Succession Crisis of 1553' (forthcoming). I am grateful to Professor Hoak for sharing his work with me in advance of its publication.

the queen or compare it with the writings of Foxe and other Elizabethan publicists. There is no evidence that Foxe had access to a copy of Wingfield's narrative. The similarities between Wingfield's and Foxe's portraits of their respective queens do not argue direct influence. But they confirm that Elizabethan writers found much to emulate as well as to refute and denounce in the eulogies of Mary Tudor.

Neither Wingfield nor Foxe recounted his subject's life from cradle to the time of writing though the 'Book of Martyrs' provided a broad historical frame for Elizabeth's story whereas *Vitae Mariae* was a stand-alone tract. Unlike de Guaras, Christopherson, and Proctor who intermittently cited episodes from Mary's life in works whose chief interests lay elsewhere, Wingfield placed Mary's character and deeds centre-stage. He pointedly eschewed delving into her tribulations during her parents' divorce or the persecution under Edward. Instead, he concentrated on Mary's fight for the throne in which he himself had played a minor role. He was one of her staunchest East Anglian supporters and it was in his sumptuous house at Ipswich that the queen stayed. Although the dedication to Waldegrave is dated 20 May 1554, the narrative effectively covers the first year of Mary's reign. It chronicles her defeat of Northumberland, suppression of the Wyatt rebellion, restitution of the old religion, and negotiations for the Spanish match.

Wingfield's Mary is not a martyr but a mighty prince and champion of the Lord. She is 'the most godly queen', 'sacred Mary', 'that most holy lady and princess', 'the blessed lady', and 'the wise queen', 'extravagant (if I may say so) in bestowing her mercy' (pp. 284, 244, 251, 253, 278, 274). Wingfield extols her 'wisdom', 'consummate judgement', 'godliness, mercy and justice', 'incomparable goodness', and 'generosity' (pp. 251, 255, 269, 271, 280). He also invokes 'the joining of these two excellent ruling Houses of Plantagenet and Tudor' as the precedent for the advent of 'sacred Mary, child of both Houses' (p. 251). Except for scriptural parallels, all the elements of early Marian panegyric are brought to bear on Wingfield's narrative of her providential accession. The author effectively magnifies the threat posed by the

On the changing views of the Marian Exclusion Crisis in Elizabethan England, see Jesse Freedman, 'A Realm "Moste Miserable": John Stow and the Succession Crisis of 1553', University of Oxford unpublished M.St. thesis in History (2007); Paulina Kewes, 'The Exclusion Crisis of 1553 and the Elizabethan Succession', in Doran and Freeman, *Mary Tudor: New Perspectives* (forthcoming).

Northumberland conspiracy to emphasize both Mary's courage and her miraculous preservation that will ensure re-establishment of Catholicism. Her enemies, he says, 'would utterly have overturned true religion if sacred Mary had not been called by divine providence to take up the reins of state' (p. 276).

For all her unwavering trust in God and gratitude for his aid the queen does not stay passive. Her firm stand against Northumberland is figured as 'Herculean rather than...womanly daring' (p. 252). When Wyatt routed her troops, 'though only a woman, she showed the spirit of her ancestors in adverse circumstances and strove with all her might to reconstruct her army from stronger material' (p. 280). The queen is 'an incomparable oratrix' (p. 281) as well as a formidable military leader. Wingfield pictures her 'passionately exhorting her followers at Kenninghall', describes as 'splendid' her Guildhall oration, and commends her 'most elegant and grave reply' to the speakers of the Upper and Lower Houses on 5 May 1554 that 'in everyone's judgement' 'surpassed' even Gardiner's speech 'for all that he is a most incisive orator' (pp. 253, 281, 291).

Wingfield's narrative repeatedly registers widespread popular support for Mary. He not only records that at the time of her confrontation with Northumberland 'men from all ranks of life were joining her every day' (p. 255) but also inserts highly effective vignettes illustrating the role of the common people in swaying their superiors to assist her cause. One of the most arresting such sketches details the conversion of the Earl of Oxford whose servants 'crowded into the ample space of the castle hall and sent up deafening shouts that they recognized no other queen but Mary'. Moved by this demonstration of popular loyalty, the Earl promptly set out for Mary's headquarters. 'And so', Wingfield concludes with a proto-Foxean flourish, 'we have the denouement of our little drama' (p. 264).

Mary's popular touch and the mutual bond of love between her and her subjects are further exemplified in the muster of the troops at Framlingham, reception at Ipswich, subsequent progress through the country, and entry into London. At Framlingham, 'Her majesty...went round both divisions of the army speaking to them with exceptional kindness and with an approach so wonderfully relaxed as can scarcely be described [so] that she completely won everyone's affections' (p. 265). Outside Ipswich's city walls she was met by the bailiffs and 'inhabitants both old and young' who gave her 11 pounds in gold that 'with her unmatched kindness she accepted...with much gratitude'. On the queen's entry into the city 'some pretty little boys presented her with a golden heart inscribed "the heart of the people"...Much delighted with this auspicious and fortunate omen, the kindly queen embraced the little token with the proverbial open arms' (p. 269).

No less compelling are Wingfield's cameos of Mary's acts of clemency. He portrays her pardoning many of those implicated in the scheme to set up Lady Jane Grey, notably Jane's father the Duke of Suffolk whom the queen forgave at the intercession of his wife Frances, 'won over by cousinly affection, by her entreaties and by her own merciful nature, never enough to be praised' (p. 271). All in all, Mary Tudor emerges from Wingfield's narrative as in every way a model prince poised to fulfil the great mission with which God has entrusted her.

What can we infer about the dissemination of Wingfield's *Vitae Mariae*? The address to Waldegrave in the concluding paragraphs indicates that the piece had been read by several of the author's friends. It is safe to assume that it thereafter circulated at court. Wingfield was a member of a humanist circle that following the transitions from Henry to Edward to Mary had become riven by confessional tensions. In the 1520s Wingfield's father, Sir Humphrey Wingfield, had educated his son at home alongside several other boys, among them Roger Ascham and John Christopherson.[33] At the time Wingfield composed the *Vitae Mariae*, the Protestant Ascham, whose patrons included Pole, Gardiner, and Paget, was the queen's Latin secretary (a post he would retain under Elizabeth); and Wingfield called on his friend to check over his Latin. Apparently, Ascham did not do a very good job and the author received 'a severe verbal drubbing by the learned for my untimely publication of the corrected copy' (pp. 284–5). The upshot was another round of revisions before the piece found its way back to the dedicatee.

Wingfield made clear that while he produced his 'little treatise...lest the famous deeds of such a godly Queen remain unknown to many', his was not a finished product. Rather, he envisaged his role as that of supplier of raw material to 'Christopherson, Ascham or to some other initiate of more accomplished literary composition' (p. 244; cf. p. 285). Ascham had been Elizabeth's tutor and maintained contact with his

---

[33] MacCulloch, Introduction, Wingfield, *Vita Mariae*, 184–5.

former charge whenever feasible. He spent two months studying with Elizabeth after she had been allowed to leave Woodstock and invited to court in late August 1555. Thereafter he was occasionally allowed to visit her at Hatfield.[34] Given that he had looked over the *Vitae Mariae*, it would be surprising if he had not communicated the contents to the princess especially regarding the allegations of her involvement in the Wyatt rebellion.[35] So Elizabeth may have been aware of the existence and general drift of Wingfield's account even if she had not read it. She was certainly acquainted with a good deal of Marian propaganda and would have seen, heard, and noted the panoply of classical, biblical, and historical epithets lavished on her royal sister. On Mary's death, Elizabeth deliberately adopted and cultivated some of them and no less deliberately shunned and discouraged others.

The response of the queen and her publicists to Catholic propaganda and the Marian past more generally took several forms. There were the attempts to suppress favourable depictions of Mary and censor writings documenting popular enthusiasm on Mary's accession and the restoration of Catholicism.[36] In November 1558, the printer of an elegy on Mary was punished, and the poem promptly reissued with an additional stanza eulogizing Elizabeth.[37] And following Mary's funeral on 14 December 1558, John White Bishop of Winchester was placed under house arrest for preaching a sermon in praise of the departed queen—and obliquely critical of her successor.[38] Then there were

[34] Lawrence V. Ryan, *Roger Ascham* (Palo Alto, Calif., 1963), 216–17.

[35] Wingfield, *Vitae Mariae*, 286.

[36] Ian W. Archer, 'John Stow, Citizen and Historian', in Ian Gadd and Alexandra Gillespie (eds.), *John Stow (1525–1605) and the Making of the English Past: Studies in Early Modern Culture and the History of the Book* (London, 2004), 13–26; 20; Marcia Lee Metzger, 'Controversy and "Correctness": English Chronicles and Chroniclers, 1553–1568', *Sixteenth-Century Journal* 27 (1996), 437–51; 442ff.; Patrick Collinson, 'John Stow and Nostalgic Antiquarianism', in J. F. Merritt (ed.), *Imagining Early Modern London: Perceptions and Portrayals of the City from Stow to Strype, 1598–1720* (Cambridge, 2001), 27–51.

[37] *The Epitaphe vpon the Death of the Most Excellent and oure late vertuous Quene, Marie, deceased, augmented by the first Author* (London, 1558?), in *Old English Ballads*, ed. Rollins, 23–6.

[38] The text survives in BL, Sloane MS 1578; a summary can be found in John Strype, *Ecclesiastical Memorials*, 3 vols. (London, 1721), iii. 465–6. For discussion, see Kenneth Carleton, *ODNB* article on White; Victor Houliston, 'Her Majesty, which is now in heaven: Mary I and the Elizabethan Catholics', in Doran and Freeman, *Mary Tudor: New Perspectives* (forthcoming).

point-blank refutations of Marian providentialism and iconography, typically accompanied by efforts to replace positive images of the Catholic queen with derogatory ones. Hales ridiculed the numerous encomia on Mary as a type of the Virgin instead insinuating a parallel with the Whore of Babylon: '[t]his Viragin rather then Virgin as she woulde bee called and taken...boasted her selfe to be sent of God, to ride and tame the people of Englande.' Hales denounced the brutality of Mary's regime as far exceeding that of 'ancient and famous tyrants and cruell murderers, Pharao, Herode, Caligula, Nero, Domitian, Maximine, Diocletian, Decius'. He also denied her femininity: 'No, no woman, but a monster, and the deuill of hel couered with the shape of a woman'.[39] Aylmer challenged the ubiquitous equation of Mary with Thomyris. She should have followed the example of the Scythian queen who rejected Cyrus's proposal of marriage, overcame him in war, and took his life, he argued, rather than accepting a foreign husband in the person of Philip of Spain, getting involved in his wars, and as a result losing Calais, Hams, and Guisnes.[40] Referring to Mary's defiance of Edward VI and his Privy Council's attempts to deprive her of the mass, Foxe castigated as 'stubbernes' what a Marian apologist would have dubbed constancy or steadfastness.[41] By far the most common and effective way of dealing with the Marian legacy, however, was to commandeer it in the service of the new dispensation. The take-over of images formerly applied to Mary such as those of Deborah, Judith, and Esther to glorify Elizabeth is one example. The troping of her preservation and accession as miraculous is another.

The providential interpretation of Mary's accession, so forcefully asserted by Wingfield in his *Vitae Mariae*, was readily available in numerous printed works in English, Latin, and Spanish. Read alongside those earlier accounts of Mary, Foxe's portrait of Elizabeth begins to

---

[39] *Oration*, in Foxe's *Actes and Monuments* (1583), 2115. Cf. Bartholomew Traheron, *A Warning to England to repente, and to turne to god from idolatrie and poperie* ([Wesel?], 1558), sigs. A3^r–A3^v.

[40] *An Harborowe*, sig. E2^r. Susan Doran, 'Mary Tudor through Protestant Eyes: Representations of Queen Mary I during the Reign of Elizabeth I', in Doran and Freeman, *Mary Tudor: New Perspectives*. I am grateful to Dr Doran for sending me her essay in advance of publication. Holinshed's *Chronicle* ridiculed encomiastic figurations of Mary as a latter-day Judith and other biblical heroines (*The Third volume of Chronicles*, marginal note, p. 1125).

[41] *Actes and Monumentes* (1563), 901.

look distinctly second-hand. Possessed of innumerable virtues—mercy, wisdom, patience, learning, generosity, courage, modesty, piety—Foxe's is a 'good godly and virtuous...Quene' and 'a chosen instrument of [God's] clemencie'. Beloved of her people, she is destined to restore the true religion. By reproducing several Marian texts—Mary's Guildhall oration, Pole's address to the three estates printed by Elder, Forrest's versified eulogies of the queen—Foxe ensures that Catholic providentialism is at once inscribed and subverted in the 'Book of Martyrs'. Mary's untimely death clinches Foxe's argument that hers is a 'tragicall storye'.[42] By contrast, Elizabeth's life is plotted as a tragicomedy or romance. Her providential accession holds out the promise of a bright future. That is exactly how Mary's arrival had been described only a few years earlier. There is a fundamental difference, however, between the uses of providentialism by Marian publicists and their Elizabethan imitators. Both sets of writers gloatingly reflected on God's suppression of their adversaries and protection of their queen. But whereas Catholics invoked Providence first and foremost to glorify Mary, Protestants deployed it at once to praise and school her younger sister.[43]

What of Elizabeth herself? She consciously exploited providential rhetoric to assert her sovereignty, and framed many of her speeches, public appearances, and political decisions with the example of Mary firmly in her mind. Reading much of recent scholarship on Elizabeth, one could be forgiven for inferring that she was England's first queen regnant or that, as Foxe's tendentious comparison with Mary urged her to be, she was in all respects unlike her Catholic sister. Little attempt has been made to consider to what uses Elizabeth put her experience

---

[42] *Actes and Monumentes* (1563), 1720; Freeman, 'Providence and Prescription'.

[43] Two Protestant works published shortly after Mary's accession praised the new queen even as they urged her to continue Edwardian reformation: Rychard Beeard's *A Godly Psalme, of Marye Queene, which brought vs comfort al, Through God, whom wee of dewtye prayse, that giues her foes a fal* (London, 1553) and the anonymous *Narratio historica vicissitvdinis rervm* ([Wittenberg], 1553) translated into English as *Historical Narration of Certain Events That Took Place in the Kingdom of Great Britain in the Month of July, in the Year of Our Lord 1553, Written by P. V. Now First Reprinted from the Latin,* trans. J. B. Inglis, ed. J. Ph. Berjeau (London, 1865). Among the Catholics, only Pole exhorted Mary to repay God's goodness to her; and he did so in private letters, not in print. See Kewes, *Drama, History, and Politics in Elizabethan England*; Thomas F. Mayer, *Reginald Pole: Prince and Prophet* (Cambridge, 2000), 205ff.; *The Correspondence of Reginald Pole*, ed. Thomas F. Mayer, 3 vols. (Aldershot, 2002–).

of Mary's reign.[44] Elizabeth's replies to parliamentary petitions that she marry could profitably be assessed alongside Mary's retort in November 1553 to the Commons's delegation who pressed her to marry an Englishman, and her speeches usefully compared to Mary's Guildhall oration. Instead of harping on Mary's lack of popular touch, we would do well to recognize similarities between Mary's gracious deportment when she entered Ipswich and her successor's conduct during her coronation entry into London or between Mary's effective muster of her troops at Framlingham and the iconic scene at Tilbury in 1588. For late Tudor queenship to be properly understood, the lives and reigns of Elizabeth and Mary Tudor, and their contemporary depictions, cannot be prised apart.

[44] For instance, recent accounts of Elizabethan conceptions of kingship and counsel routinely trace those to the Edwardian period, making little or no attempt to assess continuities and differences with Mary's reign which, if it gets a mention, is distortedly presented through the lens of evangelical attacks by Ponet, Goodman, Gilby, Traheron, and Knox. See Stephen Alford, *The Early Elizabethan Polity: William Cecil and the British Succession Crisis, 1558–1569* (Cambridge, 1998), and *idem, Kingship and Politics in the Reign of Edward VI*; Natalie Mears, *Queenship and Political Discourse in the Elizabethan Realms* (Cambridge, 2005); A. N. McLaren, *Political Culture in the Reign of Elizabeth I: Queen and Commonwealth, 1558–1585* (Cambridge, 1999). Rare exceptions include Judith M. Richards, ' "To promote a woman to beare rule": Talking of Queens in Mid-Tudor England', *Sixteenth-Century Journal* 28 (1997), 101–21; and, more recently, Louis Montrose, *The Subject of Elizabeth: Authority, Gender, and Representation* (Chicago, 2006).

10

Elizabeth on Elizabeth: Underexamined Episodes in an Overexamined Life

Leah S. Marcus

Elizabeth I has been a frequent subject for biography, from John Foxe's *Book of Martyrs* to the present. Indeed, according to biographer Paul Johnson, she 'is the first English monarch whom the evidence permits us to know with a fair degree of intimacy'.[1] There is no scarcity of detailed information: she complained, famously, that 'We princes are set as it were upon stages in the sight and view of all the world' and her contemporaries assiduously recorded her actions on that stage. But the writing of Elizabeth's life has, for the most part, been inseparable from writing the history of the nation. Her life has been of interest in so far as she was a public person, the exemplar of an age, and from early on, biographers have tended to fall into predictable patterns in interpreting it.

We have, of course, no access to Elizabeth's life outside the texts, images, personal effects, and monuments that have come down to us. But this essay will contend that we have paid too little attention to the queen's own writings as contributing evidence. Throughout her life, she was a writer, producing letters, poems, translations, and devotional materials; during her years of rule she gave a number of speeches and public prayers for which texts have survived. She received a first-rate humanist education and became a published author at the age of 15 when her translation of Marguerite de Navarre's *Miroir de l'âme pécheresse* was published on the continent (1548). Her mature writings were much admired by contemporaries for their innovative, luxuriant 'Asiatic'

---

[1] Paul Johnson, *Elizabeth I* (New York, 1974), 195.

style, their 'rare sentence and matter . . . exceedingly to be liked of'.[2] But since she was and is defined as a public person, those elements of her writings that are not directly and obviously tied to public events have tended to go unstudied.

We have sufficient evidence for a 'life and letters' approach to Elizabeth I of the sort that has been attempted for more recent literary figures. The form is outmoded, at least in so far as the 'letters' of a writer can no longer be held to offer anything approaching unmediated access to the deepest truths of the 'life'. Nevertheless, I will argue here that a closer examination of Elizabeth's less familiar writings can help us break out of the predictable patterns that have tended to structure biographies of the queen and can stimulate us to ask fresh questions about her. That is not to suggest that we will discover unknown secrets about her most private thoughts. She would not have accepted a distinction between private and public in her own life, and it would be anachronistic for us to do so here. Elizabeth often set on a public 'stage' episodes that we now would categorize as profoundly private; often material that may appear to us deeply personal leads directly into key political questions of the reign. Because I am interested in circumventing as much as possible the usual grand narratives of her life and rule, and grand narratives in general, my approach here will be deliberately fragmentary.

A TALE OF TWO LETTERS

After the death of Henry VIII in 1547, Elizabeth lived for a time in the home of his widow, Queen Catherine Parr, and Parr's new husband, Lord Admiral Thomas Seymour. During her stay, Seymour became increasingly sexually aggressive towards the 14-year-old Elizabeth, entering her bedroom unannounced early in the morning, talking intimately with her, and even being caught on one occasion with Elizabeth in his arms. Catherine Parr evidently entered into these activities at least to some degree. In one bizarre but well-documented occasion, she held Elizabeth while Seymour playfully shredded her gown. But at some

---

[2] Sir Christopher Hatton, as cited in Anne Somerset, *Elizabeth I* (New York, 1991), 158.

point during the summer of 1548, the games appear to have changed their character and Elizabeth was removed from the house. One contemporary source suggested that her precipitous departure from the Seymour household came about because Seymour 'loved her but too well, and had done so a good while; and that the queen was jealous on her and him'.[3]

According to most modern biographers, Seymour was the aggressor in these sexually titillating games and Elizabeth, the passive victim. Most recent biographers have had relatively little to say about Elizabeth's attitude towards Seymour. The documents she produced that were closest in time to the episode were two letters, one to Catherine Parr and one to Thomas Seymour. The short letter to Parr sounds apologetic and grateful, and suggests that Catherine had been helpful to Elizabeth rather than angry and rejecting in connection with the princess's departure. Elizabeth's letter, which is reproduced below, refers to Catherine's unease and poor health because the queen was pregnant with her first child. The pregnancy was evidently a difficult one and Catherine would die shortly after her delivery in September 1548. The letter has no salutation:

Although I could not be plentiful in giving thanks for the manifold kindness receive[d] at your highness' hand at my departure, yet I am something to be borne withal, for truly I was replete with sorrow to depart from your highness, especially leaving you undoubtful of health. And albeit I answered little, I weighed it more deeper when you said you would warn me of all evils that you should hear of me; for if your grace had not a good opinion of me, you would not have offered friendship to me that way that all men judge the contrary. But what may I more say than thank God for providing such friends to me, desiring God to enrich me with their long life, and me grace to be in heart no less thankful to receive it than I now am glad in writing to show it. And although I have plenty of matter, here I will stay for I know you are not quiet to read. From Cheston this present Saturday,

Your highness' humble daughter, Elizabeth

Many things could be said about this letter, but what is perhaps most interesting is Elizabeth's skill at turning what could have been interpreted as signs of rancour on Catherine's part into signs of her special

---

[3] Cited from *Elizabeth I: Collected Works*, ed. Leah S. Marcus, Janel Mueller, and Mary Beth Rose (Chicago and London, 2000) 17, n. 28. Further citations from this edition will be given by page number in the text.

friendship. The queen had evidently offered admonitions about the danger to Elizabeth's reputation posed by the situation in the Parr–Seymour household, and Elizabeth expresses thanks for the regard shown by Parr's kindness 'that all men judge the contrary' in communicating the rumours. The rhetoric of the letter wills Catherine into a continued alliance with Elizabeth, whatever Catherine's own motives may have been.

At roughly the same time she wrote to Catherine, Elizabeth also wrote to Thomas Seymour. This letter, also reproduced below, is shorter and more cryptic; its reference to an unfulfilled promise has never been adequately explained. But the letter's tone suggests that it could be interpreted as an attempt on Elizabeth's part to distance herself from the lord admiral while still preserving his friendship. It is particularly interesting that she ends this letter with greetings to be conveyed to Catherine; her letter to Catherine offered no equivalent greetings to Seymour.

My Lord,
  You needed not to send an excuse to me, for I could not mistrust the not fulfilling of your promise to proceed for want of goodwill, but only the opportunity serveth not; wherefore I shall desire you to think that a greater matter than this could not make me impute any unkindness in you. For I am a friend not won with trifles, nor lost with the like. This [thus] I commit you and all your affairs in God's hand; who keep you from all evil. I pray you make my humble commendations to the queen's highness.

                                   Your assured friend to my power, Elizabeth

Based on their texts alone, the two letters may seem to be fairly close in tone and intent, though the Seymour letter lacks the apologetic tone of the Parr letter. If anything, the Seymour letter sounds like a response to an apology from him. But in considering Elizabeth's letters, we can often learn a great deal by how they are arranged on the page. Her placement of her signature is a particularly important indicator. In ordinary business letters, Elizabeth at this stage in her life would sign a few inches below the body of the letter. But in letters of extreme abjection, like her famous later 'tide' letter pleading for her life to her sister Queen Mary Tudor, Elizabeth puts her closing and signature as far down on the page as possible. Based on the semiotics of its signature, the Parr letter (Fig. 10) is very clearly a letter of deep abjection. Even

Fig. 10. Letter from Elizabeth Tudor to Dowager Queen Katherine, PRO State Papers Domestic, Edward VI 10/2, fo. 84c.

though the letter is short, Elizabeth uses a half-folio sheet of paper, and places her signature at the very bottom as a sign of profound apology.

The Seymour letter (Fig. 11) is quite different. It is written on a small rectangle of paper, of a size that could be easily concealed, and the signature appears directly below the letter. No abjection here. Moreover, Elizabeth adorned the letter with embellishments in red ink at the top and bottom. This is the only case I have ever encountered in which Elizabeth took the time and care to decorate one of her letters. The format of the letter is one of considerable intimacy, and changes the way we are likely to view the content. It suggests that Seymour's attentions to Elizabeth may have been reciprocated by her. And indeed, a few biographers of Elizabeth have pulled out considerable evidence that she had, at the very least, an adolescent crush on Seymour.[4] Perhaps her feelings were considerably stronger than that. At this period, she reportedly loved to hear him praised and blushed violently whenever his name was mentioned. Sir Robert Tyrwhit, who later interrogated Elizabeth about her feelings for Seymour when the lord admiral was accused of treason, reported that, although she denied any interest in Seymour, he could tell by her face that she was lying. Before I had found the original of the Seymour letter at the Morgan Library, my inclination had been to believe Elizabeth and to distrust Tyrwhit. But the contrast between the Parr and Seymour letters tends to confirm Tyrwhit's view of the matter.

Why have biographers been so disinclined to consider the evidence provided by the Seymour letter? It is, of course, out of the way, part of a miscellaneous collection of autograph letters at an American library rather than part of the archive of documentary materials at the Public Record Office—materials that offer detailed records of the interrogation of Elizabeth and her household about the possibility of a planned match with Seymour because such a match, if not approved by the crown, would be further evidence of Seymour's treason. But a stronger reason for the silence of biographers is, perhaps, that Elizabeth's own complicity in the Seymour affair would complicate our sense of her moral probity and her later avowals of a lifelong commitment to virginity. It is,

---

[4] See in particular Sir John Neale, *Queen Elizabeth I: A Biography* (New York, 1957); Carolly Erickson, *The First Elizabeth* (New York, 1983); and David Starkey, *Elizabeth: Apprenticeship* (London, 2000).

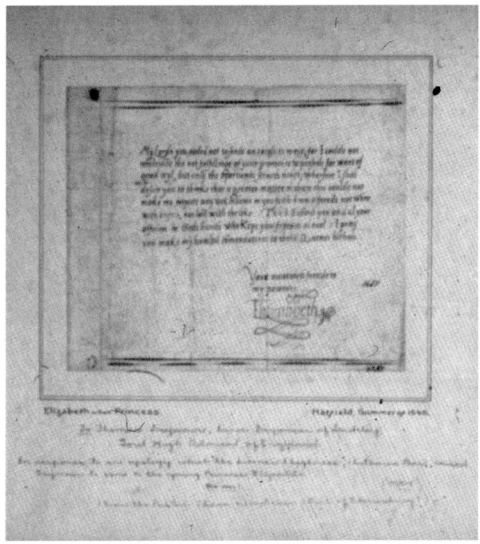

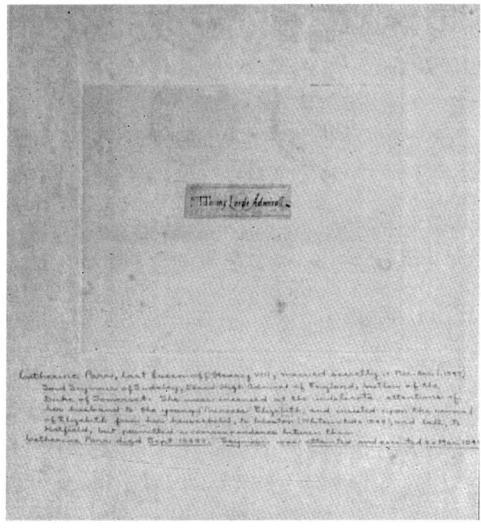

Fig. 11. Letter from Elizabeth Tudor to Thomas Seymour, Pierpont Morgan Library, MS Rulers of England, Box III, Part 1, art. 6.

of course, possible that Elizabeth's letter to Seymour was designed to mislead him into thinking she returned his affections. But it seems unlikely that Elizabeth would have risked such a communication during Catherine Parr's lifetime unless she wished it to be read by its recipient as a sign of special favour and intimacy. If we are reading the material evidence of the Seymour letter correctly, then Elizabeth later lied repeatedly under oath in denying any interest in the lord admiral at a time when other evidence suggests that she was extremely drawn to him sexually and very likely considering marriage. To imagine the 14-year-old Elizabeth as practising the duplicity and complex manoeuvring that this Tale of Two Letters suggests is to recognize the gross oversimplification of long-established iconic views of her girlhood.

STALKED BY DEATH

In 1562, the young Queen Elizabeth nearly died of a serious disease, probably smallpox. This episode intensified the demands of her subjects that she marry and declare a successor as an interim measure before she herself could produce the expected heir. Her *Private Prayers* published in Latin in 1563 may well have been designed as a thanksgiving for her recovered health. One of the prayers describes her own and the public's reaction to her close encounter with death. She acknowledges God's special benefits to her, 'Thy handmaid, whom Thou hast heaped with immense and infinite benefits from my beginning years onwards' and whom 'Thou hast placed in the highest rank of honor among mortals, not by any means because of my merit, but rather because of Thy freely bestowed goodness and kindness towards me' (p. 139). But that sense of special entitlement makes it more difficult for her to understand God's punishment of her through her illness. She surveys possible reasons— God may have wished to draw her away from worldly things, or move her to more fervent acknowledgement of her dependence on Him, or inspire her to more perfect obedience:

I say now, as Thy handmaid of late, whether by being healthfully warned or justly punished and, thus corrected and amended by grace, Thou hast affected me in this body with a most dangerous and nearly mortal illness. But Thou hast likewise gravely pierced my soul with many torments; and besides, all the English people, whose peace and safety is grounded in my sound condition as Thy handmaid nearest after Thee, Thou hast strongly disregarded in my danger, and left the people stunned. (p. 140)

Although the original of this strongly worded rebuke of God was in Latin, it is a signal example of how Elizabeth could turn her most 'private' thoughts into a public document. Her illness left her shaken in her conviction of divine favour, and had an even more powerful effect on her subjects. Over the next several years, Elizabeth, her advisers, and parliament were frequently at odds over the issue of her marriage and declaration of a successor. At one point during the 1566 sessions of parliament, which threatened to withhold subsidies unless she complied with their wishes for her marriage and settlement of the succession, Elizabeth angrily forbade them to discuss the matter further and had several MPs jailed for their impudence. Her eloquent indignation is recorded in several well-known speeches that have been so frequently discussed that I will not recapitulate them here (see pp. 70–86, 93–108), except to note a recurrent pattern. Parliamentary petitions would insist on Elizabeth's mortality as a compelling reason for settling the succession; Elizabeth would sarcastically reply that she was aware of this— 'there needs no boding of my bane' (p. 71)—and move on to other matters. The encounter with death I am interested in discussing is not the recurrent argument with parliament, but the encounter staged in her 1569 book of published devotions, *Christian Prayers and Meditations in English, French, Italian, Spanish, Greek, and Latin.*

We are not certain of the degree of the queen's participation in the publication of this second volume of devotional materials, but she certainly wrote at least some of it, and it is highly likely that she approved its publication. The volume appeared with an image of Elizabeth at prayer opposite the first page of the text (Fig. 12), and bore the royal coat of arms on the back of the title page. Many of the prayers are in the royal first person, referring to Elizabeth as 'Thy handmaid' very much in the manner of her earlier *Private Prayers*. All of these features suggest a straightforward attempt to promulgate royal piety. But the volume's format is, to say the least, unusual considering its apparent purpose. The printers placed each page within an elaborate engraved frame depicting episodes from the life of Christ and extended depictions of the Dance

Elizabeth Regina.

2. PARALIPOM. 6.

Domine Deus Israel, non est similis tui Deus in cœlo & in terra qui pacta custodis & misericordiam cum seruis tuis, qui ambulant coram te in toto corde suo.

Fig. 12. Image of Elizabeth from *Christian Prayers and Meditations* (1569).

of Death. The frames were not unique to this volume, having been used on at least one previous occasion. But they set up an interesting dialogue with Elizabeth's text. The images of death, in particular, serve as marginal commentary and critique of the devotions that share the same page. On a page where Elizabeth prays for 'the repose of men', meaning sleep, the engraving immediately below shows a dead body (Fig. 13). A page in which she particularly mentions the dignity of her place and royal crown shows death courting a crowned emperor and king (Fig. 14). These could be fortuitous correlations, but my final example surely is not. The last of the marginal images of monarchs and aristocrats stalked by death happens to be that of a queen; the expected hierarchy of images is broken by the placement of the empress and queen after the male monarchs (Fig. 15).

As historians of the book have demonstrated, it was not unusual for a sixteenth-century printed text and its marginalia to be in dialogue with or even opposition to each other.[5] But it is rather surprising to discover the words of the queen treated in the same fashion. In the context of the parliamentary debates over Elizabeth's mortality and the need for an established succession, the volume of *Christian Prayers* can easily be read as countering the queen's devotional demonstrations of her piety and concern for the spiritual welfare of her subjects with reminders of her death, much in the manner of the parliamentary petitions. The recurrent image of the Dance of Death is itself a succession of sorts, and juxtaposed with the royal prayers, establishes a counter-text that pulls against the royal text. Other elements of the volume support this interpretation. The title page, for example, just happens to depict the tree of Jesse, composed of a succession of male monarchs with the Virgin and Child at the top (Fig. 16). Of course, it would be possible to read the frames as expressing the queen's own recognition of her mortality, a theme that appears in several of her devotions. But it is likely that contemporaries read the frames as subverting the queen's voice by insisting on her mortality, her need to secure the nation's future by assuring a successor to the throne.

Who would have been responsible for the volume's unusual dialogue between the royal devotions and the marauding dance of death? Lord

---

[5] See in particular Evelyn B. Tribble, *Margins and Marginality: The Printed Page in Early Modern England* (Charlottesville, Va., and London, 1993).

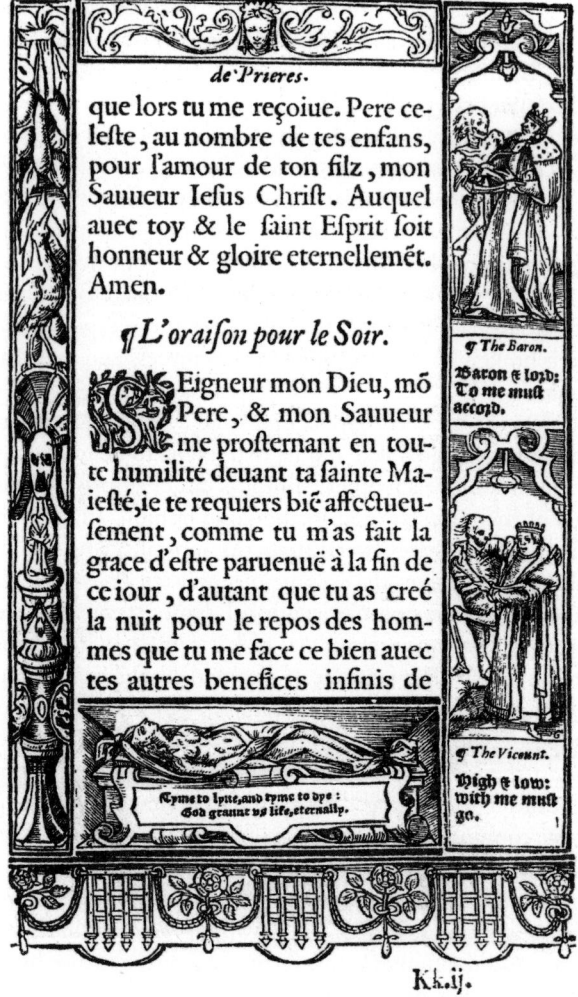

Fig. 13. *Christian Prayers and Meditations*, sig. Kk.ijr.

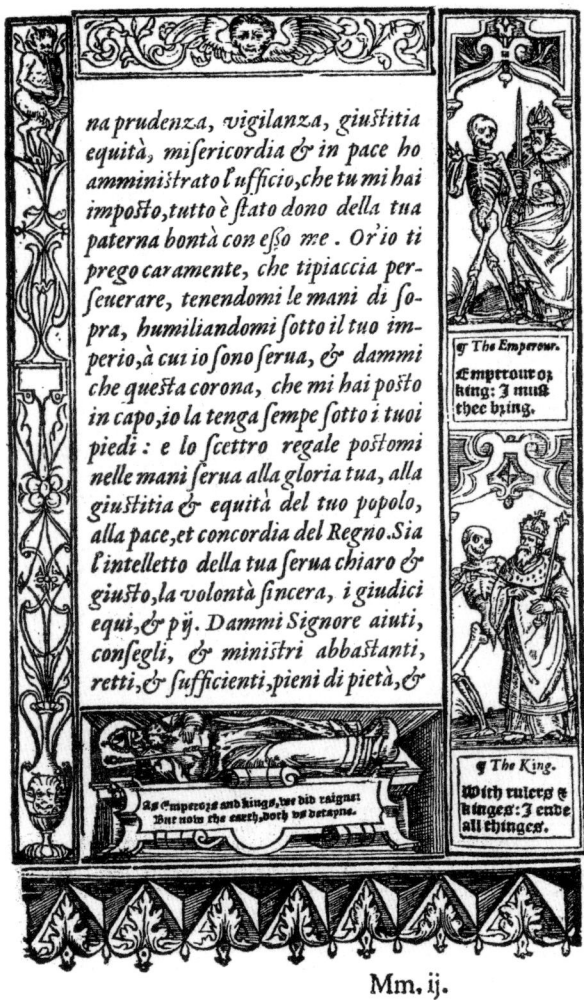

na prudenza, vigilanza, giuſtitia
equità, miſericordia & in pace ho
amminiſtrato l'ufficio, che tu mi hai
impoſto, tutto è ſtato dono della tua
paterna bontà con eſſo me . Or'io ti
prego caramente, che tipiaccia per-
ſeuerare, tenendomi le mani di ſo-
pra, humiliandomi ſotto il tuo im-
perio, à cui io ſono ſerua, & dammi
che queſta corona, che mi hai poſto
in capo, io la tenga ſempe ſotto i tuoi
piedi : e lo ſcettro regale poſtomi
nelle mani ſerua alla gloria tua, alla
giuſtitia & equità del tuo popolo,
alla pace, et concordia del Regno. Sia
l'intelletto della tua ſerua chiaro &
giuſto, la volontà ſincera, i giudici
equi, & pÿ. Dammi Signore aiuti,
conſegli, & miniſtri abbaſtanti,
retti, & ſufficienti, pieni di pietà, &

¶ The Emperour.

Emprrour oʒ
king: J muſt
thee bʒing.

¶ The King.

With rulers &
kinges: J ende
all thinges.

As Emperoʒs and kings, we did raigne:
But now the earth, doth vs detayne.

Mm. ij.

Fig. 14. *Christian Prayers and Meditations*, sig. Mm.ijr.

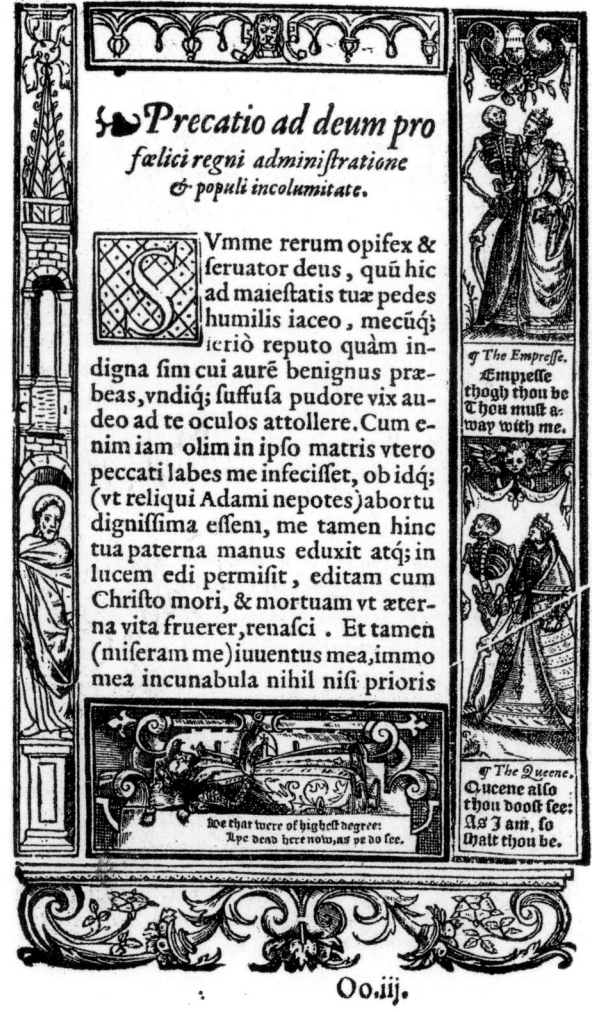

❧*Precatio ad deum pro*
fœlici regni adminiſtratione
& populi incolumitate.

Vmme rerum opifex &
ſeruator deus, quũ hic
ad maieſtatis tuæ pedes
humilis iaceo, mecũq́;
ieriò reputo quàm in-
digna ſim cui aurē benignus præ-
beas, vndiq́; ſuffuſa pudore vix au-
deo ad te oculos attollere. Cum e-
nim iam olim in ipſo matris vtero
peccati labes me infeciſſet, ob idq́;
(vt reliqui Adami nepotes)abortu
digniſſima eſſem, me tamen hinc
tua paterna manus eduxit atq́; in
lucem edi permiſit, editam cum
Chriſto mori, & mortuam vt æter-
na vita fruerer, renaſci . Et tameñ
(miſeram me)iuuentus mea, immo
mea incunabula nihil niſi prioris

We that were of higheſt degree:
Are dead here now, as ye do ſee.

¶ The Empreſſe.
Empreſſe
thogh thou be
Thou muſt a=
way with me.

¶ The Queene.
Queene alſo
thou dooſt ſee:
As I am, ſo
ſhalt thou be.

Oo.iij.

Fig. 15. *Christian Prayers and Meditations,* sig. Oo.iijr.

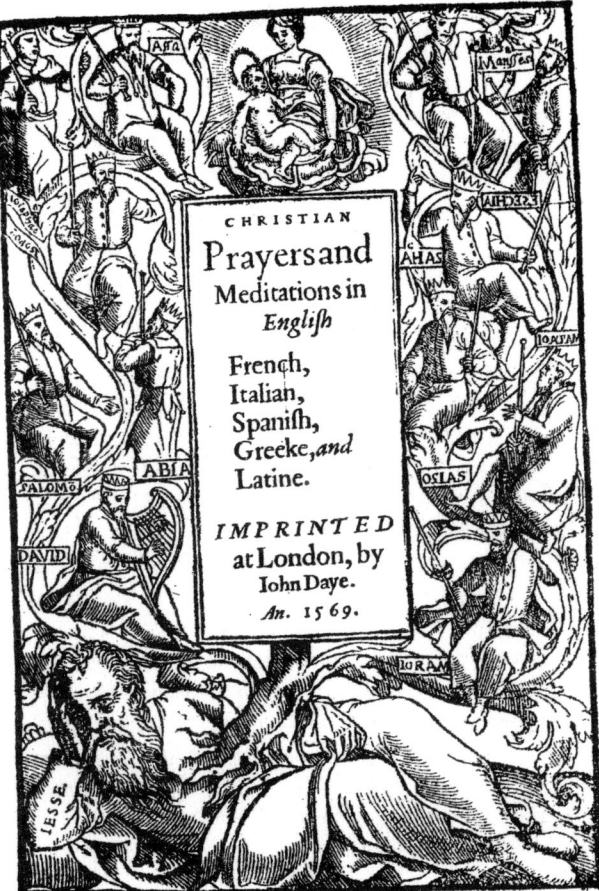

Fig. 16. Title page of *Christian Prayers and Meditations.*

Burghley would be one possibility: he was closely involved in the parliamentary petitions requiring Elizabeth to marry and name her successors, even penning drafts of one petition himself. Or it could have been another member of the government involved in the process of bringing the devotions into print. It could even have been someone in the printing house, even though the volume's printer, John Day, was an official printer to the queen. All it would have taken was a malicious gesture on the part of a single compositor to place the queen as the last of the figures stalked by death. Like the Seymour and Parr letters, the 1569 volume of devotions demonstrates the usefulness of consulting Elizabeth's writings in the form that reached her readers if we are to begin to assess their impact. In this case, that impact almost certainly included an adroit undermining of Elizabeth's public rhetoric through a visual countertext reminding both readers and monarch of the ease with which she could be snatched away.

DEFENDER OF THE FAITH

Elizabeth's religious faith is a subject understudied by biographers, despite the wealth of written evidence. Our reluctance to consider her religious attitudes in detail stems in part, I suspect, from our need to see the queen as a secular symbol. Elizabeth's name is attached to the period of English life and letters that saw the full assimilation of continental ideas of a 'Renaissance' of classical culture and a relocation of intellectual endeavour from the next world to this one. Those of us who work in the early modern/Renaissance period frequently think of it, however imprecisely, as a time of flowering secularism and nationalism as opposed to the collective spirituality and internationalism of the middle ages. Elizabeth and her courtiers are the English-speaking world's answer to the Medici merchant princes, Michelangelo and Rafael, or the burgeoning humanist culture of the courts of sixteenth-century France. Elizabeth was, of course, the head of the Elizabethan church, but her own creed and spirituality remain mysterious. This section will discuss three pieces of writing beyond her explicitly devotional material that may offer evidence of some of her religious preoccupations.

In 1576, Elizabeth gave a speech in parliament that she evidently valued particularly highly as an *apologia pro vita sua*. Numerous copies circulated at court, and she offered one to her young godson John Harrington with the words, 'Boy Jack, I have made a clerk write fair my poor words for thine use, as it cannot be such striplings have entrance into Parliament assembly as yet. Ponder them in thy hours of leisure and play with them till they enter thine understanding; so shalt thou hereafter, perchance, find some good fruits hereof when thy godmother is out of remembrance' (p. 167n.). Modern readers have found the speech difficult. Elizabeth's parliamentary historian, Sir John Neale, who explicated so many of her speeches, pronounced this one beyond his comprehension.[6] And indeed, Elizabeth had begun the speech with a recognition that she was likely to be misinterpreted: 'Do I see God's most sacred, holy Word and text of holy Writ drawn to so divers senses, being never so precisely taught, and shall I hope that my speech can pass forth through so many ears without mistaking, where so many ripe and divers wits do ofter bend themselves to conster [construe] than attain the perfect understanding?' (p. 168).

This statement is interesting for at least two reasons: she compares her own speech with scripture, and she assumes that, if probed, it will yield one meaning, 'the perfect understanding'. Anne Perry has offered a detailed reading of the speech as an account of key principles behind Elizabeth's reign, but Perry leaves out the most difficult passage, which occurs near the end. Elizabeth has been defending, yet once more, her unwillingness to name a succession, and concludes by warning:

let good heed be taken lest in reaching too far after future good, you peril not the present, or begin to quarrel and fall by dispute together by the ears before it be decided who shall wear my crown. I will not deny but I might be thought the indifferentest judge in this respect, that shall not be at all when these things be fulfilled: which none beside myself can speak in all this company. Misdeem not of my words as though I sought what heretofore to others hath been granted. I intend it not. My brains be too thin to carry so tough a matter, although I trust God will not in such haste cut off my days but that, according to your own desert and my desire, I may provide some good way for your security. (pp. 170–1)

The argument about her unique perspective for judging succession matters is clever and clear, but what does she mean when she says 'Misdeem not of my words as though I sought what heretofore to others hath been granted'? Given that she had compared her speech to scripture in its opening moments, and that she goes on to discuss the manner and timing of her death, my co-editor Janel Mueller was convinced

---

[6] Sir John Neale, *Elizabeth I and Her Parliaments*, 2 vols. (New York, 1958), i. 368.

that these words referred to the possibility of Elizabeth's being assumed directly into heaven without death, like the Virgin Mary or the prophet Elijah.

My first reaction to this interpretation was profound scepticism—how could Elizabeth be guilty of such spiritual arrogance? If Mueller's reading was right, Elizabeth's disavowal of the idea suggests that it had at least crossed her mind as a possibility. But I had no counter-reading of the lines to offer, and Janel Mueller's explication entered the notes to the speech in our edition of the writings. There are circumstantial reasons why Elizabeth might have been wondering in 1576 about her possible kinship with earlier religious exemplars. The late 1570s mark the beginnings of Elizabeth's cult of virginity in the form it took later in the reign, when she and her admiring subjects made great capital out of appropriating to the queen images and sentiments that had attached to the Virgin Mary under Catholicism. The same year that Elizabeth gave her cryptic speech, Elizabeth's Accession Day, 17 November, was officially made a feast of the English Church, with its own special liturgy that, according to some sources, Elizabeth herself had helped to compose.

The main thrust of the 1576 Accession Day liturgy is that the people should thank God for good princes and obey them as the channel of divine blessings upon the nation. To counter puritan objections that the church officially countenanced idolatry through its tolerance of popish forms like the wearing of the surplice, crosses, the use of rings in marriage, and the appropriation of Catholic imagery for Queen Elizabeth, the liturgy emphasized the role of the ruler as iconoclast and purifier of religion by offering a choice of scriptural passages about Old Testament rulers who put down idols and burned the 'high places' of the Philistines. The first of these iconoclasts is Jehosaphat; the second is Hezekiah, who defied the Assyrian conqueror Sennacherib and then became 'sicke unto death' (2 Kings 20:1 and ff.). The prophet Isaiah came to Hezekiah and said to him, in the language of the liturgy, 'Put thine householde in an order, for thou shalt dye, and not lyve.' Hezekiah prayed to God, reminding Him of his 'perfect hart' and good deeds. Isaiah had left the sickroom, but God called him back and told him to return to Hezekiah and tell him, 'I have heard thy prayer, and seene thy teares, and beholde, I wyll heale thee, so that on the thirde day thou shalt goe vp to the house of the Lorde. And I wyll adde vnto thy dayes yet fifteene yeeres, and I wyll deliuer thee and this citie, out of the hande of the kyng of Assyria, and wyl defend this citie.'[7]

The story of Hezekiah incorporated into the Accession Day liturgy gives credence to our reading of Elizabeth's speech as referring to some sort of assumption into heaven. Perhaps Elizabeth had Hezekiah and his miraculous healing specifically in mind. In its biblical context, his going up 'to the house of the Lorde' probably meant going up to the temple to offer thanks. But the passage could be understood as a reference to a temporary assumption into heaven, after which the just King Hezekiah, previously condemned to die, was brought back to earth and granted fifteen years of additional life and rule. Which came first: the ideas for Elizabeth's speech hinting at some special favour in connection with the end of her life, or the Accession Day liturgy, with its scriptural message of just such special favour for a righteous king? It is impossible to know. But the congruence of ideas suggests that we need to ask searching questions about how Elizabeth imagined her spiritual condition and destiny as God's deputy on earth. Perhaps the parliamentarians who repeatedly insisted on her mortality understood something we have not: that on some level, at some times, she speculated that she might be spared the common inevitability of death. Biographers and literary critics have tended to assume that the quasi-divine accretions that surrounded her increasingly after the 1570s are somehow inseparable from her essential nature. Clearly that cannot be the case. What did she herself think of them and to what extent did she contribute to their construction? Her 1576 speech suggests she may have viewed the process of her hallowing with some unease: 'My brains be too thin to carry so tough a matter.'

Another under-examined composition by Elizabeth is her 'Song' written after England's Armada victory and, according to the surviving manuscript from the collection of the antiquarian Henry Spelman, 'made by her majesty and sung before her at her coming from Whitehall to Paul's through Fleet Street in Anno Domini 1588'. Elizabeth's 1588 Armada speech at Tilbury has been much celebrated, but her Armada poem has been largely ignored—presumably because its political significance is less evident. It was in private hands at the time that the

---

[7] *A fourme of Prayer, with thankes geuyng, to be vsed euery yeare, the 17. of Nouember, beyng the day of the Queenes Maiesties entrie to her raigne* (London, 1576), sig. A5ᵛ. The story of Hezekiah is also told in 2 Samuel and Isaiah, but without the explicit reference to God's miraculous extension of his life.

cataloguers of the Historical Manuscripts Commission noted its existence. Since it was a literary composition, they only bothered to cite the
first two lines in their report. If it had been a royal letter, they would
unquestionably have reproduced it in its entirety. Since the poem is
relatively short, I will cite it in full, though our enquiry here will relate
primarily to the first stanza:

> Look and bow down Thine ear, O Lord.
> From Thy bright sphere behold and see
> Thy handmaid and Thy handiwork,
> Amongst Thy priests, offering to Thee
> Zeal for incense, reaching the skies;
> Myself and scepter, sacrifice.
>
> My soul, ascend His holy place.
> Ascribe Him strength and sing Him praise,
> For He refraineth princes' sprites
> And hath done wonders in my days.
> He made the winds and waters rise
> To scatter all mine enemies—
>
> This Joseph's Lord and Israel's God;
> The fiery Pillar and day's Cloud,
> That saved his saints from wicked men
> And drenched the honor of the proud;
> And hath preserved in tender love
> The spirit of his turtle dove.
>
> (pp. 410–11)

In the first stanza of the poem, Elizabeth offers herself up as a sacrifice—
in the manner of a calf or lamb among the Israelites—to be offered to
God in honour of the Armada victory. This gesture is extremely odd.
Why, particularly given that it was designed for public performance,
would she not rather have composed a song that entered more fully
into the general spirit of rejoicing that followed the Armada victory?
Biographers have noted Elizabeth's deep melancholy after the victory,
much of which surely stemmed from the death in early September of her
long-time favourite and soulmate Robert Dudley, the Earl of Leicester.
During the last few months of his life, according to a diplomatic report,
Leicester had 'usually dined with the Queen, a thing, they say, such as
has never been seen in this country before'. One contemporary letter

reports that in September after his death Elizabeth would 'not suffer any bodie to [have] accesse vnto her being verie much greiued with the death of the L. Steward' and another diplomatic report contributes the additional information that, since she had 'shut herself in her chamber alone, and refused to speak to anyone', her officials were obliged to have 'the doors broken open and entered to see her'.[8]

Some of these reports are from Spanish diplomats who would have reason to emphasize English disarray to their monarch after the humiliating Spanish loss of its armada fleet. In November, a Spanish diplomat's report observed, 'The Queen is much aged and spent, and is very melancholy. Her intimates say that this is caused by the death of the earl of Leicester'; but the diplomat's preferred explanation was that she was worn out by the burden of responsibility she had carried in connection with the war against Spain. In December, in the midst of English celebrations of the victory, English officials were reporting the same low spirits. Thomas Windebank wrote to Francis Walsingham that he 'told Her Majesty that he had sundry petitions for her signature, but she stopped him and complained of want of sleep, and unquietness'.[9] At about this same time, 19 November, St Elizabeth's Day, was made a national holiday in honour of the queen.

No doubt the juxtaposition of sudden victory and then sudden loss increased Elizabeth's disquiet in the months after Leicester's death, and her mourning was likely rendered more bitter by the fact that she suffered alone: several contemporary sources reported that the queen alone mourned the Earl of Leicester's death while her subjects celebrated the victory.[10] In a letter to the Earl of Shrewsbury in September, Elizabeth acknowledged his congratulations on the Armada victory by saying, 'Your letters written upon the good success that it plesid God lately to send us against those that sought utturly to destroye us, were very welcome.' But she refused to accept his condolences for the Earl of Leicester's death: 'As for other matter conteynid in your said letters,

---

[8] *CSP Spanish* no. 423, pp. 420–1; BL, MS Cotton Caligula DI, fo. 333 (letter dated 7 Sept. 1588, from Francis Walsingham to Sir Robert Sidney); *CSP Spanish* no. 432, p. 431 (dispatch dated 17 Sept.).

[9] *CSP Spanish* no. 470, p. 481 (dispatch dated 5 Nov.); *CSPD* 1581–90, 17 Dec. 1588.

[10] See William Camden, *Annales* (London: 1625), Book 3, p. 287; and *CSP Spanish* no. 432, p. 431.

although we doo therin accepte and acknowledge your carefull mynde and good will, yet we rather desire to forbeare the remembrance therof as a thing wherof we can admit no comfort otherwise than by submitting our will to God's inevitable appointment, who, notwithstanding his goodnis by the former prosperous nues, hath nevertheless been pleasid to keepe us in exercise by the loss of such a parsonage so deere unto us.'[11]

The resentment against God evident in this letter closely resembles her resentment expressed after her serious illness decades earlier in the *Private Prayers*. If we put the Shrewsbury letter together with Elizabeth's Armada poem, we can speculate that she resolved the deep crisis she experienced following Leicester's death by concluding that he had been the sacrifice exacted by God to enable her miraculous naval victory. In losing him, she sacrificed her own happiness to the good of the nation. She articulated that sense of sacrifice publicly in the Armada Song that was performed before her in public procession to St Paul's Cathedral. In the case of the Armada poem, we can clearly see the inseparability of private and public in the life of Elizabeth I: she commemorated her personal loss by imbedding it in a public poem of thanks and exalted praise.

As a final example of under-examined writings, we will consider Elizabeth's enigmatic 'Twenty-Seven Stanzas in French' that were discovered in a holograph manuscript by Steven W. May at Hatfield House, probably during the late 1980s, since he announced the discovery in 1991 (413n.). When did she write these verses, which seem to recount a mystical ascent into direct contemplation of God, and under what circumstances? Are they a translation or Elizabeth's own composition? May published the verses as Elizabeth's, but then, in collaboration with Anne Prescott, decided that they were a translation of an unknown original. In putting together our edition of Elizabeth's writings we cast about for an original without success, and ended up including the verses among Elizabeth's own compositions. We dated them to the 1590s on the basis of the hand. Our translation was strongly influenced by our decision to view them as the queen's own writing: at several points we interpreted

---

[11] *HMC Bath* V, p. 94 (*Calendar of the Manuscripts of the Most Honourable the Marquess of Bath, vol. v: Talbot, Dudley, and Devereux Papers 1533–1659, Preserved at Longleat, Wiltshire*, ed. G. Dyfnallt Owen (London, 1981)).

ideas relating to government and rule as political references, when the original would have allowed them just as easily to refer to the regulation of forces within the soul. As it turns out, we were mistaken. David Wootton has recently suggested that the verses were indeed a translation by Elizabeth of a poem by one of her footmen, Robert Seal, who is known to have written poetry. The poem's first two lines are 'With this blinding so strange | So contrary to my name' and suit the name 'Se-al' (see all) much better than they do 'Elizabeth', which, according to William Camden, means 'peace of the Lord' (p. 413n.). Having a name to search by, Wootton is now hunting for Seal's original poem in English from which Elizabeth translated. But the most sensational aspect of Wootton's discovery is that Seal was a follower of the heretical sect the Family of Love.[12] Assuming that Wootton's identification proves valid, why was Elizabeth translating the religious verses of a heretic? Did she find them spiritually compelling, or was she translating them merely as an exercise, in order to keep up her French? Did she know that they were the work of a Familist when she translated them? Would she have cared? She expended considerable effort on the French verses, which amount to 269 lines in total.

From the evidence we have, Elizabeth did frequently write translations as a way of sharpening her considerable linguistic skills, but she also tended to translate authors that would make a political point. For that reason she was particularly fond of working with stoic materials; famously, she let it be known that she was translating Boethius' *Consolation of Philosophy* during the difficult year of 1593. Did her contemporaries know she was translating Seal's poem, and, if so, how did they interpret her action? In the two decades since the French verses have come to the attention of scholars, we have, largely thanks to Wootton, finally been able to give them a possible provenance. But what we have managed to establish about her working with the materials only inspires a host of questions about all that we do not know. Of course we will never capture Elizabeth's thoughts and motives, or those of her contemporaries, in any way not mediated by interpretation, which has shifted and will continue to shift over time. But the discovery of the origin of

[12] David Wootton's work on the 'French Verses' will be presented at the Raleigh Lecture of the British Academy, April 2008, and subsequently published in the Proceedings of the British Academy. I am grateful to him for generously sharing his work in progress.

Elizabeth's French verses will stimulate a reassessment of her religious views, and possibly also of her willingness to entertain heterodox religious ideas during the 1590s. As the example of the French verses, and the others I have fleetingly considered here, suggest, by studying Elizabeth on Elizabeth—weighing her 'letters' as evidence of the 'life'— we can pose new and significant questions about her biography and her reign.

11

Whose Life Is It Anyway? Writing Early Modern Monarchs and the 'Life' of James II

Kevin Sharpe

What is a life? What are the materials of a life? And how do we approach the study and writing of past lives? Given the longevity and huge popularity of biography it may seem perverse to raise now such fundamental questions. But both the subject of biography—the life—and the genre of life writing have changed significantly through time. During the Renaissance, for example, lives, like histories, were published usually as moral lessons and patterns of virtue and vice. Drawing on classical models and texts, early modern lives were a predominant genre for the instruction by exempla which was fundamental to the humanist pedagogic and social programme.

During the course of the seventeenth century in England we may discern a new approach to life writing that focused more attention on capturing the peculiar character of the individual. Following the writing of new kinds of lives by Clarendon, Walton, and Aubrey, the first known use in 1683 of the term biography by John Dryden seems to acknowledge a shift in the conception of, and the writing of, a life: to signal a new, more secular sense of self, to posit the idea of self-property, and to view the self as an agent, a character and personality. Enlightenment modernity, we might suggest, fashioned a stable, rational self along with a new narrative genre for writing it that has dominated our thinking and writing about lives to our own times. The biography, or life-narrative, has been a literary (and historical) genre that has outlived many other literary fashions and forms.

Indeed biographers have largely ignored the critical moves of the last two or three decades that have transformed literary studies by challenging the stability of texts, notions of fixed meaning, and the very idea of the author or authored self. Recently, however, the biographer of Ben Jonson, Ian Donaldson, has insisted that, far from being engaged in different enterprises, the scholars of lives and texts, 'biographers and critics'—here I would add historians—'face similar and intimately related problems of interpretation which need to be pondered together'. 'Lives', he continues, 'must be read with the same subtlety that in recent years has been shown in the interpretation of texts.'[1] As his own experience must have demonstrated, Donaldson's injunction seems particularly appropriate both for the study and the writing of early modern lives. For, though contemporaries were increasingly invested in the notion of a self and the narrative of a life, in the humanist culture of early modernity selves and lives were by no means the property or script of a sole author. Ancient and contemporary lives were edited, translated, copied into commonplace books, and appropriated and quoted for use by readers: that is rendered in a myriad of textual and discursive forms by a variety of readers and writers. The texts of early modern lives, we might say, were inseparable from the lives of texts and from the multiple authorship, commerce, and free interpretation that was the culture and condition of texts in early modern England.

As the case of Jonson so obviously demonstrates, the theatre of early modern England emerged from a new interest in, a new concern with, characters and lives; but theatre also artfully staged and represented lives—including the lives of kings—not as a stable single-authored narrative, but as a series of personations and performances. In the theatre and the meta-theatre of early modern England, lives were not simply fashioned by selves but endlessly constructed, represented, and reconstituted through textual exchanges and by different actors in various forms. As John Guy recently argued, in a historical life that departed from the traditional biographical form, the humanist scholar and martyr Thomas More was not just a man for all seasons, his life was one of many different and contradictory performances and of many representations and stories. Far from trying to resolve them into one account, Guy

---

[1] I. Donaldson, *Jonson's Magic Houses: Essays in Interpretation* (Oxford, 1997), 4.

insists that these multiple representations are not just pertinent to—they are—the life of Thomas More.[2]

It is both Donaldson's urging a more textual subtlety and Guy's embracing of multiplicity that I wish to apply to a particular sub-genre of life writing where, I maintain, traditional biography has served us ill—the lives of early modern monarchs.

Despite all the obvious rewritings of early modern royal lives for our own purposes—the transformation of Elizabeth I, for example, from figure of male fantasy to inept prevaricator to feminist role model—historians, claiming objectivity, have remained reluctant to acknowledge the problems involved in their claims to find the 'real figure'.[3] Though new sensibilities have opened historical biography to dimensions of a life once ignored or repressed, such as James I's homosexuality, few royal biographies venture into the interior lives of rulers.[4] Most disappointing, traditional royal biographies (that is virtually all I know of) have taken a narrow view of what constitutes the evidence, the materials, of a royal life. In particular, they have tended to ignore royal writings and other representations except when they have the most obvious 'political' import; and even then they are read as simple statements of personal and public authority rather than as complex texts of a multiple, variable, vulnerable, and sometimes fractured, subjectivity.[5]

One of the prevalent discourses of pre-modern monarchy was the language and concept of the king's two bodies: a recognition of the human and personal as well as the public and sacred aspects of royalty. While historians have been familiar with the conceit at least since Ernst Kantarowicz's seminal study, the full implications of it—and of early modern changes in its ideological performance—for royal biography have been little explored.[6] In early modern theatre, as Kantorowicz

---

[2] J. Guy, *Thomas More* (London and New York, 2000); see Donaldson, *Jonson's Magic Houses*, 2–3.

[3] See e.g. the recent essay by George Bernard, 'History and Postmodernism', in his *Power and Politics in Tudor England* (Aldershot, 2000), 217–30.

[4] D. Bergeron, *King James and Letters of Homoerotic Desire* (Iowa, 1999); M. B. Young, *James I and the History of Homosexuality* (Basingstoke, 1999).

[5] Though for a pioneering approach, see D. Fischlin and M. Fortier (eds.), *Royal Subjects: Essays on the Writings of James VI and I* (Detroit, 2002).

[6] E. Kantorowicz, *The King's Two Bodies: A Study in Medieval Political Theology* (Princeton, 1957); A. Rolls, *The Theory of the King's Two Bodies in the Age of Shakespeare* (Lewiston, NY, 2000).

appreciated, we have rich contemporary meditations not only of a society working out new notions of identity but of a culture also newly fascinated by figures of power: in the state as on the stage. Theatre was a laboratory in which early modernity posed and pondered questions about authority, regality, and identity—what if a king goes mad or is a machiavel or heretic? Questions that we seldom find confronted in the usual materials of the biographer or historian. Such representations on the stage both reflected and fostered a theatricalization of regality that developed over the course of the sixteenth century and reached its apogee in Elizabeth's reign. While scholars readily cite Elizabeth and her successor James I comparing monarchs and actors, historians have been slow to study their royal subjects as literally that: as actors and performers who self-consciously performed on the stage of state, who for all their (and our) insistence on their integrity and transparency, recognized the tension between their private and public selves and the need to adopt personae and to perform roles.

Performance on the stage is no simple act of an authorial self. The actor's lines, albeit delivered and inflected by him or herself, are scripted usually by others and subject to revision in the context of the changing circumstances of performance—not least different audiences. It is not inappropriate to think of early modern royal performances in a similar way. Over the course of the sixteenth century, as I argue elsewhere at length, English monarchs, faced with the threat of religious war and rebellion, went to great lengths to sacralize and publicize their authority.[7] The popularity of plays about kings and courts is only one testament to their success. A growing market for copies of royal speeches and accounts of royal progresses, for royal portraits and souvenir objects evidences how regality was not only represented but increasingly observed and consumed by an audience.[8] Royal performances, as other authorial performances in early modern England, were increasingly involved in a number of dialogues, exchanges, and negotiations that complicate, to say the least, any idea either of sovereign authority—or of a sovereign self.

---

[7] K. Sharpe, *Representing Rule: Images of Power in Early Modern England 1500–1700*, 3 vols. (forthcoming). See the first volume, *Images of Tudor Monarchy*.

[8] The first books of engravings of English monarchs and of souvenir plates and other objects appear in the reign of Elizabeth I and increase rapidly thereafter.

This was nowhere more evident than in what we once readily took to be the uncomplicated authorial acts of speaking and writing—especially by rulers. Royal authority had always been heavily invested in the 'word' and Henry VIII and his successors seized the opportunity presented by print to publish the royal word and will. But print was not the preserve of sovereignty. In the divided Europe of Reformation, Henry VIII found his attack on Luther answered with excoriating wit. Increasingly too, in a humanist rhetorical culture which trained the educated laity in arguing in *utrimque partes*, all royal locutions and writings were read, debated, and answered critically. James I discovered that even his magisterial folio works were far from immune from attack. In early modern England, royal texts were not sovereign authorial acts in the sense we conceive them. As well as often being the work of more than one hand, they were, perforce, rhetorical performances scripted out of intimations of audiences and expectations of animadversion, amid the noisy contest of print.[9] They await readings as rhetorical and polemical performances, as texts, as well as documents of a public life and reign. What we also need to recognize is that if these royal texts, the representations of a royal self that was the only 'real person' most subjects perceived, had multiple lives and afterlives, the royal life itself was no more fixed but rather constituted out of texts and representations—locutions, writings, images, and rituals—and their receptions.

To apply some critical questions and approaches to lives, as Donaldson urges us, is not to undermine but to extend and enrich the project of royal biography in a number of potentially fruitful ways. In the first place a new life of an early modern monarch might benefit from reconsidering those domains of public and private that modernism has mapped and sought to define and differentiate. If today our idea of a self as something we possess outside textual and social interactions and struggles has been exposed as a fantasy, the case of early modern rulers complicates, if it does not fully discredit, such clear distinctions. As Queen Elizabeth was not the only ruler to appreciate, the royal body was not personal or private (*privatus*—that is separate from the public) but at the centre of public interest, in both the senses of curiosity

<hr>

[9] K. Sharpe, *Reading Revolutions: The Politics of Reading in Early Modern England* (New Haven and London, 2000), 27–34.

and partisanship.[10] And as James I and Charles I understood, their conscience (that which since Locke we have taken as our ultimate personal domain) was not just a personal conscience but also the public conscience.[11] In early modern England the languages of the body—of sex and marriage—and conscience, what we take to be private terms, scripted public constitutions. They need to be brought, far more than they have been, to the centre of royal lives.

A refiguring of the private and public and a questioning of the stability of sovereignty and selfhood also directs us to genres and kinds of texts too often neglected in royal biographies. For years historians of James VI and I's reign have returned time and again to C. H. McIlwain's edition of *The Political Works of James I*, leaving a host of other writings—biblical commentaries, translations, and poems— unexplored, presumably because they were held to cast little light on the public life, the royal life.[12] Only now are scholars, and still mainly critics, studying James's verse and Elizabeth's prayers and poems as processes of the construction, representation, and negotiation of both royal identity and authority. A large body of other royal texts—Henry VIII's songs and poems, Charles I's prayers, and Charles II's romance narrative—all await editing and reading as texts of sovereignty and self. New royal biography will depend not just on the inclusion of such materials but also on different approaches to reading them. As the editors of Elizabeth's works put it recently, historians and biographers have tended to read speeches and letters as 'documents of policy' and as straightforward public statements of intention and authority.[13] What we need to explore further is how they were designed and how they performed in a highly rhetorical culture to fashion identity and author- ity. Because rulers, like all authors, knew that their words were read by resistant as well as complaisant readers, they deployed devices and tropes to temper resistance and to assuage the anxieties of authority. A critical

---

[10] Elizabeth's poem to Anjou seems self-consciously to ponder this doubleness. See *Elizabeth I: Collected Works*, ed. L. S. Marcus, J. Mueller, and M. B. Rose (Chicago, 2000), 302–3.

[11] K. Sharpe, 'Private Conscience and Public Duty in the Writings of James VI and I' and 'Private Conscience and Public Duty in the Writings of Charles I', both reprinted in *Remapping Early Modern England* (Cambridge, 2000), chs. 4, 5.

[12] J. Sommerville's 1991 Cambridge edition of the *Political Writings* also omits them.

[13] Marcus, *Elizabeth*, p. xi.

rereading of all royal writings, proclamations as well as poems, which explored those tropes and the anxieties that still surface between and below the lines would, I suspect, write very different royal biographies and histories of Tudor and Stuart England.

Finally, we might observe that traditional biography, not least on account of its commitment to the biological narrative of birth to death, has paid little attention to afterlives. In early modern England, however, royal lives lived on after death in a myriad of texts, monuments, and memories that reveal much about regality, the royal subject, and his or her reign and representation. Let us again take the case of Elizabeth I whose life, contested for in her lifetime, was, over the course of the next century, appropriated by godly advocates of religious reform, critics of the Stuarts, colonizers, royalists, and republicans, Whigs and Tories, before providing a motto for Queen Anne—ironically *Semper Eadem*, always the same.[14] The history of Charles I's afterlife, as tyrant, martyr, loving husband and father, or ungodly reprobate virtually wrote the history of polemical and party conflict in the late seventeenth century and beyond.[15] The issue here is not just the polemics of memory but the openness of royal lives to such multiple deployments, the instability of the meaning of the sovereign life and reign. We need to take the opportunity that contemporaries' recognition of that instability offers to reconsider the royal life as a series of responses and readings, as receptions as well as representations.

What I propose by the application of some critical questions and perspectives is a historicizing of early modern royal lives. For address to the instabilities and multiplicities of lives as much as texts, and to the constructed nature of identity and authority; study of all the texts in and through which monarchs represented their bodies and conscience; of the rhetorics by which they sought to control how they were perceived; and the contested readings of their lives and reigns restores those lives and reigns to their early modern circumstances, which, in many

---

[14] J. Walker, 'Bones of Contention: Posthumous Images of Elizabeth and Stuart Politics', in Walker (ed.), *Dissing Elizabeth: Negative Representations of Gloriana* (Durham, NC, 1998), 252–76; Walker, *The Elizabeth Icon, 1603–2003* (Basingstoke, 2004); M. Dobson and N. J. Watson, *England's Elizabeth: An Afterlife in Fame and Fantasy* (Oxford, 2002).

[15] A. Lacey, *The Cult of King Charles the Martyr* (Woodbridge, 2003).

ways, the traditional biographical and historical projects continue to obscure.

* * *

The life and *Life* of James II present a revealing case of how a different approach can richly refigure our understanding of the man and monarch. James II is perhaps the best example of an early modern ruler whose life and history have largely been written by his enemies. After he was supplanted in 1688 by William of Orange, Whig polemicists began a determined programme to persuade English subjects that James II was a bigoted Catholic tyrant who had sought to overthrow Protestantism, liberty, and property. Their relentless propaganda campaign, conducted in writing, portraits, medals and engraved cartoons, church services and state rituals, far from suggesting the weakness of James's position and representation, evidences the anxieties of an illegitimate ruler and regime, which remained vulnerable for years after the Revolution.[16] Yet almost ever since 1688 historians have, with few exceptions, favoured Whig polemic over James's self-presentation as a believer in toleration and a custodian of the laws. And while some biographers have shown greater readiness to mute the more vitriolic denunciations, they too have painted James as a failed ruler and flawed man, indeed one who permitted his misguided personal convictions to determine public policy, with disastrous consequences.

There is an irony in the fact that the pens of James's critics and enemies have largely scripted his life and afterlife. For, here unlike his Catholic predecessor Mary Tudor who suffered a similar fate, James II took pains to present and re-present himself to his people: indeed almost uniquely to construct the narrative of his life and to determine his reputation after death. As Duke of York and then king, James, as I shall explore fully elsewhere, showed great concern over his image as a person, as a Stuart and a ruler, in all the media and genres of early modern royal representation: in portraits, on medals and coins, in rituals and ceremonies.[17] Here I concentrate on writing—not least because it is hard to think of another monarch (other than possibly James I) who

---

[16] See e.g. Tony Claydon, *William III and the Godly Revolution* (Cambridge, 1996).
[17] Sharpe, *Representing Rule*, iii (on *Images of Late Seventeenth Century Monarchy*) (forthcoming).

wrote so much at every point of his reign; and because no other ruler
so self-consciously set out to write his own life. As well as numerous
carefully crafted letters, speeches, and declarations (James made frequent
use of these and they deserve careful study), papers of devotion, and
a treatise of advice to his son, James wrote at least nine volumes of
memoirs that were evidently intended, as his latest biographer writes,
as 'a record for future generations of his thoughts, words and deeds'—
that is of the interior as well as public life.[18] Though they were mostly
not published in his lifetime, there are several indications in James's
writings from the earliest that they were intended for circulation and
publication—and probably for contemporary audiences as well as for
'future generations'. A mixture of memoir, history, and autobiography,
James's life writings convey—and were surely meant to communicate—
an image, or rather over half a century of fundamental changes in
personal and public circumstances *images*, of the king. Occasionally
plundered for data, these have yet to receive serious critical attention
as texts and acts of representation, as acts and texts of self-fashioning
and self-publicization rather than as source material.

A problem that immediately arises is that James's 'original' memoirs
have been lost and are believed to have been burned during the French
Revolution by Madame Charpentier, wife of an emissary of the Benedictine Order of Paris, who feared that the volumes would incriminate
her with the republic.[19] However, as with other acts of royal authorship
in early modern England, the simple story of loss is in fact more complicated. In the century or more before their destruction, these memoirs
were seen by a variety of actors (as well as James II and his son) some
of whom claimed to reproduce the king's own original words. Even that
notion is problematic. It appears that from the beginning of keeping a
journal, James used editorial assistants, among them his first wife, Anne
Hyde, daughter of Clarendon, and one 'Dryden', sometimes thought to
be the poet's son Charles but more likely the laureate himself.[20] These

---

[18] J. Callow, *The Making of King James II* (Stroud, 2000), 2.
[19] Callow, *Making*, 1–2; *The Life of James II*, ed. J. S. Clarke, 2 vols. (London, 1816),
i, pp. xvi–xviii.
[20] Callow, *Making*, 306, n. 5; Clarke, *Life*, p. xix; *The Memoirs of James II: His
Campaigns As Duke of York, 1652–1660*, trans. and ed. A. L. Sells (Bloomington, Ind.,
1962), 19; M. Ashley, *James II* (London, 1977), appendix, 296–301; E. Gregg, 'New
Light on The Authorship of The Life of James II', *EHR* 108 (1993), 947–65. Charles

were employed to help to turn notes hastily taken on available scraps of paper, perhaps in the midst of battle or business, into a personal and official narrative or memoir. Even in its 'original' form, then, James's *Life* was co-written by others who—literally—helped to shape it. In 1686, having assumed the throne, it seems that James intended to prepare for publication 'his' memoir and it may have been around that time that his papers began to be arranged and bound with the royal arms in readiness for such a purpose.[21] However, probably on account of the troubles which drove him from his throne soon after, the memoir was not published and probably not completed. Near death in exile James was concerned that his wife, Mary of Modena, write to 'put [his secretary] in mind of his memoirs' and was assured that John Caryll, a court poet and Jacobite conspirator, was 'hard at work about them'.[22] James himself was checking translations and the whereabouts of documents he had entrusted to others but the cherished project remained unfinished. Careful recent examination of new evidence suggests that Caryll, aided by David Nairne, clerk of the foreign office at St Germain, compiled a life based on James's original papers to 1677, which was seen and approved by the king before he died.[23] After his father's death in 1701, his son and heir commissioned a formal life to be prepared, and, perhaps because Caryll was in his mid-seventies, James Francis Edward commissioned one William Dicconson, Queen Mary's Treasurer, to write it.[24] From early in the eighteenth century, therefore, there were perhaps four versions of parts of James's memoirs—that is of his life: the originals which, though many were James's own, were themselves the work of several authors and a mix of notes, disconnected jottings and continuous narrative; the neat copies of some at least made by assistants and especially John Dryden; the hard work done by Caryll, with the assistance of David Nairne, towards an ordered life up to 1677; and Dicconson's Life, likely based on them all but supplemented and turned into a history by use of other records, including public speeches and

Dryden was but 20 and surely not the 'famous poet' referred to by Thomas, brother of Louis Innes (See Sells, *Memoirs*, 19).

[21] In 1686 James checked Dryden's fair copy, Sells, *Memoirs*, 19; on bindings, Clarke, *Life*, p. xvii.

[22] J. Callow, *King in Exile: James II: Warrior, King and Saint* (Stroud, 2004), 372.

[23] Gregg, 'New Light', 951–3.

[24] Sells, *Memoirs*, 28; Callow, *Making*, 306–7, esp. n. 9; Gregg, 'New Light', 954.

declarations of the late king. James's Life, even soon after he was laid in his grave, was a complex, multiple text but it was not always taken as such. We know that the antiquary and biographer of the Duke of Ormonde, Thomas Carte, and possibly the Whig politician Charles James Fox, used James's memoirs up to 1660, or at least a fair copy of them, and Dicconson's Life and evidently felt no need to distinguish them.[25]

The confusion about the manuscripts, that is about the text and meaning of James II's life, was translated into print in 1775. In that year James Macpherson published his *Original Papers Containing The Secret History of Great Britain From The Restoration To The Accession Of The House of Hanover To Which Are Prefixed Extracts From The Life Of James II As Written By Himself*. As his title indicates, Macpherson edited, selected, and folded James's life into a larger political narrative that traced the end of Stuart rule. He may have taken large liberties with the materials he consulted. Macpherson was a figure of dubious repute who had in 1760 fraudulently claimed to discover fragments of epic poetry relating to the legendary Ossian. Understandably therefore, his claims to have used James's original memoirs, in whatever form they were available to him, though they were at the time accepted, have since been treated with scepticism: Winston Churchill, for one, in his life of Marlborough, asserted that Macpherson had used only Dicconson's Life.[26] (Though Churchill's work was itself marred by bias and inaccuracies, on this point subsequent scholarship has supported the charge. Though he was fairly faithful to Nairne and Dicconson, Macpherson, despite his claim, never saw James's original memoirs.) The discredited reputation of their first publisher has undoubtedly discredited the first publication of James's account of himself.

Early in the next century, the text of Dicconson's Life returned to royal hands. During the Napoleonic wars, the Prince Regent, later

---

[25] Sells, *Memoirs*, 19; J. Miller, *James II: A Study in Kingship* (Hove, 1978), 244; Callow, *Making*, 6, 307; Gregg, 'New Light', 955. The notes in Bodleian MS Carte 198 seem to be based entirely on Dicconson's Life; but Carte MSS 180 and 181 contain notes from letters and memoirs in St Germain, including Caryll's correspondence (Carte MS 181, fos. 595–636) and James's devotions (Carte MS 180, fos. 57–87). C. J. Fox, *A History of The Early Part of The Reign of James II* (London, 1808). Since Fox evidently did not begin the work until 1799 (*ODNB*), it would seem unlikely he saw the original memoirs, though he refers to letters. See also Miller, *James II*, appendix, 243–5.

[26] Macpherson, *ODNB*; Miller, *James II*, 244.

George IV, bought from the estate of the Duchess of Albany, a descen-
dant of the Stuarts, a copy of Dicconson's manuscript that had belonged
to the Young Pretender. The Prince Regent commissioned an edition of
the text and appointed as editor the naval chaplain and biographer of
Horatio Nelson, James Clarke.[27] Unlike earlier scholars or users, Clarke
for the first time concentrated on the text itself and endeavoured to
check Dicconson's account and its provenance. When he published,
though he based his Life on Dicconson, Clarke printed marginal references to what he believed from studying the notes of Carte and Fox
were the (now destroyed) 'original' papers. His edition makes clear
the extent to which Dicconson's Life was cobbled together from many
different hands and materials produced for different purposes. But
it cannot finally resolve the uncomfortable question: what exactly of
James's underlines the narrative of his life? How far did he write himself
and how far did others, both authorized by him and not, script him?
To show how difficult it is even to begin to unravel authorship, we
might here note that even the shifting first- and third- person pronouns
which we might be tempted to take as evidence are problematic. For
Thomas Innes himself states that 'in the original memoirs His Majesty
speaks always of himself in the third person' and that it was only in
the 'copy of Mr Dryden he is made to speak in the first person'.[28] All
these uncertainties about authorship and the texts of James's life, as we
shall see, have fostered doubts about his authenticity as a man and his
authority as a king.

It seems likely indeed that problems about the reliability of James's
Life have discouraged historians from using it other than as a record,
to be checked against others, of the king's public actions and the history of the events of the reign. Further careful comparison of Clarke,
Macpherson, Fox, and Carte may yet ameliorate, if not remove, some
of the problems. But even as things stand we may open the texts to
different readings of James's inner life and thoughts and the king's
intended representations of his conscience and his meditations to his
subjects. For James's own actions indicate his intense conviction that his
memoirs—his represented life—were as vital to his authority and person

---

[27] Clarke, *Life*, pp. xxvi–xxvii; Callow, *Making*, 307. This, a second, copy of Dicconson, in 4 vols., once in the possession of, and annotated by, James III is now at
Windsor. Gregg, 'New Light', App.1.

[28] Sells, *Memoirs*, 19.

as his actual life. Twice indeed he risked his life to save his papers. On the first occasion, in 1682, James made good his claim to a friend that 'he would hazard his life' rather than lose his papers when his frigate ran aground off the Norfolk coast and he ensured that the strongbox containing them (we note he had them with him) was secured before he abandoned ship.[29] Then, when at short notice he resolved to flee his kingdom in 1688, 'there was nothing his majesty was more in pain for than to save his papers or memoirs'. Though he had, the account runs, only time to gather loose papers and 'thrust them confusedly' into a box, reunited with them in France, he carefully bound them with the Royal arms—a sign perhaps of a psychological connection as well as proprietal ownership.[30] And several references to the reader in parts we can ascribe to him attest that James had intended the memoirs not merely for himself but for a public audience.[31]

To follow his desire and to present James in his own preferred terms, even if not (or not necessarily) his true colours, would be to fundamentally revise our understanding of this king. But there may be more, too, in the memoirs for us than the king intended to publicize. As we read in the spirit of recent criticism we discern, for example, James's evident boyhood deep trauma during the early stages of civil war, when his captors even denied him his dwarf;[32] his lasting anxiety about republicans and 'sectaries' whom, like many others, he could not always differentiate;[33] his complex relationship with his very different brother and other members of his family;[34] his struggle with sin and faith;[35] and his combination of confidence and insecurity. All deserve a greater prominence in biographies and histories than they have received.

Though the whole of James's life deserves re-examination, in the remainder of this short chapter I want to focus on two periods for which we have accounts, both significantly written in exile, that override some of the textual problems we have encountered and which we can

---

[29] Ashley, *James II*, 143. [30] Clarke, *Life*, ii. 242–3.
[31] Ibid. i. 56, 225, 252. [32] Ibid. 2, 29–39.
[33] Ibid. 390, 395–6, 431, 439, 504, 632, 739; ii. 155; J. Macpherson, *Original Papers, Containing the Secret History of Great Britain from the Restoration to the Accession of the House of Hanover...* (London, 1775), i. 20.
[34] Clarke, *Life*, i. 49, 50, 51, 52, 386, 420, 430, 445, 449, 483, 492, 495, 509, 525, 541, 551, 557–8, 559, 596, 599, 614, 646, 673, 679, 680, 713, 745, 747.
[35] Ibid. 440–1, 452, 483–4, 539, 542, 628, 657, 701, 733.

confidently assign to royal authorship. The first is a military memoir
of James's service in the armies of first France, then Spain, between
1652 and 1660. In 1695, Cardinal Bouillon, meeting with James at
St Germain, asked the king if he would provide him with a record of his
service in the French armies under the command of the Cardinal's uncle,
the Vicomte de Turenne. James replied that he had already written his
memoirs of those experiences and offered to make extracts and have
them translated. On 27 January the next year he delivered the promised
manuscript. Though James had originally thought of translating only
those parts of his own memoirs that concerned Turenne, there was
found in Bouillon's manuscript, which was rediscovered in 1954, a
certificate signed by five members of the Scots College at Paris affirming
that 'these memoirs . . . conform to the original English memoirs written
in His Majesty's own hand'.[36] Since there is no reason to question the
statement, it would seem that they thus provide an authentic account
by James himself, and one we can use to examine language and style as
well as content as authorial decisions.

The Bouillon manuscript, though edited in 1962, has not been
used as a text of James's self-representation, perhaps because campaign
memoirs seemed to promise few insights into James's person or royal
image. In fact, the memoirs which almost certainly form the first volume
of James's life writing project reveal much about both the prince and
how he sought to present himself to other rulers and to the subjects
of the English Commonwealth from which he had escaped into exile.
Moreover, since comparison of the Bouillon manuscript with Dicconson's Life reveals no major discrepancies, we might conclude that
much later, in 1695, James was willing to endorse this youthful account
as a record he was ready to prepare for publication. For though in
1696 James urged, out of respect to Turenne, that the memoirs not
be published until after his death, all the signs of a publication intended
and imminent are scattered through the relation.[37] James deploys the
techniques of storytelling and offers tragic scenes of fraternal duels,
graphic descriptions of battles and casualties, and thumbnail sketches
of the leading characters to enliven the story.[38] Throughout phrases
such as 'before I proceed further', 'I remember an odd incident', or 'I

---

[36] Sells, *Memoirs*, 15–16, 52, 54.   [37] Ibid. 15, 19, 30–1.
[38] Ibid. 91–2, 94, 95–6, 97, 107, 138, 160, 189–90, 219–20, 248–51, 269–70, 282.

shall say more in its proper place' indicate a carefully planned narrative devised to hold the reader's attention.[39] Specific references and guides to the 'reader' leave no doubt that James wrote with a broad audience in mind.[40] It appears that at one point he intended to insert a sketch to more clearly demonstrate the movements of troops.[41]

James's war memoirs are, as well as the record of a soldier, the text of a prince, the son of a king. We must recall that in France, James was enlisted in the royal army of a king who was fighting a war against rebel Frondeurs in which the monarchy was threatened, just as it had been recently destroyed in England. Though, therefore, his relation dwells, with little emotion, on military casualties and prisoners, sieges and tactics, deeds of daring and cowardice, it is also a political memoir of a prince who suspected that he would have to fight for Stuart rights. James's contempt for rebels is not disguised. While he showed a soldier's respect for enemies who fought for their country, those who rose against their anointed monarch deserved only odium: it was, he doubted not, the hand of God that slayed more Frondeurs than loyalists in battle.[42] When James depicts his commander as the hero who saved the French crown, we cannot but hear how the prince too dreamed that he might emulate the Turenne who 'acquired immortal fame through saving the monarchy by his counsel, his conduct and his valour'.[43] Turenne's service, of course, lay most in his military brilliance. But in James's memoir, Turenne's army is figured as a little commonwealth and the commander's role is seen as not dissimilar to that of a prince. Division and disobedience, James discerned, were the principal threats to success, which usually followed on resolute courses.[44] Turenne, however, is also presented as understanding his duty always 'to consider but the public good'; to care for his men; and, while being ready to take decisions and responsibility, to heed counsel.[45] James made special note of his commander's 'familiar conversation with several officers' whereby 'the General does not only instruct them much better ... but is ready ... to answer any of their objections and to clear any doubt that may arise'.[46] Effective leadership, care for charges, taking counsel and an ability to persuade by explaining courses, were, of course, the qualities of a good

[39] Ibid. 143, 152, 193; cf. 206, 234, 279.   [40] Ibid. 184, 206.
[41] Ibid. 195.   [42] Ibid. 59, 96.   [43] Ibid. 127.   [44] Ibid. 70, 86.
[45] Ibid. 142, 151, 168.   [46] Ibid. 171.

king as well as captain. James makes clear his pride in serving such a master and cause and draws attention to his own royal status which, unlike the English rebels, even enemies respected.[47] In these military memoirs, James represents himself as a great warrior and a virtuous prince: one who, though he now fought to save a Bourbon king, was qualified by experience and character to champion the Stuart cause.

England and the fate of his royal brother, Charles II, to whom Turenne was to offer military aid, are not ostensibly the main subject of these memoirs. But in the 1650s—and again in the 1680s and 90s when they were edited and translated—their advocacy of determined leadership and resolution with consideration represented James, as he wished to be seen, as a prince fit for rule. Indeed the repetition in the Life for the period after 1660 of the need for bravery and resolution in dealing with rebels hints that not only did James regard military leadership and the conduct of rule as similar skills but that he often felt that he would make a better king than his brother to whom he nevertheless declared an unerring loyalty and obedience.[48]

The second text I want to examine briefly was written after James had lost his throne: was written, that is, in very different circumstances and, though incorporated into the Life, is of a very different genre of writing to either military relation or narrative memoir. Like the military memoir, however, we can be confident that James's devotional papers, written in exile in St Germain, are his own words. For in this case, though the papers also form part of Dicconson's Life, the manuscript escaped the destruction of the French Revolution. Preserved by James's grandson, Cardinal Henry Stuart, the papers were purchased in 1842 by a priest from Drogheda and were edited for the Roxburgh Club by the Stuart historian Godfrey Davies in 1925.[49] The largely holograph manuscript, a raw mix of reflections, prayers, and meditations, contains blank pages and unfinished sentences as well as full, even eloquent, passages.[50] Even though authentic, the bound volume is not without problems: there is some indication of another's involvement

[47] Sells, *Memoirs*, 149, 157.

[48] Ibid. 63, 100, 151; Clarke, *Life*, i. 32, 47, 420, 483, 525, 541, 551, 555, 558, 560, 563, 594, 599, 614, 633, 646, 673, 680, 713, 733; ii. 157.

[49] Callow, *Making*, 311; *Papers of Devotion of James II*, ed. G. Davies (Roxburgh Club, Oxford, 1925).

[50] Davies, *Devotions*, 26, 96.

and a smaller volume appears to have been broken up and inserted into a larger.[51] But James's Devotions, as well as helping to 'unravel the psychological enigma presented by his character', present us with the opportunity to observe James in the act of composing his life as, by the 1690s, he wished to recall, construct, and represent it; and of preparing for death, the afterlife and the judgement of memory.[52] Again, though it is unfinished and repetitive, passages such as 'I would say if I had more time' suggest that it was conceived and written for an audience, while the address to converts indicates planned publication.[53] It seems that it was by his Devotions that James wished his person and his kingship to be finally remembered.

The life past, present, and after death are the subjects of these meditations. James, the military man of youth, makes his reappearance as he records: 'I came from seeing the camp at Compiegne, a sight that was more worth seeing than any of that kind of our age.' Now, however, the commander gives way to the devout Christian who quickly moves to 'the melancholy reflection how very few amongst this great and formidable army thinks of his duty to the king of kings'.[54] James the monarch is also very present on the page of the Devotions. He writes of the duty owed to king and country; he presents himself as chosen by God to rule; he thanks God for restoring Stuart kingship and for protecting him to inherit the title; he prays that his son will succeed.[55] But kingship now takes second place to salvation and James comes close to the belief that only the loss of his kingdoms secured his eternal life by awakening him 'out of the lethargy of sin'.[56] The providence that had so often protected him from the enemy bullet and the rebel's plot now gave him the chance for a heavenly triumph and crown. James explains his conversion and faith in Catholic doctrine and liturgy. In these papers we virtually eavesdrop on a pious Christian as he prays and confesses to God, takes the sacrament, reads devotional works, meditates, and fasts. He repeats his admiration for the simple piety of the monks of La Trappe to which he retreated annually from 'the vanity of . . . worldly greatness'.[57]

---

[51] Pages 168–70 are not in James's hand. See also Davies, *Devotions*, Appendix II at end, n.p.

[52] Ibid., p. xxiv.   [53] Ibid. 3, 27.   [54] Ibid. 53.

[55] Ibid. 14, 54, 62, 90, 107, 126.   [56] Ibid. 62.   [57] Ibid. 63, 67–8.

The intensely pious and personal nature of these devotions, however, should not lead us, as they did their editor, to conclude that James in exile retreated from public presentation to private meditation. The purpose in writing is avowedly public: 'my chief design of writing this paper is to give some advice to new converts.'[58] As his grandfather had written exegeses of scripture, so James II wrote an instructional manual for the Catholic life. As his self-instruction becomes an example to others of the way to salvation, the devotions, we see, figure this exiled king as a priest.

As well as general, the spiritual advice is also specifically addressed to his children and in particular his son and heir, the claimant to the British thrones of William III. James instructs his son to avoid pleasure, to repair his faults and find God while young so as to be a good Catholic and fit ruler of three kingdoms—which he is certain he will be. For, he counsels him, while the fate of princes lay with God, it was right for his son to 'make use of all lawful means to preserve what one has or to recover what has unjustly been taken from me'.[59] As that last sentence implies, James's devotions are not a text of resignation or defeat. Though he admired monks, he was not persuaded 'to think one may not work out his salvation in the world'.[60] James prepared his son to work out his salvation as a prince and a king. For himself he hoped by a good death and advertisement of faith to advance his son's cause and to have the prospect of joining the ranks of those kings who were regarded as saints—as, of course, his father already was.[61]

Indeed reading James's Devotions, first published in 1704 as *The Pious Sentiments of The Late King James II of Blessed Memory*, we cannot but be reminded of, as we are surely meant to recall, the *Eikon Basilike* of Charles I, written on the very eve of a martyr's death. Like the *Eikon*, James's devotions are silent on most of the matters that alarmed his subjects; the account of things is very much one from the king's perspective; and defeat is re-presented as a magnificent personal and godly triumph which deprives enemies of their more mundane victory on the battlefield. In 1692, as James was writing his devotions, an edition of the *Eikon Basilike* was republished, leading to a flurry of pamphlets disputing its authorship—a sign of its continued and

---

[58] Davies, *Devotions*, 3.   [59] Ibid. 92.
[60] Ibid. 111.   [61] Ibid. 83, 89.

immediate potency.[62] The same year, *Imago Regis: Or The Sacred Image of His Majesty Written During His Retirement in France* appropriated the *Eikon* to present James as also a Christian martyr, the frontispiece engraving depicting him as a patient bearer of affliction meditating on a heavenly crown, with an earthly crown on a cushion by his side. The volume, which reproduces several of James's speeches and writings, bears on its title page a quotation from Psalm 132: 'O remember David in all his afflictions.' In his Devotions, James similarly wrote and represented himself as another David, another holy martyr and saint whose afterlife, like that of his father, might perform as a powerful political as well as devotional text—to advance the Stuarts' cause.

Whether in military memoirs written during the English republic or devotions penned in exile from his throne, James wrote to represent himself as a devout Christian, equipped by virtue, experience, and piety for the throne to which God had called the Stuarts. Even with all the difficulties surrounding their authorship, we may read them as texts of a royal person, private and public, and as a polemic for self, dynasty, and regal sovereignty. Indeed, even though the genres of military memoir and devotion appear not to suggest polemic, we must read them as artfully crafted principally to construct and underpin identity and authority. It would seem that at each stage of his life James was concerned to represent his life as a text—of different genres, changing narratives, private reflections, and public decrees and actions. In his own way, he represented his martial body (as had Henry VIII and Prince Henry) and his conscience (as had James I and Charles I) to his subjects whose real affection for him is often reiterated and apparently genuinely not doubted.

Scholars have regretted that James's life is not a complete, authoritative, and original text written throughout by the king himself. Because it is the work of imported texts, diverse hands, different genres, variant forms, and shifting pronouns they have made only the most cautious and limited use of it. In consequence they have neglected not only a prime text of an early modern monarch, his inner thoughts and faith (at least as he chose to present them) and his hopes and fears, they have

---

[62] See Lacey, *Cult of King Charles*, ch. 6; L. Knoppers, 'Reviving the Martyr: Charles I as Jacobite Icon', in T. Corns (ed.), *The Royal Image: Representations of Charles I* (Cambridge, 1999), 263–87.

failed to engage with a king who strove—though history has deemed he failed—to construct and control his representation, image, and memory. More than any other early modern monarch, James rendered his life as text. Far more than the conventional biography, a full critical examination of the texts and tropes of James's Life, and a reconsideration of his life as texts, promises a different life and history—one which may further our understanding not only of the man and monarch but of Whig and Tory polemic; and even explain why, still in the 1790s, the texts of James's life were seen to exercise such a dangerous influence.

PART V

SPIRITUAL SELVES

12

'This girl hath a spirit averse from Calvin': Reading the Life, Hearing the Voice(s)

Annabel Patterson

This chapter offers a study of a very special case of life writing. The subject of the biography, Elizabeth Carey, Lady Falkland (1585–1639) was, obviously, a woman. Second, she was one of the more notorious instances of an aristocratic woman who converted to Roman Catholicism during the reign of Charles I, so that her Life is an instance also of Catholic biography, which has its roots in hagiography. Third, she was a scholar and linguist, with something of a reputation in Europe. And last, her Life was written, as the title of the original manuscript declares, 'by one of her daughters', whose attitude to her mother was far from detached. To add to all these peculiarities, the daughter did not begin writing the biography until her mother's adventures were over, and many of them she could not have witnessed, so that the work must be in large part oral autobiography, a very special case indeed. The daughter can only have learned what happened to her mother from her mother.

If you were a seventeenth-century English woman, you had about as much chance as a highwayman[1] of having your life written by a contemporary, and published in the same century. Unless, of course, you had been a queen. Beyond heads of state, the category of persons who most frequently became the subject of lives were men of the Protestant church: Beza wrote a life of Calvin, which was published in English in 1564, shortly after Calvin's death. A life of Archbishop John Whitgift

---

[1] *The Life of Deval*, a notorious highwayman, was published in 1669.

appeared in 1612, written by the comptroller of his household, Sir George Paule. Izaak Walton wrote and published the lives of John Donne (1640), George Herbert (1651), Richard Hooker (1655), and Bishop Robert Sanderson (1670). George Carleton, himself Bishop of Chichester, wrote a life of Bernard Gilpin, his old schoolteacher, who had preached before Edward VI; the Life was published the year after Carleton himself died, in 1629. Thomas Morton, Bishop of Durham, who died in 1659, received the tribute of two prompt biographies, J. Barwick's *The Life and Death of Thomas lord bishop of Duresme* (1660), and another version by Richard Baddeley, the bishop's secretary, completed by J. Naylor, his chaplain, in 1669. Pushing the boundary of the century, Ambrose Philips published a life of John Williams, Bishop of London, in 1700.

In the meantime, Catholic life writing languished in the political shadows. Nicholas Harpsfield's life of Sir Thomas More was completed by 1555, but his hopes for its publication expired with the Catholic queen, Mary Tudor. It was not in fact published until 1932, when it was found and edited by Elsie Vaughan Hitchcock.[2] The much better-known and shorter personal memoir of More by his son-in-law William Roper was also written during Mary's reign, and initially intended to be raw material for Harpsfield's biography. Roper's Life was eventually the beneficiary of the marriage of Charles I to a Catholic queen, which caused a brief thaw in the climate for Catholic publications, and it appeared in 1628 as *The mirrour of vertue*. Richard Smith, Catholic Bishop of Chalcedon, had written his Latin version *Life of the most honourable and vertuous lady the la. Magdalen Viscountesse Montague* in 1609, the year of her death, but the English translation by Cuthbert Fursdon had to come by way of the press of the English college at St Omer, and did not appear until 1627. Sir Tobie Matthew's Life of Lady Lucy Knatchbull, though prepared for publication in 1651, never made it into print until D. D. Knowles found the original manuscript and edited it in 1931. Both these Lives of Catholic women, written by men, could make striking comparison with the Life of Elizabeth Cary, if that were our project. But it, too, suffered from unfortunate timing. Though half of her career unrolled during Henrietta Maria's reign and

---

[2] *The Life and Death of St Thomas More*, ed. Elsie Vaughan Hitchcock (London, 1932; repr. 1962).

to some extent under her auspices, Elizabeth Cary died at a very inauspicious moment for Catholic biography as such. She died just at the beginning of the English revolution. Her biography was a family project as well as a Catholic one, undertaken by one of her four daughters who had all entered the English Benedictine monastery at Cambrai in 1638 and 1639. The Life was written in 1645, but not bound until 1650, with Patrick Carey, Elizabeth's son, adding emendations *c*.1649. Perhaps he intended to have it published at some more auspicious moment, but Patrick himself died *c*.1656, too soon for the Restoration, and the Life remained unpublished until 1861, when Richard Simpson, a Catholic scholar, discovered it and published it in two issues of *The Rambler*.[3]

Elizabeth Cary became briefly famous for modern readers as the author of an original and published play, *The Tragedy of Mariam*, based on the account in Josephus of Herod the Great's troubled marriage to Mariam, a woman of royal Jewish blood. The play was rediscovered and promoted by two modern scholars, Barry Weller and Margaret Ferguson, who edited it and attached to it, for contextual purposes, the *Life of Elizabeth* as published by Simpson. Weller and Ferguson thought that for most readers the Life would only be ancillary to Mariam. In my view, however, the text of the Life is itself the prize. Elizabeth's biographer does not mention Mariam at all,[4] though she does present her mother, intermittently, as scholar, writer, translator, and poet. And the story she tells is a richly layered contribution to the genre of early biography, since it shows the conflicted experience of the learned woman in the culture of her time, made more conflicted by her independent and defiant choice of the de-authorized religion. The tensions in her real life, between her role as a wife and mother and her yearnings to be a scholar, between the pressures of Protestant aristocratic society and the allure of the shadowy Catholic presence within it—a presence which included ideas of persecution and asceticism—these tensions, I suggest, produced a Life that is radically incoherent at the level of what we would call genre. Genre is a literary concept which would not normally apply to biography; but here is an instance in which we can see, I think, where

[3] *The Lady Falkland: Her Life*, ed. Richard Simpson (London, 1861). Simpson supplies an Appendix with important letters by and about Cary, and information, some of it speculative, about what really motivated her father to disinherit her.

[4] Unless as an unnamed poem that was stolen and published against her will. See n. 9 below.

fiction comes from. Life does not imitate fiction, it provides fiction with its most powerful models and choices. The primary genre in the Life is the secular travel romance with a female heroine; but it competes, and indeed alternates, with more conventional hagiographical motifs (the deathbed vision), domestic comedy (forbidden reading in bed, food shortages), and the drier but unifying story of self-education and a scholarly career—a feminist *Bildungsroman.*

Because the Life is written, evidently, by someone unused both to writing and to narrative, it is also a textual nightmare. When Weller and Ferguson produced their edition, they naturally wished to provide a text that would be useful to modern readers. Their textual practice, however, was no more scientific than that of the Life's nineteenth-century editor, and it has subsequently been criticized by Heather Wolfe, who produced a diplomatic edition by returning, as Weller and Ferguson did not, to the original manuscript,[5] now in the Archives of the Département du Nord in Lille.[6] The contextual information in Wolfe's edition is crucial to our understanding of the Life, yet her text is unreadable for all but the most scholarly purposes. My solution has been to cite from the Wolfe edition, which retains the original spelling, but not to record the many superscript additions and deletions unless they seem of substance.

I have also provisionally adopted Wolfe's thesis that the actual writer of the Life was Lucy, the daughter who died in 1650, the year when the manuscript was bound, and who was also, according to Wolfe, the daughter whose profile best matches the attitude of the biographer, which comes across in often quite sharp criticisms of her mother. Some of the evidence for this will appear below. But I do not accept the other part of Wolfe's thesis, that, while the primary motive for writing the Life was in accordance with the devotional practice of the Cambrai monastery, there was also a penitential aspect to Lucy's work, as she tried to make up for her earlier unkindnesses. What Lucy wrote was, by and large, a realistic, anti-hagiographical life; there is something inconsistent between that result and the motive of filial penance; and since we cannot be sure who scored out some of the most reproachful or sardonic passages, it is more likely that Lucy's bent as a biographer was,

---

[5] *Elizabeth Cary Lady Falkland: Life and Letters,* ed. Heather Wolfe, Renaissance Texts from Manuscript (Cambridge, 2001).

[6] AND, MS xx. c. 1655.

shall we say, more modern, less pious, than that of her sister Anne and her brother Patrick, who can both be shown to have intervened.

Here is an outline of Elizabeth's remarkable life. Born before the Armada, the only child of Lawrence Tanfield, who was later knighted, Elizabeth might have been a significant figure of the Jacobean and Caroline court. As a child she showed prodigious intelligence and scholarly application. But she was married off to Henry Cary, who was initially interested only in her fortune, in 1602, when she was 15. Between 1609 and 1625 she had eleven children. After the second and the fourth she had a serious encounter with depression. In 1622, her husband, who had become Viscount Falkland, was sent to Ireland as James's Deputy, and three years later she left her husband in Ireland, and on returning to London made a public conversion to Catholicism. Thereafter she was disinherited by her father, discarded by her husband, plagued by poverty, and engaged in a constant but indirect struggle to have her children brought up in her own religion. In 1630 she published a translation of Cardinal Perron's reply to James I[7] in the long polemical struggle initiated by the Oath of Allegiance, and boldly dedicated it to Queen Henrietta Maria. All but a dozen copies of the impression were burned when they arrived from France, on the orders of Archbishop Abbott. After her general disgrace, and her continued separation from her husband, who tried to divorce her, she continued her scholarship, contributing to the genre of hagiography that her own biographer eschewed, writing several lives of female saints, some of them in verse.

The Life is not an easy read. By our standards it is badly written. Often it gets tangled up in very long sentences clogged with parentheses, ironically because the author struggles for precision. On the other hand the simplicity of vocabulary and dramatically reported dialogue, suggesting oral transmission, have the sound of authenticity. It is partly

---

[7] *The Reply of the most illustrious Cardinall of Perron, to the answeare of the most excellent King of Great Britaine* (Douay, 1630). Cary's personal copy of this translation, of which almost all copies were suppressed, is now in the Beinecke Library at Yale. It contains four lines of verse in her hand under the portrait of the author, a sonnet to Queen Henrietta Maria, also in Cary's hand, on a blank leaf, and some extremely careful corrections and additions. It is perhaps the presentation copy to the queen. Another copy, with identical corrections, less carefully performed, is at Harvard. These texts witness to the great importance Carey attached to her translation, as well as her hope that Henrietta Maria had created a new environment for Catholic publications. In the event, she was disappointed.

on that sound, the sound of the human voice still speaking to us over all these years, on which I shall focus.

So here are some of the things that Elizabeth must have told her daughter, and her daughter must have believed were important:

She learnt to read very soone and loved it much. when she was but fower or five yeare old they put her to learn french, which she did about five weekes, and, not proffitting att all, gave it over. after, of herself, without a teacher, whilest she was a child, she learnt french, spanish, Itallian, which she always understood very perfectly, she learnt Latin in the same maner (without being taught) and understood it perfectly when she was young, and translated the Epistles of Seneca out of it into English. . . . Hebrew, she likewise, about the same time, learnt with very little teaching; but for many yeare neglecting it, she lost it much; yet not long before her death, she againe beginning to use it, could in the Bible understand well, in which she was most perfectly well redd. (p. 106)

This paragraph tells us both that Elizabeth was a prodigy, and that she was extremely proud of this fact. She passed on to her daughter both the facts, unlikely as they seem, and the pride. You can see the child and the middle-aged woman joined, as it were, by the same linguistic ambitions, though the older speaker admits her limitations: 'for many yeare neglecting [her Hebrew], she lost it much'.

[She] having nether brother nor sister, nor other companion of her age, spent her whole time in reading, to which she gave herself so much that she frequently redd all night; so as her mother was faine to forbid her servants to lett her have candles, which command they turnned to thier owne profitt, and lett themselves be hired by her to lett her have them, selling them to her at half a crowne[8] apeece, so was she bent to reading; and she not having mony so free, was to owe it to them, and in this fashion was she in debt a hundred pound afore she was twelfe yeare old, which with two hundred more for the like bargaines and promises she payd on her wedding day; this will not seeme strange to those that knew her well. (p. 108)

Here, already, 'afore she was twelve yeare old', prodigious intellect runs smack into financial difficulties, not to say improvidence, a theme that the Life will mention frequently. But here the most interesting sentence, from a theoretical perspective, is the last: 'this will not seeme strange

---

[8] 'Halfe a crowne': an exorbitant price for candles. Her servants were blackmailing her.

to those that knew her well.' Is this Elizabeth reflecting on her own character, or is it her daughter looking back with amusement and reproof?

> when she was twelfe yeare old, her father (who loved much to have her read, and she as much to please him) gave her Calvins Institutions, and bid her read it, against which she made so many objections, and found in him so many contradictions, and with all of them she still went to her father, that he sayd, this girle hath a spirit averse from Calvin. (p. 108)

The formal sign of quotation, 'he sayd', alerts us here to the presence of another voice. Lawrence Tanfield, after many arguments with his young prodigy, can clearly be heard saying (to someone else in the room) 'this girle hath a spirit averse from Calvin'. Although we cannot be sure of his tone—was it pride or exasperation?—the remark must come to us via Elizabeth, who passed it on to her daughter.

We then learn of her early marriage, the fact that Cary 'maried her only for being an heire, for he had no acquaintance with her (she scarce ever have spoke to him) and she was nothing handsome though then very faire (i.e. blonde)'. Her new husband promptly left for Holland, she remaining in her family home, and their only communication for a while was by letters written on her behalf by others, though he thought she had written them. She then began to write to him herself, and these letters, being in a different style, he assumed were written by others, and he preferred them, but having examined her about it and 'found the contrayry, he grew better acquainted with her and esteemed her more' (p. 110). Here are the seeds of a companionate marriage, but we hear almost nothing more of this kind until her husband's death.

> From this time she writ many thinges for her private recreation, on severall subjects, and occasions, all in verse (out of which she scarce ever writ any thinge that was not translations). one of them was after stolen out of that sister inlaws (her frinds) chamber, and printed,[9] but by her owne procurement was called in. of all that she then writ, that which was sayd to be the best, was, the life of Tamburlaine in verse. (p. 110)

Now this is a surprise. Like almost all the other works of Cary mentioned in the Life, there is now no trace of this poem, but if we could find it, it would certainly complicate our view of her character.

---

[9] This was presumably *The Tragedie of Mariam* (London, 1613).

She continue to read much, and when she was about twenty yeare old, through
reading, she grew into much doubt about her religion. the first occasion of it,
was reading a protestant booke much esteemed, called Hookers Ecclesiasticall
Politie. it seemed to her, he left her hanging in the aire, for having brought her
so farre (which she thought he did very reasonably) she saw not how, nor att
what, she could stop, till she returned to the church from whence they were
come. (pp. 110–11)

In other words, Hooker's hyper-rational arguments against further
reform of the English Church led her to the logical conclusion that
Protestantism was itself an unwarranted breach with established order
and custom, those norms that Hooker invoked.

   At this point an ironic development occurs in the family. Her husband's brother (a marginal note tells us this was Adulphus), returned
from Italy 'with a good opinion of the catholick religion', Elizabeth
is suddenly involved in religious debate. Adulphus 'was a great reader
of the fathers, especially St. Augustin, whom he affirmed to be of the
religion of the Church of Rome. he persawed her to read the fathers
allso.' Her distrust of the religion into which she had been born so
increased by reading the Fathers, that twice 'she refused to goe to church
for a long while together'. This behaviour technically made her a recu-
sant. The first period of recusancy ended when she persuaded herself
that she could continue as a Protestant. The second time, beginning to
frequent the house of the Bishop of Durham, Richard Neile, she came
into contact with several learned divines, and acquired a great respect
for them. 'By them she was perswaded she might lawfully remaine as she
was' (that is, as a merely formal Protestant), 'she never making question
but for all that . . . to be in the Roman Church were infinitly better and
securer' (pp. 111–12). In this unsatisfactory state of mind she remained
for about twenty-two years.

   The Life then switches sharply to domestic issues.

She was maried seven yeare without any child, after, had eleven borne alive;
when she had some children, she and her husband went to keepe house by
themselves, where she, taking the care of her family, which att first was but little,
did seeme to shew herself capable of what she would apply herself to . . . nor
was her care of her children lesse, to whom she was so much a mother, that
she nursed them all herself, but only her eldest sonne (whom her father tooke
from her to live with him from his birth) and she taught 3 or 4 of the eldest.
(pp. 112–13)

Thus breast-feeding and home-schooling her children came to compete, heavily we must assume, with her own intellectual ambitions.

Her first care was...to have [her children] soone inclined to the knowledge, love, and esteeme, of all morall vertue; and to have them according to their capacitys instructed in the principles of christianity, not in maner of a catichisme, (which would have instructed them in the particular protestant doctrines, of the truth of which she was little satisfied) but in a maner more apt to make an impression in them (then things learnt by roat and not understood) as letting them know, when they loved any thinge, that they were to love God more then it. (p. 113)

Given this massive commitment to maternity, it is perhaps not surprising that what follows is an account of her two periods of depression:

In this time she had some occasions of trowble, which afflicted her so much, as twice to putt her into so deepe malancholy [(while she was with child of her 2d and 4th child) that she lost the perfect use of her reason] and was in much danger of her life; [she had ground for the begining of her apprehensions, but she giving full way to them (which were allways apt to goe as farre as she would lett them) they arrived so farre as to be plaine distractednesse; it is like she att first gave the more way to it, att those times, thinking her husband would then be most sensible of her trowble, knowing he was extraordinary carefull of her when she was with child or gave sucke as being a most tenderly loving father.] (p. 118)

We know now about post-partum depression; but this passage is extraordinarily interesting for its diagnosis, not of the depression, but the character. Elizabeth is remembered here as 'giving full way' to her dark feelings, especially when pregnant or nursing, because she believes her husband will be more sympathetic at those times. Diagnosis by whom? The phrase 'it is like' identifies the voice as that of Lucy, rather than Elizabeth herself; and this, if so, means that the subtle observation that her feelings were 'allways apt to goe as farre as she would let them' is also Lucy's, the 'allways' being the most critical term, and decidedly ironic, at least from this distance. Complicating the story of life writing considerably, however, is the fact that the passages between square brackets which are the most critical of Elizabeth were heavily scored out in the original manuscript.

But religious doubts continued. She 'bore a great and high reverence to our Blessed Lady, to whom, being with child of her last daughter (and still a protestant) she offred up that child, promising if it were a girle it should (in devotion to her) beare her name, and that as much as was in her power, she would indeavour to have it be a Nunne' (p. 119). Mary Cary, born in 1621, was indeed so named, though the Life has a late and confusing account of why Elizabeth did not herself carry through on this vow until Mary herself requested it. At this early point in Elizabeth's story, her husband was sent to Ireland as Deputy, and his wife accompanied him with all her children except her eldest daughter Catherine, who had recently married 'into Scotland'. In Ireland, Elizabeth attempted to make sense of this unfamiliar environment. 'She there learnt to read Irish in an Irish Bible; but it being very hard (so as she could scarce find one that could teach it) and few bookes in it she quickly lost what she had learnt' (p. 119). This would have been the New Testament, translated into Gaelic by William Daniel in 1602. And the next section of the Life describes her efforts to set up a workhouse to train Irish beggar children in useful trades; its failure; and her financial losses by fire and flood, 'all which when she was a Catholic she took to be the punishment of God for the children's going to church' (p. 121). But the biographer suggests instead that she had no head for business, a bad memory, no stability of purpose, and a tendency to be an easy mark for cheats. We are not told whether it was these failures that made her determine to leave Ireland after three years, and return to London, a decision which would have momentous results. But we have already learned that when Elizabeth made up her mind to do something, nothing would stand in her way.

The Life now takes on the strenuous and implausible tone of a romance, or of a certain kind of saint's life, beginning with the generic marker of a storm at sea:

By a violent tempest att sea they were once driven backe, being in great danger to be cast away, the child at her breast (she sitting upon the hatches) had his breath struck out of his body by a wave, and remained as dead a quarter of an hower. After arriving safe, and having first kissed her Majestys hands, (who was not long before come into England), she retired to her mothers for fear of the plague (then very hott), carrying with her (besids the rest) her maried daughter, great with child; who in the journy, being carryed over a narrow bridge by a gentleman of her mothers (who out of particular care desired to carry her) his foot slipping, fell into the watter; but he in the fall (taking only care of her) cast himself so along in the watter that she fell upright with her feet on his breast; and she seeing them all trowbled for feare of her, and he especially (who had long served her father and mother) much afflicted att it, she would not acknowledge feeling any hurt nor being frightened, but att the end of her journy the same night fell sike, and within a weeke died, being first deliverd, almost three mounths afore her time, of a daughter, which lived three howers and was christened. had it lived, the mother [Elizabeth] was resolved, to have nursed her daughters child together with her owne, not yet weaned. her daughter died in her armes. (pp. 125–6)

The drama of this narrative should not so much be regarded with suspicion as interrogated as to its source. The date was 1625. Lucy, if she were the biographer, would have been present, but only at the age of 4. So the tone, as well as the facts, must be entirely attributable to Elizabeth herself, narrating this great tale to her children in later life. After all the violence, and the complexity and delicacy of the daughter's hiding of her trauma from the family and the gentleman whose accident had caused it, the last sentence is affecting in its simplicity. I believe we can hear Elizabeth saying, in the first person: 'My daughter died in my arms.'

If so, then we also have to detect Elizabeth's voice in what follows, where again there is a generic shift, accompanied by an almost impenetrable syntax, as we are led through the deathbed scene. Here we see most clearly the peculiar effect of writing a Life almost completely without proper names, so that the referent of the female personal pronouns is often at least momentarily in doubt:

She never gave much way to greefe in any such occasion, and did heer comfort herself the more, through her daughters affirming (being perfectly awake, as they thought, and as perfectly in her sences, for all they could perceave) that there stood by her bed a bright woman cloathed in white having a crowne on her head; which she then assuredly beleeved to be our Blessed Lady, and persawded her daughter the same; but yet a litle after, dying, she often repeated with a sadd lamentable mournfull voice, Wo is me, is there no remedy; which her mother (not judging to be only the apprehension of death, she having shewed herself all the time (and when she was most in danger) much more desirous of, and carefull for, the preservation of her childs life then her owne) did persawd herself was some sight she had of what she was to suffer (as she hoped) in purgatory; (which, with all other points of catholike religion, she then believed), both which opinions she did continue to hope to be true after she was a catholike; out of the consideration of the good inclination her daughter had for Catholike religion for as much as she knew of it; which she had receaved from her, whom only she had heard speake for it, but many against it, living amongst most earnest scotch puritans. (pp. 126–7)

To translate: the daughter has a deathbed vision, which her mother persuades her is of the Virgin Mary, but the daughter remains in great distress. The mother interprets the distress not as fear of death (of which the daughter had previously shown no sign), but anticipation of purgatory. The mother is pleased by this interpretation, because it shows her daughter has absorbed her own positive views of Catholicism, despite the time she has spend 'living amongst most earnest scotch puritans'. But what of the phrase 'what she was to suffer (as she hoped) in purgatory'? Whose hope is this? The mother's, on behalf of the daughter? And the opening statement, 'She never gave much way to greefe in any such occasion', more likely signals Lucy's irony about her mother's character than her mother's assessment of herself as a stoic. The task of elucidation is complicated not only by these matters of syntax, but by the bibliographical fact, as Wolfe has shown, that this whole scene was an addition to the manuscript, tipped in before binding (p. 81). Wolfe reads this afterthought as proof that Lucy wished not only to reveal that her older sister had Catholic inclinations before her death, but that her vision 'provided for Lucy . . . a moment of providential intervention' (p. 82). But the simple piety of this construction of motive does not quite, in my opinion, square with the psychological muddle and slightly manic quality of the scene we have inherited.

Now comes the confessional showdown. You will remember that the first thing Elizabeth did on arriving in London was to kiss the hand of Henrietta Maria, a strategic gesture of female (and potentially Catholic) loyalty. That she saw the queen as a possible patron anticipates her dedication to her, five years later, of Cardinal Perron's Reply. But for the moment Elizabeth remained in a state of confessional compromise. Returning to London, she entered the circle of Bishop Neile, and spent much time with the Arminian divines. Believing these men to be in reality 'priests', i.e. closet Catholics, 'she resolved to goe to confession to one of them, making choice for the purpose of one of the Kings chaplaines (who had bene one of his Bishops)'. This person is identified in a marginal note in the manuscript as 'Doctor Cousens', that is, John Cosin (1594–1672), a protégé of Bishop Neile, and himself Bishop of

Durham. In 1627 Cosin would publish a devotional book, *Collection of Private Devotions*, which maintained that there were once again seven sacraments—of which, of course, confession was one. For this he was heavily criticized in the 1628 Parliament. Elizabeth's choice of a would-be confessor was therefore shrewd; but Cosin temporized. He 'excused himself att the present, as not being used to take confessions, but that, he would take time to prepare himself for it by studying casuists, being to goe into the country (or going a purpose) for half a yeare'. This lost him the opportunity of retaining her in the church, and caused him extreme embarrassment. For, the biographer continues, 'before his returne she had (God be thanked) made a confession somewhat more to the purpose' (p. 128).

Elizabeth's next step was to enter the circle of Walter Butler (1569–1633), eleventh Earl of Ormonde, whose devotion to the Roman religion had earned him the nickname of Walter of the Beads and Rosary. Having been incarcerated in the Tower as a result of a legal struggle over the ownership of his lands, he was in 1625 released, but only into complete poverty, and had to depend on charity for his subsistence and to pay his prison fees. His household, then, was a rich source of Catholic contacts, as well, we might infer, of the ideal of suffering for the old faith. At Ormonde's, Elizabeth met various Catholic priests, 'mr Coshet a Scotch Minum', that is a friar belonging to the mendicant order founded by St Francis of Paula, and two Benedictines, the 'Fathers Dunstans',[10] 'the white and the black' 'by whom (especially, as it is thought, by blacke Father Dunstan) she was soon convinced...of the danger and unsecurity of her present state, [on what pertence soever;][11] and had bene as soon reconciled [to the Roman church] but that she was desired by a lady her frind who had heard some of the disputations' to wait a little while, 'promising her that after hearing one more dispute, she would be reconcilled together with her' (p. 128). A manuscript insertion tells us that the 'frind' was 'My lady Denby', that is, Susan Villiers Fielding, the sister of James Villiers, first Duke of Buckingham. During the civil war she followed Henrietta Maria to France and there eventually did become a Roman Catholic. At this stage, however, Lady Denbigh was either scared or a hypocrite. She continually

---

[10] Dunstan Everard (d. 1650) and Dunstan Pettenger (d. 1665).
[11] 'Danger...soever': this clause inserted by Lucy vertically along the gutter.

procrastinated, in order to deceive her friend, and eventually trapped her in her own rooms at court, intending to prevent her access to the Catholic priests. But Elizabeth gave her the slip, and fled back to Lord Ormonde's house:

> Finding black Father Dunstan there, she was, the soonest she could, reconciled by him in my Lord of Ormonds stable...and assoone as she had done in the afternoone returnes to Court to this Lady; telling her, she was now content to stay with her as long as she pleased, for all was done. She the Lady much trowbled att it, goeth presently to a neere and powerfull frind of her owne, [identified in the margin as 'the Duke of Buckingham'] and tells him; he as instantly to the King, who shewed himself highly displeased. They strait seeke most earnestly to perswade her, that whilest it was yet unknowne she should return, but seeing her not moved nether by persawsions nor displeasurs, they lett her goe home; whether she was soone followed by secretary Cooke with a Command from the King to her to remaine confined to her house during his majestys pleasure. so as had she not done as she did, she had bene prevented, for she saw herself confind (which continued six weekes), no Catholike daring to come neere her. (p. 130)

The conversion in a stable is a nice touch, whether intentionally or not redolent of the Nativity. As for the house arrest, on 11 January 1626, Charles I had issued a Proclamation for the Better Confining of Popish Recusants According to the Lawe, so that he was in a weak position to resist when Falkland wrote to him, on 8 December, begging for the 'confinement' of his 'apostate' wife.[12] Her husband's agent (without waiting for orders) immediately stopped her allowance, which remained stopped until 18 May 1627, when Elizabeth petitioned the king to compel the agent to pay it. And her children were removed from her custody.

In the next section, the Life details the hardships Elizabeth now experienced. At this point Wolfe introduces a certain scepticism as to whether we should believe the veracity of narrative—raising a question impossible to answer. Did Elizabeth exaggerate her hardships? Lucy, who had been removed from her custody, had no way of telling. Allowed only to retain one young maidservant, Elizabeth was deprived of coal, wood, beer, and food. She sent her maid to Ormonde's to take her meals, ordering her not to reveal her plight, and the maid would bring back in

---

[12]   State Paper Office, Dublin, quoted in Appendix to the 1861 *Life*, 138.

a handkerchief 'some pieces of pyecrust or bread' to feed her mistress. Eventually the maid revealed the facts to Ormonde, who then sent her mistress food daily. But what most distressed her was her isolation. Eventually she was visited by 'a Catholike cousen of hers', Cecily, Lady Manners, second wife of Francis, Earl of Rutland, who told her plight to Lucy Hay, Countess of Carlisle, who told the king, who declared himself astonished that she was still confined, 'it having been farre from his intention...and he presently gave her leave to goe abroad at her pleasure' (p. 134).

Isolation, however, was replaced by the constant pressure of 'her frinds' to reconvert, citing as arguments:

the disgracing her Lord, undoing him and her children; seperating herself from them (for it was certaine, that as he would not permit them to live with her, no more would he ever suffer her to live with him) that she never had so much grace and favour where it was most for her advantage (even from the King himself) as before her changing her religion, and by which she might have had power most to benefitt her Lord, all which she might regain with increase by coming backe. (p. 136)

How many women would have resisted such powerful arguments? The biographer continues to describe Elizabeth's problems with her husband, her refusal to make use of the Council order for financial support from him that her friends procured for her, their displeasure at this excessive wifely obedience, and the extreme poverty in which she lived, in 'a little old house ten mile from London', and 'no other household stuff in it, than a flock bed on the bare ground...and an old hamper which served her for a table, and a wooden stool' (p. 139). It is Cinderella in reverse. But it was here that she translated Cardinal Perron's Reply to the King's Answer. It seems that Elizabeth voluntarily (or stubbornly) embraced a version of the monastic ideal of poverty and scholarship. She began at this time also to write hagiography, 'the lives of St Mary Magdalene, St Agnes Martir, and St Elizabeth of Portingall in verse, and both before and after many verses of our Blessed Lady...and of many other saints'.

When Sir Henry returned from Ireland in 1631 Charles I arranged for a reconciliation between husband and wife, although they continued to live apart. This allowed Elizabeth to have some contact with her children, 'yet never durst speake to them of religion' (p. 147). However, her husband broke his leg shooting with the king, and died of gangrene and disastrous surgery a week later. He had sent for his wife immediately the accident occurred, and she was with him till he died. The biographer claims that Sir Henry had wished for a priest that he might convert to Roman Catholicism. Here, once more, the vividness of the scene and the reported conversation has the ring of authenticity:

> He was bleeding to death more than three howers, he past the most part of it in silence, especially towards the last; she the whilest praying by him, or speaking to him; and, he being very neer death, one of the surgeons desired him to professe he died a protestant, or ells (he sayd), his Lady being there and speaking much to him, it would be reported he died a Papist; to this (which the man repeated three or fower times) he only still turned away his head without answering him; but seeing he did not cease to [bawl] the same in his eares, he said to him att last, pray, doe not interrupt my silent meditation; which shewed he could have sayd the other if he would.

What the biographer thought the most likely cause of a deathbed desire for conversion was his reading of Elizabeth's translation of Perron's Answer '(which she had given him, and was found in his clossett after his death, all noated by him)' (p. 151).

Her husband's death permitted Elizabeth to spend more time with her children, although, we are told, she had to promise them not to try to convert them. This compromise led to one of the most amusing and telling moments in the Life. Part of her strategy was to allow her children to eat meat on Fridays, without which they would have refused to live with her, though she herself tried to maintain the fast. Tried, but frequently failed:

> sometimes, having risen early and bene all morning abroad about her businesses, and finding herself att diner time (it happening often to be on fasting dayes) att some of her Protestant frinds houses, where being made stay by importunity, and forgetting the fast (there being no sign of one, to put her in mind), being sett down hungry, and ready to put her meate in her mouth, one of her children then protestant would stopp her, telling her of the fast... but with most harty thanks, she would desire her to continue to doe so, really loving her the better for having concurred to her observance of the Churches precept, though she saw well enough, she [her daughter] had no other end in it than to laugh when she had done to see how suddainly she had stopped her in her hast, and had there ether bene more fish, or she lesse hungry, she would have bene like to have lett her alone; but this happening many times, she being much subject to this forgettfullness, made her most unwilling to eate abroad. (pp. 154–5)

The humour of the anecdote is underlined by the marginal note at the phrase 'one of her children', which identifies the teasing daughter as Dame Magdalena, that is, Lucy. This is the main piece of evidence for Wolfe's identification of the biographer as Lucy. But here again an essential part of the texture, and the difficulty, of the episode, is the confusing use of the female pronouns, which brings us back to the question of voice. Does the humour come from Elizabeth's self-knowledge, or is Lucy still teasing her mother by giving this story its comic shape?

The remainder of the biography is devoted to her efforts to retain custody of her children, and to maintain them in the face of her endless poverty, bad management, and hence indebtedness. Eventually she received some help from Lucius Cary, her eldest son, even though she had kidnapped from his house her two youngest sons, Patrick and Henry. Her four daughters had already converted, and were complicit in the plans for abducting their brothers. Once again the Life decides to present itself as romance, with Elizabeth as the heroine. The narrative is extremely tangled and hard to follow, but the adventure of the kidnapping is told with much circumstantial detail, as is the subsequent legal harassment she overcame by various shrewd manoeuvres. Her two youngest sons were safely dispatched to the Convent of the Benedictine Fathers in Paris. She spent what remained of her life, until she contracted tuberculosis, in 'setting poor folks on work' and working on a translation of Blosius, the Flemish monk and mystic Louis de Blois, whose Latin treatises gave her such trouble that she had to have recourse, it is admitted, to a Spanish version.

At its conclusion, the biography moves swiftly through a series of contrasting tones and genres. First, it is the scholar's biography:

She had read very exceeding much; Poetry of all kinds, ancient and moderne, in severall Languages, all that ever she could meete: History very universally, epsically all ancient Greeke, and Romane Historians . . . Of Bookes treating of morall vertue or wisedome (such as Seneca, Plutarch's Moralls, Pliny, and of late ones, such as French Mountaine, and English Bacon) she had red very many (when she was young;) . . . (p. 212)

At this point, her reading in Seneca, Plutarch, Montaigne, and Bacon must have struck a member of her family as unseemly, for it is all heavily scored out; so that the published version, had it ever appeared, would have moved smoothly from history to theology, her intensive reading in the church fathers, especially St Augustine and St Gregory. 'Of Controversy, it may be sayd, she had red most that has bene writen', and, tellingly, from early on she was 'well red in all the workes of Sir Thomas More' (pp. 212–13).

The biographer then turns to an overview of Elizabeth's character, which proves unusually difficult, because of the contradictions in that character. We are back in social comedy. Elizabeth had clearly been completely lacking in the social graces. 'Her neglect, through forgetfulnesse, of all customary civilitys, was so noatable, that was past into a privilege.' She never remembered the names and faces of her acquaintances, to the point where the king himself, we are told, tried to see if he could make her forget who he was. An extremely absent minded professor? 'But yet she allwayes seemed to have a most harty good will to God, and his service.' She was so respectful of priests that she would ask their blessing in the public street 'afore she was aware'. Improvident all her life, just before her death 'she tooke better order for her debts, which yet remained, then could have bene expected' (p. 220). In the last stages of her tuberculosis she was 'very quiet, pliable and easyly ruled, [qualities] which were were not very naturall to her'.

And from that point on, the Life becomes what it has so far resisted being; a conventional, soothing, devotional exercise:

She was buried by her Majestys permission in her chaple, where the office was performed for her by the charyty of the Capuchin Fathers (who were in her life ever ready to doe her any courtesy...) ... and though she had not any catholike child capable of giving to have her prayed for, yet she found those, that freely of their owne accord were mindfull of her; and besides what many Moncks her frinds did privately, the Convents of Doway and Cambray did of their Charitys sing Masse solemly for her. And for what may yet be wanting to her to suffer in purgatory, may it please God to inspire his servants to assist her with their prayers and sacrifices, and of his mercy give rest to her soule. (pp. 221–2)

Perhaps all we should say in conclusion is 'Amen'. But I want to make one final point. The contradictions between different aspects of Elizabeth's life and character made her infinitely more interesting than a person less conflicted, such as Lucy Lady Knatchbull, brought up as a devout Catholic, and finding her niche as an abbess in Ghent. It was Elizabeth's intellect and her scholarship that led to her conversion. It was her enforced marriage and fecundity that made her life more difficult than her conversion alone. We can perhaps see why she was willing to consign her own daughters to a life of celibacy (though one wonders if that realization contributed to Lucy's sharpness). And to return to my title, one can emend her father's phrase to provide for her a fittingly secular epitaph: 'This girle hath a spirit averse'; or perhaps, simply, 'This girle hath a spirit.'

13

'Alchemy and Monstrous Love': Sir Robert Moray and the Representation of Early Modern Lives

Frances Harris

When Steven Zwicker first asked me to contribute this chapter on early modern life writing, he suggested putting it in a category to be called 'affective biography'. I was nonplussed by this at first. But it was certainly true that my last project had been the study of an intense platonic friendship in a religious context between a middle-aged man and a much younger woman, John Evelyn and Margaret Godolphin, called *Transformations of Love*. So 'affective biography' might mean biography with a strong love interest: the kind centred on relationships. But this also called up recollections of Francis Bacon: 'they do best, who, if they cannot but admit love, yet make it keep quarter, and sever it wholly from their serious affairs and actions of life. For if it check once with business it troubleth men's fortunes, and maketh men that they can no ways be true to their own ends.'[1] So 'affective biography', it might be supposed, would not be addressing the real end and serious purpose of men's lives: their business, their fortunes, their actions in the world.

Then I thought again. Love did mean something rather more than this to some men at the time: an idealizing force, the means by which man apprehended and reached out for the highest good, the means by which he saved his soul in fact. To some sixteenth-century cosmologists, influenced by the Hermetic writings to believe in the possibility of

---

[1] Francis Bacon, *Essays,* ed. Brian Vickers (Oxford, 1999), 23.

a recovered ancient wisdom, love was the bond that held the entire universe in cohesion and order, evidencing itself in correspondences, attractions, and sympathies between higher and lower nature (for example between the stars and the lower world), and giving rise to a comprehensive 'metaphysics of love' expressed throughout the early modern period in writings of alchemy and 'natural magic'.[2]

Here I seemed to be getting closer to one of my current biographical subjects: Sir Robert Moray, soldier, royalist agent, Hermetic philosopher, freemason, Restoration courtier, one of the founders of the Royal Society and a leading figure in the post-Restoration government of Scotland, not someone whose life lacked business or action. Yet Moray's personal emblem was a pentacle or five-pointed star with Greek letters inserted between the points, to make up what he called 'the sweet word [*Agapa*], which you know signifies love thou, or hee loves, which is the reciprocall love of God and man'.[3] Gilbert Burnet, who knew Moray well, wrote of his 'most diffused love to all mankind', adding that he was himself 'the most universally beloved and esteemed by men of all sides and sorts, of any man I have ever known in my whole life'.[4] Amongst those Moray shared his pentacle symbol with was John Evelyn, who adopted it, together with the theory of seraphic or platonic love as purveyed by their friend and Royal Society colleague Robert Boyle (whose life did not lack business and serious purpose either), for his friendship with Margaret Godolphin.[5]

In studying Evelyn and Margaret Godolphin I was overwhelmed with source material: their correspondence, diaries, and meditations, Evelyn's posthumous life of his friend, even the portrait painted to commemorate their friendship. It is much more common to find silences and ambiguities when we search out early modern lives, and this is certainly true of Moray. Yet his life seems to call to be addressed; he was not a Newton or a Boyle (though it is not always clear in any case how great works relate to the writing of lives), but he was called the life and soul of

    [2] A. J. Smith, *The Metaphysics of Love* (Cambridge, 1985), 102–12.
    [3] Moray to Bruce, 4/14 Feb. 1658, quoted in David Stevenson, 'Masonry, Symbolism and Ethics in the Life of Sir Robert Moray FRS', *Proceedings of the Society of Antiquaries of Scotland* 114 (1984), 415.
    [4] Gilbert Burnet, *History of his own Time* (Oxford, 1833), i. 109.
    [5] F. Harris, *Transformations of Love: The Friendship of John Evelyn and Margaret Godolphin* (Oxford, 2003), 80–1, 150–7. The source of Evelyn's pentacle was identified by David Stevenson, 'Masonry, Symbolism and Ethics', 417–18.

the Royal Society in its early years. His scientific networks, though they are not my focus here, are a significant study in themselves, and Burnet's description of him as the English Peiresc recognizes his importance as a connecting figure.[6] But my interest in him for the present purpose is that he lived his eventful life in a way that brings us face to face with one of the central challenges we can now have in representing early modern lives.

There have been two suggestive studies of Moray. One, by David Stevenson, focuses on the long sequence of letters he wrote to his young friend Alexander Bruce, the future Earl of Kincardine, in the late 1650s when both were in exile, Bruce in Bremen and Moray in Maestricht. These letters, as Stevenson makes clear, establish Moray's profound commitment to neo-stoicism, a philosophy which evolved, and with particular strength amongst Scottish intellectuals of this period, as an aid to the difficulties of a public career in turbulent times. Moray told Bruce in 1658 that 'it hath been my study now 31 years to understand and regulate my passions', suggesting a conscious and specific, rather than a gradual commitment. The letters also highlight the long-lasting significance for Moray of his initiation as a freemason, which took place in the Edinburgh lodge in 1641 while he was a quartermaster in the Covenanting army. His mason mark, a personal emblem deriving originally from his family crest, was the pentacle already described. He had it engraved on his seal, added it routinely to his signature and sometimes used it alone in state letters as a cipher for himself or to signal the presence of passages written in invisible ink. The pentacle of course already had a long and various history of symbolic meanings. Moray's version was to find within its angularities the five Greek letters making up *AGAPA*, which he then used as an acrostic for the five qualities: love, self-knowledge, endurance, faith, self-restraint, which summed up his 'stoic-platonic-Christian ethic'.[7]

The effect of this ethic was apparent throughout Moray's life. Gilbert Burnet remarked that he was the only true stoic he ever knew:

---

[6] Burnet, *History of his own Time*, i. 109. See also Peter N. Miller, *Peiresc's Europe: Learning and Virtue in the Seventeenth Century* (New Haven, 2000).

[7] Stevenson, 'Masonry, Symbolism and Ethics', esp. 410–20, 426–7. See also David Allen, *Philosophy and Politics in Later Stuart Scotland: Neo-Stoicism, Culture and Ideology in an Age of Crisis 1540–1690* (East Linton, 2000).

he had studied Epictetus much and had wrought up his mind to all his maxims, so that things without him seemed to make no impressions on him, and he was ever the same, so well poised that I never saw him in different tempers. He could pass from business to learning, from that to pious discourses and then go into familiar prating, and go round again, with that easiness that it was visible nothing went deeper into his thoughts than as he had a mind it should go.[8]

This seemed to be equally true of his life in prosperity as in adversity. A passionate advocate of monarchy, though of a contractual kind, he greeted the Restoration as the establishment of a new Jerusalem, was the first courtier to be granted lodgings in Whitehall,[9] and soon became a favoured companion of the king. Yet he gave the impression of being essentially disengaged from its activities. 'For myself', he told Bruce, 'I do just as I use to do, let things work out of themselves.' 'What way my staff will fall I do not know,' he added a few years later,

I am held out by a thread, yet it seemes to bind me. And I do not see how to get loose...nor indeed do I look to be left to choyce what to make of myself, though I know not what I serve for here. Proposition, project or design I have none at all more than when I first saw the light. I do not weary nor long, and these are perhaps some little masteries. But if I were at mine own disposall...know I do not at this moment what I would prefer to what it seemes you set so great value upon [that is, the opportunities of public life]. But we must let ourselves be governed by the hand that can do it best, placidly and entirely.[10]

Yet he certainly had ambitions of a kind. He had apologized to Bruce for the boldness of adopting so potent a personal symbol as a star, but in explaining the accompanying motto, 'To be rather than to seem', he pointed out that stars were far greater in magnitude than they appeared, and that their influence over inferior things was potent but not easily understood even by adepts.[11] Clearly he intended a parallel with his own life.

   [8] Burnet, *History of his own Time*, i. 109; *A Supplement to Burnet's History of my own Time*, ed. H. C. Foxcroft (Oxford, 1902), 43–4.

   [9] Osmund Airy, 'The Correspondence of Sir Robert Moray and Alexander Bruce', *Scottish Review* 5 (1885), 28, 34–5; Simon Thurley, *The Whitehall Palace Plan of 1670*, London Topographical Society Publications 153 (1998), 48.

   [10] Alexander Robertson, *The Life of Sir Robert Moray* (1922), 100; Airy, 'Correspondence', 37–8.

   [11] Stevenson, 'Masonry, Symbolism and Ethics', 414.

Hoppen, in his study of the nature of the early Royal Society, continues the story by putting Moray in the company of the alchemists Elias Ashmole, Thomas Henshaw, and Thomas Vaughan, and noting his approving references to the writings of Athanasius Kircher and the Hermetic chemist Johann Rudolph Glauber.[12] These associations allowed Moray's court opponents to represent him on occasion as a sorcery-dabbling magus,[13] but it is of course not by now news that the occult and the experimental science existed side by side and that some of the most famous practitioners of the latter, Newton and Boyle, divided their attention between the two. I am not so much concerned with the phenomenon itself as with the issues this, and other aspects of Moray's philosophy and beliefs, pose in writing about a life. I am concerned about how to represent lives in their full meaning that were lived, as it were, simultaneously in more than one dimension. In this limited context I cannot address the whole of Moray's life, but I will use two particular episodes in it to illustrate what I mean.

The first is an episode in the winter of 1665–6, when the court had removed to Oxford because of the plague. Moray usually followed the court closely. Now, with the king's permission, he left his Oxford lodgings in the house of his Royal Society colleague Dr John Wallis for long periods and holed himself up, as he put it, a few miles away at the house of one Samuel Kem, rector of Albury, a former parliamentary chaplain and army officer whom he had first encountered preaching before Charles I in his captivity at Newcastle in 1646. His reason for renewing their acquaintance on this occasion was that Kem had a laboratory with furnaces, probably those set up by his predecessor as rector, the mathematician William Oughtred. He could of course have had access to chemists' furnaces in Oxford, but this was too public for Moray, who was careful to let very few know of his whereabouts or what he was doing.[14]

---

[12] K. Theodore Hoppen, 'The Nature of the Early Royal Society, Part II', *Notes and Records of the Royal Society* 9 (1976), 245–50.

[13] *Lorenzo Magalotti at the Court of Charles II,* ed. W. E. Knowles Middleton (Waterloo, Ont., 1980), 47.

[14] Barbara Donagan, 'Samuel Kem', *ODNB* xxxi. 141–3; C. S. Terry, 'The Visits of Charles I to Newcastle', *Archaeologia Aeliana,* NS, 21 (1899), 121; *The Correspondence of Henry Oldenburg,* ed. A. Rupert Hall and Marie Boas Hall (Madison, 1966), ii. 564: Moray to Oldenburg, 11 Oct. 1665.

His task at Albury was to make metallurgical trials in connection with the exploitation of the Mines Royal in Wales. 'Mines Royal' was the name given to those which produced lead-silver ore of such richness that the silver left after burning off the lead exceeded the costs of production and the value of what was lost. The likeliest were long known to be in Cardiganshire, east of Aberystwyth, though drainage was a perennial problem and so were costs.[15] While fresh attempts were under way to make the mines workable, at Albury Moray was experimenting to make the process of silver extraction more economical; the first stage, as he explained it to a Royal Society colleague, was 'to extract from lead ore all the metall it containes, with one wash, great ease and small charge; the other to do the same with extracting silver out of the lead with the same advantages, when the lead holds so much as may be worth the paines'. 'I am the more ready to apply myself to this', he added, 'that I am in a fair way to engage my self and some of my friends in the silver mines as they call them, in Cardiganshire in Wales, which have formerly yielded much silver, & ly now under water which is to be taken off with Adits that are now carrying up to the Mines.'[16] Overtly, then, the project was a commercial speculation, involving Lord Ashley (the future Lord Shaftesbury) amongst others, and it needs no explanation why the king supported it, and why one of the few others in on the secret was Henry Slingsby of Kippax, FRS and Master Worker of the Mint.[17] Another may well have been Francis Bacon's old servant, Thomas Bushell, who had minted Welsh silver for Charles I during the civil war and was still living in London after the Restoration, an old man so deeply in debt from the costs of his former projects that he now needed the protection of court residence.[18] In April Moray was able to report to Slingsby that having 'torture[d] lead ore . . . many ways', he had produced some improvements: 'whereas in the ordinary way that ore in Cardiganshire that is called the silver or rich ore yields only 40lb of lead

[15] George C. Boon, *Cardiganshire Silver and the Aberystwyth Mint in Peace and War* (Cardiff, 1981).

[16] *Correspondence of Hartlib, Haak, Oldenberg and Others of the Royal Society with Governor Winthrop of Connecticut*, ed. R. C. Winthrop (Boston, 1878), 23–5: Moray to Winthrop, 19 Dec. 1665.

[17] K. H. D. Haley, *The Earl of Shaftesbury* (Oxford, 1967), 228; BL, Add. MS 81611: Moray to Slingsby, 27 Jan. 1666.

[18] J. W. Gough, *The Superlative Prodigall: A Life of Thomas Bushell* (Bristol, 1932); George C. Boon, 'Thomas Bushell', *ODNB* ix. 141–3.

in 100 of ore, I got 69 out of it.' As soon as the spring came he left for the mines themselves, where from Silver Mills he made a proposition to Sir Edward Harley to develop a newly discovered area with mining potential.[19]

So far, so straightforward; except that we discover (and not from Moray's letters to his Royal Society colleagues) that his partner in his experiments in torturing lead ore at Albury was Thomas Vaughan: twin brother of the poet Henry Vaughan, unbeneficed Welsh clergy-man, medical practitioner, and, most notably, one of the densest and most prolific writers of the period on alchemy as a spiritual quest; 'for Alchymie in the common acceptation, and as it is the torture of metalls', he had declared in the last of his published works, 'I did never believe; much less did I study it.'[20] Yet he died at Albury in February 1666, it was said from accidentally inhaling mercury, and was buried there by Moray, to whom he bequeathed all his alchemical books and manuscripts. There is no doubt that Moray had recruited Vaughan; his brother later told John Aubrey that he had died 'upon an imployment for his majesty'.[21] Moray's concerns, at least as he discussed them with Royal Society colleagues, appeared to be entirely practical: what kind of salts to use in extracting lead, in what proportions, where to procure them, how long it was to be in the fire.[22] Vaughan, as an experienced practitioner of iatrochemical medicine, would have been a useful partner in these experiments.[23] But the project of producing silver by intensive working on base metal also had unmistakable connections with the alchemical project as popularly understood. Vaughan's passionate commitment to its metaphysical dimension, his bequest of his books and manuscripts to Moray, and the latter's reticence about his involvement all strongly suggest that there was no clear boundary between their preoccupations.

Moray remained several weeks in Wales before returning to report on his findings. He had found 'great riches underground', he said, but the

---

[19] HMC *6th Report*, pt. 1, 338–9: P. Vaux to Slingsby, 5 April 1666; Moray to Slingsby, 9 April 1666; BL, Add. MS 70011: Moray to Harley, 8 June 1666.

[20] *Euphrates, or The Waters of the East* (1655), sig. A3. See also Jennifer Speake, 'Thomas Vaughan', *ODNB* lvi. 203–7.

[21] *The Works of Thomas Vaughan*, ed. Alan Rudrum (Oxford, 1984), 23–5.

[22] *Correspondence of Henry Oldenburg*, iii. 9: Moray to Oldenburg, 8 Jan. 1666.

[23] Vaughan's notebook, BL, Sloane MS 1741, edited as *Thomas and Rebecca Vaughan's 'Aqua vitae non vitis'*, by D. R. Dickson (2001), esp. pp. xxxix–xlix.

king refused to let him get involved further, since it would mean his being away from court eighteen months or two years, 'and I do not find after two attempts, very serious, that the King will permit me to go from him at least for so long a time'.[24] With a crisis developing in Scotland over the heavy-handed imposition of episcopal church government, the king and his secretary of state for Scotland, the Earl of Lauderdale, Moray's close associate since the last years of Charles I, had other uses for him and it was not long before he was dispatched as Treasury commissioner and confidential agent to Edinburgh.

The second matter I want to deal with arises from this Scottish connection: it is the question of Moray's wives, or rather his 'wives'. In or about 1650 he had married Lady Sophia Lindsay, sister of his friend Alexander, Earl of Balcarres, who shared both his Covenanting sympathies and his strong royalist views, and through whose influence, probably, he was then appointed Lord Justice Clerk and Privy Councillor in Scotland to the young Charles II. They also shared intellectual interests; Balcarres's father, David Lord Lindsay, had amassed a remarkable library, including a collection of alchemical manuscripts, which his son inherited.[25] It was a love match between Moray and Sophia Lindsay, but a short-lived one. His kinswoman Anne Murray, who shared a household with them in Edinburgh in the winter of 1652–3, wrote of Lady Moray's 'religious devout Life' and calm temperament, with its affinities to Moray's stoicism: 'I may with much truth averre I never in all that time saw her the least discomposed either with greefe, anger, joy or any passion.' But she was also frail in health. She went into labour with her first child during that winter, but the child could not be delivered and she died. Moray was constantly with her, '& though', Anne Murray continues, 'in health itt was the Greatest trouble that either of them had to think of Separation yett such was the great torment shee was in that itt was her question to him (who constantly held her pulse) how neere she was to her approaching death ... hee ... assuring her that every time she asked that question shee was a step nearer to itt, & hee had so many excellent arguments to strengthen her faith & increase her Confidence

---

[24] NLS, MS 5050: Moray to Kincardine, 3 July 1666 (transcript). Since this chapter has gone to press, David Stevenson's admirable edition, *Letters of Sir Robert Moray to the Earl of Kincardine, 1657–1673* has been published by Ashgate (Aldershot, 2007).

[25] J. B. Craven, 'A Scottish Alchemist of the 17th Century', *Journal of the Alchemical Society* 1 (1913), 68–75.

in her Redeemer that I found more Satisfaction in his discourse then in what the Minesters said who came to see her who were the best in Edenburgh.' When she died, 'with a grave composed behaviour [he] left her & retired himself without the shew of any immoderate greefe', the most striking testimony she could conceive of the strength of his religious faith and his stoic principles.[26]

Moray never remarried. One of his personal seals, with the device of an altar and a heart and the motto 'Une Seulle', has been interpreted by David Stevenson as a sign of his devotion to his wife's memory.[27] This may well be so, but it is not the only possibility. In one of his letters to Alexander Bruce, written when Sophia Lindsay had been five years dead, Moray mentioned having another seal cut and explained that it was for his 'wife'.[28] The term could be a euphemism for 'mistress', but this seems unlikely in Moray's case. It could also be used of a favourite female friend, and the person most commonly referred to by Moray in this way by this time was Lady Margaret Kennedy, daughter of the Earl of Cassilis. Her father was one of the most rigid Presbyterians of his time, and she shared his Covenanting sympathies. She was also learned, Gilbert Burnet (who afterwards married her, though she was eighteen years his senior) says, 'had read vastly', understood several languages, and 'was an excellent historian and knew all our late affairs exactly well'.[29] She corresponded with Lauderdale while he was in prison after the Battle of Worcester and with Moray in exile, and in their correspondence with each other after the Restoration one finds plentiful references to her as 'our wife', and much good-natured rivalry as to which of them was fittest for the role of her 'husband'. Lauderdale, for example, writing to Moray when he first arrived in Edinburgh in 1667 and was slow in visiting her, says: 'you have a wife who once undeservedly called you her kindest husband. I tell her you are not, seeing you have not yet seen her.'[30]

[26] *Memoirs of Anne, Lady Halkett, and Ann, Lady Fanshawe*, ed. John Loftis (Oxford, 1978), 69; NLS, MS 6943: Lady Halkett's journal, 1673–4, pp. 215–16.

[27] Stevenson, 'Masonry, Symbolism and Ethics', 422–3.

[28] NLS, MS 5049: Moray to Bruce, 3 Jan. 1658 (transcript).

[29] Burnet, *Supplement,* 85

[30] NLS, MS 7023, no. 309: Lauderdale to Moray, 27 July [1667]. Moray also referred to the Duchess of Hamilton and her sister Susan, Countess of Cassilis, as his 'wives'; see *The Lauderdale Papers,* ed. Osmund Airy, Camden Society, NS, xxxvi (1885), pt. 2, 37: 29 Aug. 1667.

In this case they all knew they could safely outface any gossip. Sir George Mackenzie says of the friendship between Lauderdale and Lady Margaret Kennedy:

[He] had of a long time entertained with [her] an intimacy which had grown great enough to become suspicious in a person who lov'd not, as some said, his own Lady... and the suspicion encreas'd much, upon her living in the Abbey [Holyrood, also a state residence], in which no woman else lodg'd; nor did the Commissioner blush to go openly to her chamber in his night gown: whereupon her friends, having challenged her for that unusual commerce, and having represented to her the open apprehensions and railleries of the people, received no other answer, than that her virtue was above suspicion; as really it was, she being a person whose religion exceeded as far her wit, as her parts exceeded others of her sex.[31]

We have become more aware of friendships with a religious and even sacramental dimension in the medieval and early modern periods, but they are currently perhaps receiving more scholarly attention as an aspect of same-sex relations than of relations between the sexes. 'Seraphic love' between men and women was probably just as common, and carried its own complexities.[32] The element of sublimated sexuality in all such friendships was perfectly well recognized; was the essential factor, in fact, in the progression from human to divine love. Francis de Sales, whose *Introduction to a Devout Life* and *Treatise of the Love of God* celebrated spiritual friendships between men and women and were an inspiration to many Protestants, referred unselfconsciously to 'the similarity that exists between our spiritual emotions and our physical passions'.[33] But it could not always be an untroubled similarity. Evelyn found his friendship with Margaret Godolphin a disruptive force,

---

[31] Sir George Mackenzie of Rosehaugh, *Memoirs of the Affairs of Scotland* (Edinburgh, 1821), 165.

[32] For the former, see Alan Bray, *The Friend* (Chicago and London, 2003); Laura Gowing, Michael Hunter, and Miri Rubin (eds.), *Love, Friendship and Faith in Europe 1300–1800* (Basingstoke, 2005); on the latter, Patrick Collinson, ' "Not Sexual in the Ordinary Sense": Men, Women and Religious Transactions', in *Elizabethan Essays* (1994), 119–50; Erica Veevers, *Images of Love and Religion: Queen Henrietta Maria and Court Entertainments* (Cambridge, 1989), 14–33; Harris, *Transformations of Love,* esp. 75–81, 151–7.

[33] Quoted from de Sales's *Treatise of the Love of God,* in Veevers, *Images of Love,* 24. See also Anna Baldwin and Sarah Hutton (eds.), *Platonism and the English Imagination* (Cambridge, 1994), 79–85.

difficult to contain within its spiritual context and called into question by at least one member of his (otherwise mainly supportive) circle of family and friends. Another such example occurs in one of the most notable sequences of female life writing of the period, that of Moray's kinswoman Anne Murray. Having been bred at the Caroline court, she had fled north to escape reprisals for her part in the Duke of York's escape from England in 1648, had met and married Moray's cousin Sir James Halkett in Edinburgh in the 1650s and lived on in Dunfermline as a devout widow until nearly the end of the century. Her motives for writing her remarkably novel-like autobiography, with its long passages of verbatim conversation, were never made explicit in the work itself. It is from one of her volumes of religious meditations that we learn it was begun to counter the disapproval of her Dunfermline neighbours at the friendship she formed in her fifties with a local minister. 'Wee took sweet Counsell together', she wrote, 'and Walked into the house of God in Company'; and 'I confesse I thought my designes so inocent and allowable that I gave way to intertaine myself with the advantages that I might have by the Converse of a Pious Man ... & I had not the feare of having any Suspect mee Guilty of any breach of resolution (I dare not call it vow) of holy Widowhood because all that saw or knew of my Converse with him believed as I did that his affections were placed upon another & even in that I had a satisfection because I had a kindnesse for her.' Yet as a result she met with 'disquiett both att home & abroad ... from the unjust scandals of Lying and Malicious Tongues', in her case sharpened by the knowledge that before her marriage she had allowed herself to become publicly engaged to the royalist agent Col. Joseph Bampfield for a prolonged period, despite persistent and finally undeniable evidence that he had a wife still living. Her account of her troubled life, she hoped, might 'bee of some Advantage to me if the Lord sees fit to give a seasonable opportunity to devulge it by representing my unparalleled misfortunes & the wonderfull power & mercy of God in suporting me under them; which being an evidence of the Lords compasion may incline others to the greater Charity'.[34]

The last of Moray's close female friendships brought similar difficulties. His brother-in-law Balcarres had died while still in exile in 1659, but Moray retained close ties with his surviving family: his widow

---

[34] NLS, MS 6494: Lady Halkett's journal, 1677–8, pp. 9, 30, 294.

Anna, whom Moray always called 'cummer' (who herself maintained a close friendship with the celebrated Presbyterian divine Richard Baxter), and her children, Moray's nieces and nephews by marriage. The eldest daughter greatly distressed her mother by converting to Roman Catholicism after the Restoration.[35] Of the other two, Henrietta and Sophia, it was the younger, his dead wife's namesake, who controversially became the last of Moray's 'wives'.

When he was sent by the king to Edinburgh in 1667, he immediately resumed close contact with them. Soon his letters begin to refer frequently to Sophia, her health and the journeys she made with him. Her sister Henrietta has left a long and curiously impenetrable religious memoir, made the more so by her studied avoidance of the first-person pronoun.[36] Sophia was reportedly very different: 'a creature of the daylight and brightness as much as Lady Henrietta was of twilight and reserve': witty, energetic and a risk-taker, who for a 'frolic' conducted a mock arraignment of the Provost of Stirling for his persecution of Presbyterian clergy; and much later, after her mother had remarried, smuggled her stepfather Argyll out of Edinburgh Castle under the close scrutiny of an armed guard, disguised as her page.[37] But for much of the time Moray was in Scotland she was ailing in health, and when he was recalled to London in the summer of 1668 he brought her back with him, ostensibly to undergo treatment and take the waters.

It was immediately clear that there was more to this than a straightforward act of family duty. 'What you have done with him in Scotland I know not, but truly he is much changed,' Lauderdale wrote accusingly to Lord Tweeddale, the third member of the triumvirate who effectively governed Scotland for the king at this time. Moray was seen to be spending most of his time with his niece, taking little further interest in public affairs and disregarding desperate appeals from his colleagues to return to Edinburgh and take up his post again. Soon there began to be talk of her setting up house with him, and even a suggestion that they intended to marry. Lauderdale's reaction was strong and straightforward. He and the Balcarres family were cousins, so what he called the 'horrid

---

[35] Richard Baxter, *Autobiography*, ed. J. M. Lloyd Thomas (London, 1969), 144–6.

[36] David George Mullan (ed.), *Women's Life Writing in Early Modern Scotland* (Aldershot, 2003), 204–353.

[37] Alexander, Lord Lindsay, *A Memoir of Lady Anna Mackenzie* (Edinburgh, 1868), 112.

proposition' was not just morally repugnant to him, but an affront to family propriety. He pointedly ceased to treat Lady Sophia with the civility due to a kinswoman:

I visited her very frequently, till I heard of a design that made my ears tingle; I cannot say that she harboured such thoughts, but I thought fit not to visit any more, to shew my detestation by my action as I did home by my words. I have received full assurance by words that it is given over, but I am not capable of satisfaction till there be a full separation when the weather will allow it in the spring... The young Ladies journey hither was signall folie; waters were pretended but no such thing done, and the shorter follies be it is the better.[38]

He also strongly disapproved of the other cause of Moray's abstraction from public affairs at this time: the laboratory at Whitehall, which he was helping to fit out and in which he spent hours every day.[39] What was worse, to Lauderdale's frustration, the king was very interested in what he was doing there. When he tried to persuade Charles to order Moray's return to Scotland, royal reluctance to coerce a favourite was one obstacle, but more powerful was what Lauderdale called the lure of 'the bewitching Chimestrie'. In the end, to his disgust, this combination of 'alchemy & monstrous love' prevailed. 'Yow need not expect [him] this winter', he told Tweeddale, 'his delight, his heart is heir, & so his presence wold do yow little good'.[40] All he could do was to see that Lady Sophia's mother in Scotland received highly coloured accounts of the 'scandal' in which her daughter was now involved. Although she protested that Sophia had done nothing in coming to London but obey her mother, she had no choice but to recall her as soon as spring allowed the journey.[41] Moray's concern at the 'Rhapsody of stories' finally prevailed over his stoic calm so far as to make him justify himself, though he protested that 'there are things a man should not be put to give an account of whether true or false'. 'I could have said more to her', that is, Lady Balcarres, he told Kincardine, 'but I said what was

---

[38] NLS, MS 7023: Lauderdale to Tweeddale, 7, 9, 16, 23 July 1668; *Scottish History Society*, 3rd ser., 33, Miscellany, 6 (1933), 134: Lauderdale to Tweeddale, [early 1669] (incorrectly assigned to 1666 in this edition).

[39] Thurley, *Whitehall Palace Plan of 1670*, 43; NLS, MS 5050: Moray to Kincardine, 4 Nov. 1668 (transcript).

[40] NLS, MS 7023: Lauderdale to Tweeddale, 24, 27 Oct. 1668; 17 April 1669.

[41] National Register of Archives: Report 23003, Tollemache Papers, Buckminster Park, Correspondence No. 2037: Lady Balcarres to Lauderdale, 18 Jan. 1669.

necessary. Nor will I further extend my self on the subject to you than
to repeat some words of what I said to her. I neither am married nor
do intend it. I know it is to no purpose to labour to take off jealousies
be whose they will, if once they have taken footing. . . . My Niece is to
part for Scotland with all convenient speed.'[42] Moray and Lauderdale
were reaching a parting of ways politically in any case, but their personal
relations never recovered from this episode.

How is one to interpret it? The easiest way is to accept Lauderdale's
view: it was the weakness of a middle-aged man (Moray was in his late
fifties) with a much younger woman, who perhaps reminded him of his
dead wife. He fell in love and in doing so disregarded the unsuitability
of the relationship from every point of view: kinship, disparity of age,
and conflict with public responsibilities. An intended marriage seems
implausible, but Moray's habit of referring to close female friends as his
wives lent itself easily to misinterpretation.

Yet with Moray, who invoked the motto 'to be rather than to seem',
one needs to go beyond outward appearance and (mis)representation.
There is no mass of personal documentation, such as illuminates the
friendship of John Evelyn and Margaret Godolphin, but there are hints
of another dimension. The first comes from Moray's preoccupation
with his chemical experiments. When challenged he repudiated any
intention to marry his niece in a conventional sense, but added that
he might have said more by way of explanation of their relationship if
he chose. Sophia Lindsay's ill health was genuine. As well as continuing
to 'torture metal' in the Whitehall laboratory, Moray might have been
trying to devise remedies for her, as he had formerly for her father
and as Thomas Vaughan and his wife had made their occupation in
the 1650s.[43] And Vaughan's testimony to his wife's role suggests the
possibility of something further than this. In alchemical treatises the
union of sulphur and mercury, male and female principles respectively,
to make precious metals was sometimes referred to as a marriage, a
'chymical wedding'. A female associate could be an aid to the work, and
Vaughan was passionate in acknowledging what he owed to his wife
before her untimely death:

---

[42] NLS, MS 2955: Moray to Kincardine, 25 May 1669.
[43] NLS, MS 5049: Moray to Bruce, 20 Dec. 1657 (transcript); *Thomas and Rebecca
Vaughan's 'Aqua vitae non vitis'*, pp. xxv–xlix.

To the End that wee might live well, and exercise our Charitie...I employ'd my self all her life time in the Acquisition of some naturall secrets, to which I had been disposed from my youth up: and what I now write, and know of them practically I attained to in her Dayes...and though I brought them not to perfection in those deare Dayes, yet were the Gates opened to mee then, and what I have done since, is but the effect of those principles. I found them not by my owne witt, or labour, but by gods blessing and the Incouragement I received from most loving, obedient wife, whome I beseech God to reward in Heaven, for all the Happiness and Content she affoorded mee.[44]

Lauderdale's contemptuous linking of 'alchemy and monstrous love' suggests the possibility that Moray might have adopted his niece as a kind of spiritual helpmeet in the same sense; that for both chemists the experience of transcendent human love had been a factor in transmuting iatrochemical medicine or metallurgical experiment into the realm of Hermetic philosophy.

Finally, we have one explicit comment from Sophia Lindsay herself. When Moray died unexpectedly four years later, she immediately wrote to Lord Tweeddale to let him know that she had arranged for a trust-worthy female servant to have access to the papers in his cabinet and to take away her own and Tweeddale's letters, 'without requiring them, least that should have made them too much taken notice of'. Clearly she had remained in contact with Moray herself and was also well aware that he and Tweeddale had corresponded constantly and frankly about their opposition to Lauderdale. But it is the tortuous opening sentence of her letter to Tweeddale which provides the clearest insight into her relationship with her uncle by marriage: 'Had I not known that my Redeemer Liveth & therefore your Excellent friend Sir Robert Moray Liveth also in him & By him & for him in a way transcendently elevated above the supream exultation of our most sublime apprehensions, the wounding Reflections I had on his being Dead as to me whill in this mortal state...should certainlie have proven me an instance of power rather of grief than of humane reason.' But in that mortal state, she added, he had been 'not onlie to me the best of fathers but my most Exemplarie Guid towards the Glorie that succeeded it'.[45]

[44] Gareth Roberts, *The Mirror of Alchemy: Alchemical Ideas and Images in Books and Manuscripts* (London, 1994), 84–5; *Thomas and Rebecca Vaughan's 'Aqua vitae non vitis'*, 240.
[45] NLS, MS 14406: Lady Sophia Lindsay to Tweeddale, 3 Aug. 1673.

This brings us again to what can be the ghost at the banquet in early modern lives. Where we are preoccupied with the self, they were with the soul. It seems to be easier for us now to address a commitment to neo-stoic philosophy than to passionately expressed Christian beliefs, especially in the absence of a literary and specifically clerical context to provide a framework for the discourse. Yet they are at least as insistent a presence in Moray's life. He encourages Alexander Bruce to bear his misfortunes patiently, 'knowing whatsoever your kind, wise, good and powerful father sends to you or does with you, is the very best that can befall you, how dark soever his ways be to your grief'; adding that 'one grace also, he meanes certainly to have you employ with singular industrie; that of seeking his face by prayer'. Of himself he says: 'Many such things have befallen me in the course of my life which have given me so internal an acquaintance with God's goodness in such dealings that I have much cause to thank him for stooping so farre as to give me so many and so frequent sensible experiments for confirming my faith'; and he gives this faith a greater role in conquering his passions than his study of neoclassical philosophy: 'Stoicism cannot allay griefs like Grace from on high.'[46] All this was not simply the product of solitude and exile. 'I much commend your Christian & prudent res-olutions', he writes to Henry Oldenburg, settling his affairs in London during the plague, 'the creator of man may call for the spirit he gave us when he pleases...hee is happiest that is readiest and ripest for breathing forth his Soul in his redeemers bosom'; and when he learns of the military disasters of 1667 and the deaths of the Duke of York's two infant sons: 'my heart melts as often as I reflect upon the affliction under which his Majesties spirit lyes in this conjuncture, and the sad thoughts of it get no abatement but by resolving them into prayer.'[47] John Evelyn called Moray 'my most religious friend'. 'He was as free of covetousness as a Carthusian', Aubrey says. 'He had noble and generous thoughts of God and religion', Burnet adds, and 'the chief exercise of his devotion was every night to review what had seen that day, with acts of adoration, celebrating such of the divine attributes as appeared to him in the new occurrences of providence; and this he commonly

---

[46] NLS, MS 5049, Moray to Kincardine, 8 Nov. 1657, 14 Feb., 8 April 1658 (transcripts).

[47] *Correspondence of Henry Oldenburg*, ii. 575, 19 Oct. 1665: Moray to Oldenburg, 19 Oct. 1665; BL, Add. MS 23127, fo. 56: Moray to Lauderdale, 20 June 1667.

did in an audible discourse which he said heated his fancy and fixed his thoughts'.[48]

In secular life writing a sudden death such as Moray's can seem to create a difficulty in rounding off and assessing what has been summarily truncated. Another letter of his, this time to Archbishop Sheldon shortly after his arrival in Scotland, suggests another way of interpreting it:

You will easily believe it looks a little odd to me, to see myself launched forth in a sea of businesse, after many years lying unrigged and moor'd out of reach of active employment . . . However I observe it is as easie to me to be busie now as it was to look on before. And so I am doing now one piece of my task, and then another, with all the application it requires . . . The sublunary satisfaction that usually whet other men's endeavours to attain them are still below my Horizon. I look for none that are attainable, till what is mortal be swallowed up in immortality . . . And let my exercise be all day what it will, the part of it, what only I reckon to be my own . . . is a few minutes that I am alone before I go to bed . . . And what way soever I be taken up, one care is, I be never so out of frame but that when the least moment of recess offers, I may with a becoming boldnesse turn to own bosome and entertain with a few short ejaculations the divine guest, that hath been long dressing for a temple to himself. And one of the most constant and vehement importunities that I give him is, that it may be easie for me to slip into eternity in the midst of any action, my soul or its mortal tools are employed about.[49]

If this seems too studied to accept at face value, the comment of Anne Murray, Lady Halkett, says essentially the same thing, though more succinctly: 'I'm sure his life was a continued preparation for death & therefore itt could att noe time surprise him.'[50]

Moray had an eventful life and it is easy enough to make a narrative out of it. But unless one ignores all these signs, one must also find a way also to accommodate within the narrative the reiterated lack of secular purpose and ambition, the submission to providence, the overriding commitment to Christian belief, above all the claim, endorsed by those who knew him, that the whole of this eventful life was lived provisionally, in preparation for death. If we are to understand what early modern

---

[48] BL, Add. MS 78330: Evelyn's commonplace book, fo. 12ᵛ; John Aubrey, *Brief Lives*, ed. Oliver Lawson Dick (1960), 81; Burnet, *Supplement*, 44.
[49] Bodleian Library, MS Add. C. 302: Moray to Sheldon, 14 Oct. 1667, quoted in Stevenson, 'Masonry, Symbolism and Ethics', 427.
[50] NLS, MS 6493: Lady Halkett's journal, 1673–4, p. 215.

lives meant to those who led them, and to use them fully to illuminate their times, we ought not just to set these matters aside or reduce them to post-Enlightenment or new historicist terms. Moray's 'to be rather than to seem' invokes a platonic world of essences, in comparison with which the tissue of appearances, fashioning, and contingencies which have been the focus of much academic study are the trivial things. The exercise of writing the life of an intellectually sophisticated man who believed them to be so is useful because it poses this challenge as its central issue.

I want to close with a passage from John Banville's novella, *The Newton Letter*. The narrator is a conventional biographer of Newton, who in contemplating both his subject's ambivalence about his achievements and the fascination of the ordinary lives he sees around himself, begins to doubt his project. His book was to have been, as he describes it, 'a celebration of action, of the scientist as hero'. But now he cannot cope with 'this Popovian Newton', the greatest scientist the world has known; 'not that I think it is untrue, in the sense that it is fact. It's just that another kind of truth has come to seem to me more urgent.' Why else but this realization of more urgent truth, the biographer asks, had Newton 'turned to deciphering Genesis and dabbling in alchemy? Why else did he insist again and again that science had cost him too dearly'? He envisages Newton brooding on the word Nothing 'as on some magic emblem whose other face is not to be seen and yet is emphatically there. For nothing automatically signifies everything.'[51]

In writing other early modern lives another kind of truth can also present itself as more urgent.

[51] John Banville, *The Newton Letter* (Picador, 1999), 26–7.

14

Reading Clarke's *Lives* in Political and Polemical Context

Peter Lake

The godly lives, anthologized by Samuel Clarke, have been used by generations of historians as sources for the history of puritanism and indeed for the biographies of many an individual puritan. There has, however, been no attempt to locate Clarke's lives in the generic contexts, and in the political and polemical circumstances, in which they were produced and consumed.[1] And that is what I want to make a preliminary attempt to do here. The first context in which I want to set the *Lives* is provided by the genres to which they were appended when they first appeared. For they did not appear first simply as lives, but rather as part of other, wider genres—first of martyrology and then of ecclesiastical history. They were intended to be read as codas to, indeed as culminations of, narratives that stretched through the entire history of the church, from the Old Testament or early church to the present. Second, and perhaps more importantly, I want to read Clarke's compilations against and in terms of the political and polemical situations in which they were printed and then reprinted; the situations and circumstances of 1651 and 1652, of 1660 and 1662, of 1675 and 1677, and of 1683.[2]

---

[1] P. Collinson, ' "A Magazine of Religious Patterns"; An Erasmian Topic Transposed in English Protestantism', in his *Godly People* (London, 1983).

[2] S. Clarke, *A general martyrology containing a collection of all the greatest persecutions which have befallen the church of Christ from the creation to our present time* (London, 1651); *The marrow of ecclesiastical history, contained in the lives of the fathers and other learned men and famous divines which have flourished in the Church since Christ's time to the present age* (London, 1650); *A martyrology, containing a collection of all the persecutions which have befallen the Church of England since the first plantation of the Gospel* (London, 1652); *The lives of two and twenty English divines eminent in their generation for learning,*

Clarke did not write any of the lives he collected but rather arranged and printed lives written by others. Herein lay one of their claims to authenticity. As Baxter told the readers of Clarke's 1683 compilation, 'he did not make the histories, but take them made by faithful acquaintance of the dead. And he was not to patch and paint the dead, nor to add anything of his own, but to deliver naked truths.'[3] Different combinations of lives were put together in different circumstances and each iteration of Clarke's collection was framed by different paratextual materials—dedicatory epistles, prefaces, and letters to the reader—designed to shape the reader's response and to address the particular circumstances into which the current version of these texts was being inserted.

The first generic context can be dealt with relatively briefly. The lives initially were appended to *A general martyrology*, a compilation based predominantly on Foxe, 'containing a collection of the greatest persecutions which have befallen the church of Christ, from the creation to our present times'. The resulting narrative stretched from the first ages of the world to the incarnation and then from the life of Christ virtually to the present. Clarke's account represented a continuation of Foxe, culminating in the dreadful things done to Protestants by Catholics in the French wars of religion, the Dutch revolt, the Thirty Years War, and finally the Irish rebellion of 1642, which Clarke recast not as a rebellion at all, but as rather another persecution of Protestants by Catholics. The aim of this narrative was to define the true church through persecution. 'Here thou hast a certain and infallible mark of the true church of Christ, viz. to be hated and persecuted by the devil and his instruments.'[4] On this account persecution was the work of the devil, of Antichrist and of popery and Clarke's book told how the

---

piety and painfulness in the work of the ministry (London, 1660); *A collection of the lives of ten eminent divines* (London, 1662); *The marrow of ecclesiastical history divided into two parts* (London, 1675); *A general martyrology, containing a collection of all the greatest persecutions which have befallen the church of Christ from the creation to our present times, wherein is given an exact account of the Protestants sufferings in Queen Mary's reign whereunto is added the lives of thirty and two English divines famous in their generations for learning and piety and most of them sufferers in the cause of Christ* (London, 1677); *The lives of sundry eminent persons in this later age* (London, 1683).

[3] See Baxter's 'To the reader', in *The lives of sundry eminent* (1683).

[4] *General martyrology* (1651), 'To the Christian reader', sig. aʳ.

saints have 'o'ercome both the pope and Spanish inquisition. | They conquered kings and won the crown at last'.[5]

In his *The marrow of ecclesiastical history* Clarke produced another version of the history of the church; compounded entirely of 'the lives of the fathers and other learned men and famous divines which have flourished in the church from Christ's time to the present age'. Starting with the likes of Ignatius, Athanasius, Chrysostom, and Augustine, the list stretched on through such figures as Aquinas and Lombard to include not only major reformers like Calvin, Luther, and Beza but a host of minor figures. Here were to be found not only English martyrs for Protestant truth—Bilney, Bradford, Cranmer—but also more modern divines, hammers of the papists like Jewel, William Whitaker, Knox, Foxe, Whitgift, and, more recently still, Robert Abbot and Andrew Willett. Remarkably the list concluded with two English puritan divines from the midlands, Robert Bolton and William Whateley. There could scarcely be a clearer illustration of both the global and local aspects of Clarke's work; of the international and world-historical range of his narrative and of the intensely local, English, and almost completely present-minded, focus of the *Lives* themselves. In these two books—the *Martyrology* and *The marrow*—we see a vision of the true church defined by the profession of truth in the face of persecution and error; of truth defended, often in the most difficult of circumstances, by a succession of learned ministers—'champions for scripture truths and patriots for the power of godliness'.[6]

II.

Clarke was concerned to construct and justify a particular version of the puritan tradition; 'moderate', learned, respectable, Presbyterian. In 1651 and 1652 he published two martyrologies; the first one concerned the sufferings of the international church, the second the persecution of the church in England. Appended to both of them were the lives of a number of divines, the spectrum of whose opinions reveal the dimensions of the puritan tradition that Clarke was seeking to construct. In the 1651 volume were to be found Thomas Cartwright, Hugh Clarke,

[5] Ibid., sig. a3ᵛ.
[6] *The marrow of ecclesiastical history* (1650), 'To the Christian reader', sig. A3ᵛ.

Barnaby Potter, Richard Sedgewick, Robert Balsom, John Dod, Herbert Palmer, John Ball, Richard Rothwel, Julines Herring, John Preston. In 1652, John Colet, John Coverdale, Edmund Sandys, Richard Greenham, Paul Baynes, William Bradshaw, Richard Stock, Richard Sibbes, Thomas Taylor, and Laurence Chaderton were all included. Despite their depiction by Clarke as 'moderates', many of these men had not been particularly 'moderate' at all. Indeed, some of them might be thought to have been the leading radical puritans of the period before 1640. Some—Cartwright, Bradshaw, Baynes, Herring—were unrepenting proponents of either Presbyterian or proto-Independent views of the government of the church. Others—Dod, Hildersham, Rothwell, Greenham, Herring—were overt and defiant nonconformists; men who had never finessed or evaded the demands of either subscription or conformity for a quiet life or the chance to remain unmolested in their ministry. Others—Stock, Sibbes, Preston—were neither Presbyterians nor nonconformists—but classic moderate puritans, men who had never confronted or defied the ecclesiastical authorities, but remained continuously in their ministerial posts and pulpits. Their reputation, indeed their identity, as puritans was based neither on their refusal to conform nor on their views on church government but rather on their affect, conversation, and style of divinity. And lastly some—Sandys, Coverdale, and Potter—were bishops—and one, Colet, was a Catholic.

What versions of the 'puritan tradition', what visions of the national church and of English Protestantism were being canvassed here? Here is one way in which the 'tradition' under construction in these *Lives* was characterized. John Carter was described as 'always a non-conformist, one of the good old puritans of England. He never swallowed any of the prelatical ceremonies against his conscience; so that he was often troubled by the bishops but God raised him up friends that always brought him off and maintained his liberty.'[7] Here is another, alternative description. Thomas Hill was 'sound in the faith, orthodox in his judgement, firmly adhering to the good old doctrine of the church of England, even that which in the university was taught and maintained by famous Whitaker, Perkins, Davenant, Ward and many others in their times' and 'in the other university' (Oxford) by, amongst others, Robert Abbot, the future Bishop of Salisbury whose life was, as we have seen,

---

[7] *Ten eminent divines* (1662), 5.

also to be found in Clarke's *Marrow*.[8] The aim or effect was not quite to equate these two traditions—the one classically 'puritan', centred on questions of church government and outward ceremony, the other on issues of doctrine—but rather to associate and intertwine them so inextricably that it became all but impossible to tell or to prise them apart. Thus, of Carter it was said not only that he was one 'of the good old puritans of England' but also that he was 'sound and orthodox in his judgement, an able and resolute champion against all manner of popery and Arminianism, as also against Anabaptism and Brownism'.[9] There is, of course, a via media being established here but it is one not between Rome and Geneva but rather between popery and Arminianism, on the one hand, and Brownism and sectarian heterodoxy, on the other.

The lives collected by Clarke constructed an ideal of pastoral excellence and effectiveness and of personal godliness, a perfect meld of moderation and zeal, epitomized and lived out by these men. They were all portrayed as outstandingly learned; child prodigies, many of them were described as swots of heroic proportions.[10] They were also very often presented as spiritual adepts; bringing the intensity and insight gleaned from their own spiritual experiences of conversion or despair, temptation or affliction, to bear on their study of scripture and application of scripture to the lives of their flocks.[11] This was a spiritual insight and intensity reflected not only in the power and effectiveness of their preaching but often also of their extempore prayer.[12] In their lives and works the fruits of the most abstruse scholarship, of formal divinity and the study of the scriptures in the original languages, of the church fathers and church history, were distilled into genuinely popular discourse. The high and the low met and melded perfectly in their pulpit and pastoral style. The result was a capacity to speak tellingly to the most humble of Christians.[13] They were also presented as skilful doctors of

---

[8] *A general martyrology* (1677), *The lives of thirty-two English divines*, 232.

[9] *Ten eminent divines* (1662), 5.

[10] For prodigious scholarship see *A general martyrology* (1677), *The lives of thirty-two English divines*, 475–6, for John Preston; also see *Ten eminent divines*, 2–3, for John Carter; also see *The lives of sundry eminent persons* (1683), 138, for Joseph Allein.

[11] *Ten eminent divines*, 61, for John Cotton.

[12] For extempory prayer see *Ten eminent divines* (1662), 38, for Samuel Crook; also see *The lives of sundry eminent persons* (1683), 166, for Samuel Fairclough.

[13] See ibid. 176, for John Dod's preaching style; for Fairclough's, see *The lives of sundry eminent persons* (1683), 164–5.

souls, able to handle even the most extreme and intractable spiritual crises and cases of conscience,[14] capacities which in some cases extended to an ability to wrestle with the devil himself.[15] These divines were also portrayed as sources of order and discipline, able, through their activities in the pulpit, as catechists, visitors of the laity, and regulators of access to the sacrament, to instil discipline and the rigours of properly regulated household worship.[16] In short, they were depicted as both zealous and moderate, effective defenders of both orthodoxy and of order.

And yet, as the lives proclaimed, these men had been and still were often denounced, and indeed persecuted, as disorderly; as 'schismatic', in the case of Arthur Hildersham; simply as 'puritan', in the case of John Preston; or as puritan and 'popular', in the case of Samuel Fairclough. Hildersham was in and out of trouble with the authorities—suspended, silenced, fined, and even imprisoned—throughout his career. He was denounced as 'a man refractory and disobedient to the orders, rites and ceremonies of the Church of England'; as a 'schismatic' and 'a prime ring leader of the schismatical persons in that country', but his life shows him to have been a 'moderate'; his nonconformity professed 'merely for his judgement and conscience, having done nothing either factiously or contemptuously against the government and those orders of the church that were then established'. 'Though himself was a constant nonconformist yet such was his ingenuity and Christian charity that he respected, esteemed and was very familiar with those he knew to be religious and learned, though of another judgement.'[17] Similar accounts were given of the moderation of those other iconic puritan figures and sedulous nonconformists John Dod and Richard Greenham.[18]

Just as he was not factious over the issue of conformity, Hildersham was entirely sound on the issue of schism, being a determined opponent not only of separation but also of the 'semi-separatism of Mr Jacob'. That quintessential moderate puritan Andrew Willett was quoted as

[14] *A general martyrology* (1677), *The lives of thirty-two English divines*, 14 (Greenham); 170 (Dod).

[15] *A general martyrology* (1677), *The lives of thirty-two English divines*, 72–3 (Rothwel) and 181–2 (Balsom).

[16] Ibid., 'The life of master Herbert Palmer', esp. 188–90, 195–6.

[17] Ibid., 'The life of Arthur Hildersham', 119, 120; '*Life of Dr Preston*', *passim*, see for instance, p. 87; for Fairclough see *The lives of sundry eminent persons*, 161.

[18] *A general martyrology* (1677), *The lives of thirty-two English divines*, 172 (Dod); 13 (Greenham).

hailing Hildersham as the 'hammer of the schismatics'.[19] That other radical nonconformist and Presbyterian, Julines Herring, was described as also sound on the issue of separation. Such commitments led him to lament 'the strangeness of independent brethren when they came into Holland'.[20] John Ball was similarly anti-pathetic to any hint of schism, and, just like Herring, alarmed by the rise of Independency. Again like Herring, Ball associated schism (and therewith Independency) with a slippery slope that led to all sorts of fantasies and errors. He was outspoken in his opposition to all notions of extra scriptural revelation, and while, on his deathbed (in 1640) he might prophesy the difficulties to come, predicting 'a very sharp storm'—'the last combat which we should have with Antichrist', as he termed it—when asked if he had ever enjoyed such visitations from the spirit himself, he replied, 'No, I bless God, and, if I should ever have such fantasies, I hope God would give me grace to resist them.'[21]

The *Lives* claimed that the Church of England had denied itself the full benefits of these men's ministry solely because of the episcopal persecution to which they had been subjected. For instance, William Bradshaw was portrayed as having great 'spiritual gifts', of the sort that were 'peculiar to God's favourites'. These were combined with 'natural gifts and parts' of the most outstanding order; such as rendered him 'useful and instrumental for the public good of God's people'. Yet he was 'never suffered to continue long quiet in any settled place of a more public employment'.[22] Throughout the lives an unholy alliance of jealous clergy, profane lay persons, and the bishops and their officials, was shown making the lives of these godly ministers a misery, sometimes even driving them into silence or exile. This was persecution and the response to it could be bitter; Paul Baynes was quoted as saying of the bishops 'they are a generation of the earth, earthly and savour not the ways of God'.[23]

The *Lives* showed these persecutory tendencies growing sharper in the 1630s; noting 'some flying so extremely high, the ceremonies being pressed with rigour and grievous penalties inflicted'; 'the rigour of the prelates, how it grew higher every day, how they persecuted

---

[19] Ibid., for Hildersham, p. 120.   [20] Ibid., for Herring, pp. 162, 167.
[21] Ibid., for Ball, pp. 153, 154.   [22] Ibid., for Bradshaw, p. 25.
[23] Ibid. 23.

conscientious ministers and Christ', spreading 'innovations and the book for liberty of sports on the sabbath days, tending to the fearful profanation thereof'.[24] There was also stress placed in a number of lives on the rise, at much the same time, of Arminian doctrine. Thus, of Thomas Hill it was said that

> the doctrine of God's sovereignty in his decrees: of his in-conditionate-free-electing-love: of his free grace against free will and the power of nature in spirituals: of justification by the imputed righteousness of Christ, against the perfection of inherent righteousness now attainable by us in this life: of perseverance in grace, against the apostasy of the saints and the like were not, with this pious and learned man, (as they are now called by some) sects and notions, matters only of learning and curiosity and of the presbyterian faction, but of the life-blood of faith which, at his death, (as he expressed to a friend of his) he had singular comfort from and in his life firmly believed, constantly preached and by his pen endeavoured to maintain and defend.[25]

Here we find the integral connections between doctrine and lived religious experience, between formal polemic and practical divinity, between the outpourings of the pulpit and of the press, between the world of the university and that of the parish and godly household, that were at the centre of all these lives, given compressed and concrete expression, as the earlier confrontations between Calvinist orthodoxy and Laudian Arminianism of the 1630s were associated, if not conflated, with subsequent showdowns with later varieties of (antinomian and sectarian) predestinarian error.

The master oppositions in play here are those between God and the devil, Christ and Antichrist, between the moderate puritan, incipiently Presbyterian, true church tradition being outlined by Clarke, and the popish, episcopal and later sectarian persecutors of that tradition. Again, a middle way, associated with the national Protestant church of England, is being sketched here, but it is a distinctly puritan *via media*, located between Episcopalian Arminianism, on the one hand, and later sectarian, indeed Independent-inspired, heterodoxy, on the other.

While the most prominent objects of persecution were overt nonconformists, Presbyterians, and proto-congregationalists, Clarke was concerned precisely not to isolate such men in a uniquely pure and

---

[24] *Ten eminent divines* (1662), 10, 263.
[25] *A general martyrology* (1677), *The lives of thirty-two English divines*, 232.

persecuted nonconformist or Presbyterian ghetto. On the contrary, he consistently associated the likes of Dod or Hildersham with other more moderate spirits, ministers who subscribed, and, at least after their own lights, conformed. Thus Bradshaw's life was written by his friend, the moderate Thomas Gataker, who went out of his way to quote the admiring opinion of Bradshaw held by Bishop Joseph Hall.[26]

There was only one early Stuart bishop contained in the collections of the early 1650s, and that was Barnaby Potter, 'a great favourer of zealous professors and lecturers and therefore he was accounted by many a puritanical bishop'. Potter had opposed the introduction of the book of sports into his diocese and in 1640 delivered a sermon in Westminster inveighing against the 'corruptions that were crept into the church especially in respect of ceremonies so eagerly pressed by sundry bishops as bowing to the altar and such like innovations'. When he was still denounced, in certain quarters, as a popish bishop, he died, the life implies of a broken heart.[27]

What we are seeing here was the construction of a spectrum of respectable, orthodox Protestant opinion running from Potter on the one extreme, through the likes of Sibbes, Preston, and Stock, to Greenham and Dod, Hildersham and Baynes, and Bradshaw and Cartwright, at the other. Here, then, was an orthodox English Protestant tradition being equated with a respectable puritan tradition. That tradition was connected to the version of the true church and of church history contained in the front parts of Clarke's two *Martyrologies* by the inclusion of the lives of Colet, Coverdale, and Sandys. Colet was pictured as a proto-Protestant, a connecting link between the preceding narratives and later puritanism because of the hostile attentions that his reforming activities consistently attracted from the bishops. Coverdale linked Colet to the later divines as did Sandys. Sandys, of course, became a bishop, but the account of his life in Clarke concentrated on his activities supporting Northumberland's coup against Mary, and on his subsequent imprisonment and then escape from the jaws of death in Marian England to exile and safety abroad. Sandys's preferment to the episcopate occurred in the last paragraph of the life, which concluded a matter of twelve lines later. Here was an episcopal life being put to anything but Episcopalian purposes, as Sandys's persecution at the hands

---

[26] Ibid. 60, for 'Dr Hall's character' of Bradshaw.   [27] Ibid. 156.

of the papists and participation in resistance against a popish monarch almost kicked off the collection.[28]

The prefatory materials in the 1651 and 1652 *Martyrologies* amplified these points. Clarke explained why he was continuing the *Martyrologies* with the lives 'of sundry of our modern divines ... though they were not martyrs, yet may they well be styled confessors, in regard of their persecutions and sufferings which most of them met withal whilst they lived here'.[29] The issue of persecution was particularly pertinent here because by the early 1650s the Presbyterian cause and the moderate/respectable puritan tradition delineated by Clarke were facing defeat. To prepare for what was coming and to warn the victors and their potential victims of what was in store, recourse was being had to history. Thus the reader of the 1652 English *Martyrology* was reminded that the true Christians of England had suffered persecution 'under heathens and then under Antichrist for some thousands of years and latterly under the prelacy'. But God 'through his infinite mercy and by his unresistable power' had 'in all ages preserved a church and remnant from the first plantation of the gospel to the present times'. Thus the reader was told that 'you shall here find what is that rock upon which kings, princes, prelates and other great personages have split themselves, viz. when either from a principle of innate malice, or upon the suggestions and solicitations of others they have turned persecutors of the faithful ministers and servants of Jesus Christ, and here you shall see that they'— God's children—'are preserved by the mighty power of God through faith to the salvation of their souls'.[30] 'One thing is very remarkable in this history that usually, before any great persecution befell the church, the holy men of those times observed that there was some great decay of zeal and of the power of godliness, or some mutual contention and quarrels amongst the people of God or some such sin or other that provoked God against them.' Now, it was claimed, the English church found itself in precisely that situation again. And 'if the same sins abound amongst us in these days which have been the forerunners of persecutions formerly', then surely the same outcomes were imminent now.[31]

[28] *A general martyrology* (1677), 11, for Sandys's preferment to the episcopal bench.
[29] *A general martyrology* (1651), a2ᵛ.
[30] *A martyrology* (1652), dedicatory epistle, sigs. A3ʳ–A3ᵛ.
[31] *A general martyrology* (1651), sigs. aᵛ, a2ᵛ.

After regicide and revolution had rendered the failure of Presbyterian reformation certain, the future seemed to belong to the sectarian and heterodox enemies of true religion as Clarke's *Lives* portrayed it. Ahead were almost certain assaults on all that these *Lives* held dear; on a settled, learned ministry, maintained by tithes, on the universities that produced them, on the integrity of the national church, on Protestant orthodoxy as these lives constructed it. But if persecution was just around the corner, it was a persecution to be waged not by prelates and princes, or even by papists, but rather by sectaries, schismatics, and heretics.[32]

III.

The next publication of Clarke's Lives came in 1660 and 1662. The 1660 volume comprised the *Lives of two and twenty English divines*. This reprinted the lives contained in the two *Martyrologies* of the early 1650s. The 1662 volume *A collection of the lives of ten eminent divines* contained accounts hitherto unpublished by Clarke. These were men who had been 'out' in the 1630s—prime victims of the rise of Laudianism—but very much 'in' during the 1640s, when many of them—Gouge, Hill, Herbert Palmer, Robert Harris—had moved to London livings, preached before the Long Parliament, been appointed to the Westminster Assembly and even ended up as the masters of various Oxbridge colleges. We are dealing here with an emergent 'Presbyterian' establishment, with men who had trembled on the edge of complete personal and ideological victory in the mid-1640s, faced down the prospect of equally complete defeat in the early 1650s, and managed, for the most part, to accommodate themselves to the various political and ecclesiastical establishments of the 1650s. Now, at the restoration, they were facing the prospect of defeat—of dissolution, disgrace, and expulsion—again.

Clarke's collections of 1660 and 1662 expanded the spectrum of opinions, the ideological range of the puritan tradition being defended. In a gesture towards respectable Independency and the New England Way, John Cotton came in, and, in a similar gesture towards various strands of Episcopalian opinion and conformist Calvinism, so too

---

[32] This is rendered explicit by a prefatory poem by Thomas Dugard contained in the *Martyrology* of 1652, 'On our English martyrs and martyrologers, master Fox and master Clark', sigs. a2^r–a4^r.

did that spokesman for reduced episcopacy, Calvinist orthodoxy and reformed unity against the threats of popery, Arminianism, and hetero-doxy, Archbishop Ussher.

This account of Ussher was echoed on the Presbyterian side, where not only their fearless defence of doctrinal orthodoxy but also the relative moderation of their views on church government were stressed. Thus Robert Harris was described as remaining 'not convinced of some things that were earnestly pressed about church government. He did not conceive any one external form to be so essential to a church but that it might still deserve that name, though under a presbyterian or independent or episcopal form, so long as it was kept within the general rules laid down in the scriptures. It is true, some of these had been abused to tyranny and the rest might in time be abused also, but the use and abuse of things are far different and he would not commend either the one or the other in their rigid exactions in some cases.' Harris retained doubts as to the perpetuity of lay eldership, and as for Independency, while he remained sceptical of some of its central tenets and effects, he conceded that it was in many ways 'a politic way and free from much trouble'. On the subject of the fraught relations between Presbyterians and Independents Harris decried 'the readiness of many to side and make divisions'.[33] Herbert Palmer was described as having entertained similar doubts about central aspects of the Presbyterian platform. Admittedly, he had become 'a very great instrument for the promoting' of 'presbyterian government', but only after an open-minded assessment of the debates of the Westminster Assembly.[34] Throughout, the impression being striven for was not of a doctrinaire commitment to the Presbyterian cause, but rather of a moderately held and expressed set of opinions or preferences reached after a period of doubt, discussion, and debate. This, then, remained a tradition centred on Presbyterianism, but in the formulation of 1660–2, it was a moderate Presbyterianism, modified by inclusive gestures made towards both the respectable Independency of John Cotton and the reduced episcopacy of James Ussher.

It seems reasonable to conclude that this version of the puritan tradition was a product both of the experiences of the later 1650s and of

[33] *Ten eminent divines* (1662), 317–18.
[34] *A general martyrology* (1677), *The lives of thirty-two English divines*, 428–9.

the exigencies—both the threats and the opportunities—offered by the approaching Restoration. For in many ways, during the 1650s, such a united front of respectable Independents and Presbyterians had already seen off the radical sectarian challenge. The Association Movement of Richard Baxter, which saw Presbyterians, Independents, and even some moderate Episcopalians collaborating to bend the structures of the Cromwellian church to their own evangelical ends, was only the most overt of such efforts. The popular front being constructed by Clarke's *Lives* in their 1660–2 iteration might be seen as an attempt to continue those tactics in order *both* to take advantage of the opportunities for comprehension, inclusion, and perhaps even of hegemony, if the up-coming Restoration settlement went well for the nonconformists, *and* to prepare for the exclusion and renewed persecution that would ensue if things went badly.

As the letter to the reader in the 1662 volume made clear, this was not a partisan production, intended to defend one particular faction or party, but rather to vindicate the whole English church. 'We see how diligent the papists have been to write and publish the lives of their Rome-canonised saints, though most of them were but ignes fatui that led men into bogs of error.... How much more diligent and careful should we be to perpetuate the memories of those who were fixed stars, not in the Antichristian, but in the true church of Christ. And truly, if any church of Christ in the Christian world since the reformation, much more (through God's great mercy) hath the church of England abounded with such; and now what doth the Lord require of us but that we should be followers of those who, through faith and patience, inherit the promises.' Here, then, is an explicit claim to be defending the Church of England, because of the abundance of true (puritan) saints to be found within it. That claim is being made against the counter-claims to false sanctity and sainthood advanced by the Church of Rome, but in defending the Church of England against popery that church's best self is being identified with an overtly puritan rendition of the English Protestant tradition. Moreover, elsewhere in the same letter this rendition of the puritan tradition is expressly defended against other, conformist, royalist, even 'Anglican', attempts to tar all puritans with the brush of sedition and rebellion, of sectarianism and heresy. 'This is no new thing. Indeed, it is an old trick of the devil to belie God's children and to represent them in the ugliest hue they can devise, thereby to make them the more odious.'[35] Clarke's *Lives* were designed not only to refute such claims, by emphasizing that neither the rise of the sects, and the concomitant breakdown of religious order, nor even the civil war itself, had had any thing to do with the denizens of the puritan tradition, as his works constructed that tradition, but also to type all those who persisted in making such accusations as agents of the devil, actual or potential persecutors, hell bent on suppressing the denizens of the true church; persons whose status as such could, of course, only be validated or confirmed by such treatment.

Of course, the central involvement of many of Clarke's subjects in the events of the 1640s, the inescapable fact that they were all parliamentarians, could scarcely be denied. But their political activities and commitments were ascribed always to *religion*—the pursuit of reformation and order, in the Westminster Assembly, in the colleges of the universities, or in a variety of parochial settings—and never to *politics*. The preaching of fast sermons before the Long Parliament was noted, but the contents of those sermons never anatomized or even mentioned. There is even an exception that proves this rule. One life published by Clarke in the 1650s—that of Robert Balsom— had been perhaps more than tinged with parliamentarian activism or partisanship. A chaplain in the parliamentarian garrison at Wardour Castle, Balsom had been captured by royalists and when threatened with death, unless he sued for pardon and offered to serve the king, he had spat defiance at his captors. Reprieved from execution, by, as the marginal note says, 'a special providence', he was sent to Oxford and eventually released as part of a prisoner exchange. He then served as a chaplain in Essex's army. Balsom, then, was an unapologetic, defiant, and serial parliamentarian activist. Significantly, his life is the only one from the 1650s collections omitted from those of 1660 and 1662. Similarly, the dedication of the 1651 edition of the *General martyrology* to the 'right honorable Francis Brook, baron of Beauchamp's Court', the son of that radical parliamentarian Lord Brook, with whom Clarke claimed an intimate personal connection, was also omitted from later editions.[36]

---

[35] *Ten eminent divines* (1662), 'To the candid reader', sigs. A2^r, A4^r.

[36] It was included again in 1677. For the dedication see *A general martyrology* (1651), sigs. A2^r–A4^v.

In the life of Robert Harris of Hanwel the outbreak of war is described thus—'now began those cloudy times and his saddest days'.[37] This is entirely typical; the onset of war is nearly always described in the passive voice. It is something that occurs elsewhere; something that happens *in spite of* and *to* Clarke's subjects rather than with any hint of active volition or collaboration on their part. The day of 23 October 1643 had found Harris in his pulpit at Hanwell. This was also the day of Edge Hill, 'being distant about 4 miles from him and yet it pleased God to so order it (which he took for a great mercy) that he heard not the least noise of it (the wind sitting contrary) till the public work of the day was over; nor could he believe the report of a battle, till a soldier besmeared with blood and powder came to witness it'. Harris's 'troubles' are then described as increasing 'from this very time'.[38] In fact, over the long run, Harris did very well out of the war; going first from Hanwell to St Botolph's Bishopsgate; then joining the assembly of divines, he was first offered the living at Petersfield in Hampshire before ending up as Master of Trinity College in Oxford. This led to certain 'libels' being spread in Oxford accusing him and others like him of greed, claims which Harris and his biographer went to considerable lengths to refute.[39] This was, in fact, a recurrent theme in many of these lives, as the acquisition of livings, influence, and status that their role in the 1640s conferred upon many of these divines caused them to be accused of careerism and greed, indeed of profiting from the kingdom's tragedy. Hence the stress on Harris's troubles being deepened by the war.

Moreover, just as their parliamentarianism is presented as reluctant, even accidental, such men are shown as having nothing but contempt for 'sectaries'. The efficacy of Robert Balsom's ministry was underwritten not merely by the number of people he had 'converted' to true religion but also by the number of those who, 'drawn away by sectaries', he had 'reduced' again to orthodoxy.[40] Jeremiah Whitaker 'in his public ministry' consistently expressed 'his dislike, yea his detestation thereof, to the faces of them, how great soever, who too much favoured heresies, errors and ranting courses, though he knew that thereby he did run the hazard of procuring many frowns to himself'.[41] Richard Capel

---

[37] *Ten eminent divines* (1662), 286.   [38] Ibid. 286–7.   [39] Ibid. 288–90.
[40] *A general martyrology* (1677), *The lives of thirty-two English divines*, 403.
[41] *Ten eminent divines* (1662), 166.

took a similarly intransigent stance against the doctrinal innovations of the day. As for his own pulpit practice Capel was described as having 'kept close to the footsteps of our choicest worthies, as famous Mr Dod...Mr Cleaver, Mr Hildersham and such other holy men of God, led by the self same spirit'.[42]

In passages like these we can watch the English puritan and reformed tradition, constructed and asserted in these lives, feeding upon and reproducing itself. Equated with the public Christian profession of the Church of England and with the beliefs and practises of 'our choicest worthies' and most 'orthodox divines', that tradition provided the basis for a thoroughgoing rejection not only of the innovations of Laudianism and Arminianism but also, rather more pressingly in 1660, of the sectarian chaos of the 1640s and 1650s. The lives printed in 1662 reiterated the previous claim that this version of the English puritan and reformed traditions represented a true *via media* between popery and Laudianism, on the one hand, and schism and sectarian heresy, on the other. After the defeats of the later 1640s, the earlier hopes for reformation and partisan energies of the civil war period have been suppressed, and after the accommodations of the 1650s, partisan divisions between Presbyterians and Independents are being laid aside in favour of a common front against the dual threats of sectarianism and heresy, on the one hand, and of a renewed episcopal 'persecution', on the other. These claims to moderation, the selective amnesia and the common 'puritan' front were just as effective as pitches to be comprehended within, as they were as preparatives for exclusion from, the restored Church of England. When Clarke was writing the epistle to the reader for his second volume on 'October 10, 1661', in 'my study in Threadneedle Street' the renewed exclusion and persecution that, in fact, followed St Bartholomew's Day 1662 must have seemed anything but inevitable.[43] There was still much to play for and, arguably, in publishing these lives, in this form, then, Clarke was playing for it.

IV.

Of course, the Restoration settlement did not include—indeed it might be said, in the end, to have been expressly designed to exclude—the style of churchmanship delineated in Clarke's volumes. And the next time

---

[42] Ibid. 252.   [43] Ibid., 'To the reader', sig. A4ᵛ.

we find Clarke's lives being reinserted into the public discourse about
conformity, comprehension, and persecution is in the mid-1670s; in
1675 and 1677, to be precise, when he reprinted, first his *Marrow of
ecclesiastical history* and then, two years later, in one volume both his
General and *English martyrologies* and all the clerical lives that had been
appended to or published separately in his previous volumes. Again, the
timing may not have been an accident, as doubts about the rise of popery and arbitrary government began to increase and Danby continued
to play the church and king card to rally support for the regime. His
dedication of the reprint of *The marrow* to Philip, Lord Wharton and
his wife, with the former, 'though my personal acquaintance with your
lordship be not great', hailed as someone who had 'publicly espoused'
'the interest of religion' and 'as eminent in appearing for a generation
of people everywhere spoken against', certainly betokens an attempt
both to stir up and to advert to political support for the cause of
nonconformists in a time of trouble.[44]

The last publication by Samuel Clarke of a collection of lives came in
1683, after the crisis presaged by the 1677 volume and the outbreak of
renewed nonconformist political activism that had attended that crisis
were over, and the Tory reaction that those events had provoked was in
full swing. This book retained essentially the same agenda as the previous volumes; the maintenance of respectable puritan or nonconformist
unity and the refutation of the conformist and Anglican accusation that
all puritans were in effect sectaries, heretics, and rebels. Such accusations
had, of course, received a new lease of life during the Exclusion Crisis
and the Tory reaction that had followed it. Thus in an epistle to the
reader Richard Baxter explained that

we live in a time of mental war, when it is the devil's great and daily business to
belie the best of men and make the ignorant believe that they are a generation of
walking plagues, movers of sedition, teaching men to worship God contrary to
the law, enemies to Caesar, preaching up another king, one Jesus, and turning
the world upside down, not keeping the traditions of the fathers. The cry is
loud, away with such fellows from the earth. It is not fit that they should live.
Most odious lies are published of them with so great confidence as that strangers
may think they are bound to believe them, lest they should censure the reporters

---

[44] *The marrow of ecclesiastical history divided into two parts* (1675), 'the epistle dedicatory', signed 'from my study in Hammersmith August 2nd 1675', sig. b2^{v}.

to be what they are. . . . Thousands are hardened in sin, yea in enmity against a
holy life, yea in persecution, by believing serious godly men to be as bad as the
carnal world, a humorous, proud, seditious, hypocritical sort of people. . . . It is
the custom of the devil to write infamous lies of the best men when they are
dead, which would be believed if those that knew them while they lived did not
say that which should refute the lies.[45]

This passage repeated, in compressed form, the schema of the previous
martyrologies. The master oppositions here were those between God
and the devil; true religion and popery; the godly and the persecution
of princes and prelates, but those polarities were now being applied
to the current struggle between the puritan godly, whose pedigree,
identity, and virtues formed the subject of Clarke's tomes, and their
contemporary (church and king, 'Anglican') critics and enemies. For, on
this unforgiving binary logic, if the calumny of the godly was the work
of the devil, then, conversely, telling the truth about them was God's
work; its status as such confirmed, as Clarke himself claimed, by the
fact that his works had been so generally accepted 'of the saints and
with the church of Christ'.[46]

The 1683 volume was composed entirely of lives hitherto unpublished by Clarke. The chronological range spanned the life of Hugh
Broughton from the late Elizabethan and early Stuart periods and ran
more or less up to the present. The emphasis, however, was placed
heavily on men who had come into the ministry in the 1650s and died
in the 1660s and 1670s. It represented an account, therefore, of the
re-entry of respectable Presbyterian puritanism into an age of exclusion
and of persecution and told of the drift of even the most moderate of
puritans towards 'dissent'.

The claims from the volumes of the 1660s about the relation of such
puritans to both the civil war and with the sects were repeated in spades.
Baxter repeated the anecdote about unknowingly preaching while battle
raged at Edge Hill, only this time about himself.[47] That leading parliamentarian Richard Vines—a clerical adviser at treaties with the king
at Uxbridge and the Isle of Wight, Essex's chaplain and memorialist,
a member of the assembly of divine—was described as being forced by
the outbreak of hostilities to 'retire for his safety' to that parliamentarian

[45] *The lives of sundry eminent persons* (1683), 'To the reader'.
[46] Ibid., 'The preface with the life of the author', sig. A^r.
[47] Ibid., 'To the reader'.

stronghold of Coventry, where the subsequent lectures and exercises in which he participated were presented as having nothing to do with the war.[48]

The same sort of denial, of selective but intense amnesia, was in play whenever the lives turned to the relation of the strand of puritan churchmanship which they were designed to celebrate with the rise of the sects and the collapse of ecclesiastical order and puritan unity. Just like the civil war itself, that, Clarke claimed, had had nothing to do with *us*. Clarke had left his Warwickshire living at Alcester at the start of the 1640s. When the course of hostilities had allowed him to return, he had found that many members of his flock having taken refuge in Warwick had been tainted with Anabaptism, so that 'many young men, whom I looked upon before as children begotten by my ministry to God, were turned preachers'. Clarke prevailed upon these unfortunates to desist and agree to submit themselves to his ministry again, if he returned, but 'these sectaries, under hand, wrought against me', and he was forced to return to London.[49] A similar story was told of Thomas Wilson, in Maidstone.[50] The claims being made here are clear enough; civil war, regicide and revolution, schism and heresy, were none of their doing, but rather things that happened to these men and against which they had struggled mightily.

Opposed, as they were, to the extremities and heresies of the sects, the divines included in Clarke's 1683 compilation were nevertheless shown to be men of intense spirituality and personal charisma. The baroque emotionalism of high puritan pietism echoes through these pages. Perhaps significantly, the best or most extreme example of this tendency—provided by the life of John Janeway—was also the most overtly a-political and frequently reprinted of the lives. Janeway died in his early twenties; there was therefore not much life to describe and the account concentrated on the spiritual potency, the charisma, of this young prodigy. His life was full of spiritual ejaculations, of letters of counsel and rebuke sent to his brothers, indeed to his father, who was himself a minister. The narrative was finished off by an elaborate account of a deathbed full of 'ecstasies of joy', of 'tastes of heaven' and 'joy unspeakable'.[51] Some of the same characteristics can be seen in

---

[48] Ibid. 48; for a similar story about Samuel Fairclough, see ibid. 173–4.
[49] Ibid., 'The preface with the life of the author', sig. aʳ.   [50] Ibid. 35–6.
[51] Ibid. 60–81, for the deathbed see esp. 77–8.

the more conventional life of Dr Samuel Winter, in which great play
was made with the 'prevalency' and 'power' of Winter's prayer. Winter's
wife was tempted with Anabaptism, going so far as to be dipped, she
still hesitated to go public because of the damage this would do to
her husband's reputation. A day of prayer was arranged to settle her
conscience in the matter, but Winter told her that, because of a pressing
dinner engagement, they could not attend. When she protested, he told
her 'I have been praying for thee and God hath assured me that thou
shalt be satisfied and that quickly too'. And so it turned out; she was
indeed 'satisfied from heaven and afterwards able to dispute with female
Anabaptists, yea and to confute them'.[52]

This story makes, in short compass, a number of claims about the
nature of Winter's style of piety and its relation to order. The enthusiasm, the claims to spiritual insight and prophetic power, habitually
made by the sects, are being matched here by the powers and achievements of the prayerful Winter; through his exercise of those powers he
is able to reimpose clerical authority and orthodox profession on one
tempted by error and schism and to reimpose male patriarchal power
on an errant woman and wife and to do all these things by spiritual
persuasion rather than by force of mere command.

As that story shows, if these lives display the spiritual intensity, the
spirit-drenched charisma, the intercessionary and prophetic power, of
the godly clergy, they are also about the capacity of such clergy to
create and sustain order. Both before the civil war and after the defeat
of Presbyterian hopes for full reformation in the 1640s these men are
shown creating the moral and social effects of Presbyterian discipline
through the simple exercise of their skill and power as pastors. Wilson is
described as having reduced the hitherto profane town of Maidstone to
sobriety and order. These effects paralleled those wrought by the private
visits to all the households in his parish undertaken by Joseph Allein, or,
before the war, by Samuel Fairclough's attempts to regulate access to the
communion.[53]

V.

All this, of course, had been thrown away in 1662. All the divines
whose lives were collected in Clarke's 1683 volume, and who were

---

[52] *The lives of sundry eminent persons* (1683), 104, 106–7.
[53] Ibid. 35, 144, 169.

alive in 1662, had refused to conform and thus left the church and
their ministry. The result was a more systematic repeat of the situation
pertaining before 1640, as his earlier volumes had portrayed it, with
the Church of England denied, or rather denying itself, the services of
some of its most exemplary ministers, its most effective savers of souls
and creators of order. But if they all 'left', all these men, in one way or
another, continued to exercise many of the functions of a minister of
the word. The most passively law-abiding response came from Clarke
himself who held that after that 'black act for conformity' that 'turned
me, and almost 2000 godly and painful ministers and schoolmasters out
of their places' 'I durst not separate from the Church of England nor was
satisfied about gathering a private church out of a true church, as I judge
the Church of England to be, yet'. He withdrew from London to Isle-
worth and appears to have eschewed all ministerial activity, restricting
his activities to the printing press.[54]

Clarke's subjects in *Sundry eminent persons* were, for the most part,
more active; continuing to expound the word, praying and fasting in
their own or other people's households. Thus, after he was expelled
from his Suffolk living, Samuel Fairclough led a peripatetic life moving
from the household of one son to another. There he would attend the
parish church in the morning and preach himself in the family in the
evening. As a marginal note put it, 'he doth preach in private and hear
in public'.[55] Edmund Staunton made an even more finely calibrated
withdrawal and re-engagement with the ministry. For all the emphasis
placed, throughout Clarke's account, on the 'private', household- and
family-based nature of Staunton's activities after 1662, and the delineation of his carefully variegated withdrawals from 'public ministry', it
is clear that, despite having been silenced as a nonconformist, Staunton
had continued to exercise many of the central functions of a public
ministry, albeit in 'private'; preaching and ministering, both in his own
household and abroad, to all comers, while using a network of gentry
connections in Hertfordshire and London to defy the authorities—
without, of course, ever himself separating from the national church
or attempting to gather a separated church or congregation from out of
that church.[56]

Others were yet more assertive; Thomas Tregoss having been
'excluded from the public place of prayer and preaching' 'ceased not

---

[54] Ibid. 11.   [55] Ibid. 176.   [56] Ibid. 163–5.

to preach in his own family twice every lord's day, which, being known in the neighbourhood, diverse, who had the comfort of his ministry in public, could not but thirst after it in private'.[57] Owen Stockton, having been given 'the liberty of his pulpit' by the non-resident and then entirely delinquent minister of Chattisham in Suffolk, took immediate advantage of the Indulgence of 1672 by accepting the call of an Ipswich congregation.[58] Tregoss and Joseph Allein eventually chose to preach publicly and to evangelize openly both at home and abroad. Tregoss adopted this course in 1665 at what he took to be the direct prompting of God. Thereafter, he returned to the public pulpit in various local churches, only immediately to attract the attention of the authorities; a local JP, Thomas Robinson, apprehended Tregoss when he was preaching in his own house, took the names of all those attending and bound Tregoss over to present himself to the constable in a week's time. Thus began a period of what was, in Clarke's terms, something like full-on persecution, the experience of which allowed both Tregoss and his biographer to parallel his sufferings to those 'of the saints departed, martyred for the testimony of Jesus' under Mary Tudor and immortalized by Foxe.[59] The lives of both Tregoss and Allein were full of stories of run-ins with local JPs and deputy lieutenants, the persecuting gentry, and church courts. That of Tregoss was laced with accounts of the providential punishments and judgements visited upon his persecutors.[60] Both Tregoss and Allein spent a good deal of time in court, and indeed in jail. But whenever they secured their release they returned to the struggle and ended up in trouble again. Both men had their health broken by a combination of their extreme pastoral exertions and their time in prison.

We have, then, a spectrum of responses to the Restoration church settlement running from Clarke's own passivity through publication, through the combination of private defiance and public compliance perfected by Fairclough or Edmund Staunton, Stockton's use of Indulgence to embrace the identity of a 'dissenter', to the full-on defiance of Allein or Tregoss. And yet despite the wide range of reactions on display here, it was claimed of all of these men that they were, in some sense, 'moderate'. Their moderation consisted in the maintenance of a

[57] *The lives of sundry eminent persons* (1683), 110.   [58] Ibid. 193.
[59] Ibid. 112, 116.   [60] Ibid. 113, 115–16.

charitable communion with all those who maintained the root of true godliness within them, in a refusal to allow the partisan espousal of particular views about church polity or outward ceremonies or observances to disrupt the unity of the godly and a concomitant refusal to seek out or to prosecute, for their own sake, disputes about such matters. Even that firebrand, Joseph Allein, was so described.[61]

In the Life of Allein, these attributes were distributed under the marginal heading of his 'holy prudence'. Next to 'his moderation', however, we find the opinion that 'separation in a church was many times necessary, from the known corruptions of it. But allowed not separation from a church where active compliance with some sinful evil was not made a condition of communion.'[62] That, of course, was a view in direct contrast to that of Clarke himself. Thus, by reading between the lines, we can discern, even in Clarke's own text, a division within the ranks of English Presbyterians, between those, like Allein, who were willing, perhaps even eager, to separate themselves from a church that made 'active compliance with sinful evil' 'the condition of communion' and those, like Clarke himself, who 'durst not separate', nor even 'gather a private church out of' the 'true church that he judged the Church of England to be'. On the one hand, by stressing the 'moderation', the mutual forbearance and Christian charity, pertaining between men of these different opinions and approaches, and indeed between them and other 'saints' with 'the root of the matter in them', Clarke's collection of lives represented a closing of the ranks, the construction, in the face of exclusion and repression, of a popular dissenting or puritan front. On the other hand, for all its elaborate claims to moderation, its professed and apparent refusal to take sides in the disputes between those excluded in 1662 over what to do next, we might take Clarke's books, both of 1677, and particularly of 1683, to be *sotto voce* contributions to subsequent intra-puritan debates; contributions that came down squarely on the side of nonconformist unity in the face of persecution and of 'dissenting' readiness to be reincorporated within a suitably modified national Protestant church; that is to say, that came down firmly on the side of comprehension, rather than of toleration or of de facto separation.

---

[61] For Machin, see ibid. 90; for Owen Stockton, p. 197; for Edmund Staunton, p. 170; for Thomas Tregoss, p. 121; for Joseph Allein, pp. 142–3.

[62] Ibid. 142, for his 'holy prudence; p. 143, for 'his moderation'.

Thus in 1683, just as in 1662, despite the overwhelmingly Presbyterian tenor of the collection, through the inclusion of Richard Mather, a reconciliatory gesture was made towards respectable Independency, at least as it was represented by the New England Way. The stress on the refusal of all these men to make a fuss about 'things disputable', about the 'dividing controversies of our age', represented an attempt to draw a veil over the internal disputes of the 1640s and 1650s, to build on the links of cooperation and support that had united some Presbyterians and Independents in the 1650s in order to play up both the unity and the moderation of those excluded at 1662. As with the involvement of an earlier generation in the civil war—represented here in the lives of Vines or Fairclough, Wilson or Stockton—great stress was laid upon the exclusively religious, entirely non-political, nature of these men's disobedience and dissent. Thus the insistent accusations that that serial nonconformist, Thomas Tregoss, was 'a dangerous and seditious person' were turned aside with the claim that 'neither in his preaching nor conference' had he ever 'meddled with the present discipline or liturgy of the church, much less with any state affairs. Nay, he persuaded others to be obedient to the higher powers and, in his daily exercises, he put up many fervent petitions for the King's Majesty.'[63]

It is clear, then, that Clarke wanted his essentially Presbyterian version of puritanism or dissent to appear moderate, inclusive, and tolerant. When confronted with such claims, it is essential to ask just who was it that was beyond the pale? What hints do these texts give as to the identity of those who were not 'sound in the fundamentals of religion'? Just whose 'practice' *did* destroy 'their profession of Christianity'? On the nonconformist side of the equation, the one group that these lives were prepared to identify in this role was the Quakers. One of the anecdotes told to illustrate the peculiar efficacy of John Machin's prayers involved his praying at the deathbed of a Quaker. 'The more earnestly he prayed with the sick person, the more he raged, which was an argument to him and to several other of the company then present that Quakerism was a degree of possession.'[64] Not even the common experience of persecution could elide or reduce these differences. While in prison, Joseph Allein and his fellows had been much afflicted by the profane prisoners who, with 'the rattling of their chains, the blaspheming of

---

[63] For Machin, see ibid. 114.   [64] Ibid. 84.

their tongues, their roaring and singing', disrupted their devotions. But the 'quakers also much molested them disturbing them with their cavils in the times of prayer, preaching and singing and would come and work in their callings just by them at such times, to their great grief'.[65]

But if the Quakers were 'out', at least some conformist divines were (sort of) 'in'. Two of the 1683 lives have certificates of spiritual authenticity, expressions of admiration and acceptance, from nameless conformist divines appended to them. 'A reverend conformist' preached Fairclough's funeral sermon, passages from which were quoted at length at the end of the life.[66] At the conclusion of the life of John Machin, 'a pious divine who at this time is a dignitary in the church' was cited as giving a wholly admiring 'character' of Machin's spiritual qualities and pastoral effectiveness.[67] But if such sympathetic conformist spirits might be included, undoubtedly excluded from the English Protestant tradition, the Church of England way, delineated by these texts, were the Bonner-like persecutors of the subjects of Clarke's *Lives*; such men (and women) had been and still were performing the devil's work, persecuting the godly just like the papists had before them. For all the moderation and irenicism that had gone into Clarke's Protestant tradition-building for such as these—for unrepentant sectaries like the Quakers, and for equally unrepentant persecutors like Thomas Tregoss's tormentor, the JP Thomas Robinson, who had been gored to death in his own tenement by his own (and otherwise entirely pacific) bull—these were scarcely moderate or unpolemical texts, but rather messages of defiance and warnings of divine judgement and revenge.

The common puritan front that Clarke was constructing here was thus Janus-faced. On the one hand, we might see it as a hunkering down before the prospect of a renewed persecution, and, as such, as a step along a road that led inexorably from 'puritanism' to 'dissent'. Born of Presbyterian defeat in the 1640s, and again of incipient non-conformist exclusion in 1660–2, Clarke's collections had always had that tendency or potential within them. But it would be a mistake to see them moving either enthusiastically or unequivocally in that direction. While Clarke's version of 'puritanism' might indeed provide a basis from which to resist and frustrate the renewed pressure—in Clarke's terms, the 'persecution'—all too likely, in 1683, to be visited on the saints at the height of the Tory reaction and under a popish prince, it might also function as a perfect launching pad for the final comprehension within the national church of the last and best of the Church of England—that is to say, of the puritan tradition of thought and feeling being constructed and defended in Clarke's books. Then, at last, true and national church could coalesce. Then, at last, could the Church of England extract the full credit for, and benefit from, the many saints and martyrs that she had created and sustained and who, in their turn, had created and sustained her, even in the darkest days of popish (and then of prelatical and even of sectarian) 'persecution' and of bitter civil war. Thus, in and through the experience and witness of these both saints and martyrs, could the church in England and the Church of England become one and return to full unity with the true church of Christ conjured and described in Clarke's *Martyrologies* and *Church Histories*.

The tendency over the years has been for historians to use Clarke as a source either for the study of individual lives or of puritanism, and later of dissent, more generally conceived. Full as they are of rich anecdotal and narrative materials, the lives certainly lend themselves to such purposes. But they need to be used with caution and reading them together and in context is a necessary corrective against taking many of their claims and tendencies, their recurrent structures and assumptions, at face value. (Here the constant interplay between zeal and moderation, noted throughout, is a case in point.) But, read critically and contextually, they are a wonderful source for something else as well; not only for the study of the lives and events they recount, but also for the study of the ways in which, and of the purposes for which, early modern people wrote and read their own, and other people's, lives.

15

The Servant and the Grave Robber: Walton's *Lives* in Restoration England

Andrea Walkden

From George Herbert prostrate before the altar of the tiny parish church in Bemerton to John Milton waiting to be milked of his poetry by his amanuensis, many of the most enduring and arresting vignettes of early modern experience appear in Restoration lives. Restoration writers did not invent the life, which existed in many guises from classical antiquity onward, but they did endow it with new and urgent purpose: to debate the legacy of the civil wars and to establish their relevance for present political argument. One writer, in particular, exploited the formal resources of the life narrative to bind recent history and current controversy into complex and highly divisive configurations. Izaak Walton wrote five lives between 1640 and 1678. His subjects were the poet and Dean of St Paul's John Donne (1640), the diplomat and provost of Eton Henry Wotton (1651), the Elizabethan apologist Richard Hooker (1665), the Jacobean minister and poet George Herbert (1670), and the Restoration bishop Robert Sanderson (1678). Ideological battles pushed the resources of the life narrative harder and farther: the range and creativity of Waltonian biography—its status as literature—is a product of embittered partisanship; its historiographical sophistication, a response to polemical need.

Walton's lives served more than one function and therefore took more than one form during their early publication history. They appeared separately as free-standing works, as prefaces attached to the writings of their biographical subjects (helping the reader to arrive at the correct understanding of the materials before him), and as a single, composite work. This final form owes something to the popularity of biographical collections such as those of Thomas Fuller, Clement Barksdale, and Samuel Clarke, but it derives also from Walton's long-standing ambition to write an updated version of Plutarch's *Lives*, one that would replace Greek and Roman statesmen with loyal English churchmen, military service with pastoral service, and secular with sacred ambition. Samuel Johnson would take up Walton's vision of a national literary biography in his *Lives of the Poets* (1744–83). T. S. Eliot would take up his vision of an Anglican seventeenth century in his New English Canon.[1] Despite, or perhaps because of, their extraordinary impact upon a literary tradition now superseded by the rise of Milton studies, the *Lives* have received little attention in recent studies of the later Stuart period. Nonetheless, Walton is the single figure who marks out most centrally the ambitions and vocabularies of life writing during the post-revolutionary era. His *Lives* demonstrate not only the contribution of biographical narratives to Restoration public discourse, but also the competition they posed to rival modes of historiography and political manoeuvre.[2] This chapter traces the pattern of Walton's career from 1640 to 1678. It focuses on the series of self-inscribing servant figures that Walton uses to define and legitimate the biographer's public role. More broadly, it illustrates how the construction of politico-religious identities—new, old, and new pretending to be old—stimulated the growth of biographical writing in the decades following the Stuart Restoration.

LIVES

The improbable Anglican triumph of 1661–2, improbable because of the apparent strength of the comprehension party just one year earlier,

---

[1] Eliot's essay 'The Metaphysical Poets' originally appeared in the *Times Literary Supplement* on 20 Sept. 1921 as a review and endorsement of Herbert J. C. Grierson's *The Metaphysical Lyrics and Poems of the Seventeenth Century: Donne to Butler* (Oxford, 1921).

[2] For Restoration historiography, see Royce MacGillivray, *Restoration Historians and the English Civil War* (The Hague, 1973), and Daniel R. Woolf, 'Narrative Historiography in Restoration England: A Preliminary Survey', in G. W. Marshall (ed.), *The Restoration Mind* (Newark, NJ, 1997), 207–51. For the development of public discourse, see Peter Lake and Steven Pincus, 'Rethinking the Public Sphere in Early Modern England', *Journal of British Studies* 45/2 (2006), 270–92.

returned the bishops to the centre of national politics.[3] Religious uniformity was soon enforced by a series of acts, passed between 1661 and 1665, that removed the possibility of comprehension and made toleration conditional upon the royal indulgence. Despite their victory the bishops remained on the offensive; as John Spurr has shown, the 1660s witnessed an outpouring of Anglican apology intended to restore prestige to the resettled church.[4] Orchestrated by Gilbert Sheldon, first as Bishop of London and then as Archbishop of Canterbury, the campaign sought to make the historical as well as scriptural case for a national church with a set liturgy, prescribed ceremonies, and episcopal government. At the same time, Presbyterians who had fought and lost the campaign for Protestant comprehensiveness, and who now faced expulsion from their parishes, continued to argue their case in print. At stake for both parties was the coveted centre ground of English religion, the occupation of which allowed Anglicans to stigmatize all nonconformists as extremists. If Presbyterians could contest the middle ground by distinguishing moderate nonconformity from sectarian radicalism, they could undermine the Anglican position and strengthen their claim for inclusion in the national church.

The celebration and appropriation of church luminaries were tasks central to these rival campaigns, and biography was particularly suited to accomplish both. Clement Barksdale's *Memorials of Worthy Persons*, first published in 1661, reprinted in 1662, and expanded in two further editions in 1662 and 1663, collects brief lives of exemplary English Anglicans (and in the case of Lady Falkland a high-profile convert to Catholicism) and from them constructs an ecclesiastical *via media* for the Restoration church to inherit and continue.[5] Protestant dissenters are conspicuous mainly by their absence. It is likely that the *Memorials* were a calculated response to a rival collection of lives chosen and edited by the Presbyterian Samuel Clarke. Clarke's *Lives* were of long

---

[3] I use the term 'Anglican' and its cognates to describe any party hostile to a comprehensive religious settlement. I do not use it in its broader sense to describe a member of the Church of England.

[4] Paul Seaward, *The Cavalier Parliament and the Restoration of the Old Regime, 1661–1667* (Cambridge, 1989); John Spurr, *The Restoration Church of England 1646–1689* (New Haven, 1991), 29–61.

[5] A committed royalist, Barksdale was ejected from his parish in Hereford by parliamentary forces in 1646. In 1653 he defended the Anglican prayer book and articles in a public disputation with the Independent divine Carnsew Hulme; John Coffey, 'Barksdale, Clement (1609–1687)', *ODNB* (Oxford, 2004).

standing: having first appeared in 1640 in response to Laudian persecution, they were reissued during the 1650s as a response to the growth of
religious sects and again in 1660 and 1662 as a response to the Anglican
settlement. Subsequent editions in 1677 and (posthumously) in 1683
reacted to the state persecutions of the 1660s and 1670s.[6] Walton's
Life of Donne appeared in 1640, the same year as the first of Samuel
Clarke's biographical collections. It is not clear if Walton was aware of
Clarke at this stage—his interest in Protestant dissent appears to have
been limited to the puritan preacher Richard Sibbes—but he would
certainly have been aware of him by the time he collected his lives (of
John Donne, Henry Wotton, Richard Hooker, and George Herbert)
and published them together in 1670. For it is no exaggeration to
say that between 1660 and 1665 Barksdale's *Memorials* and Clarke's
Lives were locked in a battle of the books; their rival constructions
of a national church vying for public allegiance while Parliament sat
debating and legislating the religious settlement. The two collections
appeal to many of the same historical figures—lives of John Colet, John
Whitgift, and James Ussher appear in both—as well as to a common
standard of piety and pastoral duty. For Clarke, whose desire is not
for conquest but for incorporation, this shared heritage is precisely the
point. But the more important point, at least for this discussion, is that
the two collections also share a methodology: both seek to recover and
to canonize a tradition of worship rather than to celebrate particular
individuals. Following the example of earlier forms such as the martyrology or ecclesiology, to which in their early publication history Clarke's
Lives were attached, both collections organize their godly communities into historical narratives that span the sixteenth and seventeenth
centuries.

Barksdale's *Memorials* and Clarke's *Lives* suggest how useful a tool
biography had become for the re-establishment of group identities as
well as for their defence and recruitment during the years immediately
following the Restoration. But not all biographical works proved as
successful as theirs at creating and fostering communal loyalties; indeed
one of the more significant failures, John Gauden's *Life of Richard
Hooker*, marks the entry of Walton into the culture of Restoration life
writing.

---

[6] See Ch. 14 by Peter Lake.

In January 1662 John Gauden, the ghost writer of *Eikon Basilike*, published a handsome folio edition of Richard Hooker's *Of the Laws of Ecclesiastical Polity* as a new year's present for Charles II. Gauden's edition included the seventh book of the *Laws*, not previously published because of its controversial discussion of episcopal authority.[7] As was becoming customary, Gauden prefaced the *Laws* with a life of Hooker, an expanded version of Thomas Fuller's brief life in his posthumous biographical collection, *The Worthies of England* (1661). Prominent Anglican leaders, Gilbert Sheldon and Walton's long-term patron, George Morley, judged Gauden's life negligent on numerous counts: for its thinly veiled criticism of the Laudian church; for its factual errors and emphasis upon the less enobling aspects of Hooker's career, including an encounter with a prostitute; and, perhaps most of all, for its atrocious prose. Of the famous Hookerian style, Gauden writes that it was 'at once *liberal* and *elegant*, copious and comely, with a majestick kind of *ampleness*, and stately luxuriancy, as the ancient Roman Buildings: or as bodies that are *fair* and *full, sinewy* and *beautiful*, handsome and yet *athletick* . . . as was said of *Pindars Odes,* he is both *full, fluent* and *sublime,* yet *serene* as the firmament: a Torrent indeed, but untroubled, carrying all before him with weighty and convincing *reasonings*'.[8] Gauden's own torrent continues to mix metaphors for many more lines.

Hooker needed to be rescued as much from Gauden's failings as a writer as from his failings as a party Anglican, and Walton was the man appointed by Sheldon and Morley to perform both operations. Walton's *Life of Hooker* appeared as a separate work in 1665, but when a second edition of the *Laws* was seen through the press one year later, it was Walton's life not Gauden's that served as its preface. Hooker's

---

[7] The first five books of Hooker's *Laws* had been published in Hooker's lifetime, and James Ussher saw books 6 and 8 into print in 1648. As David Novarr has noted, the irregular pagination of Gauden's edition suggests that book 7 was a late insertion, added only once printing had begun, *The Making of Walton's Lives* (Ithaca, NY, 1958), 220. For the posthumous reception of Hooker, see, among other, C. Condren, 'The Creation of Richard Hooker's Public Authority: Rhetoric, Reputation, and Reassessment', *Journal of Religious History* 21 (1997), 35–59; Peter Lake, 'Business as Usual? The Immediate Reception of Hooker's *Ecclesiastical Polity*', *Journal of Ecclesiastical History* 52 (2001), 456–86; and D. MacCulloch, 'Richard Hooker's Reputation', *English Historical Review* 117 (2002), 773–812.

[8] John Gauden, *The Works of Richard Hooker* (London, 1662), 14.

seventh book with its compromising arguments about church government had entered the public domain and could not now be recalled, but
an appendix to Walton's biography casts doubt upon the authenticity
of the final three books of the *Laws*. Engaged in a cover-up, Walton
makes only one reference to Gauden, and it is disingenuous: 'I think
it necessary to inform my Reader that Dr. Gauden (the late Bishop of
Worcester) hath also lately wrote and publisht the Life of Mr. Hooker;
and though this be not writ by design to oppose the Life of Mr. Hooker
written by him, yet I am put upon a necessity to say, That in it there
be many Material Mistakes, and more Omissions.'[9] Walton corrects
Gauden's biographical errors, certainly, but he also recreates Hooker in
the Anglican image, directing attention away from theological controversies toward the simple, primitive piety of the man himself.

Five years later, Walton wrote his next life, of the Jacobean church-
man George Herbert whose collection of poems, *The Temple. Sacred
Poems and Private Ejaculations*, appeared within months of his death
in 1633. Herbert had an affiliation to Laud, and his lyrics speak
to the external rituals of worship, but the dramatic and devotional
energy of his poetry turns towards the internal conflict of the sinner
and his relation to a recognizably Calvinist God. For this reason both
Anglicans and nonconformists claimed Herbert's lyrics as expressions of
their own religious experience. The Anglican interpretation began with
Herbert's friend and first editor Nicholas Ferrar and was continued by
poetic imitators such as Christopher Harvey, whose own collection *The
Synagogue, Or, The Shadow of the Temple* (1640) was often published and
bound with Herbert's original. Richard Baxter claimed Herbert for the
nonconformists in *The Saints Everlasting Rest* (1650); Oliver Heywood,
Faithful Teat, and John Bryan, among others, repeated and reinforced
Baxter's reading during the Restoration.[10] The publication of Walton's
Life of Herbert in May of 1670 coincided with an upsurge of religious

[9] *Life of Mr. R Hooker* (London, 1665), A7ᵛ. Walton gives a fuller account of how
he became 'ingaged' to write the *Life* in his address 'To the Reader' in the 1670 collected
Lives, A5–A6.
[10] Ray Robert, 'Herbert's Seventeenth-Century Reputation: A Summary and New
Considerations', *George Herbert Journal* 9 (1986), 1–15; Daniel Doerksen, 'The Laudian
Interpretation of George Herbert', *Literature and History* 3 (1994), 36–54; Sharon
Achinstein, *Literature and Dissent in Milton's England* (Cambridge, 2003), 200–8, and
'Reading George Herbert in the Restoration, *English Literary Renaissance* 36/3 (2006),
430–65.

persecution after the successful passage of the Second Conventicle Act through parliament.[11] Given this political occasion, the cleverness of Walton's narrative lies in its apparent retreat from polemic into pastoral, its celebration of a country piety far removed from the power struggles of church, parliament, and state. Characterized in the preface as 'a free-will offering', at once unsolicited and admiring, the *Life* belongs, nonetheless, to a recognizable political programme; its task is to reclaim Herbert, and by extension the pre-civil war ministry, for an Anglican tradition of worship. Walton's stimulus upon the Restoration reputation of Herbert was immediate: the *Temple* was reprinted three times during the next decade, in 1674, 1678, and 1679, each time with his *Life* securely attached.

In 1678 Walton came out of retirement to write his fifth and final life of the Laudian divine, Cromwellian collaborator, and Restoration bishop Robert Sanderson.[12] The work displays all of Walton's political acumen, his brilliance at stretching the formal parameters of the life to accommodate topical debate. Most important, it shows how the pressure of theological politics led him to clarify his own biographical calling as it moved away from its original Plutarchan foundation. Reading backwards from the *Life of Sanderson* (1678) to the *Life of Donne* (1640) emphasizes the coherence of Walton's project, the subtlety with which it accommodates its own changes of direction, and the ambition of its overarching claims about the relation of biography to history and the relation of the biographer to his subject.

THE GRAVE ROBBER

In the *Life of Sanderson,* the biographer's reluctance to write history neatly coincides with his subject's reluctance to participate in it. Both Walton and Sanderson are isolationists, both wish to be left alone in Sanderson's Lincolnshire benefice of Boothby Pannel, and both are constantly thwarted in that wish by the incursion of national events.

---

[11] Achinstein, 'Reading George Herbert', 446–7.
[12] Peter Lake, 'The Calvinist Conformity of Robert Sanderson', *Journal of British Studies* 27/2 (1988), 81–116.

'I cannot lead my Reader to *Dr. Hammond* and *Dr. Sanderson* where we left them at *Boothby Pannel*', explains the narrator, 'till I have look'd back to the long Parliament, the Society of Covenanters in *Sion Colledge*, and those others scattered up and down in *London*, and given some account of their proceedings and usage of the late learned *Dr. Laud*, then Archbishop of *Canterbury*.'[13] When the narrator does finally return to Boothby Pannel, he discovers that the life—as opposed to the *Life*—of Sanderson has been proceeding in his absence. Abducted by parliamentary soldiers and imprisoned at their garrison in Lincoln, Sanderson has been carried out of his own biography.

Walton orchestrates this missed appointment not to show that history and biography are antithetical projects, but to show their interconnection. Having established Sanderson's rural parish as a place of refuge—akin to the riverside of his famous interregnum treatise, *The Compleat Angler* (1653)—Walton promptly undermines his own pastoral designation. Sanderson's capture relocates the parish to the frontline of the civil wars, breaking down the geographical opposition between city and country and the generic one between public and private history. In order to tell the story of Sanderson, an Anglican minister who stayed in England and complied with the Commonwealth regime, Walton must of necessity broach the larger, national story.

Walton had been toying with the idea of writing a life of Sanderson, whom he had known personally, at least since 1670.[14] No doubt the deteriorating political situation as the decade wore on strengthened his resolve. Sharpening divisions between parliament and the king led to expectations of an alliance between, as one contemporary pamphlet puts it, 'the High Episcopal Man and the Old Cavalier', threatening to return the nation to the crisis of the early 1640s. Allied to the government through the leadership of Thomas Osborne, the Earl of Danby, church leaders tried to strengthen their exclusionary interests. They pursued an uncompromising legislative programme in the parliamentary session of 1677–8, including a bill that proposed to safeguard the Protestant

---

[13] *The life of Dr. Sanderson* (London, 1678), sig. h3ᵛ.

[14] Walton praises Sanderson in the Epistle to the collected *Lives*, asking 'who, if they love vertue, would not rejoyce to know that this good man [Sanderson] was as remarkable for *the meekness and innocence of his life*, as for his great learning', *The Lives of Dr. John Donne, Sir Henry Wotton, Mr. Richard Hooker, Mr. George Herbert* (London, 1670), sig. A7.

religion in the event of a Catholic succession by transferring the power of ecclesiastical preferment from the king to the bishops.[15] This bill and other related measures were attacked with vitriol by Andrew Marvell in his relation of Anglican–royalist policy from 1675 to 1677, *An Account of the Growth of Popery and Arbitrary Government.* Licensed for the press on 7 May 1678 Walton's *Life of Sanderson* entered into and sought to influence these ongoing debates over Catholicism, absolutism, and Anglican conformity, debates that would only intensify in the months immediately following with the outbreak of the Popish Plot, the dissolution of the Cavalier Parliament, and the beginning of parliamentary attempts to prevent James, Duke of York, from succeeding to the English throne.

Given the political context, it is perhaps not surprising that the *Life of Sanderson* is the most avowedly argumentative of all of Walton's biographies. It is also formally the most self-conscious. Walton adopts a bifurcated first-person voice that switches between a younger self, who witnesses the horrors of the rebellion first hand, and an older self, who recalls the horrors from the vantage of the 1670s—'But when I look back upon the ruine of Families, the bloodshed, the decay of common honesty...'.[16] Through this narrative technique, Walton asserts continuity between the religious fanatics of the 1650s and the dissenting communities of the 1670s, defending the principle of a uniform church on political as well as on theological grounds.[17] His *Life* is a deliberate attempt to stir the national history memory, to defend the right of the state to mandate religious practice by making that right a matter of national security, not simply one of spiritual unity. Nowhere is this polemical objective more apparent than in his report of a foolish parish and a looting Presbyterian minister.

And in the way thither [from London to Lincolnshire] I must tell him, That a very Covenanter and a Scot too, that came into *England* with this unhappy Covenant, was got into a good sequestred Living by the help of a Presbyterian Parish, which had got the true Owner out. And this Scotch Presbyterian being

[15] Spurr, *The Restoration Church of England*, 61–80; Mark Goldie, 'Danby, the Bishops, and the Whigs', in Tim Harris, Paul Seaward, and Mark Goldie (eds.), *The Politics of Religion in Restoration England* (Oxford, 1990), 75–105.

[16] *The life of Dr. Sanderson*, sig. e2ᵛ.

[17] Walton uses this same technique in his pamphlet, *Love and Truth in Two Modest and Peaceable Letters Concerning the Distempers of the Present Times* (London, 1680).

well settled in this good Living, began to reform the Church-yard, by cutting down a large Ewe Tree and some other Trees that were an ornament to the place, and very often a shelter to the Parishioners; who excepting against him for so doing, were answered, *That the Trees were his, and 'twas lawful for every man to use his own as he, and not as they thought fit.*[18]

The anecdote opens as a matter of historical record, but, as so often in Walton's work, an allegorical reading quickly becomes necessary. Walton arranges the unnamed parishioners and the hewn trees into an emblem of Presbyterian destruction—an act of desecration postures as an act of reform. Unwilling to let the Presbyter have the last word, the narrator continues:

I have hear'd (but do not affirm it) That no Action lies against him that is so wicked as to steal the winding sheet of a dead body after 'tis buried; and have heard the reason to be, because none were supposed to be so void of humanity, and that such a Law would vilifie that Nation that would but suppose so vile a man to be born in it: nor would one suppose any man to do what this Covenanter did. And whether there was any Law against him, I know not; but pity the Parish the less for turning out their legal Minister.[19]

With no indication that he has made a remarkable transition, Walton switches to a second act of desecration: the theft of a winding sheet from a buried corpse. According to the reported logic, there exists no legal redress for grave robbery because in order to devise one the nation would have to concede the possibility of an unthinkable crime being committed by one of its members. In such a case, responsibility may rest with the malefactor, but culpability, and the shame that accompanies it, must be shared by all. After laying out this reasoning, Walton makes the identification between grave robber and Covenanter explicit: 'nor would one suppose any man to do what this Covenanter did'.

The analogy functions in two ways. First, it serves as a counter-example to the Presbyter's legalistic definition of right and wrong—'Twas lawful for every man to use his own as he and not as they thought fit'. Like the grave robber, the Presbyter has the sanction of the law's silence, but this does not grant him moral sanction. Sanderson has already formulated the extra-legal principle of *caritas* for a rent-racking landlord earlier in the narrative: 'That the Law of this Nation (by which

---

[18] *The life of Dr. Sanderson*, sigs. g1ᵛ–g2ʳ.   [19] Ibid., sigs. g2ʳ–g3ᵛ.

Law he claims his Rent) does not undertake to make men *honest* or *merciful*; but does what it can to restrain men from being *dishonest or unmerciful*, and yet was defective in both.'[20] Second, it exposes the danger of legal denial. Should England refuse to legislate against an exceptional evil (because 'such a Law would vilifie that Nation that would but suppose so vile a man to be born in it'), what happens when 'vile' men commit crimes without prospect of redress? Here the analogy comes close to assuming the status of historical allegory, bringing the reprobate minority and the consenting majority into uncomfortable relation for a Restoration audience with recent memories of regicide and rebellion. It is no accident that the animus of the tale recoils back upon the congregation—'pity the parish the less for turning out their legal minister'.

With this ending Walton makes his parable serve a further purpose: the justification of Sanderson's willingness to serve under a rebel regime. For in Walton's scenario, in the scenario of the marauding Scotch Presbyter whose destructive licence the law is powerless to redress, it is Sanderson the collaborator, and not his Anglican brethren in exile, who emerges pristine and removed from blame. Newly schooled by the parable of the Presbyter and the parish, the reader is primed to greet Sanderson, still the benevolent master of his own churchyard, with gratitude and with relief. It is at this point in the narrative that Walton discusses Sanderson's decision to take the Oath of Engagement and abandon the prayer book in order to keep his living and his parish safe.

In 'The Case of the Liturgy' (1653) Sanderson defended the decision of ministers who, like himself, had elected to conform and keep their livings by reminding the Anglican leadership of the alternative: the 'delivering over the sheep of Christ, that lately were under the hands of faithful shepherds, into the custody of ravening wolves', who 'will be sure to mistreat them one way or other, either by instilling into them Puritanical and Superstitious Principles...or else, by setting up new lights before them, to lead them into a maze of Anabaptistical confusion and frenzy'.[21] No doubt Walton knew of Sanderson's tract and decided to dramatize it in his account of its author's life. But the tale derives also

---

[20] Ibid., sig. d3ᵛ.
[21] *The Works of Robert Sanderson*, ed. William Jacobson, 6 vols. (Oxford, 1884), v. 47–8.

from Walton's treatment of a similar scenario—that of a misled Anglican parish and a rapacious Presbyterian minister—composed thirteen years earlier for his *Life of Richard Hooker* (1665). The repetition is no doubt deliberate, anticipating the connection between Hooker and Sanderson established by the inclusion of one of Hooker's sermons among Sanderson's tracts at the end of the life.[22] Unlike a Plutarchan parallel, Walton's pairing of Hooker and Sanderson is never made explicit, but its underlying intention is clear: to establish continuity between the Elizabethan and the Restoration churches and to parallel the religious polarization of the 1590s with that of both the 1640s and the 1670s. Sanderson and Hooker are both absent from their respective civil war tales although for very different reasons: Sanderson because he is busy attending to his own parish, Hooker because he has been dead for over forty years.

Walton surmounts the narrative terminus of his subject's death by introducing the figure of Hooker's superannuated parish clerk. At the beginning of the civil war, the clerk still lives in Hooker's final benefice at Bishopsbourne in Kent. He watches as the Anglican rector is expelled and replaced by a Presbyterian minister who quickly converts the parishioners to new ways of worship. On the day appointed for the congregation to receive communion for the first time by sitting up rather than kneeling in the Anglican manner, the clerk is ordered to bring some joint-stools into the church. He complies but then protests the changes to church ceremony, grounding his protest upon the authority of his former master: 'for all men will say my Master *Hooker* was a good Man and a good Scholar and I am sure it was not used to be thus in his days.'[23] Having said his piece, the clerk walks out of the church, goes home, and dies: 'I do not say died immediately,' adds Walton, 'but within a few days after.'[24] Walton knows that he is about to push his material over a melodramatic brink. He needs to endow the clerk with the stature and dignity of a latter-day John of Gaunt, but the tragic register comes at the expense of some narrative embarrassment.

Hooker's parish clerk, however extraneous to the plot of the biography, articulates the rationale behind the writing of it—'All men will say ... it was not used to be thus'. The clerk's voice, raised in argument

[22] *The life of Dr. Sanderson*, sig. S2ʳ.
[23] *The life of Mr. Rich. Hooker, the author of those learned books of the laws of ecclesiastical polity* (London, 1665), 132.
[24] Ibid. 132.

in a place where it would normally be hushed with reverence, carries clearly to us an idea of a lost order. The lamentation has authoritative force not simply because it invokes the near-legendary figure of Hooker, but because it derives from the living memory of the speaker. The clerk becomes the reader's witness to the past, he authenticates the past for us, and he delivers its death knell before exiting in order to die himself. Read in this way and despite Walton's apologetic fumble, the clerk's death makes good symbolic sense. A relic of a better age whose loss he articulates, the speaker cannot long survive his own elegiac utterance.

The outspoken clerk enlarges upon a customary role in Waltonian biography, that of the grateful servant who officiates over the abandoned body of his dead master. Considered chronologically from the *Life of Donne* (1640) to the *Life of Herbert* (1670), Walton's servant figures trace the development of his biographical art from its first classical expression, modelled on Plutarch's *Lives,* to its final Christian one, modelled on the sacred biography of the gospel narratives. The theoretical claims advanced through these servant figures inform the replacement of Hooker's parish clerk in the first scenario with the grave robber in the second. They also reveal how the analogy of the grave robber, the extravagance of which appears purely opportunistic, becomes the occasion for Walton's final statement about biography as both an ethical practice and as a form of art. In order to see how this is so, we need to turn back to the beginning of Walton's literary career, to 1640, to Donne, and to Plutarch.

THE SERVANT

If I shall now be demanded as once *Pompey's* poor bondsman was, (The grateful wretch had been left alone on the Sea-shore, with the foresaken dead body of his once glorious lord and master: and, was then gathering the scatter'd pieces of an old broken boat to make a funeral pile to burn it (which was the custom of the Romans;) *who art thou that alone hast the honour to bury the body of* Pompey *the Great?*[25]

---

[25] *The Lives,* 10. Although the *Lives* were published jointly each *Life* has its own title page, signatures, and pagination, perhaps suggesting that they were sold separately as well as together.

The allusion to Plutarch takes the form of a modesty topos in which Walton identifies himself with Pompey's former slave who has the honour, out of all proportion to his station, of burying the famous general he has served. Plutarch contrasts the loyalty of Philip—Walton's 'poor bondsman'—with the treachery of Septimus—an old servant of Pompey's now in the employ of Pompey's Egyptian assassins—who strikes the first blow (from behind) against his former master. The arrival of a third servant figure, an army veteran, clarifies the moral opposition between the loyal Philip and the perfidious Septimus. The veteran approaches Philip to ask him: 'O friend, what art thou that preparest the funerals of Pompey the Great?' Walton reiterates this question and then applies it to himself: '*so* who am I that do thus officiously set the Authors memorie on fire?'[26] By matching the incredulity of his reader to the incredulity of Plutarch's superannuated soldier, Walton casts himself in the role of Philip. The Plutarchan anecdote enables Walton to authorize his own biographical practice—he is not Plutarch, but he is a Plutarchan character. Most important, Walton presents himself as the dutiful servant whose loyalty extends beyond the lifetime of his master. Represented by a carefully selected vocabulary of *gratium* (grateful) and *officium* (officious duty), Pompey's bondsman establishes a model for his Christian counterparts in later *Lives,* the parish clerk in the *Life of Hooker* and, in the *Life of Herbert,* Mary Magdalene.[27]

The *Life of Herbert* first appeared in 1670, both separately and in a volume that collected Walton's four lives and published them together for the first time.[28] In the preface to the *Life,* Walton locates Donne, Wotton, Hooker, and Herbert in a genealogy of Christian biography stretching back to its first illustrious subject, the Christ of the gospel narratives. Meditating upon the example of Mary Magdalene, he recalls how, when she anointed Jesus in the house of Simon the Leper, Jesus

---

[26] Thomas North, *The Lives of the Noble Grecians and Romans* (London, 1579), 718. The Plutarchan allusion is also discussed by Jessica Martin, *Walton's Lives: Conformist Commemorations and the Rise of Biography* (Oxford, 2001), 41.

[27] The early modern and now obsolete meaning of 'officious'—active or zealous in the exercise of an office; dutiful—carries none of the negative connotations later attached to it (*OED* s.v. 'officious' 1a and 1b).

[28] David Novarr argues convincingly that the separate publication of the *Life of Herbert* pre-dated the joint publication of the *Lives,* although both share the same Imprimatur, Appendix D in *The Making of Walton's Lives,* 510–12.

assured her that her sins would be forgiven. But this was not all that Jesus promised her.

She also had from him a testimony, that her alabaster box of precious oyntment poured on his head and feet, and that Spikenard, and those Spices that were by her dedicated to embalm and preserve his sacred body from putrefaction, should so far preserve her own memory, that these demonstrations of her sanctified love, and of her officious, and generous gratitude should be recorded and mentioned wheresoever his Gospel should be read: intending thereby, that as his, so her name should also live to succeeding generations, even till time shall be no more.[29]

Walton's account expands upon Matthew 26:13, rendered in the King James Bible as: 'Verily I say unto you. Wheresoever this gospel shall be preached in the whole world, there shall also this, that this woman hath done, be told for a memorial of her.' Although Mary is a different kind of servant from Pompey's bondman Philip, the same vocabulary is used to describe her: she too is grateful, and her actions are officious. Mary's service to Jesus is needful since no man, not even the Son of God, can prepare his own body for the grave. Through the figure of Pompey's servant, who makes preparations for the decapitated trunk of his master to be burnt, as through the figure of Mary Magdalene, who anoints Jesus in preparation for his crucifixion, Walton claims for himself this sublimated role as the guardian of great men after death.

Walton makes the same point rather differently in a famous episode added to the *Life of Donne* for the second edition of 1658 and expanded for the edition of 1670, which also contained the Magdalene preface. Close to death, Donne poses for a final portrait as the corpse he will soon be. The preparations for his sitting are described as a progression of deliberate actions, each one a mortification of the living flesh: 'He brought with him into that place his winding-sheet in his hand; and, having put off all his cloaths, had this sheet put on him, and so tyed with knots at his head and feet, and his hands so placed, as dead bodies are usually fitted to be shrowded and put into the grave.'[30] The economy

---

[29] *The Lives*, 7. Clayton D. Lein briefly discusses the Magdalene preface in 'Art and Structure in Walton's *Life of Mr. George Herbert*', *University of Toronto Quarterly* 46/2 (1977), 162–76; 76.

[30] *The Lives*, 75. For a reading of this scene, see Richard Wendorf, ' "Visible Rhetorick": Izaak Walton and Iconic Biography', *Modern Philology* 82 (1985), 269–91.

of the repeated verb with its changing prepositions—the 'put[ting] off' of clothes and the 'put[ting] on' of the winding sheet before being 'put into' the grave—parses the progression of the body into the ground. Of course, Donne is not quite dead, and so he is able to rehearse his own funeral rites, but even he cannot stop the movement towards the passive voice when the action becomes the habitual and general one of the living fitting the dead man for his grave. The process is repeated at Donne's actual death when, Walton tells us, 'he closed his own eyes; and then disposed his hands and body into such a posture as required not the least alteration by those that came to shroud him'.[31] The power of both scenes, the rehearsal and the final performance, comes from the dignity with which Donne reconciles his body to death. Are we to imagine him reaching up to close his eyes with his hands, as a mourner would do, rather than simply letting them close of their own accord? The contrast between the well-disposed body in these scenes and the abandoned body in Walton's Plutarchan preface could not be more striking. But in each case Walton's interest is drawn towards the moment at which the dying man loses control over his body and its fate, even if, like Donne, he exerts that control to the last possible moment, the 'minutes latest point', of his life.[32]

Donne's winding sheet has a prominent afterlife. Memorialized in Donne's funerary monument, which stood in St. Paul's cathedral until the fire of 1666, and in the frontispiece to Donne's final sermon, *Deaths Duell* (1632), the winding sheet is also the structuring conceit of John Marriot's verse 'Hexastichon Bibliopolae', which formed part of the complex paratext to the 1633 posthumous edition of Donne's collected poems:

> I See in his last preach'd, and printed booke,
> His Picture in a sheete; in *Pauls* I looke,
> And see his Statue in a sheete of stone,
> And sure his body in the grave hath one:
> Those sheetes present him dead, these if you buy,
> You have him living to Eternity.[33]

---

[31] *The Lives*, 78.

[32] John Donne, Holy Sonnet 6, 'This is my playes last scene'.

[33] *Poems by J.D. with Elegies on the Authors Death* (London, 1633), sig. e2ᵛ. Marriot's verse is also discussed by Leah Marcus, *Unediting the Renaissance: Shakespeare, Marlowe, Milton* (New York, 1996), 194–5.

Marriot refers first to the frontispiece to *Deaths Duell* ('his picture in a sheete') then to the monument at St Paul's ('a sheete of stone') before turning to the original winding sheet from which portrait and sculpture are modelled ('And sure his body in the grave hath one'). What follows is tantamount to a resurrection as the sheets of the printed book replace those other sheets—of cloth and of stone—that shroud the body of Donne. 'For books', as Milton will insist eleven years later, 'are not absolutely dead things.'[34] John Marriot (or 'Jo. Mar.' as he appears on the page) was the printer and bookseller responsible for the publication of the 1633 *Poems*, to which Izaak Walton, one of Donne's parishioners at St Dunstans in the West, contributed an elegy.[35] His son Richard would publish Walton's *Life of Donne* some seven years later, and it was perhaps from John Marriot that Walton took the conceit of the winding sheet, not, as Marriot employs it, in punning reference to sheets of paper, but in larger and looser reference to the humble biographer whose job it is to dress the exemplary dead.

If the grave robber who steals a winding sheet in the *Life of Sanderson* can be traced to Donne's deathbed portrait and the 1633 *Poems*; if he can also be tied to a series of self-inscribing servant figures—Pompey's poor bondsman, Hooker's parish clerk, Mary Magdalene—whose service to the dead preserves what others would desecrate, then the symbolic precision of Walton's analogy between the grave robber and the Presbyterian may also start to be understood. The Presbyterian is likened to a grave robber because he too defiles a past he does not respect: the 'graves' that he is robbing belong to his Anglican forebears, men like Hooker, and Herbert, and Donne. For his fifth and final life, Walton reverses his own procedures of generic and authorial representation. Instead of imagining another servant and surrogate biographer, he creates an adversary against whom he defines himself and his craft. Artistic and ideological convictions coalesce in the figure of the grave robber, and through him Walton advances his final understanding of the life narrative as the battleground of the Restoration, a space in which to fight for and to canonize the Anglican interpretation of history.

[34] John Milton, *Areopagitica* (1644), in *John Milton: Complete Poems and Major Prose*, ed. Merritt Y. Hughes (New Jersey, 1957), 720.
[35] *Poems by J.D.*, 382–4.

Writing some forty years after Walton, Joseph Addison would emphasize not the opposition between the biographer and the grave robber, but
their resemblance:

There is a Race of Men lately sprung up among this sort of Writers, whom
one cannot reflect upon without Indignation as well as Contempt. These are
our Grub Street Biographers, who watch for the Death of a Great Man, like so
many Undertakers, on purpose to make a Penny of him. He is no sooner laid
in his Grave, but he falls into the Hands of an Historian.[36]

Motivated by the possibility of a quick and easy profit, Addison's 'Grub
Street Biographer' exists at the farthest possible remove from Walton's
loyal and disinterested servant. Yet the increasing politicization of biography during the later Stuart period, the traffic in men (and women)
of the recent past for ideological rather than for economic profit, is not
so very far from the commercialization that Addison derides. Walton's
grave-robber analogy contains a specific attack upon the Presbyterians
and their disrespect for church tradition, but it may also attack the larger
cultural practice of ransacking the past for immediate and self-serving
gain, a practice in which the biographer (and arguably Walton himself)
is deeply implicated. If this is indeed the case, then the analogy does not
simply oppose Anglican tradition and Presbyterian destruction, but two
rival versions of biography, suggesting that the passage from the grave
to Grub Street was one that Walton, as well as Addison, was anxious to
resist.

[36] *The Freeholder* for Friday, 20 April 1716, no. 35. Quoted in Donald Stauffer, *The
Art of Biography in Eighteenth Century England* (Princeton, 1941), 530–1.

PART VI

TOWARDS BIOGRAPHY

16

Biography, Fiction, and the Emergence of 'Identity' in Eighteenth-Century Britain

Michael McKeon

BIOGRAPHY, FICTION, AND THE COMMON

Like their predecessors, early modern historians made ample use of concrete examples to teach abstract precept, a rhetoric of exemplarity that moves from the local instance to the general application. In traditional use, this rhetoric is persuasive because its examples are taken not from the realms of the local and the lowly but from the public precincts of greatness: only the lives of illustrious men and women can teach a pattern of virtue. By the same token, the distinction between historical and biographical writing, although traditionally understood as one between a regard for the public and for the private life, nonetheless took for granted that the exemplars even of private life would be great men, figures of public importance.

In the later seventeenth and eighteenth centuries, however, biographical exemplarity underwent a revolution in which the illustrious was challenged by the private or common example. At mid-century Samuel Johnson wrote that 'the business of the biographer is often to pass slightly over those performances and incidents, which produce vulgar greatness, to lead the thoughts into domestick privacies, and display the minute details of daily life, where exterior appendages are cast aside, and men excel each other only by prudence and virtue'. Johnson justifies this focus on the domestic because he believes that moral precepts are most reliably learned from the ethical examples of specifically private life: 'The good or ill success of battles and embassies extends itself to a

very small part of domestick life: we all have good and evil, which we feel
more sensibly than our petty part of publick miscarriage or prosperity.'[1]
Contemporaries seconded Johnson's assessment of the business of the
biographer. According to Oliver Goldsmith, 'The relations of great
events may surprize indeed; they may be calculated to instruct those
very few, who govern the million beneath, but the generality of mankind
find the most real improvement from relations which are levelled to the
general surface of life; which tell, not how men learned to conquer, but
how they endeavoured to live.' And towards the end of the century John
Bennett addressed 'a young lady' on the topic of biography in similar
terms: 'Instead of wars, sieges, and victories or great atchievements,
which are not so much within the province of a female, it presents
those domestick anecdotes and events, which come more forcibly home
to her bosom and curiosity.' The language of interiority ('home to her
bosom') strikingly discloses here the generality of human nature in the
ultimate particularity of private sentiment. Another biographer writes
that whatever people's outward differences, 'yet follow them close, enter
with them into their cabinets, or, which is still more, into their private
thoughts, and the dark recesses of their minds, and they will be found
pretty much on a level.'[2]

What I have called a revolution in the rhetoric of exemplarity involves
a revaluation of exemplary particularity from a means to the end of
preceptual generality to an end in itself—that is, to an exemplification
of the general in the sense not of qualitative greatness but of quanti-
tative representativeness and inclusion. The most obvious cause of this
revolution was the early modern decay of status hierarchy, a long-term
process that challenged on several fronts the tacit coextension of lineage and virtue, birth and worth.[3] Personhood was disembedded from

[1] Samuel Johnson, *Rambler* 60 (13 Oct. 1750), in *The Yale Edition of the Works of Samuel Johnson*, ed. W. J. Bate and Albrecht B. Strauss (New Haven, 1969), iii (*The Rambler*), 321; Johnson to Joseph Baretti, 21 Dec. 1762, in James Boswell, *Life of Johnson* (1791), ed. R. W. Chapman (Oxford, 1980), 269.
[2] Oliver Goldsmith, *Life of Richard Nash* (1762), 2–3; John Bennett, *Letters to a Young Lady* (1789), 184; and *Memoirs of the Life and Times of Sir Thomas Deveil* (1748), 1, quoted in Mark Salber Phillips, *Society and Sentiment: Genres of Historical Writing in Britain, 1740–1820* (Princeton, 2000), 135, 133, and 136, respectively; on these matters, see generally ch. 5, *passim*.
[3] The following paragraph is elaborated in Michael McKeon, *The Origins of the English Novel, 1600–1740* (Baltimore, 1987), ch. 4.

social practice, moral being became detachable from social rank, and the categories of birth and worth were explicitly reconceived as distinct, respectively 'external' and 'internal', manifestations of what traditionally had seemed a multiform but integral whole. As Bennett's language reminds us, the consequent valorization of interiority had profound implications for ideas of gender difference; it also was deeply rooted in Protestant doctrine. Of course Christianity as such was founded on the paradox, exemplified by the life of Christ, that spiritual elevation was to be discovered among the lowly. Although this pattern was reflected often enough in Roman Catholic lives of the saints, in his *Book of Martyrs* (1563, 1570) John Foxe overlaid Roman Catholic absolutism with the state absolutism of the Marian persecutions so as to throw the spiritual authority of the English saint into the high relief of socio-political subjection, which Foxe reinforced with a plenitude of humble and homely details. Moreover, Protestant soteriology itself argued a degree of private responsibility that was emphasized by the triumphantly parodic figure of an aristocracy not of 'honour' but of 'grace'. Thus Alice Driver is a common woman who 'was an honest poor man's daughter, never brought up in the university... but I have driven the plough before my father many a time'. And after his conversion Roger Holland, formerly an apprentice, tells his persecutors that he has replaced 'that liberty under your auricular confession, that I made no conscience of sin, but trusted to the priest's absolution', by the strenuous conscientiousness of discipline in the calling.[4] In the seventeenth century Foxe's work was extended by practitioners of 'spiritual biography' like Samuel Clarke, who collected and published scores of puritan lives between 1650 and 1683. Clarke also augmented the association, already apparent in Foxe, of the spiritually sanctified social humility of the saint with the historical authenticity of his or her life story. As Richard Baxter writes in the preface to Clarke's last collection, 'He did not make the Histories, but take them made by faithful acquaintance of the dead... To have made Stories himself had been unworthy a Historian.'[5]

Energized by Protestant doctrine, by the middle of the eighteenth century common and domestic examples were thought able to do the

---

[4] *The Acts and Monuments of John Foxe* (1563, enlarged 1570), ed. Stephen R. Cattley (London, 1839), viii. 493–5, 473–6.

[5] Samuel Clarke, *The Lives Of sundry Eminent Persons in this Later Age...* (1683), Baxter's 'To the Reader', a4ʳ.

sort of epistemological work that formerly had seemed to require a ped-agogic fulfilment in the realm of the public. Or to put this differently, the aim to teach ethico-epistemological precepts of a general nature was no longer thought to depend on using examples of socio-political greatness. In one of the passages just quoted, Johnson commends biography for preferring 'domestick privacies' to 'vulgar greatness' because the differences that owe to 'exterior appendages' are there 'cast aside' and we confront more directly the realm of the ethical—of 'prudence' and 'virtue'—that we all inhabit in common. And a few lines earlier Johnson makes clear that the ultimate end of biographical particularization is generalization: '[T]here is such an uniformity in the state of man, considered apart from adventitious and separable decorations and disguises, that there is scarce any possibility of good or ill, but is common to human kind.' Johnson's remarks are relevant to the question of when and how the modern sense of identity—of the 'self', the 'person', the 'subject', the 'individual'—came into being.[6] Does the self-conscious experience of Renaissance 'self-fashioning' express, as has been widely argued, the modern idea of coherent and integral identity—even more, a destabilizing scepticism about this already conventional idea? By Johnson's way of thinking, selfhood appears to be entailed not in the performance of particular social roles but in the constancy and uniformity revealed by stripping them away—or rather, in the dialectic between external particularity and internal generality that constitutes the self as a singular instance of a common kind. Indeed, 'the common' is a fruitful term in this emergent sense of the self because its semantic richness mediates between these two realms. On the one hand, the common refers to what is 'common to humankind', what is uniform in human nature and general to us all. On the other hand, the common inheres in 'domestick privacies' and 'the minute details of daily life', through whose legible familiarity we can learn more about a man, 'by a short conversation with one of his servants', 'than might be collected from publick papers'.[7]

---

[6] The terms are obviously distinct but to different degrees overlapping: for an illumi-nating historical semantics of these and related categories see Amélie Oksenberg Rorty, 'Characters, Persons, Selves, Individuals', in *Mind in Action: Essays in the Philosophy of Mind* (Boston, 1988), 78–98.

[7] Johnson, *Rambler* 60 (13 Oct. 1750).

We would be wrong to see Johnson as arguing either that the private lives of commoners or the testimony of common servants offers a privileged exemplary means for sifting the general from the particular. And yet both points seem implicit—even more so in Johnson's essay about the new species of fiction, written in the same year, 1750, as his commentary on 'the business of the biographer'. Here Johnson contrasts the 'fiction' that is popular with 'the present generation', which 'exhibits life in its true state, diversified only by accidents that daily happen in the real world', with the fiction of the past, which had easy recourse to giants, knights, and 'imaginary castles'. 'In the romances formerly written, every transaction and sentiment was so remote from all that passes among men, that the reader was in very little danger of making any application to himself', since their protagonists 'had neither faults nor excellencies in common with himself'. 'But when an adventurer is levelled with the rest of the world, [he] acts in such scenes of the universal drama, as may be the lot of any other man.' 'The task of our present writers ... requires ... that experience which ... must arise from general converse, and accurate observation of the living world ... Other writings are safe, except from the malice of learning, but these are in danger from every common reader; as the slipper ill executed was censured by a shoemaker who happened to stop in his way at the Venus of Apelles.' Johnson's momentarily confusing analogy would stress not the special knowledge of the artisan but on the contrary the authority of the average man. Like the common shoemaker, that is, the 'common reader' has an epistemological advantage that bears some relation to his socio-political status, which is that of the lowest common denominator, one to whose place the rest of the world has been levelled.[8] Like the idea of the common, the language of levelling Johnson shares with Goldsmith ('relations which are levelled to the general surface of life') and the anonymous biographer ('they will all be found pretty much on a level') points in two directions. On the one hand, the levelled is common in the sense of being general; on the other hand, the levelled has a socio-political commonness that gains access to the general by virtue of its being that 'part of the universal drama' which, stripped of all status distinction, is truly universal.

[8] Johnson, *Rambler* 4 (31 March 1750). Johnson alludes to Pliny's *Natural History*, 35. 36. 85.

BIOGRAPHY, FICTION, AND THE ACTUAL

So for Samuel Johnson, both modern biography and modern fiction appeal to their readers by featuring protagonists who are common in both senses of the term. Yet, in the common appeal of fiction, Johnson finds a danger that receives no such emphasis in his treatment of biography: 'But if the power of example is so great... care ought to be taken that... the best examples only should be exhibited... It is therefore not a sufficient vindication of a character, that it is drawn as it appears, for many characters ought never to be drawn.' From a modern standpoint Johnson's distinction is unimpeachable. A branch of history, biography draws life 'as it appears' in actuality; whereas in Johnson's words, 'historical veracity has no place' in fiction. In fact the orthodoxy of this distinction, although as old as Aristotle, is a recent development in European culture. Until the Renaissance, history and romance were, epistemologically speaking, only ill-distinguished from each other. Their modern divergence, and the emergence of 'fiction' in the modern sense of the term, were determined by a range of factors, but the most evident cause was the scientific revolution and the rise of empiricist epistemology—at least in the long run. In the short run and until the middle of the eighteenth century, the authority of empiricism was so general that it had the opposite effect and carried all before it. We can see this in the seemingly contradictory tendency to empiricize even religious narrative: for example, Baxter's insistence on the historicity of Clarke's puritan biographies, which implicitly functions as a material guarantor of their spiritual authenticity. We also can see this tendency in the way religious 'apparition narratives' like Defoe's famous story about the ghost of Mrs Veal stake their truth value on elaborately circumstantial claims to historicity.[9] This sort of appeal to the evidence of the senses also played a central role in what with hindsight we may recognize as the first and crudest phase of novelistic 'realism'. Defoe's *Robinson Crusoe* (1719) and *Moll Flanders* (1722), Swift's *Gulliver's Travels* (1726), Eliza Haywood's *The Fair Hebrew* (1729), and Samuel Richardson's *Pamela* (1740), to name only the best-known authors, self-consciously present themselves as 'historical' in the sense of being about

---

[9] Daniel Defoe, *A True Relation Of the Apparition of one Mrs. Veal The next Day after her Death To one Mrs. Bargrave at Canterbury The 8th of September, 1705* (1706).

events that actually occurred, and they are narrated, either in the first or the third person, so as to appear either autobiographical or biographical. As their titles suggest, these narratives also are about the private lives of common people, and to different degrees they adduce the accessibility of their characters as testimony to their pedagogic exemplarity. So the first wave of 'realism' entails a kind of naive empiricism, an insistence on factuality so literal as to bespeak not a literary convention of realism but the more-or-less transparent narration of the real.

BIOGRAPHY/FICTION AND THE VIRTUAL

But as a radical denial of conventionality, the claim to historicity, if compelling, was also short-lived. Richardson's second novel—indeed, the second edition of *Pamela*, published three months after the first— already had compromised the claim, and authors like Swift indulged it only with a patently parodic motive. Such a motive is obvious in the very title of Henry Fielding's first narrative, *Shamela* (1741). So if the claim to historicity was the first attempt to practise the emergent genre of the novel according to empiricist protocols that crudely conflated the novel with biography, parodies like Swift's and Fielding's rejected that practice no less ostentatiously. And in the year after *Shamela* was published, Fielding's formal critique of the claim to historicity modulated into what is recognizably an early version of the modern doctrine of realism, a technique that accommodated the new genre to the normative standards of empiricism, but strictly in its own terms. In the middle of *Joseph Andrews* (1742), Fielding reflects on this practice, strikingly enough using the word 'biography'—according to the *OED* a neologism less than sixty years old—to name the form he is writing. 'I describe not Men but Manners,' Fielding declares; 'not an Individual, but a Species.' 'Notwithstanding the Preference which may be vulgarly given to the Authority of those Romance-Writers, who intitle their Books, the History of *England*, the History of *France*, of *Spain*, &c. it is most certain, that Truth is only to be found in the Works of those who celebrate the Lives of Great Men, and are commonly called Biographers, as the others should indeed be termed Topographers or Chorographers.' According to Fielding, the latter two justly describe the place and time in which the persons they treat have their existence. 'But as to the Actions and Characters of Men, their Writings are not quite so authentic'— which for Fielding pointedly means they get their 'facts' wrong. 'Now with us Biographers the Case is different, the Facts we deliver may be relied on, tho' we often mistake the Age and Country wherein they happened.' 'Perhaps it will be answered, Are not the Characters then taken from Life? To which I answer in the Affirmative; nay, I believe I might aver, that I have writ little more than I have seen. The Lawyer [in *Joseph Andrews*] is not only alive, but hath been so these 4000 Years.' Whereas what is commonly called history is 'confined to a particular Period of Time, and to a particular Nation; [biography] is the History of the World in general'. In this way Fielding's 'general' factuality, not limited to the 'particular' details of time and place, lays claim to a different kind of historicity and factuality, which become available only when the exemplary truth of action and characters is dis-embedded from the obfuscating details of a strictly empirical or actual particularity.[10] Clearly this is not the modern meaning of 'biography'. But it is interesting that Fielding should have chosen that term to name the sort of narrative that, while historical, nonetheless is not slavishly tied to the actualities of time and place. And it is no accident that this dyad recalls the debate over the pseudo-Aristotelian dramatic 'unities', since Fielding's amusingly pedantic rejection of 'chorography' and 'topography' is consistent with the tendency, at least in England, to debunk the unities of time and place as a 'rule' that misconceives the psychology of aesthetic response by confusing it with strictly empiricist standards of cognition.

In this generalization of actual particularity Fielding's purpose is not only epistemological but also ethical and pedagogic. He aims 'not to expose one pitiful Wretch, to the small and contemptible Circle of his Acquaintance; but to hold the Glass to thousands in their Closets, that they may contemplate their Deformity, and endeavour to reduce it, and thus by suffering private Mortification may avoid public Shame. This places the Boundary between, and distinguishes the Satirist from the Libeller; for the former privately corrects the Fault for the Benefit of the Person, like a Parent; the latter publickly exposes the Person

---

[10] Henry Fielding, *Joseph Andrews* (1742), iii, ch. 1, in *Joseph Andrews/Shamela*, ed. Douglas Brooks-Davies and Thomas Keymer (Oxford, 1999), 164, 162.

himself, as an Example to others, like an Executioner.'[11] Fielding's discrimination between libel and satire participated in a general debate that flourished for a half century or so and that drew comment also from Dryden, Shadwell, Congreve, Addison, Steele, Defoe, Swift, Pope, and Haywood, among others. And although the superiority of satire to libel frequently was rationalized on an ethical basis, the terms of the debate were generated by the state's legal efforts to subject the libel of public figures to prosecution. The direct effect of these efforts was limited, since attacks on well-known figures continued; but the danger of legal prosecution may have contributed to the ethical and epistemological arguments for detaching exemplary teaching from the realm of actuality.[12]

But if naive empiricism and the threat of libel prosecution might be overcome by reconceiving factuality as general not particular, virtual not actual, how could this be compatible with the emergent sense of biographical and fictional exemplarity as possessing the down-to-earth concreteness of private and common example? In the doubleness of the common, we recall, the concreteness of the local and familiar example is instrumental in ensuring its generalizability. Over the course of the seventeenth century, the unprecedentedly normative force of empirical actuality had both re-empowered exemplary concreteness and mandated the idea that concreteness depends on empirical—that is, actual—particularity. But Fielding's 'biography' and non-libellous satire are able to generalize about the individual life beyond the temporal and spatial registers of actual particularity only because they possess the concreteness of characterization needed to ensure that generalization. The demise of the naive claim to historicity marked the separation of fiction from biography, but it thereby encouraged a deeper recognition of their similarity. The concrete particularity of the narrative subject, until now assumed to inhere in and depend on his or her historico-personal actuality, became available as a species of virtuality, modelled on the particularity of the empirical subject but detached from the necessity of actual existence. To contemporaries this had important

---

[11] Fielding, *Joseph Andrews*, iii, ch. 1, 164–5.
[12] On the critique of the unities of time and place from the perspective of an emergent aesthetic doctrine and on the contrast between libel and satire see Michael McKeon, *The Secret History of Domesticity: Public, Private, and the Division of Knowledge* (Baltimore, 2005), 368–72 and 95–9, respectively.

pedagogical implications. Only within the general realm of the virtual, it came to appear, could the private transaction of ethical improvement be achieved. To remain in the realm of actual particularity is, on the contrary, to resign oneself to libel, to the public exposure of the private, sacrificing the private to the public instead of bringing the private into public discourse. More broadly, the separation of virtual from actual particularity aided in the emergent division between the 'literary' and the 'biographical-historical' by substituting for the actual particularity of the novelistic claim to historicity the concrete particularity of probabilistic 'realism', permitting literature to be 'personal' in the sense of privacy and the familiarity of the common without also being 'personal' in the sense of actual reference.

THE SELF BEHIND SELF-FASHIONING

As the interplay of epistemological, ethical, and legal motives makes clear, this division between the literary and the historical was broadly overdetermined. Nor was it forced only by modernizing developments like empiricism and the proliferation of print. In 1698, the Jacobite non-juror Jeremy Collier ignited a major cultural controversy over what he called 'the profaneness and immorality of the English stage'. As Collier's assault makes clear, the public exposure of the personal met ethical opposition regarding not only print but also dramatic performance, and not only on the grounds that it injured exposed individuals but also because even if the exposure had no actual referent and made no pretence to personal representation, it nonetheless publicized and disseminated vicious example. For a poet 'to descend to Particulars, and fall to Characterizing', Collier wrote, 'is no better than Libel, and Personal Abuse'; hence '[a]ll Characters of Immodesty (if there must be any such) should only be hinted in remote Language, and thrown off in Generals'. But Collier's position was even more extreme than this. He flatly asserted that ''tis the Poet that speaks in the Persons of the Stage', and when those are vicious, the poet's 'private Sentiments fall under Censure'. Collier's insistence that the characterization of an evil person is necessarily an evil characterization forced his antagonists to make explicit the protocols of interpretation that tacitly obtained under customary conditions of theatrical performance and publication. According to William Congreve, nothing should be 'imputed to the Persuasions or private Sentiments of the Author, if at any time one of these vicious Characters in any of his Plays shall behave himself foolishly, or immorally in Word or Deed'. Similarly, James Drake warned against confusing the poets' 'private or real sense' with the 'Sentiments, which they are obliged sometimes to furnish Villains and Extravagants with in conformity to their Characters'.[13] Again, what is new here is not the capacity to make a tacit distinction between fictional character and biographical author but the explicit separation out of character from author, of projected or performed self from self as such. Collier's antagonists hypostasize for literary characters a distinct realm of virtuality. For Collier, however, characters are simple empirical extensions of actual particularity, of actual authors, hence authors and characters constitute a continuous and homogeneous personality.

From Elizabethan through Enlightenment culture, the figure of the theatre exercises a fascination for English people, expressing an extraordinary, perhaps even an increasing, power in the ontological intuition that to be in the world is to 'act' on the 'stage' of the world. By metaphorizing life as art, the figure of theatrical performance, like that of self-fashioning, gives voice to the understanding that actual persons are creatures, whether by the Creator or by the internalization of sociocultural 'role' not naturally given but artfully made. Early on, the stress in the figure falls not on the nature and agency of the making but on the fact of madness. But the increasingly explicit and general application of the figure of the theatre also increased explicit enquiry into the empirical nature of the agency it implied. The gradual replacement of 'soul'-by 'self'-terms over the span of this period is one measure of that increase, as are the growth of both secularization and the sociological imagination. Of more immediate relevance here, however, is the way questions of agency increasingly broach questions of 'identity' that posit a quasi-'natural'

---

[13] Jeremy Collier, *A Second Defence of the Short View of the Prophaneness and Immorality of the English Stage* (1700), 104; *idem, A Defence of the Short View of the Prophaneness and Immorality of the English Stage* (1699), 10–11. See William Congreve, *Amendments of Mr Collier's False and Imperfect Citations, &c.* (1698), 9; James Drake, *The Antient and Modern Stages Survey'd* (1700), 222. All quoted in Aubrey Williams, *An Approach to Congreve* (New Haven, 1979), 61, 78.

self anterior to the artificial self that has been made. In the earlier period, the experience of role-playing derives from the experience of having played other and different roles on other occasions. In the later period, the experience of role-playing derives from the sense of difference between any given role and the constant and continuous identity that it and all roles momentarily displace. The singularity of self-identity presupposes a 'naturalness' of selfhood, conceived as a statistical generalization, of which it is a singular instance. The modern category of the self is constituted by this relationship between the singular and the general. 'There is such an uniformity in the state of man', Johnson writes, 'considered apart from adventitious and separable decorations and disguises, that there is scarce any possibility of good or ill, but is common to human kind.' Collier's insistence that 'the poet speaks in the persons of the stage' articulates, in the ethical and epistemological continuity between author and character, an assumption more local than but analogous to the assumption that the performance or fashioning of the self is coextensive with the self. The dramatists' rebuttal separates out the agency of author and character on analogy with the separation Johnson will argue between general selfhood and singular self-identity. But to formulate this analogy is also to recognize one dimension of disanalogy. There is a fundamental difference between the way authorial agency fashions virtual characters and the way actual, empirical persons exist apart from all such fashioning.

FROM SECRET HISTORY TO NOVEL

A summary overview of the changing relationship between biography and fiction during this period is provided by the fortunes of what contemporaries called the secret history.[14] The idea of a secret history presupposes the idea of a manifest and official but necessarily partial version of things. In the midst of civil war the Leveller Richard Overton posed the rhetorical question, 'If the King conquer, the Parliament

---

[14] For a fuller discussion see McKeon, *Secret History*, pt. 3.

will be Traytours to posterity by Cronicle; for who writ the Histories of the Anabaptists but their Enemies?'[15] The secret history is both a logical entailment and of a solution to the problem of the fact that history gets written by the winners. The phrase 'secret history' itself became familiar to Anglophone culture through the 1674 English translation of the *Anecdota* of Procopius (*c.* AD 550), whose title means 'unpublished things'.[16] The Procopian precedent quickly provided a popular model for the disclosure of state secrets. The material prefatory to a Restoration translation from the French praises the author for having written 'a sort of Cabinet, Historical Inquisition' that 'has refin'd upon Procopius his Pattern'. But the 'Author's Preface' to this translation also makes clear the broader relevance of the secret history to the turn of biography toward the private and the common:

[T]he Historian considers almost ever Men in Publick, whereas the Anecdoto-grapher only examines 'em in private. Th' one thinks he has perform'd his duty, when he draws them such as they were in the Army, or in the tumult of Cities, and th' other endeavours by all means to get open their Closet-door; th' one sees them in Ceremony, and th' other in conversation; th' one fixes principally upon their Actions, and th' other wou'd be a Witness of their inward Life, and assist at the most private hours of their leisure: In a word, the one has barely Command and Authority for Object, and the other makes his Main of what occurs in Secret and in Solitude . . .

Not but that the Writer of *Anekdota* draws a Picture of Persons, as exact, and as faithful, at the least, as can be done by the Historian; but he does it after his own Mode: He represents only as much of the Man's Out-side, as is necessary to know his Inside; and as the good and bad dispositions of the Mind, are only to be disclos'd in the Manners, 'tis also for the Manners that he reserves his liveliest Colours, and finest Materials. . . . I pretend likewise . . . to relate with a serious Air, the smallest trifles, when they have been th' Origine or occasion of the greatest Matters.

In the words of the translator, 'Irresolution and Passion prevail equally in the Great, as in the Vulgar. And often a little Cabinet-pique, or

---

[15] Richard Overton, *The Arraignement of Mr Persecution* (1645), in *Tracts on Liberty in the Puritan Revolution, 1638–1647*, ed. William Haller (New York, 1933), iii. 230.

[16] Procopius, *The Secret History of the Court of the Emperor Justinian . . .* (1674).

Bed-Chamber Quarrel, occasions a rumbling World, and is the source of the greatest Transactions.'[17]

As these words suggest, the significance of the private and the trivial in secret histories is that they bear an illuminating motivational relationship to great and public happenings. But the allure of the secret history was also that it might entail a stealthy political allegory: read aright, what appears to be an exotic tale or history turns out to have present and public application. Indeed, this may be the implication of the decision to reissue the 1674 translation of Procopius in 1682, although too late to fan the flames of the Exclusion Crisis, as *The Debaucht Court. Or, the Lives of the Emperor Justinian, and his Empress Theodora the Comedian*. In other words, the mode of secret history that is inspired by the translation of Procopius draws strength from, and dovetails with, the mode of the *roman à clef* that had flourished at least since the beginning of the seventeenth century, which signals its secrecy through allegorical, amatory 'romance' plots that sanction techniques of close reading to uncover their deepest public meaning. (Sometimes keys to the actual identities of the romance characters were published soon after the *roman* itself.) That is, the substantive, motivational relationship between the trivial–private and the great–public that organizes the Procopian secret history is expressed, in the *roman à clef*, as a formal relationship of signification between the trivial romance plot we read and the great historical plot we take it to mean. Once the historical meaning of the romance plot has been disclosed, however, the resulting public scandal may be either high or low, either political or sexual—or both by turns, as the *roman à clef* allegorizes state politics through the 'sexual politics' of amatory intrigue and erotic romance. Indeed, in a nation state like England, where royal sovereignty depends on familial–dynastic inheritance, the metonymic contiguity of the political and the sexual guarantees that political secrets will be understood in terms of sexual secrets. But as patriarchalism—the customary and tacit analogy between the family and the state—becomes increasingly explicit, hence strained, over the course of the seventeenth century, the separation out of the family from the state exerts pressure on their traditional metonymic relation as well. Under this pressure, the

---

[17] [Antoine Varillas], *Medicis. Written Originally by that Fam'd Historian, the Sieur de Varilles. Made English by Ferrand Spence* (1686; French 1685), 'Epistle Dedicatory', A4^v–5^r, A6^r, and 'Author's Preface', a4^v–a5^r, a8^r.

sexuality of political dynasty, the intimate privacy of the body natural that grounds the body politic, acquires the potential to undermine it, to desublimate the secret and scandalous truth of sovereignty so as to reveal that the 'deepest meaning' of the story is in fact not public but disreputably private.

So the secret history operates along the differential axis of the public and the private, and in its gradual modulation towards the private realm it parallels the joint development of biography and fiction I have already described. What bearing might this development have on the differential axis of actual and virtual particularity, in whose terms biography and fiction have, by the mid-eighteenth century, parted ways? The major *romans à clef* in the English tradition include Philip Sidney's *Old Arcadia* (1579–81), John Barclay's *Argenis* (Lat. 1621, trans. 1625, 1629), Mary Wroth's *The Countesse of Montgomeries Urania* (1621), the anonymous *Princess Cloria; or, the Royal Romance* (1661), Aphra Behn's *Love-Letters between a Nobleman and his Sister* (1684, 1685, 1687), and Delarivier Manley's *New Atalantis* (1709). By the time of Haywood's secret histories of the 1720s, a subtle, century-long transformation has been completed. This transformation has three interlocking features: the secrets concealed and revealed by the secret history have become primarily private and personal rather than public and political; the bi-levelled allegorical signification of public by private in the *roman à clef* has largely been displaced by a single literal narrative about private (that is, domestic and sexual) affairs; and the resulting literal narrative retains the virtual particularity it possessed when it was no more than the signifier of actual particulars: history has become fiction. Although this is a work of time, Behn's *Love-Letters* is the single most consequential stage in this transformative process and may be summarized in its terms. Published in the aftermath of the Exclusion Crisis, Behn's *roman à clef* sets out to reveal and to vindicate the conditions of political subjection that should obtain under Restoration monarchy, using the disparate exemplary models available in her private, virtual plot as multiple and alternative foils for the normative subordination of actual subjects to actual king. But the circumstantial and affective detail with which Behn thickens her account of private, amatory affairs increasingly vies for attention with the political and military affairs it purports to signify. The result is less the direct 'political' correlation of private character with public personage (of, for example, Cesario with the Duke of Monmouth) than the construction of a broadly 'ethical' grid of concrete examples that have both public and private relevance. Questions of state policy come to seem internalizable as questions of familial ethics. Over time, epistolary form gives way to third-person narration as the documentary and existential secrecy of letters is found to be less compelling than the subjective and psychological secrecy of the motives that lie behind and beneath them. In the end, the 'key' that seems to open Behn's *roman à clef* is not the political identity of actual people but an ethical identification between readers and characters.

In modern practice, the difference between telling the stories of actual people and telling the stories of virtual people defines the boundary between biography and fiction. Indeed, it is our very confidence in this boundary that encourages us to experiment inventively at the borders of those two genres in a way that is not thinkable when the sense of borders is not explicit or coherent enough to make their crossing a fully stable concept. The tacit porousness of categories that is common in a culture that has not yet experienced a fundamental division of knowledge is very different from the self-consciously reactive conflation of categories in a culture that has been marked by such division. But how do we bring this generalization into chronological specificity? We can draw a line at a specific point anywhere from 1550 to 1750; but by its very nature this falsifies the character of historical process, which at every moment consists in both continuity and discontinuity. Still, the implausibility of a parallel between early modern and postmodern culture may help where chronological precision does not. It seems implausible to me that readers of Foxe, Sidney, or Barclay experienced something akin to postmodern knowingness about the mixture of fact and fiction, whether an anxiously uncertain or (to use the term that has become mandatory in recent years) a boldly 'transgressive' sort of knowingness. Rather, they and those they read seem to move back and forth along the continuum of fact and fiction, life and art, nature and nurture, uncoloured by the demystifying scepticism that fuels the very different sort of sophistication of postmodernity. But we do not need to wait until the twentieth century to see the latter mode in operation. I have already mentioned the fiction of Fielding and Sterne. As for biography, one of the ways in which the indefatigably opportunistic and intrusive James Boswell set the standard for the future in his *Life of Johnson* (1791) is expressed in the modern maxim that all biography is also autobiography. The maxim would have no point if we lacked a firm and abiding conviction that the subject and the object of knowledge are separable from each other. This conviction takes shape, over the course of the seventeenth century, in conjunction with the scientific revolution and the rise of empiricist epistemology. The socio-ethical conviction that is analogous to and intertwined with this epistemological belief is the separability of self and society, a conviction that takes shape in conjunction with the seventeenth-century crises of status inconsistency and social mobility. It is also to these developments, I think, that we owe both the formation of, and the challenge to, the notion of self-identity. To look no deeper than the great philosophers, it was not until 1690 that the basic principle of empiricist epistemology was formulated, by John Locke, as the notion that the probable knowledge of an object requires that it be separate from the subjective process by which it is known. And although he knew that under normal circumstances the 'Understanding…takes no notice of it self: and it requires Art and Pains to set it at a distance, and make it its own Object', Locke also affirmed the activity of reflection as one in which 'the Understanding turns inwards upon it self, *reflects* on its own *Operations*, and makes them the Object of its own Contemplation'. In 1739, David Hume remarked of Locke and others that '[t]here are some philosophers, who imagine we are every moment intimately conscious of what we call our SELF; that we feel its existence and its continuance in existence; and are certain, beyond the evidence of a demonstration, both of its perfect identity and simplicity'. On the contrary, Hume continues, it is 'successive perceptions only, that constitute the mind'. We have a great 'propension to ascribe an identity to these successive perceptions, and to suppose ourselves possest of an invariable and uninterrupted existence thro' the whole course of our lives'. And so 'we feign the continu'd existence of the *perceptions* [my italics] of our senses, to remove the *interruption* [my italics]; and run into the notion of a *soul*, and *self*, and *substance*, to disguise the variation'.[18] In the fifty years between Locke and Hume, English thinking about the self made the transition from modernity to what we like to call 'postmodernity'.

---

[18] John Locke, *An Essay concerning Human Understanding* (1690), ed. Peter H. Nidditch (Oxford, 1975), bk. I, ch. 1, para. 1, p. 43; David Hume, *A Treatise of Human Nature* (1739), ed. L. A. Selby-Bigge, 2nd edn., rev. P. H. Nidditch (Oxford, 1978), bk. I, pt. iv, sect. 6, pp. 253, 254.

Notes on Contributors

Alastair Bellany is Associate Professor of History at Rutgers University. He is the author of *The Politics of Court Scandal in Early Modern England* (2002) and (with Andrew McRae) is the editor of *Early Stuart Libels: An Edition of Poetry from Manuscript Sources* (2005). He is currently completing *England's Assassin: John Felton and the Murder of the Duke of Buckingham*, co-written with Thomas Cogswell, and is beginning a book on the portraits of Buckingham and the presentation of the courtly self.

Thomas N. Corns is Professor of English at Bangor University. His work includes *The Development of Milton's Prose Style* (1982), *Milton's Language* (1990), *Uncloistered Virtue* (1992), *Regaining 'Paradise Lost'* (1994), and *John Milton: The Prose Works* (1998). His most recent publications are *A History of Seventeenth-Century English Literature* (2006) and (with Gordon Campbell, John Hale, and Fiona Tweedie) *John Milton and the Manuscript of De Doctrina Christiana*. He is the editor of the prize-winning *A Companion to Milton* (2001) and the new *Milton Encyclopedia* (forthcoming). He is also General Editor, with Gordon Campbell, of *The Complete Works of John Milton* (forthcoming). His *John Milton: Life, Work and Thought*, co-authored with Gordon Campbell, will be published in 2008.

Andrew Hadfield is Professor of English at the University of Sussex. He is the author of numerous works on Renaissance literature and culture, including *Shakespeare and Republicanism* (2005), which was awarded the 2006 Sixteenth-Century Society Conference Roland H. Bainton Prize for Literature; *Shakespeare, Spenser and The Matter of Britain* (2003), and *Spenser's Irish Experience: Wilde Fruit and Salvage Soyl* (1997). He has also edited *The Cambridge Companion to Spenser* (2001), and a special Issue of *Textual Practice: Were Early Modern Lives Different?* (forthcoming).

Frances Harris is Head of Modern (post 1603) Historical Manuscripts at the British Library. She is author of *A Passion for Government: The Life of Sarah, Duchess of Marlborough* (1991), *Transformations of Love: The Friendship of John Evelyn and Margaret Godolphin* (2003), and editor with Michael Hunter of the essay collection, *John Evelyn and his Milieu* (2003). She is working on a study of Anglo-Scottish courtiers under the Stuarts, with focus on the career of Sir Robert Moray.

Lisa Jardine, CBE, is Director of the Centre for Editing Lives and Letters and Centenary Professor of Renaissance Studies, at Queen Mary, University of London. She is a Fellow of the Royal Historical Society and Honorary Fellow of King's College, Cambridge, and Jesus College, Cambridge. She holds honorary doctorates from the University of St Andrews, the Open University, and Sheffield Hallam University. For the academic year 2007–8 she will be seconded to the Royal Society as Adviser to its Collections. She has published over fifty scholarly articles in refereed journals, and seventeen full-length books, both for an academic and for a general readership, including *Worldly Goods: A New History of the Renaissance* (1996), *Ingenious Pursuits: Building the Scientific Revolution* (1999), and biographies of Sir Christopher Wren and Robert Hooke. Her book on Anglo-Dutch reciprocal influence in the seventeenth century (March 2008) is entitled *Going Dutch*.

Paulina Kewes is a Tutorial Fellow in English Literature at Jesus College, Oxford. Her publications include *Authorship and Appropriation: Writing for the Stage in England, 1660–1710* (1998), *Drama, History, and Politics in Elizabethan England* (forthcoming), and two edited volumes, *Plagiarism in Early Modern England* (2003) and *The Uses of History in Early Modern England* (2006). She is a General Editor of the Oxford Holinshed. Her new project is a study of the late Elizabethan succession crisis.

Peter Lake is Professor of English History at Princeton University. His most recent book, written with Michael Questier, is *The Antichrist's Lewd Hat* (2002). He is currently working on Shakespeare's history plays and the politics of the 1590s and Catholic critiques of the Elizabethan regime as a conspiracy and a tyranny.

The late Harold Love was Professor of English at Monash University, Melbourne, the author of a number of distinguished volumes on early modern and Restoration literature, including *Scribal Publication in Seventeenth-Century England* (1993), *Attributing Authorship* (2002), and *English Clandestine Satire, 1660–1702* (2004) and the editor for Oxford University Press of *The Works of John Wilmot, Earl of Rochester* (1999), (with Robert Jordan) *The Works of Thomas Southern* (1988), and (with Robert D. Hume) *The Plays, Poems, and Miscellaneous Writings Associated with George Villiers, Second Duke of Buckingham* (2007).

Michael McKeon is a Board of Governors Professor of Literature at Rutgers University, New Brunswick. He is the author of *Politics and Poetry in Restoration England* (1975), *The Origins of the English Novel* (1987), and *The Secret History of Domesticity* (2005), and he has edited *Theory of the Novel*

(2000). He is currently working on the idea of the aesthetic in the eighteenth century.

Julia Marciari Alexander is Associate Director for Exhibitions and Publications at the Yale Center for British Art. In 2001 she curated with Catharine MacLeod of the National Portrait Gallery, London, the exhibition *Painted Ladies: Women at the Court of Charles II, 1660–1685* and co-wrote and edited the corresponding exhibition catalogue; the exhibition took place both in London and at Yale. She has curated a number of exhibitions for the Center and other institutions, published widely in her field, and taught courses in the History of Art Department at Yale University. A specialist in seventeenth-century British and French portraiture, she received her Ph.D. from Yale University.

Leah S. Marcus is Edwin Mims Professor of English at Vanderbilt University. She is the author of *Childhood and Cultural Despair* (1978), *The Politics of Mirth* (1986), *Puzzling Shakespeare* (1988), and *Unediting the Renaissance* (1996) as well as editions of the writings of Queen Elizabeth I, co-edited with Mary Beth Rose and Janel Mueller (2000 and 2003) and *The Merchant of Venice* (Norton, 2006). She is presently at work on an edition of *The Duchess of Malfi* (scheduled to appear from Arden in 2009).

Annabel Patterson is Sterling Professor Emerita at Yale University. Her most important books were *Censorship and Interpretation* (1984), *Pastoral and Ideology* (1987), *Shakespeare and the Popular Voice* (1989), *Reading Holinshed's Chronicles* (1994), *Early Modern Liberalism* (1997), and the Yale edition of *Marvell's Prose Works* (2003). A new book, *The Long Parliament of Charles II*, is forthcoming.

Kevin Sharpe is the author and editor of eleven books, including *The Personal Rule of Charles I* (1992), *Criticism and Compliment* (2nd edn., 2003), *Reading Revolutions* (2000), *Remapping Early Modern England* (2000), and, with Steven Zwicker, *Reading, Society and Politics in Early Modern England* (2003). He is Leverhulme Research Professor and Director of the Centre for Renaissance Studies at Queen Mary, University of London. He is completing a three-volume study of *Representations of Rule in England, 1500–1700*.

Stella Tillyard is Senior Visiting Research Fellow at the Centre for Editing Lives and Letters, Queen Mary, University of London, and a biographer. She is the author of *The Impact of Modernism* (1987), *Aristocrats* (1994), *Citizen Lord* (1998), numerous articles and reviews, and, most recently, *A Royal Affair* (2006).

Andrea Walkden is assistant professor of English at Queens College, the City University of New York. She is the author of articles published or forthcoming on allegorical insubordination in Spenser's *Faerie Queene* and the thematics of self-authorship in Milton's *Paradise Regained*. Currently, she is completing a book-length study on life writing in later Stuart England.

Steven N. Zwicker is Stanley Elkin Professor in the Humanities at Washington University in St Louis. He is the author or editor of *Politics and Language in Dryden's Poetry* (1984); *Lines of Authority: Politics and English Literary Culture, 1649–1689* (1993); *The Cambridge Companion to English Literature: 1650– 1740* (1998); *The Cambridge Companion to John Dryden* (2004); and, with Kevin Sharpe, *Reading, Society and Politics in Early Modern England* (2003) and *Refiguring Revolutions: Aesthetics and Politics from the English Revolution to the Romantic Revolution* (1998). He is currently finishing a book on Marvell's poetry with Derek Hirst.

Index

Note: page numbers in *italic* indicate illustrations.

WRITING LIVES

nil me poenitet

DUGDALE

ODNB

ex libris

Jan Broadway Ph. D

Writing Lives

Biography and Textuality, Identity and
Representation in Early Modern England

KEVIN SHARPE AND STEVEN N. ZWICKER

OXFORD
UNIVERSITY PRESS

OXFORD
UNIVERSITY PRESS

Great Clarendon Street, Oxford OX2 6DP

Oxford University Press is a department of the University of Oxford.
It furthers the University's objective of excellence in research, scholarship,
and education by publishing worldwide in

Oxford New York

Auckland Cape Town Dar es Salaam Hong Kong Karachi
Kuala Lumpur Madrid Melbourne Mexico City Nairobi
New Delhi Shanghai Taipei Toronto

With offices in

Argentina Austria Brazil Chile Czech Republic France Greece
Guatemala Hungary Italy Japan Poland Portugal Singapore
South Korea Switzerland Thailand Turkey Ukraine Vietnam

Oxford is a registered trade mark of Oxford University Press
in the UK and in certain other countries

Published in the United States
by Oxford University Press Inc., New York

British Library Cataloguing in Publication Data
Data available

Library of Congress Cataloging in Publication Data
Data available

Typeset by SPI Publisher Services, Pondicherry, India
Printed in Great Britain
on acid-free paper by
Biddles Ltd., King's Lynn, Norfolk

ISBN 978–0–19–921701–4

1 3 5 7 9 10 8 6 4 2